THE MANLY MASQUERADE

The Manly Masquerade

MASCULINITY, PATERNITY, AND CASTRATION

IN THE ITALIAN RENAISSANCE

Valeria Finucci

DUKE UNIVERSITY PRESS

DURHAM & LONDON

2003

© 2003 Duke University Press
All rights reserved
Printed in the United States
of America on acid-free paper ∞
Designed by Amy Ruth Buchanan
Typeset in Adobe Jenson by Tseng
Information Systems, Inc.
Library of Congress Cataloging-in-
Publication Data appear on the last
printed page of this book.

To Anna Ferrarotti, Giuseppe Gerbino,
Carmel Mullin, and Rosamaria Preparata,
true friends

CONTENTS

ACKNOWLEDGMENTS ix

INTRODUCTION

Body and Generation in the Early Modern Period 1

CHAPTER 1

The Useless Genitor: Fantasies of Putrefaction
and Nongenealogical Births 37

CHAPTER 2

The Masquerade of Paternity: Cuckoldry and Baby
M[ale] in Machiavelli's *La mandragola* 79

CHAPTER 3

Performing Maternity: Female Imagination, Paternal Erasure,
and Monstrous Birth in Tasso's *Gerusalemme liberata* 119

CHAPTER 4

The Masquerade of Masculinity: Erotomania
in Ariosto's *Orlando furioso* 159

CHAPTER 5

Androgynous Doubling and Hermaphroditic
Anxieties: Bibbiena's *La calandria* 189

CHAPTER 6

The Masquerade of Manhood:
The Paradox of the Castrato 225

SELECTED BIBLIOGRAPHY 281

INDEX 307

ACKNOWLEDGMENTS

The making of this book has spanned almost a decade, and in the course of it I have incurred many, many debts. Friends and colleagues from a variety of disciplines have through the years discussed, read, offered detailed criticism, and otherwise been very supportive of this project in numberless ways. I wish to thank for their unstinting generosity Giuseppe Gerbino, Elizabeth Clark, Marina Scordilis Brownlee, Kevin Brownlee, Ronald Martinez, Walter Stephens, Susan Noakes, and Dino Cervigni. I am also indebted for spirited conversations to Giuseppe Mazzotta, Eduardo Saccone, Elissa Weaver, Mary Ann Frese Witt, Ronald Witt, Franco Fido, Daniel Javitch, Regina Schwartz, Tim Carter, Victoria Kirkham, Eric Nicholson, Antonia Arslan, Daria Perocco, and Robert Bonfil.

This project has been generously supported by a number of grants and by a sabbatical leave from Duke University. I wish to thank Harvard University for a year fellowship at their Renaissance center, Villa I Tatti, in Florence in 1994–95, where I wrote parts of chapters 3 and 4. Other grants from the Lila Wallace/Reader's Digest Endowment Fund, the American Philosophical Society, the Trent Foundation, the Research Council, and the European Studies Center of Duke University have helped the research along by freeing time or by sponsoring trips to archives in Italy. Special thanks go to the staff of the Interlibrary Loan Office at Duke University for unfailingly pursuing all kinds of obscure requests and to the staff of the Biblioteca Marciana in Venice and the Biblioteca Nazionale in Florence.

For their timely generosity and enthusiasm, I wish to thank my many students and colleagues at Duke University, and the students and colleagues at the University of Pennsylvania and at Johns Hopkins University, where I briefly taught as a visiting professor. The members of the North Carolina Research Group on Medieval and Early Modern Women, the members of the Renaissance Workshop of the University of North Carolina at Chapel Hill, and the fellows at I Tatti have all in one way or another kept me focused. Other friends have provided me with an extraordinarily supportive and nurturing atmosphere; my thanks go to Rosamaria Preparata, Anna Ferrarotti, Gianfranco Finucci, Carmel Mullin, Julie Linehan, Mark Sosower, Silvia Ross, Edda Dussi, Rosalind Coleman, James Rolleston, Caroline Bruzelius, Margaret Greer, Joan Hinde Stewart, Philip Stewart, and Luciano Donato.

I am deeply grateful to Reynolds Smith of Duke University Press for his long-standing support, to the press readers for their very helpful suggestions, to Maura High for her careful editing, to Justin Faerber for his wit, and to Sharon Torian for her cheerfulness. An earlier version of chapter 4, titled "The Masquerade of Masculinity: Astolfo and Jocondo in *Orlando furioso*, Canto 28," appeared in *Renaissance Transactions: Ariosto and Tasso* (Duke University Press, 1999), which I edited; and an earlier version of chapter 3 titled "Maternal Imagination and Monstrous Birth: Tasso's *Gerusalemme liberata*" appeared in *Generation and Degeneration: Tropes of Reproduction in Literature and History from Antiquity to Early Modern Europe* (Duke University Press, 2001), which I coedited with Kevin Brownlee.

INTRODUCTION

Body and Generation in the
Early Modern Period

For the man is not of the woman; but the woman is of the man.
— SAINT PAUL, 1 Corinthians 12.8

Conception is indeed a dark business . . . full of shadows.
— W. HARVEY, *Disputations Touching*
the Generation of Animals

Where were ferments and microbes before Pasteur? One can make sense of the world after Pasteur, as well as of the world before him, only through what Bruno Latour calls a "work of retrofitting—which includes history telling, textbook writing, instrument making, body training, and the creation of professional loyalties and genealogies."[1] I want to take Latour's critical urge to retrofit the past and bring it to bear on the issues of sex and generation by examining a time before words such as "genetics" and "ovulation" had entered the vocabulary, a time when medical books in the vernacular were, nevertheless, already teaching people how to reproduce "right" (or not to reproduce), and when newly fashionable conduct books were explaining how to behave correctly according to society's expectations and embedded class values.

For this purpose I plan to assemble, interpret, and contextualize the array of discourses on masculinity and paternity, as well as femininity and maternity, that informed Italian literature and culture from roughly the late fifteenth through the middle of the seventeenth century, with occasional forays into earlier and later times. I will examine plays, novellas, treatises, travel journals, *historiae*, poems, anecdotes, myths, and chivalric romances, because literature, being a reflection of the culture to which it belongs, has always displayed an interest in sexuality and in the organization of gendered identities. Given that it routinely gives a sexual meaning to a sexual act, literature has also been a fertile ground for the definition of what at any given time can be considered "normal" or otherwise. Since a practice of deductive inquiry was brought to bear in the early modern period on all epistemology and the gap between scientific and aesthetic knowledge was narrow, I will use medicine, theology, juridical law, and other culturally pregnant but historically "insignificant" incidents to make sense of my examples. Those among us who have a sense of history as providential can easily agree that it took too long for science to refute the notion that women are sexually poisonous or to dispel the anxiety about spontaneous generation that gripped the imagination of people at the dawn of our age. On the other

---

1. Bruno Latour, *Pandora's Hope: Essays on the Reality of Science Studies* (Cambridge: Harvard University Press, 1999), 170. Latour continues: "Without beginning to rework part of the philosophy of technology and part of the myth of progress, we won't be able to shake off the moral and political burden that the modernist settlement has so unfairly placed on the shoulders of nonhumans" (172).

hand, the study of how our predecessors dealt with these issues, and why they were obsessed with them, can be both illuminating and humbling, especially for those who see them as hardly different from modern fears — that expectant mothers can, for example, imprint on their unborn babies the sign of what they desire and that airborne germs cause disease.

It has become axiomatic that gender is constructed, that is, that masculinity and femininity are not fixed but are aligned with historical contingencies and prevalent sociocultural values through a process of constant retooling and watchfulness.[2] The standards, of course, are by definition shifting, because they hinge on social, religious, medical, juridical, philosophical, and historical variables. In the West, masculinity has been routinely identified with the universal — a definition that puts a great deal of pressure on men to behave "like men," while conferring some obvious advantages. Conversely, women have been the object of constant vigilance to make sure that they understand what is culturally expected of them within the limits of their sex. Ironically, proper gender alignment has been more relevant to men than to women, no matter the discrepancy in the amount of legislation meant to enforce decorum on maidens, wives, widows, and nuns (the four possible states of womanhood in the period that is my focus in this book). We know that men rarely dressed in women's clothes, unless in jest or during the Carnival season. We also know that women used male disguise, although not how many did so. For example, a successful play of the period, Gl'Intronati's Gl'ingannati (The Deceived), tells the audience almost offhandedly that nuns cross-dressed often, that convents were notoriously full of male clothing, and that women wore male clothes to go about their affairs at night.[3] In the city of Ferrara a statute authorized any man to check under a woman's dress to see whether she was wearing pants ("calzoni"). To control possible improprieties, however, the statute ordered the man's hand cut

2. Criticism on the subject is vast. See, for example, Judith Butler, Gender Trouble: Feminism and the Subversion of Identity (New York: Routledge, 1990); and Joan Scott, Gender and the Politics of History (New York: Columbia University Press, 1988), esp. 28–52.

3. In Gl'ingannati, the main female character, an adolescent called Lelia, chooses, for safety while traveling, to wear a male outfit lent to her by her relative, the mother superior, when she moves out of the convent where her father was temporarily keeping her. See Gl'Intronati, Gl'ingannati, ed. Ireneo Sanesi (1538; Bari: Laterza, 1912), 1.3. Gl'Intronati were a group of intellectuals from Siena who wrote under this collective (and self-deprecating) name.

off ("tagliata la mano") if he was wrong.[4] Never shy about divulging his sexual practices, the poet Pietro Aretino in a letter of 1547 thanked the generous Zufolina—a courtesan with a name her mother certainly did not give her—for having come to his house dressed once as a male and once as a female, with the objective of playing both.[5] But then in Venice it was a common practice for prostitutes to wear male clothes under their more gender-specific accoutrements, since they were paid more when they wore outrageous costumes.

Renaissance culture liked to project a fully empowered and virilized image of masculinity and encouraged frequent gestures toward male self-fashioning. Paintings of the time, for example, portray men in short hair and plumed hats, beards and rigid collars, their bodies erect and stiff, their eyes firmly beholding the onlooker. Gentlemen, courtiers, merchants, and youths often dressed in black, wore codpieces, and carried daggers pointing suggestively upward and swords placed firmly between their legs. In fact, all fashionable young men in the 1530s, we are told by the character Gherardo in Gl'ingannati, swagger around town with plumes in their caps (standing up stiffly in the Guelph style), their swords at their sides, and their daggers behind.[6]

This display of a strong erotics of masculinity contrasts with the representation of men frequently seen after the 1640s, when the Spanish style gave way to more ornamented and ostentatious French fashions. In the upper classes, this shift meant long, blond, powdered wigs, tight stockings, high heels, makeup, powder, beauty spots, and plucked eyebrows.[7] Extravagant as it may seem, the redundant, bewildering, hedonistic, baroque, bombastic poetry of, say, Giam-

4. See Alessandro Luzio and Rodolfo Renier, "Il lusso di Isabella d'Este marchesa di Mantova," Nuova Antologia 68 (1986): 463.

5. "Due volte la mia sorte bona ha mandato la vostra persona bella in casa mia e d'altri: una vestita da uomo, essendo donna, e l'altra, vestita da donna, essendo uomo. . . . Certo che la natura vi ha in modo composta in l'utriusque sesso, che in uno istante vi mostrate maschio, ed in subito femina . . . il favellar di voi è di donzella, e il proceder vostro di garzone." Aretino's letter is quoted in Lynne Lawner, Le cortigiane (Milan: Rizzoli, 1988), 23.

6. Gl'ingannati, 1.1.

7. The first French wig was introduced in Venice in 1665. See Rosita Levi Pisetzki, Storia del costume italiano, 3 vols. (Milan: Istituto Editoriale Italiano, 1964), 3:319–23. Arcangela Tarabotti gives a satirical catalogue of the feminized male lifestyle in Antisatira in risposta al lusso donnesco (Venice: Valvasense, 1644; reprinted in Satira e antsatira, ed. Elissa Weaver (Rome: Salerno Ed., 1998). See also Gabriele Martini, Il "vitio nefando" nella Venezia del Seicento: Aspetti sociali e repressione di giustizia (Rome: Jouvence, 1988), 95–97.

battista Marino, was liked because it provided an escape from an existence marked by political submission, rampant poverty, waves of epidemics, and the plague. The feelings of disempowerment and of demasculinization that these events must have created nourished in turn a divide between illusion and reality and encouraged fantasies of frivolity and impermanence. A new desire for the unusual started to inform a semiotics of masculinity that proclaimed the beauty of excess, the sensuality of the effeminate, the magic of the artificial, and the lure of caprice. To wit, the new fashion for opera theater, which began at that time, propelled to the forefront the languorous figure of the castrato, dressed at times as a woman and at times as a man, as the most successful and sought-after man on the Italian stage.

But then the sixteenth century too was concerned with gender slippages, so much so that cross-dressing became one of the most common features in both plays (for some critics, *the* most common feature) and chivalric romances. The newly invented genre of conduct books constantly reiterated what it takes for a man to behave like one or to be taken for one; and sumptuary legislation, although usually concerned with class prerogatives, offered repeated glimpses on what rituals confirmed or had to be followed to assure proper gender alignment. No matter how much men liked to project themselves as take-charge *pater familias*, the early modern period constantly showed fissures in this construction.

And then there was the castrato. As I will argue in the last chapter, the castrato started to be manufactured by surgeons and barbers for the sake of a voice uncannily and studiedly feminine, not in the "decadent" seventeenth century but as early as the middle of the supposedly manly sixteenth century. The presence of these sexually mutilated men in courts and in churches before they took the stage in large numbers problematizes not only the issue of how much men who call themselves men truly possess all characteristics of the male sex but also the issue of the gender with which castrati could or would align themselves. Their presence must have fostered a high level of sexual panic in men who had apparently little reason to worry about their own masculinity, at least in public, for a strong revulsion against the practice of prepubertal castration was often recorded. Castrati were known to wear items of feminine clothing in public, such as corsets and veils, especially at the height of their fashion; they carried makeup and rouge and were often called "prima donna" or "signora."[8] What gender were

8. See, for example the film *The Castrato Farinelli* (1995), an Italian and French coproduction directed by Gérard Corbiau, which reconstructs liberally the career of the most

they embodying or performing, and how much did surgical manipulation of their sex impinge, if at all, on their object choice?

Unlike gender, sex has been given in culture as something stable, that is, a man is a man when he possesses male and not female sexual organs. In cases when nature seems to have been more ambiguous, surgeons now literally carve a sex most resembling that which best follows an individual's predominant characteristics. But in the early modern period the stability of sexual categories was always at risk, and I am not talking here of castrati. Doctors were able to explain with more credibility than would be imaginable in our times how, for example, by running after a pig and jumping over a ditch, a fifteen-year-old French woman called Marie Germain became a man (later known as Germaine Garnier), recognized and certified as such upon medical investigation.[9] Responsible for the mishap were changes in bodily heat caused by Marie's unfeminine chase. Apothecaries, charlatans, midwives, and barbers were all called upon, alongside medical experts, to interpret and possibly correct the mechanisms of bodies in which fluctuating humors could produce havoc, where fears of engendering through putrefying and fermenting matter could infect the psyche even of educated men, and individuals whose femininity or masculinity had previously appeared unproblematic could suddenly discover themselves in limbo.

Genitalia, in short, did not constitute a clear-cut sign of difference, and a sex could always assume the features and the functions of the other: a man could, in effect, be constructed. Such is literally the claim that Angelo Dovizi da Bibbiena makes, as we will see in chapter 5, when he shows the character Calandro in La calandria to be made of detachable parts and prosthetic additions. The fact that the episode is awash in compensatory irony does not dispel the anxiety that sexual difference may be difficult to pinpoint or to secure. Such is also the evidence suggested by the practice of castration, which in freely "remaking" male sexuality invited questions on what the input of socialization was in making a man a man and whether beliefs in biological determinism were tenable.

As I concentrate on identity and generation in this book, I am aware that it is difficult to destabilize the male body as the site of sexual difference, since

---

famous castrato singer ever and consistently shifts between representations of Farinelli as a man with, on the one hand, strong heterosexual interests and, on the other, a fascination for feminine bric-a-brac.

9. See Ambroise Paré (1517–90), *On Monsters and Marvels*, trans. Janis Pallister (1573; Chicago: University of Chicago Press, 1982), ch. 7.

through the centuries it has been constituted as the standard, because of the sexism inherent in much philosophical and biological enquiry. Still, I think it fruitful to investigate the performative nature of masculinity to show how problematic indeed it is for men to be virile, phallic, and active. Women's bodies have always been constructed as marked and incapable of fitting any cultural mold for good, even when restrained to their most deterministic function of bringing a pregnancy to fruition. Women, that is, unlike men, have always been supposed to perform femininity and construct their selves in accordance with a masculine ideal of what "women" are like. As Jacques Lacan famously put it, womanhood and masquerade are made for each other: "It is in order to be the phallus, that is to say, the signifier of the desire of the *Other*, that the woman will reject an essential part of her femininity, notably all its attributes through masquerade. It is for what she is not that she expects to be desired as well as loved."[10] But then, should we not ask who is in charge in such a masquerade?

Engendering in the Early Modern Period

Let me pause here and contextualize my argument by tracing the discourse on the functions of the male and female bodies as they were reflected in texts on reproduction in the early modern period. We know that medical pronouncements on engendering contained in the Hippocratic corpus, a collection of information dating from the end of the fifth century to the beginning decade of the fourth century B.C., still influenced Renaissance thought. The major Greek voice on the subject was of course Aristotle, specifically the Aristotle of *Generation of Animals*, as read in the early Middle Ages by the Arabic doctor Avicenna.[11]

10. Jacques Lacan, "The Meaning of the Phallus," in *Feminine Sexuality: Jacques Lacan and the Ecole Freudienne*, ed. Juliet Mitchell and Jacqueline Rose (New York: Norton, 1982), 74–85, esp. 84. For a fuller analysis of the masquerade of femininity focused on the Italian Renaissance and for a reconstruction of the critical thinking on the subject, from Joan Rivière to Sigmund Freud, Friedrich Nietzsche, Luce Irigaray, and Mary Ann Doane, see Valeria Finucci, "The Female Masquerade: Ariosto and the Game of Desire," in *Desire in the Renaissance: Psychoanalysis and Literature*, ed. Valeria Finucci and Regina Schwartz (Princeton: Princeton University Press, 1995), 61–88.

11. Aristotle (384–322 B.C.), *Generation of Animals* [hereafter GA], trans. A. L. Peck (Cambridge: Harvard University Press, 1990); Avicenna (ibn-Sina, 980–1037), *Canon* (*Liber Canonis*) (Venice, 1507; facsimile, Hildesheim: Olms, 1964). For Avicenna's influence in the period, see Nancy Siraisi, *Avicenna in Renaissance Italy: The Canon and Medical Teaching in Ital-*

Roman gynecological thought also weighed in with Soranus of Ephesus, who wrote in the second century A.D.[12] Medieval Latin treatises on generation and obstetrics attributed to Trotula and the school of Salerno and heavily influenced by Soranus had a large circulation and were translated into a number of vernacular languages before they were printed in 1544.[13] But the figure towering above all practitioners and influencing every single aspect of embryology at the time was undoubtedly Galen of Pergamum, personal physician to the Roman emperor Commodus, who united the Hippocratic and Aristotelian traditions and forcefully impacted the West after the translation of his work (almost 120 medical treatises) into Latin in the eleventh and twelfth centuries.[14] Galen's views were held and confirmed through newly fashionable anatomical explo-

---

ian Universities after 1500 (Chicago: University of Chicago Press, 1987). The widest circulation of the Canon occurred between 1470 and 1520.

12. Soranus, Gynecology (Gynmaeciorum libri IV), trans. Owsei Temkin (Baltimore: Johns Hopkins University Press, 1956).

13. Trotula, The Disease of Women (De mulierum passionibus), trans. Elizabeth Mason-Hohl (Los Angeles: Ward Ritchie Press, 1940). See also Monica Green, "Women's Medical Practice and Health Care in Medieval Europe," Signs 14 (1989): 434–73.

14. Galen (130?–199?), On the Usefulness of the Parts of the Body (De usu partium corporis), 2 vols., ed. and trans. Margaret May (Ithaca: Cornell University Press, 1968), vol. 1, bk. 14: "Reproductive Tract." The Opera Galeni was produced in Venice, first in Greek (the Aldine edition) in 1525 and then in Latin (the Giunta edition) in 1541–42, and was soon rendered in a number of vernacular languages. Robert Durling assesses 630 editions or translations between 1473 and 1600. See Durling, "A Chronological Census of Renaissance Editions and Translations of Galen," Journal of the Warburg and Courtauld Institutes 24 (1961): 230–305. Galen's De anatomicis administrationibus became important for the anatomical studies of Vesalius in the 1540s; his Thrasybulum, however, impacted only later. Although by the end of the sixteenth century, as a result of anatomical observations and following attacks by Vesalius, Paracelsus, and Fracastoro, Galen's influence on medical thought started to wane, the best medical university in Italy, Bologna, still made him the only authority in surgery in 1586 through a change in curriculum. See Durling, "A Chronological Census," 245. The three major medical texts taught in Italian medical schools from the sixteenth century through the eighteenth were Hippocrates's Aphorisms, Galen's Ars medica, and Avicenna's Canon. The standard medical book, Articella, which appeared continuously after 1476 and from which all students studied, favored Galen over the other two. When Paracelsus's work became known, Hippocratic medicine gained favor. See Siraisi, Avicenna. Another influence on medical teaching was Cornelius Celsus's De medicina (first century A.D.), rediscovered in the fifteenth century, which contained sections on pharmacy, dietetics, and surgery.

rations by the majority of Renaissance doctors, including Andreas Vesalius.[15] Highly respected were the *praecepta* on fertility by Albertus Magnus, who combined Aristotelian and Galenic sources; and at the local level the observations of the fifteenth-century Paduan doctor Michele Savonarola.[16] In general, Aristotelian thought dominated philosophy and Galenic thought influenced medical research.

For Aristotle, woman was a passive creature who desired sexual union with man in order to complete herself.[17] Her body was a vessel that received and

15. Andreas Vesalius (1514–64), *On the Fabric of the Human Body* (*De humani corporis fabrica*), trans. William Richardson (1543; San Francisco: Norman, 1998). See also Prospero Borgarucci, *Della contemplazione anatomica, sopra tutte le parti del corpo humano* (Venice: Valgrisi, 1564); and Giovanni Valverde (1525–88) *Anatomia del corpo humano* (Rome: Salamanca et Lafréry, 1560). Dissection was forbidden in earlier times but was possible by the fourteenth century, although embalming was not. Male bodies were more easily available than females, since the cadavers permitted for dissection were those of criminals. Doctors preferred drowned subjects to those hanged because they were thus assured that the bone structure had not been compromised. See Roger French, *Dissection and Vivisection in the European Renaissance* (Aldershot: Ashgate, 1999). Since dissection was performed to instruct on known human physiology rather than to discover more about it, it did very little to displace philosophical givens on bodily functions. See Nancy Siraisi, *Medieval and Early Renaissance Medicine: An Introduction to Knowledge and Practice* (Chicago: University of Chicago Press, 1990), 89; and William Brockbank, "Old Anatomical Theatres and What Took Place Therein," *Medical History* 12 (1968): 371–84.

16. Albertus Magnus (1193?–1280), *De secretis mulierum* (Lyons: De Marsy, 1595); Michele Savonarola (1385–1466?), *Practica Major Jo Michaelis Savonarolae* (Venice: Giunta, 1559); and *De regimine pregnantium et noviter natorum usque ad septennium*, now in *Il trattato ginecologico-pediatrico in volgare*, ed. Luigi Belloni (Milan: Stucchi, 1952). For a voluminous excursus on medical opinions on the uterus and its function from Greek times to the beginning of this century, see Felice La Torre, *L'utero attraverso i secoli: Da Erofilo ai giorni nostri* (Città di Castello: Unione Arti Grafiche, 1917).

17. For the Renaissance medical discourse that I put forward in these pages, I am particularly indebted to the work of Thomas Laqueur, *Making Sex: Body and Gender from the Greeks to Freud* (Cambridge: Harvard University Press, 1990); Ian Maclean, *The Renaissance Notion of Woman: A Study on the Fortunes of Scholasticism and Medical Science in European Intellectual Life* (Cambridge: Cambridge University Press, 1980); Londa Schiebinger, *The Mind Has No Sex? Women in the Origins of Modern Science* (Cambridge: Harvard University Press, 1989); Nancy Tuana, *The Less Noble Sex: Scientific, Religious, and Philosophical Conceptions of Woman's Nature* (Bloomington: Indiana University Press, 1993); Danielle Jacquart and Claude Thomasset, *Sexuality and Medicine in the Middle Ages*, trans. Matthew Adamson (Princeton: Princeton

cultivated the male seed until it discharged a fully formed infant. The importance of the mother for Aristotle was therefore accidental: she provided the
"matrix," but her mate gave everything else: seed, a sensitive and rational soul,
and physical features. The man, because he was hotter than the woman, also
determined the sex of the newborn — the better sex being male, of course, since
only male fetuses were complete for Aristotle, though females were necessary
to the reproduction of humans. Even in the middle of the sixteenth century the
Venetian anatomist Niccolò Massa took pains to explain that the word "matrix"
does not come, as we would imagine, from the Greek noun *meter* (mother) but
from *metra*, "resembling a vessel which preserves the foetus."[18] For Aristotle the
signs of man were the penis and scrotum and the active principle to generate,
that is, the seed; those of woman were the uterus and a passive, nongenerating
principle, the *catamenia*, that is, menstrual discharge. Although both seed and
catamenia are identified as surplus bodily productions, only men were able to
produce a secretion potent enough for engendering. Paternity is what defines
men, and maternity what defines women: he reproduces in her, and she hosts
the generated embryo.[19]

University Press, 1988); Stephen Greenblatt, "Fiction and Friction," in *Shakespearean Negotiations: The Circulation of Social Energy in Renaissance England* (Berkeley and Los Angeles: Univer-
sity of California Press, 1988), 66–93 and 175–84; and Helen Lemay, "Human Sexuality in
Twelfth- through Fifteenth Century Scientific Writings," in *Sexual Practices and the Medieval
Church*, ed. Vern Bullough and James Brundage (Buffalo, N.Y.: Prometheus Books, 1982),
187–205. For a visual excursion into discourses of the body, see Zirka Z. Filipczaz, *Hot Dry
Men, Cold Wet Women: The Theory of Humors in Western European Art, 1575–1700* (New York:
American Federation of Arts, 1997). Rudolph Bell's book *How to Do It: Guides to Good Living
for Renaissance Italians* (Chicago: University of Chicago Press, 1999) (see esp. chs. 2 and 3) unfortunately appeared after I had completed the relevant medical sections of this book but
should certainly be consulted.

18. Niccolò Massa (1485–1569), *Introductory Book of Anatomy* (*Liber introductorius anatomiae*)
(Venice, 1536), reprinted in *Studies in Pre-Vesalian Anatomy: Biography, Translations, Documents*,
ed. Levi Robert Lind (Philadelphia: American Philosophical Society, 1975), 174–253, esp.
204. For a hilarious survey of literature on the activity of the male sperm and the passivity of
the female ovum, see Emily Martin, "Body Narratives, Body Boundaries," in *Cultural Studies*,
ed. Lawrence Grossberg, Cary Nelson, and Paula Treichler (New York: Routledge, 1992),
409–19.

19. See Maryanne Cline Horowitz, "Aristotle and Women," *Journal of the History of Biology*
9.2 (1976): 183–213; and Vern Bullough, "Medieval Medical and Scientific Views of Women,"
Viator 4 (1973): 485–501.

Unlike Aristotle, the Hippocratics believed that women contributed to generation, although because of their relative lack of body heat their contribution was not exactly equal: the male produced a stronger sperm and the female a weaker one. But males and females tended to produce differently at any given time, which explained the difference in sexes. Quantity was also important, and abundant albeit weak sperm could still produce a boy. It all depended on the mixture. For Galen, women, like men, produced semen, but theirs was colder and therefore less determinant than male semen, given that women's nature was cold and humid, in contrast to the hot, dry nature of men. He thus clearly assigns a role in generation to women, although not as strongly as the Hippocratics before him.

These views were reflected widely in the learned literature of the period. Dante described procreation as a sequence of events in which male activity meets female passive materiality. The semen mingled with menstrual blood, as in Aristotle:

> Ivi s'accoglie l'uno e l'altro insieme,
> l'un disposto a patire e l'altro a fare
> per lo perfetto loco onde si preme.

> There the one is mingled with the other, one designed to be passive, the other to be active, by reason of the perfect place whence it springs.[20]

In the most influential treatise on the politics of court life in the Renaissance, Baldassarre Castiglione's *Il libro del cortegiano*, the view expressed is predominantly Aristotelian on issues of form and matter, but Galen creeps in: Castiglione assigns to a misogynist character by the name of Gasparo the view that the birth of a woman constitutes a mistake or defect and is contrary to nature's wishes; he then counters this view with another, assigned to a liberal, the Magnifico Giuliano, who answers that both man and woman are necessary to engendering:

> nè so come possiate dire che la natura non intenda produr le donne, senza le quali la specie umana conservar non si po. . . . Perciò col mezzo di questa compagnia di maschio e di femina produce i figlioli; . . . [e] l'una e l'altro

---

20. Dante Alighieri, *Purgatorio*, in *The Divine Comedy*, ed. and trans. Charles Singleton (Princeton: Princeton University Press, 1973), 25.46–48.

insieme vengono a generare, la qual cosa far non possono alcun di loro per se stessi.

> You cannot possibly argue that Nature does not intend to produce the women without whom the human race cannot be preserved. . . . For by means of the union of male and female, she produces children; . . . both join together for the purpose of procreation which neither can ensure alone.[21]

In Giovan Battista Gelli's *La Circe*, women are unable to generate, but they provide the "vegetative soul" ("l'anima vegetativa") that makes the new being grow. The process is identical to that of a hen, which can make, as well as grow, the egg, but cannot bear offspring unless she has consorted with a cock.[22]

As many historians of science have pointed out, the issue of who contributed what was important, not because it was biological but because it was political: woman needed to be postulated as inferior and man as superior, no matter what a scientific investigation might prove.[23] The issue, in short, had nothing to do with women as real beings. Emilia Pio, who directs the courtiers' conversation in the *Cortegiano*, recognizes that much when she asks the courtiers to stop their useless debate on matter and form: "Per amor di Dio, — disse, — uscite una volta di queste vostre 'materie' e 'forme' e maschi e femine e parlate di modo che siate inteso" (3.17.222; "In heaven's name, leave all this business of matter and form and male and female for once, and speak in a way that you can be understood"). Undaunted, the men resume the conversation and start expounding on hot men and frigid women. In fact, although Galen's theory that women were needed in

21. Baldassarre Castiglione, *Il libro del cortegiano* (1528; Milan: Mursia, 1972); translated as *The Book of the Courtier*, ed. and trans. George Bull (London: Penguin, 1976), 3.14.220; and 3.16.222 [hereafter in the text; the numbers refer to book, section, and page number]. For Gasparo's ideas on women, see 3.11.218.

22. Giovan Battista Gelli (1498–1563), *La Circe*, in *Trattatisti del Cinquecento*, 2 vols., ed. Mario Pozzi (Milan: Ricciardi, 1978), 1:1067–1158, esp. 1117. No matter the import of this observation, Renaissance medicine did not know the female ovum. It was discovered in 1651; spermatozoa were identified in 1670. William Harvey, the father of modern embryology (*De generatione animalium*, 1651), thought that the ovum was the result, and not the cause, of conception. He also noticed that women could conceive without emission of fluids. See Angus McLaren, *Reproductive Rituals: The Perception of Fertility in England from the Sixteenth Century to the Nineteenth Century* (London: Methuen, 1984), 22.

23. See, for example, Laqueur, *Making Sex*; Schiebinger, *The Mind Has No Sex?*; Jacquart and Thomasset, *Sexuality and Medicine*; and Tuana, *The Less Noble Sex*.

procreation because they provided more than passive semen was already quite modest, thinkers such as Taddeo Alderotti and Cesare Cremonini, both Neo-Aristotelians, downplayed the woman's role further. Kaspar Hoffman, a Galenist, denied woman had semen at all.[24] A woman who could produce semen—like a man—and also provide the body for the fetus to develop—which man could not—had too much power. So these early theorists devised a weakness: her organs were inferior to those of the male because she had less body heat and higher humidity. This view that the male body was superior to the female's persisted as late as the eighteenth century, even though available data, dissection, and study of both male and female cadavers (including their brains), seemed to show otherwise.[25]

If medical thought was adamant in denying woman too much importance in procreation even while postulating the two-seed theory, it was even more adamant in denying that woman's body, and therefore her functions, could be independent from men's. Male and female organs were considered homologous—as a number of medical treatises of the time reiterated, even those written in the vernacular, which the middle class preferred—no matter what visual, medical, and anatomical surveys could reveal. The only difference between the organs of women and men was that female organs were inside the body (because women lacked heat) and those of males were outside.[26] Since the standard was male, it was woman's body, not man's, that had ostensibly to be constructed and explained. The vagina was considered a "spermatic vessel," like the penis, and was in fact thought to be an inverted penis cavity; the ovaries stood for male testes

24. On Alderotti (1223–1303), see Nancy Siraisi, *Taddeo Alderotti and His Pupils: Two Generations of Italian Medical Learning* (Princeton: Princeton University Press, 1981), 188–200; on Cremonini and Hoffman, see Maclean, *The Renaissance Notion of Woman*, 36.

25. In *The Anatomy of the Human Bones*, Alexander Munro, for example (already in 1726), wrote that "The Bones of Women are frequently incomplete, and always of a Make in some parts of the Body different from those of the robust Male." See Schiebinger, *The Mind Has No Sex?*, 193. A favorite bone was the pelvis, for its relation to woman's maternal functions. Plenty of explanations had to be given to the fact that female craniums appeared larger than those of the males; doctors and cultural historians who had argued that women were naturally predisposed to maternity, given the relative largesse of their pelvises, had now to come up with creative reasons to justify what difference in brain size meant for this sex.

26. As Galen put it, "All the parts, then, that men have, women have too, the difference between them lying in only one thing . . . that in women the parts are within [the body], whereas in men they are outside." See *On the Usefulness of the Parts of the Body*, 2.14.628.

and were called *testiculi* well into the eighteenth century; the female prepuce was compared to the foreskin; and the uterus corresponded to the scrotum.

Whatever men did, women did as well: since conception required that men had an orgasm and ejaculated, women had to experience the same. Female secretions thus were thought to be female sperm; they were necessary to conception—up to a point.[27] Only at the end of the sixteenth century did women

27. New discoveries did not dislodge the firmly held view of the one-sex body: as Laqueur writes, Vesalius's realization that the left testicular vein comes from the kidney and not from the vena cava, and therefore that the watery fluid it carried might have some bearing on conception, made no difference to the then current theory; the fact that Leonardo da Vinci found that uterine vessels did not lead to the breast and that milk could not be concocted from blood in the womb to form a fetus also made no impact; the discovery (or recovery) of the clitoris in 1559 by Realdo Colombo or Gabriele Falloppio and Fallopio's discovery of the Fallopian tubes also changed nothing. Neither did the discovery of the prostate, which would have proved male and female bodies different. Drawings of the period show the two sexes as identical. In fact, even observations made during dissection of female cadavers generally did not challenge those postulated theoretically: the anatomist Alessandro Achillini (1463-1512) dissected two women and still did not see where the left seminal vessel enters the kidney, a discovery that would have disproved the view that females were inferior to males because their blood was not cleansed when exiting the vena cava. See *Anatomical Notes* (*Annotationes anatomicae*, 1520) in Lind, *Studies in Pre-Vesalian Anatomy,* 49; and Tuana, *The Less Noble Sex*, 138. At other times anatomists added to the female body what was not there. Vesalius, for example, even though he had, by his own recognition, access to a good number of female cadavers for dissection, thought for a while that horns came from the side of the womb, just as Galen had asserted. See Andreas Vesalius, *Tabulae anatomicae*, in *The Illustrations from the Works of Andreas Vesalius of Brussels*, ed. J. B. de C. M. Saunders and Charles O'Malley (1538; Cleveland: World Publishing, 1950), pl. 87, fig. 2-4. Also inaccurate is the uterus drawn by renowned anatomist Jacopo Berengario da Carpi (pseud. Giacomo Barigazzi, ca. 1460-ca. 1530) in his *Carpi commentaria cum amplissimus additionibus super Anatomia Mundini* (Bologna: De Benedictis, 1521). See Loris Premuda, *Storia dell'iconografia anatomica* (Milan: Martello, 1957), 98. Recently Gianna Pomata has contested the theory of the one-sex body by demonstrating that the naturalness with which men accepted spontaneous bleeding—often confused with menstruation when it had a certain regularity, no matter from which part of the body blood was exiting—speaks for a way of constructing the male body not as the standard but as modeled on the female (considered here as better because able to get rid of extra blood). See "Menstruating Men: Similarity and Difference between the Sexes in Early Modern Europe," in *Generation and Degeneration: Tropes of Reproduction in Literature and History from Antiquity to Early Modern Europe*, ed. Valeria Finucci and Kevin Brownlee (Durham, N.C.: Duke University Press, 2001), 109-52. Janet Adelman's objection to Laqueur's

cease to be seen as failed men, and only in the late seventeenth century were the sexes considered no longer homologous and hierarchically placed but simply different, with the movement toward preformationism (as embodied, for example, by Nicolas Malebranche and Marcello Malpighi) and the concept that fully formed individuals existed within ova or spermatozoa.[28]

The rules of generation were relatively simple: in the economy of anatomical similarity, women conceived when there was suitable heat, correct body position, adequate arousal, sufficient rest, proper food, satisfactory concoction of semen, fitting psychological state, right moment of the month and of the day, and appropriate phase of the moon. When the combination was optimal, a male child was the guaranteed outcome.[29] For Aristotle, male sperm equaled female menses. Both came from blood, but due to their heat deficiency females were less able than males to reduce its quantity and purify it; males, by contrast, had the heat to make it turn whitish. Women contributed no semen, since they discharged it all in their menses. True, they seemed to have a discharge following genital stimulation, but not all women, only the fair-skinned and the most femi-

---

model—that theories advocated by Galenist doctors of continental Europe were not really received in England—obviously does not apply to Italy. But her point, that "the elevation of the one-sex model to hegemonic status . . . sometimes turns out to be only the most recent way of reinforcing lack," is well taken. See her "Making Defect Perfection: Shakespeare and the One-Sex Model," in *Enacting Gender on the English Renaissance Stage*, ed. Viviana Comensoli and Ann Russell (Urbana: University of Illinois Press, 1999), 23–52, esp. 25.

28. Even then the struggle between proponents of ovism (who thought that the female ovum contained a preformed being) and proponents of animalculism (who thought that the male sperm held within itself a miniature being) settled in favor of the male. In fact, the view that females are colder than males still has its committed followers today. In psychological parlance, for example, a woman can be characterized as a sexually frigid creature. Freud himself, reflecting the nineteenth-century obsession with the uterus, had no problem in connecting vaginal frigidity "to the essence of femininity" and in considering woman, as a result of humors induced by her uterus, more prone to melancholia, mood shifts, and depression. See Sigmund Freud, "Three Essays on the Theory of Sexuality," *Standard Edition* [hereafter *SE*], 24 vols., ed. and trans. James Strachey (1905; London: Hogarth Press, 1953–74), 7:125–243 (1953), esp. 221.

29. How to do it was even illustrated by that singular reporter of bodies, limbs, and musculature, Leonardo da Vinci. In "Coitus" he carefully sketched how copulation works from inside the body. See *Leonardo nelle biblioteche milanesi: Edizioni e riproduzioni*, ed. Giulia Bologna (Novara: Istituto Geografico de Agostini, 1983), 78.

nine types.[30] Women could also conceive without experiencing pleasure: they simply needed to be excited. According to Galen, a baby's sex was determined by both parents in tune with their body temperature. Male seed produced from the right testis combined with female seed produced from the right ovary and deposited in the right side of the uterus engendered a boy; the process was reversed for a girl.[31] Male fetuses were also formed faster than female fetuses and moved earlier. Conception could take place only if the man actively aided the woman.[32]

Premature ejaculation or having a uterus too moist or too dry constituted a problem. How to explain then that some women became pregnant even without having an orgasm or as a result of being raped? Soranus and many doctors after him argued that such women must have somehow enjoyed intercourse, even if they were unaware of it in their desire to keep the experience out of their mind.[33] The degree of wishful thinking that the theory of necessary female

30. *GA* 1.20.728a.

31. Galen, *On the Usefulness of the Parts of the Body*, 2.14.626–28. In the pseudo-Galenic *De spermate* (*The Seed*) in circulation during the Middle Ages, the combination of weak or strong male and female seed was fraught with risk: a weak male and a strong female seed could engender a hermaphrodite; a strong male and a weak female seed could give the same results. See Jacquart and Thomasset, *Sexuality and Medicine*, 141. For a sense of how haphazard and complicated the combination of humors of men and women could be at any given time, see the treatise on how to engender an intelligent boy from an intelligent father—not an easy task—by Juan Huarte de San Juan (1529?–1588), *Essamina de gl'ingegni de gli huomini accomodati ad apprendere qual si voglia scienza* (Venice: Barezzi, 1600). The original Spanish text, *Examen des ingenios para la ciencias*, was published in 1575; the first Italian edition in 1582. The book was placed in the Index after the Jesuit Antonio Possevino criticized its determinism.

32. The woman must enjoy sex in order to conceive, as Michele Savonarola notes, "la dona engravidare non se può senza suo gran dilecto recevuto in tal acto." See *Trattato utilissimo di molte regole, per conservare la sanità, dichiarando qual cose siano utili da mangiare, e quali tristi, e medesimamente di quelle che si bevono in Italia* (Venice: Eredi di Gioanni Paduano, 1554), 40. See also Realdo Colombo (1515?–59), *De re anatomica* (Venice: Bevilacqua, 1559), 242–43 and 246. Unfortunately for women, early in the nineteenth century female orgasm started to be considered irrelevant to conception; later it came to be understood that women ovulate whether or not intercourse has taken place. Ovulation was discovered in the nineteenth century.

33. Soranus, *Gynecology*, 36. See also Ann Hanson, "The Medical Writers' Woman," in *Before Sexuality: The Construction of Erotic Experience in the Ancient Greek World*, ed. David Halperin, John Winkler, and Froma Zeitlin (Princeton: Princeton University Press, 1990), 309–37, esp. 315. McLaren notices that only from the nineteenth century on, did courts of law no

orgasm requires is indeed staggering. Were philosophers and theoreticians so out of touch with reality as not to know what was going on in the bedroom? Or were women just as experienced in the art of faking it as they seem to be today? The only difference between the sixteenth and the twenty-first centuries is in their agenda: in the Renaissance, orgasmic behavior would have shown that they were "real" women, that is, proper procreative partners; in our days, that they are "real" women, that is, sexually liberated companions.[34]

In his treatise on gynecology, Antonio Guainerio recommended not only that women be submitted to some amount of foreplay for the purpose of conceiving, but that men too, if necessary, use stimulants; an example was crushed pepper, to be chewed and then spread with saliva on the penis before intercourse.[35] Reflecting the culture of his times, the Venetian doctor Giovanni Marinello suggested that men prepare themselves with sweet-smelling "suffumiges" and oil their penises with civet, musk, or other substances one hour before going to bed. They should avoid cold drinks to avoid chilling the sperm.[36] Gabriele Falloppio urged parents to work early with their hands on their boy's penis to assure that it would become sufficiently long and serviceable with an eye to future adult engagements.[37] Another doctor, Girolamo Cardano, recommended that men remain active, eat roasted rather than boiled food, recharge themselves with good bread, and drink wine.[38] Giambattista della Porta extolled the power of satyrion (orchid), because it gave men plenty of sperm, lengthened intercourse, and excited women, though lettuce had to be avoided, he warned, and saffron

---

longer assume that a pregnant rape victim had enjoyed forced intercourse. See *Reproductive Rituals*, 27.

34. For a witty discussion on the pleasures of faking it in the Renaissance, see Marjorie Garber, "The Insincerity of Women," in Finucci and Schwartz, *Desire in the Renaissance*, 19–38.

35. Antonio Guainerio (Anthonius Guainerius, d. 1448), *Tractatus de matricibus (Treatise on the womb)*, in *Opera Ommia* (Pavia: n.p., 1481), fol. z4va–b. On Guainerius, see Helen Lemay, "Anthonius Guainerius and Medieval Gynecology," in *Women of the Medieval World*, ed. Julius Krishner and Suzanne Wemple (London: Blackwell, 1985), 317–36.

36. Giovanni Marinello (d. ca. 1576) *Le medicine partenenti alle infermità delle donne* (Venice: Francesco de' Franceschi, 1563), 2.1 and 2.8; abridged version in *Medicina per le donne nel Cinquecento: Testi di Giovanni Marinello e di Girolamo Mercurio*, ed. Maria Luisa Altieri Biagi et al. (Turin: UTET, 1992).

37. Gabriele Falloppio (1523–62), *Secreti diversi e miracolosi* (Venice: Bonfad, 1658).

38. Girolamo Cardano (1501–76), *De subtilitate libri XXI: De hominis natura et temperamento* (Basel: Henricpetri, 1582), 376.

could kill conception altogether.[39] Niccolò Machiavelli too believed in satyrion to further male virility. Fantasizing in the play *Clizia* on the best way to fortify himself for his upcoming encounter with the virginal Clizia, the character Nicomaco announces that he will take "satirione" and a dinner of onions, fava beans, spices, and pigeon meat cooked rare.[40]

Woman's position in assuring conception was also deemed important. To nobody's surprise, all doctors and commentators agreed that what has come to be known as the missionary position was most conducive to the purported goal: the woman was to lie below the man, but in such a way as to allow her body to participate in the sexual act. Showing some penchant for gymnastics, Guainerio recommended that the woman put her head low, her hips high, her left foot under her hip, and her right leg extended.[41] Reading the position positively for women, Lodovico Domenichi argued that it was nobler for women, after all, to look toward heaven during intercourse than down below, like men, which was more like what beasts do ("come le bestie fanno").[42] Michele Savonarola was specific on what parts of the woman's body needed to be touched: breasts, nipples, and everything below, plus clitoral stimulation, he said, were

39. Giambattista Della Porta (1535-1615), *Magiae naturalis* (Naples: S. Abbati Stampatori, 1558; reprint, Palermo: Il Vespro, 1979), 113-14. Satyrion was the root of choice to restore sexual desire and potency in men because its form mirrored the male organ. Paracelsus (1493?-1541) recommended it. See Walter Pagel, *Paracelsus: An Introduction to Philosophical Medicine in the Era of the Renaissance* (New York: Karger, 1958), 149.

40. Nicolò Machiavelli, *Clizia*, in *Mandragola/Clizia*, ed. Riccardo Bacchelli (Milan: Feltrinelli, 1995), 4.2.

41. Guainerio, *Tractatus de matricibus*, fol. z4va-b. See also Lemay, "Anthonius Guainerius," 332. Sins against nature were harshly condemned by canon and civil law. Augustine had specifically called the sin worse in a wife than in a prostitute: "when a man seeks to exploit a woman's sexual parts beyond what is granted in this way, a wife becomes more basely if she allows herself rather than another to be used in this way." See Augustine, *The Good of Marriage*, in *De bono coniugali, De sancte virginitate*, ed. and trans. P. G. Walsh (Oxford: Clarendon Press, 2001), 27.12. Thomas Aquinas also spoke against unnatural intercourse like onanism, sodomy, and bestiality. He deemed those acts worse than rape of a virgin because they entailed the use of the wrong vessel, the wrong body, and the wrong species respectively. See *Summa Theologica*, trans. Fathers of English Dominican Province (New York: Benziger Brothers, 1947), 2.2, qu. 154, arts. 11 and 12. See also Vern Bullough, "The Sin against Nature and Homosexuality," in Bullough and Brundage, *Sexual Practices and the Medieval Church*, 55-71.

42. Lodovico Domenichi (1515-64), *Della nobiltà delle donne* (Venice: Giolito, 1551), 112r.

good spots on which to concentrate in order to have woman "spermatize" ("spermatizare").[43] Girolamo Ruscelli suggested that the couple follow a collaborative technique. Insertion in the vagina of essences such as incense, for example, immediately after intercourse was a proven therapy. A woman could also increase her chances for pregnancy by eating tiny *polpi* (octopuses) roasted without oil.[44] In his *Secreti medicinali*, Pietro Bairo advised women to lie still for an hour after intercourse with their thighs together. Then for three days they had to treat the vagina with a solution of tar, frankincense, and oil to ensure conception.[45] Consumption of complicated apotropaic preparations, such as uteruses of rabbits and hares, was deemed effective, but drinking something as simple and ubiquitously available as cold water had to be avoided because it could cause barrenness or the birth of a female.[46] In general it was recommended that woman lie on her right side during or at least after intercourse to ensure conception of a boy and on the left when a girl was desired. Falloppio also advised women to keep their legs up as an extra insurance for proper engendering. By touching his wife's neck after intercourse, a husband could also know whether he had made his partner pregnant: a hot neck was a good sign.[47]

43. "Se debeno tocare l'uno l'altro, specialiter l'huomo la dona, quella tochendo e frichendo cum le decta il luoco fra il sexo e la natura: il perchè quello è il luoco exteriore nel quale le done ricieve più piacere, per la proximità di quello al collo de la matrice, dove hanno tuto el suo delecto; e per tal fricare si iritano più facilmente a spermatizare. Da puo' prolungare la coniunctione, quella tochendo pur cum le mane le mamelle e lezieramente i capi de quelle, iungendo basso a baxo per le galte, buocha et altri lochi, tochare spetialmente il luoco di sotto l'omblico." In *Il trattato ginecologico*, 41. For intriguing Renaissance recipes on how to stimulate sexual passion in men and women, see Emanuela Renzetti and Rodolfo Taiani, "Le cure dell'amore: desiderio e passione in alcuni libri dei segreti," *Sanità, scienza e storia* 2 (1986): 33–86; and Enrico Malizia, *Ricettario delle streghe: Incantesimi, prodigi sessuali e veleni* (Rome: Edizioni Mediterranee, 1992).

44. Girolamo Ruscelli (d. ca. 1566), *De secreti del R. D. Alessio Piemontese* (Venice: Bonsadino, 1611), bk. 1, 16v and bk. 2, 8r.

45. Pietro Bairo (1468–1558), *Secreti medicinali* (Venice: Tebaldini, 1602), 194v. See also Piero Camporesi, *The Incorruptible Flesh: Bodily Mutation and Mortification in Religion and Folklore*, trans. Tania Kroft-Murray (Cambridge: Cambridge University Press, 1988), 233.

46. For example, Della Porta recommends the uterus of a hare, to be used eight or ten days after the onset of a woman's period. See *Magiae naturalis*. For other recipes, see Malizia, *Ricettario delle streghe*, 260. On the effects of cold water in Aristotle, see *GA* 4.2.767a. On cold water affecting heat in men's semen, see Marinello, *Le medicine partenenti*, 2.1.

47. Falloppio, *Secreti diversi*, 3:300–1. See also Ruscelli, *De secreti*, 3, 46v.

Men too were encouraged to assume a lifestyle that would help to make their wives pregnant. Too much sex was counterproductive, the philosopher and doctor Marsilio Ficino felt, since each ejaculation wounded the mind ("ferisce la mente").[48] In Castiglione's *Cortegiano* it is explicitly stated that men dry out more than women in copulation; as a result, they do not live as long as their companions (3:18.224). Prospective fathers, Savonarola wrote, following Avicenna, should be neither too young nor too old and not drunk or too sexually active.[49] Guainerio was more specific: to engender a son men must be robust, with large testicles (especially large right ones), and produce plenty of hot seed.[50] Penis size seemed to have something to do with conception. Perhaps addressing unspoken male fears, Aristotle asserted that shorter penises were better than longer ones because with short penises semen would have had less chance to cool when traveling down to the uterus.[51] Lean men also produced more sperm than fat ones because their nutrients did not become fat but were used up in copulation.[52] Avicenna, however, warned that too small a penis was perhaps insufficient to guarantee pleasure in women: the result could be disastrous for reproduction, since lack of female ejaculation meant no procreation. Moreover, he added, women might be left tempted to relieve themselves otherwise.[53] For Giovanni Marinello the problem was technical: a short penis, he worried, might be unable to get to the neck of the "matrix" (cervix) to engender, regardless of what the woman did.[54]

The time of the year most conducive to impregnation was spring; the best time of the day was six or seven hours after digestion had started. Savonarola suggested the very early morning hours ("la hora dil matutino").[55] Moon phases

---

48. Marsilio Ficino (1433–99), *Della religione christiana* (Florence: Giunti, 1563), 16. See also Antonio Dal Fiume, "Medici, medicine e peste nel Veneto durante il secolo XVI," *Archivio veneto* 62 (1981): 33–58. Intercourse was specifically discouraged at times of disease or sickness in order to conserve energy.

49. Savonarola, *Il trattato ginecologico,* 9.

50. See Lemay, "Anthonius Guainerius," 333.

51. *GA* 1.7.718a.

52. *GA* 1.19.727a.

53. Avicenna, *Canon,* 3.20.1.44. See also Laqueur, *Making Sex,* 50.

54. Marinello, *Le medicine partenenti,* 2.1.

55. Savonarola, *Trattato utilissimo,* 23. For hours, see also also Inge Botteri, "Ars amandi: Il galateo della procreazione responsabile," in *Educare il corpo, educare la parola nella trattatistica del Rinascimento,* ed. Giorgio Patrizi and Amedeo Quondam (Rome: Bulzoni, 1998), 123–63.

were also important, and those who wanted to become pregnant were advised to avoid engaging in sex when there was no moon. For Tommaso Campanella, not only should men and women wait for the right conjunction of stars and planets but also the uterus had to be clean, so that it would not taint the semen ("non ammorbi il seme col menstruo").[56]

Most doctors agreed that woman's best time for conceiving was at the very end of her menstrual cycle, when the vaginal canal was still moist but she was dry, when no corrupted blood was in circulation and the "matrix" was clean — and, as Savonarola describes it, hungry for man's semen ("il seme cum più apetito e dilecto riceve").[57] Timing intercourse for the second week after menstruation (as we now know, the time women actually ovulate) was considered a poor choice for couples hoping to have a boy; Girolamo Mercurio deemed eight or ten days before a woman's period the best for engendering males, because there was plenty of hot and humid blood in the uterus.[58]

Unfortunately, even in the best of circumstances, some women would not conceive. Sterility was considered mostly a female problem, and beautiful women were assumed to be less fertile than plain ones. Those least likely to engender were women who had not restrained themselves from having too much sex, Guglielmo de Conches wrote, for repeated use of the vagina caused inter-

---

56. Tommaso Campanella (1568–1639), *Del senso delle cose e della magia*, ed. Antonio Bruers (Bari: Laterza, 1925), 4.18.305.

57. Savonarola, *Trattato utilissimo*, 24–25. Among Savonarola's many contributions to gynecology, it pays to mention his invention of the "sella perforata," a half-moon-shaped birth chair that became widely used. See Ynez Violè O'Neil, "Giovanni Michele Savonarola: An Atypical Renaissance Practitioner," *Clio Medica* 10.2 (1975): 77–93, esp. 86.

58. Girolamo Mercurio (Scipion Mercurii, d. 1615), *La commare o riccoglitrice* (Venice: Ciotti, 1596), 1.13. An abridged version of this treatise is in Altieri Biagi, *Medicina per le donne nel Cinquecento*. Women were recommended to have sex at the end of their menses to maximize their chances of conceiving as late as the turn of this century. See McLaren, *Reproductive Rituals*, 46. Of course, if engendering had so many rules, keeping a woman from aborting was a never-ending preoccupation. Sperone Speroni instructed his pregnant daughter, Iulia, not to eat fresh cheese, not to have fish and fowl, not to get her legs cold, and not to warm her kidneys unduly by overdressing or by sleeping on her back. While garlic, fennel, and parsley were good, carrots and capers had to be cooked first, and lettuce, radicchio, endive, and pears had to be avoided altogether. See Sperone Speroni (1500–88), "Alla Magn. M. Iulia De' Conti a Padova," letter 16 (1561) in Pozzi, *Trattatisti del Cinquecento*, 1:809.

nal incrustations, which in turn made the sperm leak out.[59] There were saints invoked expressly to help against infertility in women, but none to plead for furthering the male generative potential.[60] To enhance chances of pregnancy, doctors concentrated first and foremost on menses or a lack thereof. Problematic periods were not an uncommon phenomenon at the time, since amenorrhea (*madrazza*) was rampant, due to improper or substandard nourishment. It is difficult to imagine today the depth of past physicians' concern with fluids that remained inside the body when they were supposed to be expelled; only too often they reverted to esoteric therapies to avoid, as Niccolò Massa put it, "the suffocation of the matrix" due to retention of the menses.[61]

Menstruation was theorized as discharge of impure blood or, better, as discharge of plethora unnecessary to woman at a time in which she was neither pregnant nor breast-feeding. Being traditionally connected with uncleanliness, especially from a religious point of view (during the Middle Ages menstruating women were not allowed in church and could not receive communion), women with menses were considered carriers of disease, especially smallpox.[62] The connection between woman and unpleasant smell was invoked straight from Latin: "foemina" came from "foetidas," the lore went, just as man had inscribed in his name his own virtue: "vir"/"virtus."[63] Sex had to be avoided during menses

59. Guglielmo de Conches, *Dialogus de substantiis physicis* (Strasbourg: Rihelius, 1567), 253.

60. See Evelyne Berriot-Salvadore, "The Discourse of Medicine and Science," in *A History of Women in the West: Renaissance and Enlightenment Paradoxes*, ed. Natalie Zemon Davis and Arlette Farge (Cambridge: Harvard University Press, 1993), 348–88. According to Marinello, a man might seem sterile but in fact be perfectly able to procreate with a different woman, and a better combination of humors. He also wrote that semen could be inactive if it was too liquid or if the man was melancholic, and therefore too cold. See *Le medicine partenenti*, 3.3.

61. See *Introductory Book of Anatomy*, 207. Massa declares that he saw this suffocation in the year 1526. Therapies to bring on menses were often herbal; radicchio and chamomile were recommended; more invasive practices included bloodletting and manual dilation of the uterus. See Maria Pia Casarini, " 'La madrazza': Malattia o occultamento della gravidanza," in *Il corpo delle donne*, ed. Gisela Boch and Giuliana Nobili (Bologna: Transeuropa, 1988), 87–101, esp. 94–95. Men were thought to expel their humors through sweat.

62. See Patricia Crawford, "Attitudes to Menstruation in Seventeenth-Century England," *Past and Present* 91 (1981): 47–73, esp. 60–61.

63. Changing the etiology around in order to defend women, Galeazzo Flavio Capra (1487–1537) argued instead that woman is not "foetida" but is ritually purged every month

because the male seed would not attach itself properly to female blood and a monstrous birth or leprosy in the infant could occur.[64] A number of Renaissance doctors, following the Hippocratics, recommended that to stabilize their menses girls should marry early and married women have regular intercourse.

One reason why some women were not fertile, physicians postulated, was that their wombs might have become displaced. Lack of intercourse, for example, caused problems, because a womb that was not kept sufficiently moist might wander in order to attach itself to moister organs such as the liver, the heart, and the brain. The womb was like an independent animal within a woman's body for Plato, though not for Galen.[65] Galen thought that the uterus moved as muscles contract and relax; it also influenced women's mood (*hystera,* whence "hysteria," is Greek for "womb") and made them desire sex. A good way of drawing the womb back to its proper position was through fumigations, Guainerio recommended: a midwife would have a woman smell substances with foul odors and the womb that had been, for example, attached to the head would draw away as a result. Sweet-smelling substances were to be positioned in the meantime close to the vagina to attract the uterus back to its proper place. Rest and a therapeutic bath were to follow.[66] For Aristotle, lack of intercourse could not only displace a womb upward but also downward, since a prolapsed womb could be the result of lack of moisture, that is, of intercourse.[67] A displaced womb could also be the result of chills.

"d'ogni ribaldaria e d'ogni altra cosa che la potesse macchiare per sì fatta via." See *Della dignità e eccellenza delle donne,* ed. Maria Luisa Doglio (1525; Rome: Bulzoni, 1998) 110. An abnormally large and dark "menstrual vein" was deemed responsible for the homicidal behavior of a woman improbably named Sancta who, having suffocated her twins, was condemned to die by the same method. When the anatomist Colombo dissected her, he had no problem in connecting her psychical disorder to her physical monstrosity. See Colombo, *De re anatomica,* 173.

64. See Ottavia Niccoli, "*Menstruum quasi monstruum*: Monstrous Births and Menstrual Taboo in the Sixteenth Century," in *Sex and Gender in Historical Perspective: Selections from Quaderni Storici,* ed. Edward Muir and Guido Ruggiero (Baltimore: Johns Hopkins University Press, 1990), 1–25, esp. 2. At the very least, Jacquart and Thomasset write, a child conceived during a woman's period would have red hair. See *Sexuality and Medicine,* 73.

65. Plato, *Timaeus,* 91b–d.

66. Guainerio, *Tractatus de matricibus,* fol. y2ra.

67. Aristotle, *The History of Animals* [hereafter *HA*], in *The Complete Works of Aristotle,* 2 vols., ed. J. Barnes, trans. A. W. Thompson (Princeton: Princeton University Press, 1984),

Even with the womb in the right place and with menstrual flow regular, women might be unable to become pregnant, it was feared, because their body passages were not correctly open. Since all passageways were connected, whatever could be smelled through the nose or mouth should also have been smelled through the vaginal canal. Thus, one way to check for proper opening, Marinello suggested, was to have the woman sit over something strongly smelling; the doctor would try to detect that odor directly from her mouth. If that was unsuccessful, pessaries were recommended.[68] Thorough cleansing of the vagina with fumigations, baths, and ointments were also highly advised to combat sterility. Bairo's counsel was to put a bag of "mercury herb" inside the vagina for three days and then to take a bath containing sufficient herbs to titillate any apothecary's greed: "feverfew, wormwood, oregon, wild mint, motherwort, camomile flowers, cloves, wild rue, storax, wood of a balsam tree, costmary, fruit of balsam, madder."[69] Another solution for Bairo was to fumigate the vagina with a concoction of dried testicles of fox, boar, or male pig combined with rennet and the wombs of hares, mixed with half that quantity of sugar and ground ivory. This potion had to be taken on an empty stomach.[70] Ruscelli recommended a vaginal fumigation of boiled mint repeated ten or twelve times to guarantee results; Leonardo Fioravanti opted for a purge, a syrup for the uterus, an electuary, and a bath. Sex had to follow right away.[71]

7.582b. The fact that by the sixteenth century anatomists had clearly shown that there was no place in the body for the uterus to move had very little impact on either practitioners or lay people. See Laqueur, *Making Sex*, 110.

68. A woman with bad breath had of course problems in this respect. Pessaries were also used to cause abortions, with remedial pessaries then recommended to stop pain or heal ulcerations in the uterus. To precipitate an abortion in a woman who was afraid that she was pregnant, a Hippocratic practitioner recommended that she jump up and down, heels touching her bottom seven times, because she had not felt the semen slip out, unlike other times. This she did, whereupon "there was a noise, the seed fell out on the ground, and the girl looked at it in great surprise" (quoted in Hanson, "The Medical Writer's Woman," 322).

69. Bairo, *Secreti medicinali*, 193r–v. Translation in Camporesi, *The Incorruptible Flesh*, 231–32.

70. Bairo, *Secreti medicinali*, 914r.

71. Ruscelli, *De secreti*, 3.38v–39r; Leonardo Fioravanti (1517–88), *De capricci medicinali* (Venice: Avanzi, 1573), 1.50. See also Domenico Furfaro, *La vita e l'opera di Leonardo Fioravanti* (Bologna: Società Tipografica Editori, 1963), 152.

No matter the amount and the detail of medical counsel available to rich and middle-class people, generation was at times feared as taking place beyond the control of both mothers and fathers, beyond the help of magical engendering herbs, and beyond God's providential plan. Many people—not just the uneducated—believed that a child could be born without a paternal imprimatur, or through a woman's encounter with an animal, or as a result of an incorrect disposal of semen, or by fiendish couplings and "chemical" concoctions. Sexual practices aimed at reproduction have been notoriously difficult to control, more so at a time in which the environment was thought to proliferate with insects and animals born without mothers and fathers, straight out of fermented and putrefied matter, and godly or devilish interventions in human affairs were believed to determine fetal abnormalities and the most worrisome changes in a newborn's physical features. Even the psyche of expectant mothers, it was widely believed, could play tricks, willed or unwilled, on the baby being formed, to say nothing of unfavorable climatic changes, unreliable menstrual patterns, or interracial and interspecies couplings.

Registered at all levels of the populace, such fears of ever present pollution and uncontrolled generation were less strange than they may appear to our eyes, since they were based on apparently sound scientific principles. For Aristotle locomotion is eternal, as is generation, which, by being necessary, is cyclical for simple bodies.[72] In the presence of heat, matter is continuously formed, and thus generation, even unorganized spontaneous generation, can be put in motion at any time, for act is potency. When the sun is near, what is generated is superior to what gets destroyed; the opposite happens when the sun moves further away from matter.[73] Aristotle, who deemphasized the importance of male orgasm in postulating that it did not by itself produce generative matter, did

72. Aristotle, *De generatione et corruptione*, in Barnes, *The Complete Works of Aristotle*, 2.9.335b and 2.11.338a.

73. Beside *De generatione*, see Aristotle, *On the Heavens*, in *The Complete Works*, 2.7.289a; and *GA*, appendix A, n. 7. Pneuma for Aristotle is both internal and external and its presence "heats air. . . . For air, by nature, is moist and cold. . . . Add heat to this and one has a substance that is hot, moist, and frothy." Quoted in Michael Boylan, "The Digestive and 'Circulatory' Systems in Aristotle's Biology," *Journal of the History of Biology* 15 (1982): 89–118, at 96.

however say that it produced the most heat, which in turn caused generation (boys and old men could also have orgasms, he argued, but did not generate because their sperm was insufficiently heated). But lower beings, including some animals and fish, lack heat and are born without coital congress, from putrefying and fermenting substances.

Following the Stoics, ancient medical theorists believed that something they called pneuma was carried with the blood through arteries and veins, imparting motion and sensation. But at times the mixture of inner and outer pneuma caused problems. As Dale Martin writes,

> The whole body is endangered when the pneuma is corrupted by the inhalation of bad air, and the pneuma may be affected by poison from things like snakebites. . . . The pneuma was considered the stuff of rationality, thought, and sensation, and as such it was dangerously susceptible to pollution and corruption . . . ; it permeated other forms of nature and therefore could be acted upon, damaged and even altered by other natural elements.[74]

When the balance among various fluids present in humans (bile, phlegm, blood, water) is disturbed, or the mechanisms of hot and cold, dry and humid are disrupted, when one's unstable, fluid body is affected by the environment, the body loses its equilibrium. Changes in temperature, improper digestion, delay in appropriate purging, contact with polluted substances, alteration of internal factors, invasion of hostile outside elements, inhalation of miasmic air, immoderate use of the flesh, and a frenetic lifestyle—all contributed to corruption, degeneration, and disease.

The problem was worse in women because their flesh was thought more humid, wet, porous, and penetrable than men's, and they had too many orifices; thus they were more able to pollute and be polluted. But then male semen, being refined blood, was theoretically always putrefiable (female semen, of course, was already putrefied as menstrual blood); and blood too could become corrupted through mixture with, say, bile.[75] Even mother's milk, so necessary to guarantee

---

74. Dale B. Martin, *The Corinthian Body* (New Haven: Yale University Press, 1995), 23–24. I am indebted to Martin for my understanding of pneuma.

75. On corrupted semen, see Jacobus Silvius (Jean Dubois, 1478–1555), in *Hippocratis et Galeni physiologiae partem anatomican isagoge* (1542; Basel: Derbilley, 1556). Like some doctors of the period, Silvius held that semen was manufactured by the whole body.

a newborn's survival, was thought to be another version of putrefied blood. To ensure growth, the lore went, male children had to be given to nurse to mothers who had generated boys and had the best milk; lactating mothers of girls were traditionally offered lower wages.[76] Books on putridity and the horrors of corruption were everywhere, from Gerolamo Accoramboni's *Tractatus de putredine* (Venice, 1534) to Mario Sanbarolitano's *Degressio de putredine* (Venice, 1535) and *De simplici generatione, putredine, coctione, concretione et liquefactione mistorum corporum et perfectorum* (Mondovì, 1565), on to Giuseppe Daciano, *Trattato della peste* (Venice, 1576).

The excremental quality of natural conception, as defined by medicine, was easily buttressed by the Church's reading of sex as a degraded act, of the sexual organs as polluted and dirty (female genitals were commonly referred to as *turpitudo foeminarum* or *pudenda*, from Latin *pudere*, to be ashamed), and of engendering as taking place, so to speak, in *spurcitia* and next to fecal matter. Doctors did not know about the urethra, as separate from the vagina or birth canal, so every birth could be seen as analogous to a release of urine; it was common lore that menstrual blood could kill and sterilize, so every child concocted from it is flawed; the fetus was believed to be nourished in the fermentation and miasma of a womb, where worms self-generated even during pregnancy (because women had more phlegm), so all humankind seems indeed to have been fully punished for the sin of Adam.[77]

76. As in this song by Giulio Cesare Croce (1550–1609) in which wet nurses advertise their skills in their search for newborns to breastfeed: "Chi ha bambini da lattare? / Tanto più, state a udire, / fian migliori i nostri latti, / poichè tutte al partorire / figli maschi abbiam fatti." In "Mascherata Terza," in *Storie di vita popolare nelle canzoni di piazza di G. C. Croce*, ed. Monique Rouch (Bologna: Cooperativa Libraria Universitaria, 1982), 203. Breast milk was also a cure for deafness, earaches, and fevers. In Germany it was used to procure abortions. See Londa Schiebinger, *Nature's Body: Gender in the Making of Modern Science* (Boston: Beacon Press, 1993), 60. To keep women young, as well as to cure all sorts of skin disease ("lepra"), Caterina Sforza has a recipe that requires a mixture of metals such as silver, gold, iron, lead, and bronze to be kept one night in warm white wine, one night in juice of fennel, a third night in the milk of a mother feeding a male infant ("in lacte de donna che dia lacte a putto maschio"), and so on. See Caterina Sforza (1463–1509), *Ricettario di bellezza di Caterina Riario Sforza*, ed. Luigi Pescasio (Verona: Wella italiana, 1971), 67.

77. As Giovan Battista Codronchi (1547–1628) wrote on a treatise on the legions of worms infesting the city of Imola, "many unrefined humours are to be found in them [women] as a result of imperfect digestion; and these humours give rise to worms." See *De*

Until the discovery of modern genetics the biological connection between a father and a son could not be confirmed. Thus legal and philosophical practices provided whatever links were missing in the medical and religious discourses on reproduction. In nature, many wild beasts do not have fathers with which they are connected through social structures; they have mothers. But in human society men have asserted their link to the children their female companions were bearing through the invention of the family unit and the legal enforcing of the institution of marriage. As Pierre Vernant argues, marriage allows men to "have legitimate children who 'resemble their father' despite being the issue of their mother's womb, and who will thus be able, on the social and religious level, to continue the line of their father's house to which they belong."[78] To counter the notion that women could inseminate themselves, Aristotle declared that children in principle will resemble both mothers and fathers.[79] Eunuchs presented a special problem. Since what distinguishes men is their ability to father, Aristotle classified castrated males as "almost" female, because the active male principle that would have distinguished them from women had been lost through surgery.[80] Every philosopher, in fact, has given paternal right legal value as well a religious or quasi-religious status.

But here is the rub. If all hinges on appearing like one's father, how can a progenitor fully control the reproductive process that is so central to his being considered manly in his cultural milieu? Legally this issue was hardly problematic, since in Roman (and soon in Italian) law it was incontrovertibly stated that a father, but not a mother, had a legitimate tie (*legitima cognatio*) with his offspring, a tie that could also be natural, like that of mother and child, but not necessarily so. Only men, in short, had *patria potestas*, because only men had rights of *consanguinitas* (consanguinity) and *agnatio* (agnation, male line of descent) and could as a result bequeath property, name, and lineage.[81]

---

morbis qui Imolae (Bologna: n.p., 1603), 22. Translation in Camporesi, *The Incorruptible Flesh*, 82. It seems that the Hippocratics knew of women's urethra but that knowledge had been lost until dissections of the early modern period found it again.

78. Jean Pierre Vernant, *Myth and Society in Ancient Greece*, trans. Janet Lloyd (Brighton: Harvester Press, 1980), 138.

79. GA 1.18.722b. For the influence of this idea among Italian doctors, see Siraisi, *Taddeo Alderotti*, 197–98.

80. GA 1.2.716b.

81. *Corpus juris civilis: Digesta*, ed. Theodor Mommsen (Berin: Weidmann, 1895), 38.10.4.

In reality the issue was more complicated. When property was divided among brothers — mostly until the first half of the sixteenth century, after which a new regime of patrilinear descent started to be implemented — it was perhaps less important for a father to know which of the children he thought he had generated were in fact legitimate than it was later, when property started to be bequeathed to the first son.[82] This may explain the profusion of early modern literary texts centered on the male fear of cuckoldry, or the amount of sumptuary legislation enacted to condemn instances of unwarranted, feminine acts of freedom; it even perhaps explains the publication and sale of popular medical texts on reproductive technologies, written in Italian for an audience without the sophistication and learning needed to read Latin treatises but with plenty they needed to know on the topic. A casual affair could lead to engendering, but paternity and maternity were generally complicated businesses: legal matters, inheritance practices, and social standing were all, one way or another, connected with the practice and the externalization of desire.

82. Sisters inherited differently in Italy. Unlike brothers, who could legally divide their father's property among themselves, sisters relied on dowries accessible to them at the time of marriage or at their entrance in a convent — although administrative matters were usually left to their husband or guardian, since women were neither emancipated through marriage nor when they reached a specific age. Their legal incapacity was decreed in both civil and canon law. Dowries could occasionally be more substantial than the share of a brother's inheritance, because a sister's marriage above her social class through a tempting dowry could be important to a family's strategic alliance, but there was no assurance that all sisters would be provided for equally, and in fact such cases were rare. Dowries were usually made up of liquid assets so that the family ancestral "casa" and all landed property could remain bequeathed to the household's males. For Florentine customs, see Christiane Klapisch-Zuber; *Women, Family, and Ritual in Renaissance Italy* (Chicago: University of Chicago Press, 1985), 230–46; for the Venetian, see Stanley Chojnacki, *Women and Men in Renaissance Venice: Twelve Essays on Patrician Society* (Baltimore: Johns Hopkins University Press, 2000). For family structures in general, see Marzio Barbagli, *Sotto lo stesso tetto: Mutamenti della famiglia in Italia dal XV al XX secolo* (Bologna: Mulino, 1984), ch. 4; for issues of *patria potestas*, inheritance, and legal guardianship concerning women, see Thomas Kuen, *Law, Family and Women: Toward a Legal Anthropology of Renaissance Italy* (Chicago: University of Chicago Press, 1991), esp. 197–257; and Samuel Cohn, *Women in the Streets: Essays on Sex and Power in Renaissance Italy* (Baltimore: Johns Hopkins University Press, 1996). For the Veneto region, see Sergio Lavarda, *L'anima a Dio e il corpo alla terra: Scelte testamentarie nella terraferma veneta, 1575–1631* (Venice: Istituto Veneto di Scienze, Lettere ed Arti, 1998), ch. 5.

All the themes I have outlined, from how to control engendering to when to enforce proper gender choices, will play their part in this book as I examine paradigmatic literary texts. My first and last chapters take a free-wheeling, high-speed ride through an array of sources (mostly novellas) on all sides of the issues; the other four chapters explore complementary problems by centering on single literary texts. The problems I study are present in almost all works of Italian literature of the period, so I have chosen texts with an eye to their exemplary quality and canonical status. The two plays I examine, for example, Niccolò Machiavelli's *La mandragola* and Bernardo Bibbiena's *La calandria*, were the best known and most frequently reprinted plays of the sixteenth century; from the two chivalric romances I consider, Ludovico Ariosto's *Orlando furioso* and Torquato Tasso's *Gerusalemme liberata*, both sixteenth-century bestsellers, I chose two well-known stories: the episode of King Astolfo and the knight Jocondo in Ariosto was among the most imitated in the Renaissance, and the story of the woman warrior Clorinda in Tasso has been the prototype for numberless representations of womanhood in the early modern period.

The genre that lent itself most readily to an investigation of sex and generation, then as now, is undoubtedly the novella. Even Renaissance plays were derived from the novelistic tradition (for example, the story that Shakespeare used for his *Romeo and Juliet* traces back to novellas by Masuccio Salernitano, Luigi Da Porto, and Matteo Bandello). Machiavelli's *La mandragola* and Bibbiena's *La calandria* have clear ties to Boccaccio's fool Calandrino in the *Decameron* (in Bibbiena's case, this connection is inscribed in the name of the main character as well as in the title). The plot of Ariosto's story of Astolfo and Jocondo comes from a series of novellas about the two men; and the story of Clorinda's origin is indebted to a work by Heliodorus, *An Aethiopian Romance*, recovered and translated in the sixteenth century. But the place where the novelistic tradition is strongest is in the material I explore in chapters 1 and 6; the topics dealt with there were not accorded a higher literary treatment by contemporary authors because civic and ecclesiastical printing norms would not have allowed it. Chapter 1 looks at cases of self-engendering and births attributed to putrefaction, which come to us from the low genre of the novella. Along the same lines, the figuring of real castration, which I trace in chapter 6, is restricted to the novella, although representations of psychological castration are found in all genres (in this book castration anxiety is a recurring theme, whether in discussing the pains of paternity in Machiavelli's *Mandragola* or the surgical jokes in Bibbiena's play). Here again Bandello, as in chapter 1, proves a rich source, together with other fantasized accounts coming from travel literature.

My book begins by looking at reproductive issues during the Renaissance and then turns to a deeper examination of masculinity in this period. The first three chapters treat, in turn, the widespread preoccupation that a child could be born without a fully "normal" maternal and paternal sexual participation, the way in which a man's desire to produce an heir could be fulfilled through an unorthodox contract, and how a mother's contribution to the reproductive process appears to cancel the father's imprimatur. Chapter 1, "The Useless Genitor: Fantasies of Putrefaction and Nongenealogical Birth," concentrates on miscegenation and fears of violating species distinctions in an unstable, humor-based, and pneuma-controlled world. Building on contemporary philosophical and medical discourses, I give examples of strange births and engenderings, of male gestation, and spontaneous generation from putrefaction and fermentation, as they are registered in popular texts.[83]

Some people may just have laughed at these notions, but many scholars and lay people believed that peculiar ways of conceiving were possible, because in their world the boundaries between male and female biology were permeable, and miasma, inner fermenting matter, misuses of the body, or interacting humors imbued every sexual act with unknowns. We cannot be sure to what extent noncoital reproduction was part of the cultural imaginary, but it is clear that these fears were not found only among the uneducated—among, for example, people like the inquiring miller Menocchio trying to make sense of chaos.[84] In fact, philosophers and doctors often reported specific cases and argued for the possibility of birth without seed more than popular literature itself did.

Chapter 2, "The Masquerade of Paternity: Cuckoldry and Baby M[ale] in

83. Until the publication of Johannes Joachimi Beccheri's *Physica subterranea profundam subterraneorum genesim* (1669), there was no sure understanding of the difference between putrefaction and fermentation. See Piero Camporesi, *The Anatomy of the Senses: Natural Symbols in Medieval and Early Modern Italy,* trans. Allan Cameron (Cambridge, Mass.: Polity Press, 1994), 42.

84. For the idea (as theorized by Menocchio, a miller condemned by the Inquisition) that the world, God, and man were created from chaos and this creation was intimately linked to spontaneous generation, see Carlo Ginzburg, *The Cheese and the Worms* (Baltimore: Johns Hopkins University Press, 1980).

Machiavelli's *La mandragola*," focuses on an example of surrogate parenthood in an Italian comedy so bawdy that it ended up in the Index of Forbidden Books, and the morality of its main female character had to be defended as recently as the play's first representation after World War II.[85] My purpose is to see what is, culturally speaking, behind Machiavelli's construction of the story, in which a man becomes a father without sexual intercourse with his wife, by delegating the risky business to another man. The story feeds on and amplifies the mysogynistic legend of the venomous "spider woman," who can kill while making love, while she herself, unaffected by the poison in her body, can produce a child—a male one, at that, as her cuckolded husband wistfully hopes. Arachnophobia reached epidemic proportions in Italy in the sixteenth century, and doctors outdid themselves to invent cures for it (one cure was vigorous dancing, which gave the *tarantella*, still danced today, its name).

Recommendations on how to control maternal imagination to ensure proper development of the fetus, and therefore proper lineage, are examined in chapter 3, "Performing Maternity: Female Imagination, Paternal Erasure, and Monstrous Birth in Tasso's *Gerusalemme liberata*." In this chapter, my interest is on the vagaries of pregnancy. Specifically I examine the fear that a mother with a too active imagination can engender a child not resembling her husband (or her lover, for that matter) and give birth to a baby with the wrong racial features and a monstrous body. The woman warrior Clorinda in Tasso's epic is a monstrous, disorderly woman, whose utter otherness comes from the "fact" that her father's generative input was canceled by maternal fancy during pregnancy, thus she was born white though her parents were black Ethiopians. But being "Ethiopian" had just as many cultural as geographical connotations at the time of Tasso's writing. Tasso makes Clorinda's womanhood so unconventional, her nature so "hermaphroditic," in the sense given at the time to the word, that he has to kill her off before she marries and has children. Writers whose theme is dynasty (and in the *Liberata* Tasso was celebrating the Este family) could not associate the lineage of the ruler employing them with anything like miscegenation, so Clorinda has to exit the story.

In chapters 4 through 6 I consider constructions of masculinity and its

85. The defender was no less than the secretary of the communist party, Palmiro Togliatti. See Mario Baratto, *La commedia del Cinquecento: Aspetti e problemi* (Vicenza: Neri Pozza, 1975), 26.

variants, with the goal of connecting masculinity to maleness and fathering. Chapter 4, "The Masquerade of Masculinity: Erotomania in Ariosto's *Orlando furioso*," focuses on an embedded novella in Ariosto's romance of chivalry, in which two men, Astolfo and Jocondo, merrily crisscross Europe with the purpose of making love to more than a thousand women in revenge for having been betrayed by their respective wives. I concentrate on issues of narcissism, fantasy, doubling, and repetition to show that just as femininity in culture is something women put on to conform to social requirements, so masculinity is not only unstable but unhinged, both a performance and a masquerade, even (or especially) in sexually obsessed men.[86] My two Don Juans abruptly end their heterosexual adventures after they realize that even by triangulating desire they cannot control its effects. What I find interesting in Ariosto's characterization of masculinity is that constant sexual activity ends up making men less manly, as if expenditure of that "dramma" of concocted blood uncoupled from an imperative to reproduce not only weakens the body but also has the power to feminize.[87] The two men regain their power only when they stop performing masculinity and keep the phallus veiled. Back home, they maintain their self-deluding fantasies free from the disruption and emasculation—the metaphorical castration—that heterosexual desire brought them in the past and reassume control over their environment.

Chapter 5, "Androgynous Doubling and Hermaphroditic Anxieties: Bibbiena's *La calandria*," explores the moment in late adolescence when cross-dressing allows challenges to gender arrangements before a "proper" adult object choice is made, marriage is entered, and lineage comes into the picture. I examine the unsteadiness of sexual and gender categories in a story of eighteen-year-old twins of opposite sex, each of whom likes to pass for the other. *Calandria* mourns a loss—of parents, of country, of identity, of social standing—by visualizing it as a lack: lack of truth, lack of a sexual core, lack of place, thus the almost out-

86. For femininity as a masquerade, see Joan Rivière, "Femininity as a Masquerade," in *Formations of Fantasy*, ed. Victor Burgin, James Donald, and Cora Kaplan (London: Methuen, 1986), 35–44.

87. For Daciano, an orgasm was worthy forty bloodlettings of equal quantity: "la vacuazione fatta per un coito più noce et più indebolisce il corpo che se quaranta volte tanta quantità di sangue li fussi dalla vena estratto." See Giuseppe Daciano, *Trattato della peste et delle petecchie* (Venice: Zanetti, 1576), 55.

of-control use of fetishistic cross-dressings that defines it. In this chapter I use psychoanalysis as well as medical accounts of hermaphroditism to see what to make of moments in the action when sexual organs are lost and recuperated or dizzily taken away in imaginary crossings and then put back. Building on Peter Stallybrass's examination of prostheses in the construction of an unstable gender, I claim that sex too is unstable in this play full of *membra disjecta* and then work through the complex restructuring that drives and sublimations undergo as a consequence.

Obsessive sex only metaphorically unmans the men in *Orlando furioso*, and body parts are lost only in jest in *La calandria*, but organs are lost for good and sexual performance becomes questionable in chapter 6, "The Masquerade of Manhood: The Paradox of the Castrato." Here I reconstruct the beginning of the phenomenon of castration of singers that swept Italy from the late sixteenth through the eighteenth century, when an interest in soprano voices required the collaboration of doctors to create another kind of "man." Symbolic, rather than literal, castration has always been at the forefront of psychoanalytical criticism, since, as Freud states, "the *castration complex* . . . is of the profoundest importance in the formation alike of character and of neuroses," and any individual of whatever sex needs to journey through it to reach adulthood.[88] Following Freud, Jacques Lacan makes castration not only the signifier of a man's or woman's entry into subjectivity, but also the sine qua non of gender difference and desire.[89]

Yet, how can one theorize castration when it is literal rather than — or as well as — symbolic? And within literal castration, how does one reconcile what is important within culture: the castrato's scrotum or the Freudian penis, manhood or the "legal" visibility of manhood? Until recently male researchers in cultural studies have been unwilling to uncover forms of "debilitated" masculinity, more so since *evirati* (castrated boys) had often little choice in the matter and this practice was repudiated at the start of modernity.[90] Women critics, for their part, have not had much at stake in examining castrati's sexual choices and gender

88. Sigmund Freud, *An Autobiographical Study,* in SE 20:7–74, esp. 37. See also *Symptoms and Anxiety,* in SE 20:87–175.

89. Jacques Lacan, "The Meaning of the Phallus," in Mitchell and Rose, *Feminine Sexuality,* 74–85.

90. Castration for musical purposes was outlawed by Napoleon as soon as he conquered Italy. By then, in any case, the phenomenon was on the wane, and impresarios were no longer venturing everything on feminized male voices.

alignment, given their more important task of questioning and redefining their own position within the Law of the Father.

In focusing on what makes a man a man—not a penis, in my reading, but testicles; that is, not phallic potency but the power to make progeny for society's sake—I turn my attention to the first ecclesiastical pronouncement addressing specifically male sexuality in the late sixteenth century. A 1587 papal bull in which canon law has been interpreted with more *frisson* and historical freedom than a literary text legislated that men unable to emit seminal fluid because they lacked testicles could not marry, although they may have been able to have sex, may have desired only a partner of the opposite sex, and may have provided sexual satisfaction.[91] Unlike gender, which was consistently legislated and impugned in the period, sex had not been a significant preoccupation for the Church until this specific edict. By equating male impotence with male sterility and by making sexuality coterminous with reproduction, the Church thus disqualified castrati from entering a marriage contract. A new subject, the unmanned man, was produced and legitimated in Italy as it became the focus of the law.[92] Through an examination of "rejected" men, those denied the possibility of signifying their own masculinity through fathering, I challenge in this chapter the social link between one's experience of the body and one's given sexuality and reconstruct the shifts and realignments that object choices and gender preferences undergo in men for whom such reassignments of sex meant a life in limbo, or perhaps in culture's hell.

My discourse on sex and gender, it turns out, is a discourse on power, identity, lineage, paternal right, and patriarchal might. Needless to say, as it moves from procreation without a genitor and without sex, to sex without identity, and from there to sex without procreation, it is also a discourse on anxiety and decay, on faddish medical interventions and on gender-biased philosophical cover-ups, on the disorder that manufactured and fantasized sexual parts create, on the

91. Archivum Secretum Vaticanum, Fondo Secretariatus Brevium, Spagna, vol. 129, fol. 82. I thank Giuseppe Gerbino for first alerting me to the importance of this document and for our many conversations that followed.

92. As Foucault has repeatedly argued, sex is always the effect of a regime of sexuality created by society through language ("sex is the most speculative, most ideal, and most internal element in a deployment of sexuality organized by power in its grip on bodies and their materiality, their forces, energies, sensations and pleasures"). See Michel Foucault, *The History of Sexuality*, vol. 1: *An Introduction* (New York: Vintage, 1980), 155.

panic that fear of castration and metamorphosis engenders, and on the regulatory regimes of sexuality that are put in place to keep behaviors on track. Thus it is thoroughly and always a discourse on women.

To return to the discovery of the microbes by Louis Pasteur with which I started, we have always known that fermentation and putrefaction were among the greatest fears of people of the early modern period, who were unable to distinguish between the two. They dreaded aerial, "miasmic" transmission to the point of washing rarely in order not to open skin pores; they worried that "decaying substances" in the air would shorten their lives; they imagined hell in terms of the pungent smells of cheese factories and the fumes of tanneries and abandoned family duties and parental practices when plagues and choleric epidemics struck home.[93] In this sense Pasteur discovered nothing. But only with Pasteur's research on lactic acid did fermentation and putrefaction become friends, life-givers rather than death warrants. With Pasteur it became possible to historicize the event and finally put to rest, two centuries after it had been scientifically demonstrated as impossible, the theory of self-generation.[94]

Discarding a theory does not mean that the psychic trauma connected to its application can be dismantled. It took centuries, after all, for bloodletting to be discredited as a health-bestowing technique; just as the modish and ubiquitous practice of tonsillectomy has passed away, though many adults still wear the scar on their psychoses as well as on their throats. In these post-Pasteur times, to reread ancient and early modern texts that describe male and female orgasm as corruption ("corrompimento"), and semen as polluted ("sperma foetidum") by the time it was used for engendering; that claim that women could impregnate themselves by concocting *molae* from putrefied menstrual blood and that they were themselves poisonous; that believed that castrated boys were necessary to society because their angelic voices uplifted people's spirits — to reread all this is to walk through the web-like myth of progress and the time-tested culture of solidarity with open eyes and a wondering mind.

93. "It is clear and obvious to the natural physicists," Immanuel ben Salomon of Rome boasted, "that air that is pure and free from impurities, and bright and cleansed of the ill effects of decaying substances, is a powerful factor in the length of life." See *On Longevity,* in Robert Goldstein, "Longevity, the Rainbow and Immanuel of Rome," *Hebrew Union College Annual* 42 (1971): 244.

94. On Louis Pasteur's study of lactic fermentation, see James Bryant Conant, *Pasteur's Study of Fermentation* (Cambridge: Cambridge University Press, 1957).

CHAPTER I

The Useless Genitor:

Fantasies of Putrefaction and

Nongenealogical Birth

Putredini dixi: "Pater meus es, mater mea vermibus"
Oh dear worms, mother of my spirit who is reborn!
—R. MARCHELLI, *Prediche quaresimali*

Sempre natura, se fortuna trova
Discorde a sè, com'ogni altra semente
Fuor di sua region, fa mala prova.
—DANTE, *Paradiso*

"What's he / That was not born of woman?" Macbeth asks in Shakespeare's tragedy, knowing that only such a man will bring about his undoing. Macbeth does not question whether a baby can gestate outside of a woman's womb or whether a human could be born other than as a result of sexual intercourse between a man and a woman.[1] As a fantasy, however, the possibility that one can be born without a mother, without a father or, for that matter, without either parent, that birth can be the result of self-insemination, parthenogenesis, or autogenesis is present in our cultural imaginary. The aim of this chapter is to see how questionable but entirely plausible ideas of reproduction were corroborated in the early modern period by medical, philosophical, and legal or pseudolegal pronouncements informed by Aristotelian and post-Aristotelian thinking on generation and degeneration, and how they were played out in Italian literature, especially in the novella tradition. For this purpose I provide examples of birth without a father or a mother, of bestial begetting, of women's self-gestation, and even of male pregnancy before I bring to the fore stories of spontaneous generation from pollution and putridity.

What is a child made of? Not much, Nicolò Serpetro offers, just three drops of semen and a bit of blood spread like milk and curdled like cheese.[2] Obviously a number of things could go wrong in this deceptively simple, homey mixture: fantasies of miscegenation and boundary confusion, disquietudes about utter sameness or utter alienation, and misconceptions about distinctions among species proliferated. What if semen was not sufficiently warm to mature in a womb? What if woman's blood was too impure? Could things other than human babies be in a womb? Could a woman engender through an encounter with an animal or through spontaneous generation? Could a man become pregnant or a mother be substituted by a mechanical womb? Using literature as a way of producing knowledge, on a par with the writings of medicine, juridical law, theology, and philosophy, is a complicated endeavor, since while narratives of engendering

---

1. "Untimely ripp'd," Shakespeare writes, meaning that the child was extracted from his mother's womb and not born vaginally. See William Shakespeare, *Macbeth*, in *The Complete Works of William Shakespeare* (New York: Random House, 1975), 5.7.2–3.

2. "Tre gocce di seme e d'un tantino di sangue sparsi in guisa di latte e quagliati in modo di cascio," in Nicolò Serpetro, *Il mercato delle meraviglie della natura: Overo istoria naturale* (Venice: Tomasini, 1653), 1–2.

can reflect overall acceptance of variously explained reproductive mechanisms (no matter the bafflement), they may just as well parody them.[3] My task is to recreate a poetics of engendering that takes into account facts and fantasies and remains aware of the uneasiness with which each story is told and satirized at the same time.

To stress the point I will start with the Greek satirical writer Lucian. His description of the reproduction of people on the moon in *Vera historia* is no more than a fantasy of extraterrestrial origins. Lacking women, men marry each other on the moon, he writes; in fact any man until the age of twenty-five acts as a wife; after that, he gets the role of a husband. When a man gets pregnant, he carries the child in the calf of his leg and gives birth by cesarean section. No reader would consider this account of engendering realistic, although Lucian's reasons for why the younger man takes a feminine role in a homosexual relationship must have sounded plausible to a man of the third century A.D., just as bloodletting from the calf of one's leg was a common medical practice in those times.[4] Pliny, whose work became fashionable in the Renaissance, offers a similar reproductive fantasy in his tale of the unorthodox origins of Servius Tullius, one of the Roman kings, conceived when a penis emerged from the ashes and impregnated the captive servant Ocresia, who was sitting close to the hearth.[5] And a biographer of the empire explained the cruel and lecherous ways of Commodus as the result of his mother Faustina's douching herself just before conceiving him with the recently spilt blood of a gladiator.[6] These

3. Bridging the gap between scientific and aesthetic knowledge, Celsus declared, for example, that the birth of medicine was the result of developments in the discipline of literature. See Aulus Cornelius Celsus, "Proemium," in *De medicina*, ed. and trans. W. G. Spenser (Cambridge: Harvard University Press, 1935–38), 4. For the humanist Angelo Poliziano (1454–94), medicine was the pupil ("alunna") of natural philosophy. See *Panepistemon*, in *Opera omnia* (Venice: Manuzio, 1498).

4. See, for example, Nancy Siraisi, "In Search of the Origins of Medicine: Egyptian Wisdom and Some Renaissance Physicians," in *Generation and Degeneration: Tropes of Reproduction in Literature and History from Antiquity to Early Modern Europe*, ed. Valeria Finucci and Kevin Brownlee (Durham, N.C.: Duke University Press, 2001), 235–61.

5. Caius Pliny, the Elder, *Natural History: A Selection*, ed. and trans. John Healy (London: Penguin, 1991), 364. See also Felice La Torre, *L'utero attraverso i secoli: Da Erofilo ai giorni nostri* (Città di Castello: Unione Arti Grafiche, 1917), 97.

6. See Mathew Kuefler, *The Manly Eunuch: Masculinity, Gender Ambiguity, and Christian Ideology in Late Antiquity* (Chicago: University of Chicago Press, 2001), 29.

stories were accepted only because the origins of mythical kings, warriors, and tyrants have always been fanciful; explanations of how such births were possible were conveniently put aside. Along the same lines, the thirteenth-century poet Matazone da Caligano proposed that uncouth men were the product of donkeys' wind ("malvoxio vento"); the Renaissance macaronic writer Teofilo Folengo made a similar coprophiliac association between poor men and human excrement ("Surge, villane, . . . disse Giove allora / e 'l villan da que' stronzi saltò fuora").[7] Here we seem to be in the realm of parody, and yet Piero Camporesi argues that we should not discount the cultural background of these stories, since there was a strong, even documented, belief in medieval agrarian culture that souls could issue from unconventional sources.[8]

In *La prima veste degli animali,* the sixteenth-century writer Agnolo Firenzuola retells a story by Aesop in which a wife convinces her husband that the son she bore came from her eating snow. The husband does not question her argument, but when the child disappears he ducks any responsibility in the matter by arguing that the boy must have melted in the sun.[9] Firenzuola's is an ironic tale of adultery in which the joke links snow and semen. But the hint that eating can engender is not that innocent, since it was thought that ingested semen could cause a woman to become pregnant without intercourse. Even dreaming of snow could lead to an unorthodox engendering, as in the often cited case of the African queen who gave birth to a white child because her mind wandered while she was asleep.[10] When the sixteenth-century novelist Matteo Bandello

7. "L'istoria / de soa natevità" writes Matazone da Caligano, "voyo che vu indendà. / Là zoxo, in un hostero, / sí era un somero; / de dré sí fé un sono, / sí grande come un tono: / de quel malvaxio vento / nascé el vilan puzolento," in *Poeti del Duecento,* ed. Gianfranco Contini (Milan: Ricciardi, 1960).

8. Piero Camporesi, *Il paese della fame* (Bologna: Mulino, 1985), 27; in English, *The Land of Hunger,* trans. Tania Kroft-Murray (Oxford: Blackwell, 1996). According to the anthropologist Gilbert H. Herdt, the Sambia, a tribe in New Guinea, believe in anal birth. See *Guardian of the Flute* (New York: McGraw-Hill, 1981), 154.

9. This story is told many times by different writers. See Antonfrancesco Doni (1513–74), *Tutte le novelle* (Milan: Daelli, 1863), novella 41; and Giovanni Sercambi (1347-1424), *Novelle,* 2 vols., ed. Giovanni Sinicropi (Bari: Laterza, 1972), novella 127. See also Dominic Rotunda, *Motif-Index of the Italian Novella in Prose* (Bloomington: Indiana University Press, 1942), 199.

10. See Londa Schiebinger, *Nature's Body: Gender in the Making of Modern Science* (Boston: Beacon Press, 1993), 136.

writes that children were told that newborns come out of their mother's armpits, readers know that he was explaining the mystery of birth in culture by metonymy, just as in fantasy children believe in anal birth.[11] When François Rabelais has Gargantua born after an eleven-month pregnancy through an unconventional opening (his mother's left ear), because she no longer had available for delivery the normal birth canal after her sphincter was sown up following an appropriately Gargantuan meal, we know that the author is deriding Christianity.[12] But when Jacopo Sannazaro describes the auricular impregnation of Mary, where the Virgin's blessed body swells immediately upon hearing God's *verbo*, he is deadly serious, and Christianity accepted long ago the dogma that Christ was conceived "of the Holy Spirit."[13] Yet how can one believe in engendering via the ear or ashes any more than in birth via the anus, the leg, or the armpit?

In his essay on childbirth, "Dialogo del tempo del partorire delle donne," Sperone Speroni argues that some things happen rarely in generation but they are still within the norm.[14] He cites the case of a virgin who engendered a child although she has never had sex, together with the often rehashed story, told by Averroes, that it is possible to become pregnant by bathing in water in which a man has just ejaculated. Speroni's dialogue is in many ways emblematic of the

---

11. Matteo Bandello (1485-1561), *Tutte le novelle*, 2 vols., ed. Francesco Flora (Milan: Mondadori, 1934-43), 3.3, p. 264.

12. Rabelais coyly begs his story to be believed: "I doubt whether you will truly believe in this strange nativity but an honest man, a man of good sense always believes what he is told and what he finds written down." See François Rabelais (1490?-1553?), *The Histories of Gargantua and Pantagruel*, trans. J. M. Cohen (Baltimore: Penguin, 1955), bk. 1, pp. 4-6, for the whole episode.

13. Jacopo Sannazaro, *De partu virginis*, ed. Charles Fantazzi and Alessandro Perosa (Florence: Olschki, 1988), 163-69. A distinction is in order between the "Immaculate Conception," which is the belief (to become dogma in 1854 with Pope Pius IX's bull "Ineffabilis Deus") that Mary was conceived without the original sin inherited by all humankind since the fall of Adam and Eve (so she could be the perfect receptacle for Jesus), and the belief in the "Virgin Birth," or divine impregnation of Mary by God and her delivery of Jesus, as recounted in the Gospels. The latter has been dogma since the earliest days of Christianity and became part of the Nicene Creed as early as 325. I would like to thank Lance Lazar for pointing out the need to make this distinction.

14. Sperone Speroni, "Dialogo del tempo di partorire delle donne," in *Opere*, 2 vols. (Rome: Vecchiarelli, 1989), 1:64-74.

befuddlement surrounding birth in the early modern period. Can a six-month female fetus remain alive, Speroni asks? Yes, he answers. Is it possible that pregnancies last up to fourteen months? Of course, he writes, citing cases of babies born with teeth.[15] Does menopause stop generation? He says no, citing women who gave birth at seventy-two, not to mention the biblical cases of Elizabeth and Sara. How early can a woman conceive? Five-year-old girls seem sufficiently mature to engender among certain people, Speroni says.[16] How many children can be carried in a single pregnancy? Seven at most, he hypothesizes, but there have been cases in which women miscarried up to seventy fetuses at a time ("tale ve n'ebbe, che 'n una volta dieci, dodici, trenta, e settanta ne disperdette").

Speroni was hardly the only sexologist of the period. His contemporary Gianfrancesco Pico della Mirandola expounds on a woman named Dorotea who had nine children in a single pregnancy and eleven in a second; not much later Ambroise Paré illustrates how difficult it was for Dorotea to walk with her huge belly.[17] Along the same lines, the anatomist Berengario da Carpi relates that a Genoese woman gave birth to sixteen fetuses, all formed like babies, each as large as the palm of one's hand.[18] Not to be upstaged, Tommaso Garzoni describes, among others, the case of Margherita of Holland, who gave birth to three hundred and sixty children in just one pregnancy, although he finds it hard to believe.[19]

15. For Aristotle too human gestation had variable length, from seven to ten months, an inconstancy only registered in the human race, he wrote, since all other animals had uniform gestations. See *Generation of Animals* [hereafter *GA*], trans. A. L. Peck (Cambridge: Harvard University Press, 1990), 4.6.775b.

16. For Giovanni Marinello, young women are also more apt to generate males, since they are warmer, less fat, and less humid than older women. See *Le medicine partenenti alle infermità delle donne* (Venice: Francesco de' Franceschi, 1563), bk. 3, p. 3; abridged version in *Medicina per le donne nel Cinquecento: Testi di Giovanni Marinello e di Gerolamo Mercurio*, ed. Maria Luisa Altieri Biagi et al. (Turin: UTET, 1992).

17. Gianfrancesco Pico della Mirandola (1469–1533), *Examen vanitatis doctrinae gentium et veritatis Christianae doctrinae* (Basel: Henricpetri, 1601), 1.16, p. 524; and Ambroise Paré, *On Monsters and Manners*, ed. and trans. Janis Pallister (1573; Chicago: University of Chicago Press, 1982), ch. 5.

18. Jacopo Berengario da Carpi, *Carpi commentaria cum amplissimus additionibus super Anatomia Mundini* (Bologna: De Benedictis, 1521), 221r.

19. Tommaso Garzoni (1549?–1589), *La piazza universale di tutte le professioni del mondo*, 2 vols., ed. Paolo Cherchi and Beatrice Collina (1585; Turin: Einaudi, 1996), 1:663.

To be sure, confusion about issues of engendering was fed by a wide array of sources at the popular level. The teeming night population of incubi, succubi, goblins, imps, werewolves, basilisks, vampires, fairies, witches, elves, nightriders, and demons was believed able to disrupt the engendering process at any time. The unregulated mixture of herbal remedies, plasters, infusions, fumigations, poultices, suppositories, and ointments, and the frequency of bloodletting, purges, leeches, clysters, frictions, sudatories, and vomitories that women were prescribed throughout their fertile years continuously interfered with the reproductive agenda by keeping the body in a state of flux. The disease of "oppilation" ("mal d'oppilazione"), for example, an ubiquitous and gender-neutral infirmity frequently named as causing an array of bodily related afflictions but nonexistent today, required a liberal amount of purges and pills and could last for over half a year, as Sister Celeste Galilei reveals in a letter to her father Galileo, enough to deplete healthy bodies, let alone sick or even pregnant ones.[20] Widespread poverty and illiteracy, the rituals of self-flagellation, the seemingly never ending famines, the common belief in the divinatory power of dreams, and the public display of rotten, quartered, flayed, headless, and castrated bodies, stirred the people's fascination for the macabre, the horrid, the supernatural, the devilish, and the uncanny that multiplied with a vengeance fears about gestation and parturition. When brains of unbaptized newborns or skulls of decapitated criminals are recommended for their aphrodisiac powers and children's fat is supposedly used by witches to oil their bodies on the way to devilish encounters, the boundaries between life and death, birth and rot appear to us moderns dangerously blurred.[21] When a man's discarded semen was thought to generate

20. Celeste refers to the cure of a certain Dr. Ronconi who gave her a pleasing purge ("purga piacevole") to be followed by unspecified pills the morning after. See Celeste Galilei, *Lettere al padre* (Genoa: ECIG, 1992), 62. Along the same lines, the "mal dello scimmiotto," a life-threatening disease affecting numberless children, perhaps because incorrect nutrition caused premature wrinkling of the skin, was cured by oiling the chest with pork fat; if some pig's bristles appeared, the child was cured. See Mario Turci, ed., *La culla, il talamo, la tomba: Simboli e ritualità del ciclo della vita* (Modena: Panini, 1983), 55; and more generally, Pericle Di Pietro, "Le antiche patologie," in *Cultura popolare nell'Emilia Romagna: Medicina, erbe e magia*, ed. Piero Camporesi et al. (Milan: Silvana Editoriale, 1981), 33–51.

21. A recipe would recommend, for example, reducing the cranium of hanged men to powder ("cranium hominis suspensi in pulvere reduce") for a variety of medical problems. See Piero Camporesi, *Il sugo della vita: Simbolismo e magia del sangue* (Milan: Edizioni di Comunità, 1984), 14. Fat of butchered children used as ointment was a staple in accounts of

"lemurs" or, by impregnating marine creatures, produce mermen, mermaids, merdogs, and merspiders; when an unspecified but equally threatening "sperm from the stars" bred monsters in the air, as Paracelsus claimed, neuroses and psychoses had a fertile ground on which to establish themselves.[22]

Pope Sixtus V's 1588 bull on abortion, *Effraenatum* (a decree that was annulled by his successor Gregory XIV), which criminalized interventions on the female body on the part of midwives, herbalists, witches, *materculae,* and charlatans, can thus be contextualized as a concerned, if overly paternalistic, response from above to irrational fears of panspermic birth.[23] The measure made it more difficult for women to abort on the grounds of supposed or simply declared

---

witchcraft. See Giovan Battista Codronchi, *De morbis veneficis ac veneficijs* (1595; Milan: Jo. Bapt. Bidellium, 1618), 158. Enrico Malizia gives some mind-boggling recipes to aid or impede sexuality and pregnancy. A recipe using the brain of a newborn baby is attributed to a witch of the British Isles. See Malizia, *Ricettario delle streghe: Incantesimi, prodigi sessuali e veleni* (Rome: Edizioni Mediterranee, 1992), 163–64.

22. For a remarkable account by Paracelsus of birth from discarded sperm, see Walter Pagel, *Paracelsus: An Introduction to Philosophical Medicine in the Era of the Renaissance* (New York: Karger, 1958), 217.

23. Most witchcraft trials in Italy took place between 1580 and 1620, the years between 1575 and 1590 being the most frenetic. The trials of the "Benandanti," for example, started in 1575. See Carlo Ginzburg, *The Cheese and the Worms* (Baltimore: Johns Hopkins University Press, 1980). Still, the Inquisition in Rome maintained a healthy skepticism in most cases of witchcraft brought to its courts, in contrast to what was happening in other parts of Europe. In Venice, for example, the most typical physical punishment inflicted on persons accused of entertaining devilish thoughts was just whipping. See Ruth Martin, *Witchcraft and the Inquisition in Venice, 1550–1650* (Oxford: Blackwell, 1989), 33; and Paul Grendler, *The Roman Inquisition and the Venetian Press, 1540–1605* (Princeton: Princeton University Press, 1977), 58–60. With *Coeli et terrae* (1586), Pope Sixtus V chose to criminalize astrology and learned magic, which were clearly more dangerous to church's doctrine than the witches' sabbat. See Giovanni Romei, *Inquisitori, esorcisti e streghe nell'Italia della Controriforma* (Florence: Sansoni, 1990), 250–54. The same year the pope enacted the most detailed sumptuary legislation of the time in Rome, *Reformatio circa immoderatos sumptus,* bull 78; he also issued bull 70 against the dissolution of the family. For the many interventions on criminality of "er papa tosto," as Sixtus was called by lay people, see Franca Sinatti D'Amico, "La qualità della vita nella concezione di Sisto V," and Ombretta Fumagalli Carulli, "Sisto V e la 'questione criminale,'" both in *Sisto V. Roma e il Lazio,* 2 vols., ed. Marcello Fagiolo and Maria Luisa Madonna (Rome: Istituto Poligrafico e Zecca dello Stato, 1992), 1:161–84 and 1:85–94.

devilish interventions on their generative apparatus and punished those who terminated a pregnancy as well as those who assisted the deed or simply provided the abortifacients. Until this papal intervention—as the next chapters will show, this pope, a former inquisitor, intervened more than any other to regulate sexuality and gender during the five short years of his papacy—the abortion of an embryo was not proscribed, and therefore getting rid of a forty-day-old male fetus or of an eighty-day-old female fetus (in fact, of any fetus, since no sexual difference could in those days have been ascertained) was not punishable with excommunication.[24] As Machiavelli's character the parasite Ligurio sees it in *Mandragola*, an embryo was, after all, only an unborn piece of meat ("un pezzo di carne non nata").[25] But doctors at that time had few opportunities to check the women whose gynecological problems they were describing, because morality required that a parturient be seen only by midwives or expert women in her neighborhood. The case of the German doctor Veit, burned at the stake because he cross-dressed to intervene at women's bedside, has remained famous, but it must not have been so unusual if the Roman physician Girolamo Mercurio, too, suggests that in extreme cases a doctor should be introduced in the darkened delivery chamber dressed as a woman, silently, and with a veil over his head ("fosse introdotto senza parlare, travestito in abito di donna con la testa bendata") for the purpose of saving one or perhaps two lives.[26]

24. The rule of forty days for males and eighty days for females is based on the theological understanding of the descent of the soul in a human being, which was thought to be different for the two sexes. See Uta Ranke-Heinemann, *Eunuchs for the Kingdom of Heaven: Women, Sexuality, and the Catholic Church* (New York: Doubleday, 1990), 249. The decree was repealed in 1591.

25. Niccolò Machiavelli, *La Mandragola*, ed. Gennaro Sasso (Milan: Rizzoli, 1980), 3.4.

26. Girolamo Mercurio, *La commare o riccoglitrice* (Venice: Ciotti, 1596), 2.16; abridged version in Altieri Biagi, *Medicina per le donne*. Although Mercurio cites a number of wondrous pregnancies, the only uncommon delivery he witnessed was that of quintuplets, who died at birth in the city of Forlì (1.13). For more information on Veit, see the introduction of Altieri Biagi in *Medicina per le donne*. Watchfulness is paramount in things related to parturition, Tommaso Garzoni warns, since it is known that some midwives press on the baby's skull to adjust it, or suck the baby's blood and take its breath away—the danger of what takes place behind closed doors magnified here by male fears of exclusion. See Garzoni, *La piazza universale*. Giambattista Della Porta cites Hippocrates in relating the case of people living along the river Phasis, whose very long heads were reportedly shaped through the generations

The documented paranoia caused by the spread of syphilis among all social classes from the end of the fifteenth century onward also strongly contributed to fears about improper engendering. Syphilis manifested itself with small chancres on the sexual organ that spread to the groin and was accompanied by a perceptible stench and pustules, scabs, and lesions. "A caries, born amidst squalor in the body's shameful parts," Girolamo Fracastoro states, "became uncontrollable and began to eat the areas on either side and even the sexual organs."[27] Conjugal relations reached new levels of anxiety, since this "serpentine" disease was caused by a "poison" intrinsic to menstruation, according to Fracastoro, and thus not only caused birth defects, repeated miscarriages, and future sterility, but also reinforced the view that sex was a conclave of polluted seed, inflamed organs, and pus-like or urine-like release. Only the milk of a woman who had given birth to a daughter was able to cure this epidemic in men, Gabriele Falloppio writes, regaling us with an unusual construction of salvific womanness.[28] Anatomists complained that they no longer had good cadavers to dissect because, unlike Galen who had lived in the youthful moment of God's creation and thus had perfect bodies around him, now degeneration was reflected in the decline of

---

by repeatedly squeezing and binding them to make them less round. See *Magiae naturalis* (Naples: S. Abbati Stampatori, 1588; reprint, Palermo: Il Vespro, 1979); English version in *Natural Magick*, ed. and trans. Derek Price (New York: Basic Books, 1957).

27. Geoffrey Eatough, *Fracastoro's Syphilis* (Liverpool: Cairns, 1984), 55–57. See also Gabriele Falloppio, *De morbo gallico* (Padua: Bertellus, 1564); and Niccolò Massa, *Liber de morbo gallico* (Venice: Bindoni ac Pasini socii, 1536). To be sure, astronomers in northern Italian universities also attributed the appearance of syphilis to a conjunction of the planets Jupiter and Saturn in November 1484, but the cause for the disease was soon correctly tied to sexual contact. See Sheldon Watts, *Epidemics and History: Disease, Power and Imperialism* (New Haven: Yale University Press, 1997), 127; John Henderson, Jon Arrizabalaga, and Roger French, eds., *The Great Pox: The French Disease in Renaissance Europe* (New Haven: Yale University Press, 1997); and Peter Lewis Allen, "Syphilis in Early Modern Europe," in *The Wages of Sin: Sex and Disease, Past and Present* (Chicago: University of Chicago Press, 2000), 41–60. The spread of syphilis has also been linked to the witch craze that swept Europe, since the two appeared almost contemporaneously. See Stanislaw Andreski, "The Syphilitic Shock: A New Explanation of the Witch-Burning," *Encounter* 58 (1982): 7–26. On attempts at regulating the diseased body because of leprosy, plague, and syphilis, see Suzanne Hatty and James Hatty, *The Disordered Body: Epidemic Disease and Cultural Transformation* (New York: SUNY Press, 1999).

28. Falloppio, *De morbo gallico*, 22r.

the human bones and flesh. Even the most perfect bodily concoction, the male semen, called "spuma" (foam), was just fermenting matter (Aristotle's *aphrodes*), and to have an orgasm was to harvest corruption ("corrompimento").[29]

People took seriously such things as putrefaction and worms, believing that generation was too delicate a matter to work dependably, since the evidence was all around them: it was a time when human refuse piled up in the street, and contagion was thought to spread aerially rather than by touch. Marsilio Ficino, a strong believer in holistic medicine, recommends that people regulate humors to avoid putrefaction, through a sober life and a diet lacking soft fruits and herbs, but full of licorice. It was also important to wash one's face and hands with a solution of water and vinegar, to oil the body in cold days, and walk in the sun rather than in the shade.[30] Blood needed to be expressed for the body to work properly and fight rottenness, following the "salus erat in sanguine" ("health was in the blood") dictum, and bloodletting was the most common recommendation for any health-related problem. Expelling excrement had to be part of a daily regimen, one that needed to be aided by baths, encouraged by massages, or supervised by colonic irrigation specialists so that the irresistible rush of the human physique toward decay could be kept in check. At court, the days in which purges and laxatives were administered to the prince and his family were carefully registered.

Patients were advised to be watchful and avoid grubs, bugs, and all sorts of earthworms in order to counter fermentation and were reminded by well-meaning doctors of the importance of a regulated life.[31] Children were especially subject to worms, which mothers could detect by the smell ("puzzo di vermi")

29. Time did not help, as in Spallanzani's "vermicelli spermatici." See Lazzaro Spallanzani (1729–99), "Osservazioni e sperienze intorno ai vermicelli spermatici," in *Opuscoli di fisica animale e vegetabile* (Modena: Società Tipografica, 1776).

30. "Come à l'ombra diventiamo putridi e marci, così all'aria aperto, e al lume veramente viviamo," in Marsilio Ficino (1433–99), *De le tre vite. A qual guisa si possono le persone letterate mantenere in sanità. Per qual guisa si possa l'huomo prolungare la vita. Con che arte, e mezzi ci possiamo questa sana, e lunga vita prolungare per via del cielo* (Venice: Tramezzino, 1548), 2:4, 32r–v. For a recent English translation, see *Three Books on Life*, ed. Carol V. Kaske and John R. Clark (Binghamton: State University of New York, Medieval and Renaissance Texts and Studies, 1998), 174–75.

31. See Fernando Salando, *Trattato sopra li vermi, cause, differenze, pronostico e curatione* (Verona: n.p., 1607).

coming from them. The condition was cured by a concoction made of artemisia ("seme santo") or by hanging a sack of garlic on their neck.[32] Moderate exercise was also called upon to fight inner deterioration. In his treatise *De arte gymnastica,* Girolamo Mercuriale recommends exercises suitable not only for men but also for women.[33] A house whose windows faced east and north was optimal for the summers of "a civilized and intelligent man," Platina assures his readers, because it was "lighted by morning sun and cleared, as it were, of all nighttime disease."[34] For Alessandro Petronio, early marriage and therapeutic use of intercourse were sufficient to keep degeneration away.[35] Electuaries *de sanguine* were recommended all over by pharmacists to restore health. Timoteo Rossello suggests fermenting the blood of young men with red hair, the sperm of whales, and the marrow of bulls for a perfect restorative, the "oil" of life.[36]

But how many people could afford such cures? Daily reality was quite stark. Water, for example, was the most suspect of beverages, easy to contaminate in stagnant pools and tainted wells, responsible when drunk cold for nervous diseases and bouts of sterility—unlike wine, the recommended dietary liquid, "the blood of the earth."[37] The knee-deep mix of urine and oil in which workers

32. See Di Pietro, "Le antiche patologie," 40.

33. Girolamo Mercuriale (1530–1606), *De arte gymnastica* (Venice: Giunta, 1569).

34. Platina (Bartolomeo Sacchi), *On Right Pleasure and Good Health* (*De Honesta Voluptate et Valetudine*), ed. Mary Ella Milham (ca. 1470; Binghamton: State University of New York, Medieval and Renaissance Texts and Studies, 1998), 105.

35. Alessandro Petronio (d. 1585), *Del vivere delli Romani et del conservare la sanità* (Rome: Basa, 1592), 274. Other recipes are in Leonardo Fioravanti, *Capricci medicinali* (Venice: Avanzi, 1568); and Isabella Cortese, *I secreti della signora Isabella Cortese ne' quali si contengono cose minerali, medicinali, arteficiose, e alchemiche. Et molte de l'arte profumatoria, appartenenti a ogni gran signora. Con altri bellissimi secreti aggiunti* (Venice: Cornetti, 1584). Cortese's book went through a remarkable number of reprints, but it is unclear whether she was a woman or a man who passed for a woman in order to appeal to a female audience.

36. Timoteo Rossello (fl. 1561), *Della summa de i secreti universali in ogni materia si per huomini e donne di alto ingegno, come ancora per medici* (Venice: Miloco, 1619), 14r–15v. For centuries, medicine remained at best uneven in achieving results, at worst downright harmful. For example, in the official death register ("Libro dei Morti") of a parish outside Padua, Battaglia Terme, the cause of death of a woman named Carlotta Tinello is registered on August 21, 1871, as the full-fledged stupidity ("asinite") of her doctors. We can only surmise the suppressed anger of this document's scribe, who, in relating a death caused by malpractice, came up with a sarcastic pseudo-scientific term as the official cause.

37. A regimen of wine has a long tradition. Platina recommends that children and people

in cloth factories were immersed all day must have reminded many, moreover, that the oozing and vile stench that clerics described as belonging to the ante-chamber of hell could not have been much worse than what these airless and pungent shops were already offering.[38] Putrefaction was everywhere. It took the discovery of the ovum in 1688 by the anti-Aristotelian Francesco Redi to understand that any living being, from the lowest form to the human being, needs a mother and a father to be generated, and that putrefaction or devil-ish interventions do not produce anything that lives. Still, although these find-ings constituted a monumental step in the understanding of the mechanisms of conception, Redi's work did not have an immediate impact.[39] In fact, even when Lazzaro Spallanzani moved one step further to demonstrate that with-out semen there could be no reproduction, the reaction to his discovery was less dramatic than could have been anticipated, because of preconceived ideas about the ovum.[40]

---

with an abundance of blood drink it diluted, young and middle-aged people drink it straight, and older people choose a strong variety. See *On Right Pleasure and Good Health*, 465.

38. For an almost contemporary view of the ugly and grueling working conditions of many professions, see Bernardino Ramazzini (1633–1714), *Le malattie dei lavoratori* (*De morbis artificum diatriba*), ed. Francesco Carnevale (Rome: La Nuova Italia Scientifica, 1982), esp. 84–145. On food, see Ken Albala, *Eating Right in the Renaissance* (Berkeley: University of California Press, 2002).

39. Francesco Redi, *Esperienze intorno alla generazione degli insetti*, in *Scienziati del Seicento*, ed. Maria Luisa Altieri Biagi and Bruno Basile (Milan: Ricciardi, 1980). Even Redi found an ex-ception to his own theory in the "gallozzole"—woody excrescences from which mosquitoes and other insects seemed to hatch in spring; he claimed these insects reproduced asexually by self-generation. This mistake was later corrected by Antonio Vallisnieri (1661–1730). See the chapter titled "Riflessioni intorno la maniera sinora creduta del nascere degl'insetti," in his *Opere fisico-mediche* (Venice: Sebastiano Coleti, 1733); but see also Marcello Malpighi (1628–94), *Opera omnia, seu thesaurus locupletissimus botanico-medico-anathomicus*, 2 vols. (Leiden: Petrum van der Oa, 1687), 2:112–30. More generally on spontaneous generation, see Bruno Basile, "Polemiche sulla generazione spontanea: Redi, Buonanni, Malpighi," in *L'invenzione del vero: La letteratura scientifica da Galileo a Algarotti*, ed. Bruno Basile (Rome: Salerno, 1987), 125–67. For the related issue of how to control insemination and pregnancy, see John Noonan, *Contraception: A History of Its Treatment by the Catholic Theologians and Canonists* (Cambridge: Harvard University Press, Belknap Press, 1965).

40. See Spallanzani, *Opuscoli*. For a recap of controversies over ovism and spermism, see Clara Pinto-Correia, *The Ovary of Eve: Egg and Sperm and Preformation* (Chicago: University of Chicago Press, 1997).

A joke recounted to me by a learned colleague a few years ago tells of a Sicilian woman who writes to her faraway husband the news of her pregnancy. Having been away at war for a couple of years, the husband is understandably surprised and asks how this could be possible. She writes back reminding him that he had sent her a photograph of himself a few months earlier. By looking intensely at the picture, she explains, she became pregnant. In his reply the husband does not question his wife's conclusion that it is possible to engender a child just by looking at the manly figure the picture displays, but explains that such could not have been the case in this particular instance: after all, what he sent her was not a full-length reproduction of his body but one that stopped at the waist.

The thought that pregnancy was possible, or at least imaginable, without paternal participation has a long genealogy. In Ovid's *Fasti*, Juno asks Flora why it should not be possible for a woman to have a child without man's intervention: "Cur ego desperem fieri sine conjuge mater, / Et parere intacto, dummodo casta, viro?"[41] Philosophically speaking, the notion that a woman could engender in a semen-free environment was not nonsensical. Generation starting without a man's actual presence was in fact theoretically possible for Aristotle, who believed that the heat of the stars could begin the generative process, just as lack of heat could accelerate degeneration. The notion that woman could conceive on her own, without a man, can be inferred also from the teachings of Galen, who gave females an important, although lesser, role than males in forming an embryo. For Galen, a woman had semen and that semen was an active element in conception; she also had menstrual blood, which played a necessary though passive role. Thus, in the Galenic system, women could be thought of as theoretically, if not actually, able to start a pregnancy on their own and bring it to term.[42]

---

41. Ovid, *Fasti*, 5. Juno's question becomes a reality, at least in the realm of myth.

42. "From the moment one supposes that female sperm possesses the power to bring order into matter—as Galen had done—there are in women two humours capable of taking part in reproduction: the one actively (the sperm) and the other passively (the menses). Thus, if one reasons in philosophical terms, women ought to be capable of conceiving all by themselves." In Danielle Jacquart and Claude Thomasset, *Sexuality and Medicine in the Middle Ages* (Princeton: Princeton University Press, 1988), 65. For Aristotelian and Galenic views on engendering, see chapter 1.

Cornelius Agrippa von Nettesheim traces the history of this possibility: "Her organ, called a womb, is so well adapted to conception that a woman, one reads, sometimes has conceived without uniting with a man."[43] Following Ottoman beliefs that women called Nefesogli conceived without male semen, Agrippa makes his point first through Origen, who wrote that "some females are fecund without the participation of the male, as female vultures," and then through Virgil, by recounting the story of mares impregnated by the western wind, Zephyr.[44] Neither Origen nor Virgil, however, unlike Agrippa, claimed that this way to parenthood was possible for human beings, although winds were considered important for generation—according to Albertus Magnus northern winds led to the engendering of males because it was pure, and southern winds to females because it was moist.[45] Openly plagiarizing Agrippa, Lodovico

43. Cornelius Agrippa Von Nettesheim (1486?-1535), *Declamation on the Nobility and Preeminence of the Female Sex*, ed. and trans. Albert Rabil (Chicago: University of Chicago Press, 1996), 58. The original Latin text, *Declamatio de nobilitate et praecellentia foeminei sexus*, was written in 1509 and circulated in Italy at least by the 1540s.

44. Agrippa (Von Nettesheim), *Declamation on the Nobility*, 60. No matter what he said about women's self-conception in this book, Agrippa proceeded to say the opposite in his *Opus paramirum*, written between 1531 and 1533. See Arlene Miller Guinsburg, "The Counterthrust to Sixteenth-Century Mysogyny: The Work of Agrippa and Paracelsus," *Historical Reflexions/Réflexions Historiques* 8.1 (1981): 3-28. Constance Jordan notes that Agrippa's *De Nobilitate* was "often thought to be facetious." See her "Renaissance Women and the Question of Class," in *Sexuality and Gender in Early Modern Europe*, ed James Grantham Turner (Cambridge: Cambridge University Press, 1993), 90-106, esp. 105. Virgil's story is in *Georgica* (*Georgics*), ed. Richard Thomas (Cambridge: Cambridge University Press, 1988), bk. 3, pp. 273-75.

45. Albertus Magnus, *De secretis mulierum* (Lyons: A. De Marsy, 1595). See also Ranke-Heinemann, *Eunuchs for the Kingdom of Heaven*, 188. The story of mares who, when wanton and uncoupled, are impregnated by the wind, is first in Aristotle, *The History of Animals* (*Historia animalium*), in *The Complete Works of Aristotle*, 2 vols., ed. J. Barnes, trans. A. W. Thompson (Princeton: Princeton University Press, 1984), 6.572a. It is not surprising that one of the authorities most cited in writings of female self-generation among philosophers is a poet, Virgil. Here the same source is put to a different use in a satirical contribution by John Hill, who published a pamphlet titled *Lucina sine concubitu* under the name of Abraham Johnson. Written at the peak of the philosophical discussion on the preformation of eggs and spermatozoa, this booklet addresses a highly debated issue: if men and women both carry all possible semen for all future generations, it was asked, where do they carry it? Everything is in the air, Hill laughingly hypothesizes. He thus sets out to demonstrate

Domenichi too makes man a passive partner in generation: evoking the metaphor of cheese production, a link that seems to have been particularly liked by Italians, he characterizes men's semen as a kind of coagulant. For Domenichi, women do all the work, since they already have seed for generation and can concoct blood for the fetus's nourishment.[46]

A highly debated account of panspermic birth, believed at first to be true by lawyers and supported by doctors, involved a woman from Grenoble called Magdeleine d'Auvermont. It was published in Paris on February 13, 1637, in a booklet eight pages long.[47] According to the account, Magdeleine was accused of adultery and brought to trial by her husband Auguste de Montléon's relatives, who sought to declare her offspring illegitimate. It was reported that she had lived in chastity for four years following the departure of her husband of whom no news was available. Then one night she dreamed of having sex with him. The dream made a big impression on her mind, so much so that the morning after she started to feel the telltale signs of pregnancy. The child, called Emmanuel, was born nine months later. During the trial, four local matrons, all dutifully named,

---

that women can become pregnant by the wind, by inhaling animalcula, and cites his success in making his own servant, Lucina, pregnant. The idea for the experiment came to him not so much from science as from literature, he writes. Following Virgil, who had sung of mares made pregnant by the western wind, he declares that preformed germs are floated by the eastern wind into women, who then carry their pregnancy to term without intercourse (*sine concubitu*). Although Hill's pamphlet was written to satirize academicians and doctors, it struck a chord by addressing the belief that it could be possible that a father was useless in the engendering process. See *Lucina sine concubitu: A letter humbly address'd to the Royal Society* (London: Cooper, 1750).

46. "Vedese anchora che l'huomo non concorre alla generatione, altramente che faccia il quaglio o presame a fare il caccio. Onde essendo nella donna il seme per la generatione, e il sangue per fomentare e nutrire la creatura; l'huomo col suo seme aiuta a unire queste cose insieme." In Lodovico Domenichi, *Della nobiltà delle donne* (Venice: Giolito, 1551), 44r. The comparison of the action of the semen on woman's secretion to that of rennet on milk had already been used by Aristotle, with different implications. See GA 2.4.739b. Aristotle also argued that some species of fish are only female and generate themselves (GA 2.5.741a).

47. *Arrest notable de la Cour de Parlament de Grenoble, donné au profit d'une Damoiselle, sur la naissance d'un sien fils, arrivé quatre ans après l'absence de son mary, & sans avoir eu cognoissance d'aucun homme. Suivant le Rapport fait en ladite Cour, par plusieurs Médecins de Montpellier, Sage-Femmes, Matrones, & autres personnes de qualité* (Paris, 1637). A translation into Italian is in *Libertine o madri illibate*, ed. Lynn Salkin Sbiroli (Venice: Marsilio, 1989), 138–40.

declared that they themselves had become pregnant without intercourse, and the opinion of four midwives and four doctors from the University of Montpellier corroborated their pronouncements. The judges voted in favor of the woman and the son was declared legitimate.

On June 16, 1637, after reviewing the sentence, the Parliament of Paris declared it spurious.[48] The consensus was that this birth without insemination was a joke, given the names of mother and son, which suggest a topsy-turvy reenactment of Christ's gestation without physical paternal presence, and given the fact that the sentence from Grenoble came on Carnival day. Yet even after the event was erased from official documents, a number of scientists including the renowned anatomist Thomas Bartholin asserted that engendering could occur in such circumstances, for the power of maternal imagination was believed to be such that the possibility of birth from parthenogenesis could not be easily discounted.[49]

Engendering Things Other than Babies

Is it possible for a woman to gestate a nonhuman fetus? Or, to put it another way, can a woman's belly contain only babies? In a pro-woman treatise, *Della eccellenza e dignità delle donne*, Galeazzo Flavio Capra declares women superior to men in generation because they are able to create without a male ("senza il maschio suo") a living fetus, called *mola*, which although it dies soon after birth, still

---

48. Parlement (France), *L'Arrest veritable du Parlement de Grenoble, par lequel le faux Arrest supposé donné au meme Parlement au proffit d'une Damoiselle, sur la fausse naissance d'un sien fils quatre ans apres l'absence de son mary, sans avoir eu cognoissance d'aucun homme, a esté condamné d'estre lasseré & biffé, & mis au feu par la main de l'executeur de haute justice, le 13 du mois de Iuille, 1637* (Paris, 1637).

49. Thomas Bartholin (1616–80), "Ex imaginatione natus," in *Historiarum rariorum Anatomicarum* (Copenhagen: Martzani, 1654–61), pt. 6, no. 61; Thomas Bartholin, "De narrationis fabulosis," in *Epistolarum medicinalium a doctis vel ad doctos scriptarum*, 3 vols. (Copenhagen: Godicchen, 1663–67), vol. 3, letter 83 (May 19, 1662); and "De mirabilis in partibus humani," vol. 3, letter 84 (Aug. 29, 1662). For modern readings of the episode, see Salkin Sbiroli, *Libertine o madri illibate*, 138–40; U. Floris, "Beffa a Grenoble," *Storia e Dossier* 10 (1989): 29–33; Massimo Angelini, "Il potere plastico dell'immaginazione nelle gestanti tra XVI e XVIII secolo: La fortuna di un'idea," *Intersezioni* 14 (1994): 53–69; and "Grenoble 1637: Una sentenza memorabile," *Abstracta* 48 (1990): 58–65.

stands as a demonstration of the privilege given to woman by nature.[50] *Molae* are cysts that both sexes can have, although the phenomenon seems to affect women more often than men. In the past, they were considered pathological forms of pregnancy: a fleshy mass was produced in the uterus or in the ovarian tubes and was later expelled. Aristotle attributed *molae* to a lack of heat specifically in women; only human females produced *molae*, he asserted, because among all female animals, women alone had an abundant menstrual discharge.[51] It is very likely that a number of early-stage aborted fetuses were disposed of as *molae* in those times. In a salacious novella by Girolamo Morlini, titled "Filomena giovinetta," a monstrous *mola* turns out to be a motif of phallic empowerment. A fourteen-year-old girl residing in a convent while her father is arranging her marriage falls prey to a violent fever with horrible pain investing her lower abdomen. Anguished by her cries for help, her parents call the most renowned herbalists, doctors, and midwives, all to no avail. Finally they summon surgeons, with the understanding that they relieve her of whatever noxious substance is collecting in her womb. What the surgeons see coming out of the incision they perform is not, however, some putrefied excrescence, but an *immensus priapus*. The nuns would have been very happy at the discovery of this stupendous penis, the author concludes, had it happened in private; as it was, they had to let the "hermaphrodite" go.[52] This story confirms, misogynistically perhaps, the notion that the stability of sexual features is always at risk in a world obsessed with the

50. "Deve essere superiore eziando la donna quanto alla generazione, perciò che essa senza uomo può generare uno parto vivo che si chiama mola, la quale cosa a niuna altra specie è conceduta che la femina senza il maschio suo possa concipire e partorire; e quantunque tal parto non possa vivere lungamente, non per tanto in esso si lascia de considerare il privilegio datogli da la natura." In Galeazzo Flavio Capra (1487–1537), *Della eccellenza e dignità delle donne* (1525–26), ed. Maria Luisa Doglio (Rome: Bulzoni, 1988), 105.

51. *GA* 4.7.776a. Today the term "mola" describes tumors that seem to display hair or teeth because of the composition of their cells.

52. Girolamo Morlini, *Novelle e favole*, ed. Giovanni Villani (Rome: Salerno, 1983), 103–5. This story is also in Firenzuola's *Le novelle*, 12. Firenzuola relates another story of sex change, "Fulvio s'innamora in Tigoli." Here the switch from female to male is invented by the author to circumvent a husband who is made to believe that his maid turned into a man and that such a transformation was possible because Pliny had stated that much. See Agnolo Firenzuola, *Prose*, 2 vols., ed. Lorenzo Scala and Lodovico Domenichi (Florence: Giunta, 1548), 1:2.

proper meshing of humors or in which the seminal energy of Aristotelian and Neoplatonic heat is able to fashion matter. It also demonstrates how, in a culture where every female is a man *manqué*, nature could be imagined to work toward its most advanced form of development by producing a man even in unlikely circumstances.

That it was possible for females to become males is attested by a number of philosophers and doctors. Tommaso Campanella is sure that sexual self-arousal can change women into what Ludovico Ariosto's Ricciardetto calls the better sex ("miglior sesso") and tells women to use sex only for procreative reasons. He himself had witnessed these sexual metamorphoses, he writes.[53] Tommaso Garzoni tells similar stories of sex changes, with male members coming out of women's wombs at inappropriate times. He cites the case of a girl from Cassino who became a boy under the eyes of her parents and as a result was relegated to a deserted island, and that of a woman in Argo who grew a beard, became a man, and married. A maiden in Eboli also developed a priapic addition on the night of her wedding, he writes, and was able to have her dowry back and live as a man.[54] In general it was believed that hermaphroditism in human beings meant a sterile adult life with no possibility of conception. And yet the Roman doctor Paolo Zacchia, the founder of forensic medicine, whose authority was invoked in cases involving ecclesiastical jurisprudence for the next two centuries, writes of a fertile "hermaphrodite," a soldier named Daniel who was married and became pregnant by a comrade. For Zacchia this man was actually a woman even though he appeared to have a penis. But a specific organ is no proof of sex, since Daniel, he reasons, could have had a prolapsed uterus.[55]

Penises or *molae*, in any case, are not the only things that can emerge from

53. "e vidi femine, maschi farsi dopo nate per fricarsi affettuosamente," in Tommaso Campanella, *Del senso delle cose e della magia*, ed. Antonio Bruers (Bari: Laterza, 1925), 4.18, p. 307. See also Ludovico Ariosto, *Orlando furioso* (1532), 2 vols., ed. Marcello Turchi (Milan: Garzanti, 1974), 25.42.

54. Garzoni, *La piazza universale*, 1:663. Most of Garzoni's stories are taken from Pliny, the Elder. See Pliny, "Changes of Sex," 81. Many accounts are also present in Lodovico Domenichi, *Historia varia* (Venice: Giolito, 1564), 4:217–18. For other examples, see chapters 1 and 5.

55. Paolo Zacchia (1584–1659), *Quaestiones medico-legales* (Lyon: Huguetan and Ravaud, 1661). See also Thomas Laqueur, *Making Sex: Body and Gender from the Greeks to Freud* (Cambridge: Harvard University Press, 1990), 140.

female organs: there are reports of combs, hair, serpents, toads, wood, glass, stones, nails, aborted fetuses, and monsters. Paré writes that women's wombs can generate animals such as frogs, snakes, lizard, harpies, and hairy worms, and this happens because of "the corruption of certain excrements being retained in their womb."[56] Della Porta reports that women can produce toads through their purgations; they grow in maternal bellies just like children.[57] Leonardo Fioravanti recounts that he treated a sixty-two-year-old Spanish woman who, thanks to his preparation, vomited a *mola* as large as a hand, which remained alive for two days.[58] In his Italian translation of a Spanish text by Antonio Torquemada, Celio Malespini explains that in the kingdom of Naples some women are afraid to deliver because two or three little animals "like frogs" would emerge from their wombs before the actual human child. If perchance these animals start to walk on the ground, the parturient would die.[59] In certain regions of Italy, such as the area around Pisa and in Apulia, where unsanitary diets were said to be common, it was believed that women expelled strange animals from their wombs — though not harpies, as people feared, because such animals have only a vegetative life. Making a reference to Nicola Florentino, Paré asserts that the ancients called harpies "Lombard brothers" because harpies are born to women in Lombardy alongside healthy babies. It also happens to Neapolitan women, he adds, because their diet is based on fruit and herbs, and the resulting mass of putrefying elements in the digestive tract is conducive to the generation of animals.[60]

Lorenzo Gioberti, a French court doctor whose treatise on generation was very popular in Italy, agrees that harpies are excrescences spontaneously generated in women's wombs.[61] The chief culprit for such births, he explains, is

---

56. Paré, *On Monsters*, ch. 16.

57. "dal sangue mestruo delle donne è cosa malagevole non nascerno rospi, perchè le donne sovente ne generano in corpo con i figli." Della Porta, *Magiae naturalis*, 55.

58. See Domenico Furfaro, *La vita e l'opera di Leonardo Fioravanti* (Bologna: Società Tipografica Editori, 1963), 97.

59. Celio Malespini (1531-1610?), *Giardino di fiori curiosi, in forma di dialogo* (Venice: Ciotti, 1597), bk. 1, 8v-9r.

60. Paré, *On Monsters*, ch. 16.

61. Lorenzo Gioberti (Laurent Joubert, 1529-83), *La prima parte de gli errori popolari. Nella quale si contiene l'eccellenza della medicina e de medici, della concettione, e generatione, della gravidanza, del parto, e delle donne di parto, e del latte, e del nutrire i bambini* (Florence: Giunta, 1592), bk. 3, ch. 7. The English translation by Gregory de Rocher, *Popular Errors* (Tuscaloosa: Univer-

corrupted semen around which menstrual blood has accumulated. At other times harpies are produced by women via a kind of putrefied self-engendering, when they concoct their own semen and menstrual blood. This would explain, I suppose, why harpies look like women. Gioberti's source does not come from scientific or medical information, but from literature: a reference to harpies in Ariosto's *Orlando furioso*, which Ariosto took from Virgil to use in connection with the story of a king of Ethiopia, Senapo. Although extravagantly rich, this king was unable to eat because foul-smelling harpies stole or defecated on his food any time he was tempted to relieve his hunger. Such was the divine punishment for arrogance:

> Se per mangiare o ber quello infelice
> venia cacciato dal bisogno grande,
> tosto apparia l'infernal schiera ultrice,
> le mostruose arpie brutte e nefande,
> che col griffo e con l'ugna predatrice
> spargeano i vasi, e rapian le vivande;
> e quel che non capia lor ventre ingordo,
> vi rimanea contaminato e lordo. (33.108)

> Every time the poor unfortunate was driven by dire necessity to eat or drink, at once a swarm of infernal avengers would appear — those obnoxious brutes, the harpies. With their predator's snouts and talons they would scatter the dishes and snatch the food; and what their greedy bellies could not hold was left contaminated and befouled.

The description of harpies as female animals possessing a sort of *vagina dentata* and expressing their ire through defecation fits with a view of women as castrating viragos full of rot inside. Femininity that refuses male power is rendered as monstrous, just as harpies, generated by and from women without the corrective admixture of male semen, are rendered as grotesque excreta.

Prostitutes, in fact, are nothing but cesspools, Ferrante Pallavicino writes in *La retorica delle puttane*, once more linking women to excrement: men who have a superabundance of seed could use them as toilets and urinals made accessible for the community's benefit ("cacatoi e . . . orinali esposti al beneficio

sity of Alabama Press, 1989), comes from the French version, *Erreurs Populaires* (1579). On Gioberti, see also Rudolph Bell, *How to do it* (Chicago: University of Chicago Press, 1999).

comune"). Being unable to generate, these women can be of use as receptacles of decomposing garbage ("cloache al ricettare quelle immondizie che con sordita tamutazione ivi corromponsi").[62] Campanella does not let up either on the topic, for women's genitals are for him the most revolting hole of dirt ("buca di sporchezze"), a fetid place.[63] As Matteo Bandello notices, even Caesar Augustus called his daughter a piece of cancerous meat full of putridity and decay ("un pezzo di carne cancherosa e piena di putredine e di marcia").[64] Women incarnate the cult of disintegration. Sometimes a womb is just a tomb, as in the notorious story related by Giovanni Imperiali, in which a live fetus from flesh becomes a stone inside his mother's uterus.[65] In another case, recounted by Paré, a dead child emerges not whole but in dismembered pieces from all the mother's orifices: her uterus, her anus, even her umbilicus—leaving the mother's body by every possible way.[66]

Born of Woman and Animal

There is no cross-breeding in nature, Torquato Tasso states in *Il mondo creato*, because God's will is to make every offspring resemble the parent.[67] He reiterates this opinion in another treatise, "Il messaggero," in which the Minotaur, the centaur, and the siren are called poetic inventions. Tasso's reasoning is that experience and reason prove that it is possible to have a mixed breed, but only in species that resemble each other and do not have the gift of reason ("privi di ragione"), such as wolves and dogs, donkeys and horses. Men, on the other hand, are so different from animals that there is no possibility of breeding anything

---

62. Ferrante Pallavicino (1615–44), *La retorica delle puttane*, ed. Laura Coci (1647; Parma: Guanda, 1992), 129.

63. Tommaso Campanella, "Lettera a Cristoforo Pflug," July 1607, in *La città del sole e altri scritti*, ed. Franco Mollia (Milan: Mondadori, 1991), 185.

64. Bandello, *Novelle*, 1.36, p. 445.

65. "s'è già notoriamente veduto un infante nell'utero materno esser tramutato di carne in pietra." In Giovanni Imperiali (d. 1653), *Le notti beriche overo de' quesiti, e discorsi fisici, medici, politici, historici, e sacri* (Venice: Baglioni, 1663), 69.

66. Paré, *On Monsters*, ch. 17.

67. Torquato Tasso, *Il mondo creato*, in *Le opere*, 5 vols., ed. Bruno Maier (Milan: Rizzoli, 1964); English version in *The Creation of the World*, trans. Joseph Tusiani (Binghamton: State University of New York, Medieval and Renaissance Texts and Studies, 1982), 6.369–75.

human as a result of interspecies coupling.[68] *Pace* Tasso, opinions on whether a woman could carry an animal-like form in her belly varied across the board.

Man's fascination with animal pedigree and interbreeding, plus the abundance of mythical tales with gods in the shape of animals and the prevalence of an agrarian way of life, could have easily affected at the time fantasies of cross-species sexual joining. People thought, for example, that a woman eating food walked on by a cat emitting semen would become pregnant with cats. One would imagine that such a set of circumstances was difficult to replicate, but we know that there were abortifacients made of herbs specifically to address this possibility in any well-stocked apothecary store.[69] Pliny, for example, believed that a cat could engender in a woman, which explains the necessity of the remedy.[70] Cases of hybrids existed, it was thought, because the mother's imagination could change the fetus into the animal that had frightened her. Even Voltaire, to give a later example, believed a story in which a pregnant woman frightened by a dancing dog in a circus gave birth to a "petit animal" just like the dog she saw.[71] Fortunio Liceti thought that a woman could engender a being with the features of a dog or monkey through an encounter with those animals.[72] Paré too presumes that dogs can reproduce successfully in human beings and refers to a case cited by Gerolamo Cardano of a child born in 1493 who looked like his mother from the navel up and like his father, a dog, from the navel down. Paré illus-

68. Torquato Tasso, "Il Messaggero," in *Dialoghi*, ed. Bruno Basile (Milan: Mursia, 1991), 82.

69. Such a case happened in Scotland, for example, in 1654. See John Riddle, *Eve's Herbs: A History of Contraception and Abortion in the West* (Cambridge: Harvard University Press, 1997), 118. For the case of the English woman Mary Taft, whose declaration that she had given birth to seventeen rabbits in 1726 was believed by doctors and citizens alike, see Dennis Todd, *Imagining Monsters: Miscreations of the Self in Eighteenth-Century England* (Chicago: University of Chicago Press, 1995).

70. Recently David Cressy has examined the case of a woman who claimed to have given birth to a cat in Leicestershire in 1569. See *Travesties and Transgressions in Tudor and Stuart England: Tales of Discord and Dissention* (Oxford: Oxford University Press, 2000), 9–28.

71. Voltaire (1694–1778), *Oeuvres complètes*, 13 vols. (Paris: Furne, 1836–38), 7:732. For other cases, see chapter 3.

72. Fortunio Liceti (1577–1657), *De monstrorum caussis, natura et differentiis* in *De la nature, des causes, des différences des monstres*, ed. Francois Houssay (1616; Paris: Editions Hippocrate, 1937), 84. Houssay's translation is highly idiosyncratic.

trates in detail, as he often does, the particularities of this body in his book on monsters and marvels.[73] There was also the case in Avignon in 1543 of a woman burned at the stake with her dog because her newborn had a combined body shape: human and canine.[74] Bestial births attributed to diabolical interventions meant often that the mother was burned alive in Italy too, as happened in Messina at the end of the sixteenth century.[75] At the same time there were people whom nobody had personally seen but who were rumored of being perhaps too much like animals and not enough like men: the pygmies, for example, called baboons ("babuini") by Berengario da Carpi. Pygmies were thought to be two feet in height, to live in Upper Egypt, to reproduce at the age of three, and to die at seven. The Paduan anatomist Gabriele de Zerbis claimed that they had speech and some imagination, and were therefore human and not animal, but that they lacked all sense of morality and sociability.[76]

For Aristotle the problem of generation through the union of animals of different species was the length of gestation, so he rejected the possibility.[77] Vincent of Beauvais, however, disagreed. He thought it was possible to engender through the union of man and animal, although such an unnatural copulation could generate monsters: "Sometimes when the movement of the active virtue is weak . . . an animal is formed; but this may have the head of a boar or a bull, or else in a similar way a calf with the head of a man is engendered, or a lamb with the head of a bull."[78] Zacchia firmly believed that it is possible to have living births by coupling of humans, animals, and demons.[79] Paracelsus insisted

73. Gerolamo Cardano (1501–76), *De rerum varietate* (Avignon: M. Vincentius, 1558), bk. 14, ch. 64; and Paré, *On Monsters*, ch. 20.

74. See Benedetto Varchi (1503–65), *Lezzione . . . sopra la generazione de' mostri, e se sono intesi dalla natura o no*, in *Lezzioni di M. Benedetto Varchi* (1548; Florence: Filippo Giunti, 1590), 85–132, esp. 99–100.

75. Ottavia Niccoli, "*Menstruum quasi monstruum*: Monstrous Birth and Menstrual Taboo in the Sixteenth Century," in *Sex and Gender in Historical Perspective: Selection from Quaderni Storici*, ed. Edward Muir and Guido Ruggiero (Baltimore: Johns Hopkins University Press, 1990), 1–25, esp. 5.

76. Jacopo Berengario da Carpi, *Carpi commentaria*, fol. 13v; Gabriele de Zerbis, (1445–1505) *Liber anathomie corporis humani* (Venice: Locatello, 1502), 3–4.

77. GA 4.3.769b.

78. Quoted in Jacquart and Thomasset, *Sexuality and Medicine*, 163.

79. See in this context, Angelini, "Il potere plastico," 68.

that the result of coupling a human being and an animal is not a monster but a human being.[80]

In popular literature, the fantasy of the union of a woman and an animal gave origin to a beast-like child who in adult life becomes a subhuman tyrant. In a novella by Sebastiano Erizzo that soon found itself in the Index of Forbidden Books, "Del nascimento di Attila, re degli Unni," the daughter of the king of Hungary, Ostrubaldo, lives secluded in a tower with some servants and a beloved dog while her father waits to marry her properly. One night, while resting naked in bed, this libidinous young woman ("libidinosa giovane") is taken by a burning incontinence and a bestial appetite ("da focosa lussuria e bestiale appetito stimolata"). Putting her judgment aside, she couples with her dog. The result of this immensely grave sin and abominable excess ("peccato gravissimo e abominevole eccesso"), as the author writes in censorious fashion, is pregnancy.[81] When he hears the news of her status, her father summons her. She

---

80. Paracelsus, *De Natura Rerum*, bk. 1 of 9 bks.: *De Generationibus Rerum Naturalium*, in *Operum medico-chimicorum sive paradoxorum*, 11 vols. (Frankfurt: Collegio Musarum Palthenianarum, 1603), 6:201; abridged English translation by Franz Hartman, in *The Life of Paracelsus and the Substance of His Teachings . . . Extracted and Translated from His Rare and Extensive Works* (London: Kegan Paul, 1887).

81. "Ignuda nel letto giacendo, da focosa lussuria e bestiale appetito stimolata, come rea e malvagia femina, operando contra il natural corso, rivolse il suo corpo verso il cane, il quale, il caldo piacevole della donzella sentendo, in tal modo coll'opera della libidinosa giovane a lei s'appressò, che seco usò carnalmente. E, sì come fu questo, in che ella cadde, peccato gravissimo e abominevole eccesso, così [in] maggiore e più periglioso danno ne risultò; però che non sì tosto fu dal cane la donzella tocca, ch'ella di quel seme ingravidò." In Sebastiano Erizzo (1525-95), *Le sei giornate* (Rome: Salerno, 1977), 314-15. This work was composed of thirty-six novellas. The excised novella of Attila was substituted with another in the only edition printed during the Renaissance of Erizzo's work (Venice: Varisco e compagni, 1576). The manuscript of this novella was then discovered and published for the first time in 1795. See Paul Grendler, *The Roman Inquisition*, 155. See also the introduction by Alessandro D'Ancona, *Studi di critica e storia letteraria* (Bologna: Zanichelli, 1880), 475-77.; C. Grimaldo, "Una novella di S. Erizzo proibita dalla censura," *Archivio veneto* 96 (1965): 35-43; and Rinaldo Rinaldi, "Le novelle-pretesto di Sebastiano Erizzo ovvero un'utopia mancata," in *Metamorfosi della novella*, ed. Giorgio Barberi Squarotti (Foggia: Bastogi, 1985), 145-78. The story of Attila's bestial origin comes from popular tradition and was printed the first time in Venice in 1472. See Alessandro D'Ancona, "Attila flagellum Dei. Poemetto in ottava rima riprodotto nelle antiche stampe," in *Poemetti popolari italiani raccolti e illustrati da*

defends her behavior along the lines of Ghismonda's defense of her choice of a lover in Boccaccio's *Decameron* and accuses the king of failing to provide for her sexual needs.[82] The father keeps her alive and marries her off while hiding the news of her pregnancy from the groom. When the baby Attila is born with the face of a human being and the body of a dog, the husband is tempted to kill both wife and child, but is told that she could not have helped herself, for she had seen a dog during pregnancy, and this image had remained in her mind so much that it impressed itself on the offspring she was carrying.[83] I will discuss in more depth in chapter 3 the link between maternal imagination and birth defects. Here I simply point out that female lasciviousness is punished for violating not only the Law of the Father but also the laws of nature. Erizzo's story reflects the cultural obsession of locating the monstrous in woman: civilized beings are begotten by man, but for the monstrous a woman has no need of one, the logic of the *animal rationale* turned upside down.

A similar example, with less of an emphasis on female desire, describes the origin of the tyrant Ezzelino in the early humanistic tragedy *Ecerinis* by Albertino Mussato, written in Latin and heavily influenced by Seneca. Here Adelheita tells her son Ezzelino (Ecerinus) how she was raped and made pregnant by a bull who came to her in a cloud of smoke. In this revisionist account of Jupiter's rape of Io, Adelheita endures a sorrowful, ten-month-long pregnancy, until she brings her monstrously shaped, bloody child into the light of day.[84] Bandello too has a novella in which a monster is born of the union of a non-Christian ruler, Cassano, king of Tartary, and Caterina, a beautiful Christian Armenian. The husband thinks that such a horrid monster ("più a fiera e orrendo mostro rassemblava che a criatura umana") must be the result of adultery and condemns

---

A. *D'Ancona* (Bologna: Zanichelli, 1889), 167–309. On the fortune of this legend, see A. H. Krappe, "La Légende de la naissance miraculeuse d'Attila, roi des Huns," *Moyen Age* 41 (1931): 96–104.

82. Giovanni Boccaccio, *Decameron* (Milan: Mursia, 1974), 4.1.

83. "quando giace carnalmente la donna con l'uomo, se a lei cadesse alcuna cosa in desiderio della quale non lo potesse adempire, era necessario che nel prodotto parto qualche simiglianza rimanesse della cosa desiderata nella concezione sua della madre" (320).

84. Albertino Mussato, *Ecerinis*, ed. Luigi Padrin (1314; Munich: Wilhelm Fink Verlag, 1975). For the myth of Pasiphae, mother of the Minotaur, which this story replicates, see Ovid, *Metamorphoses*, trans. A. D. Melville (Oxford: Oxford University Press, 1986), 175.

both wife and son to die at the stake. But then she asks that the baby be baptized first, and suddenly the monster turns into a handsome boy resembling his father. At this point the king reconciles with Caterina and converts to Christianity.[85] Monstrosity here, not unexpectedly, is the symptom that gives away the Muslim other.

In the novelistic tradition there are cases of women engendering from an animal without any contact but as a sort of punishment. Giovan Francesco Straparola writes of a tuna that impregnated a twelve-year-old girl because it was asked to do so by a simple man, Pietro, whom she had rebuffed.[86] That a fish can engender in a woman is attested by the doctor Juan Huarte, who relates the case of a maiden walking in a rape-prone countryside and finding herself impregnated by a fish that jumped out of the water. Huarte wonders how a being can be generated in the absence of a father, when men, and not women, are the prime agents in engendering. His explanation is that women with strong semen need less male seed than others to procreate, and "animals without reason" such as fish, dogs, monkeys, and bears can provide sufficient nourishment for the purpose. The child coming out of such unions looks like a human being, he concludes, but eventually betrays a bestial pedigree in his mental equipment and habits.[87]

Other stories of human transmutation or of bestial engendering abound both in realistic and visionary accounts, from Homer's tale of Circe changing

85. Bandello, *Novelle*, 4:12, 718. The urtext of such novelistic births from human and animal unions is the story of Alexander, often retold in the Middle Ages. The lore had that Alexander was born from the union of Olympias with the god Ammon (the Egyptian Jupiter), who was represented as having horns and the head of a ram. Alexander's monstrous origin was evident in his sharp teeth and eerie eyes. See David Williams, *Deformed Discourse: The Function of the Monster in Mediaeval Thought and Literature* (Montreal: McGill-Queens University Press, 1996), 232.

86. "Non passarono molti giorni e mesi, che 'l verginal ventre cominciò crescere alla fanciulla che ancora il duodecimo anno tocco non aveva: e vedevansi segni evidentissimi di donna gravida." In Giovan Francesco Straparola (1480-1557), *Piacevoli notti*, 3.1, in *Novelle italiane: Il Cinquecento*, ed. Marcello Ciccuto (Milan: Garzanti, 1982), 49-59. In 4.3, Straparola also reports the case of a woman accused of having given birth to animals. In fact, her children were taken away and animals substituted for them, to make her believe the story.

87. Juan Huarte, *Essamina de gl'ingegni de gli huomini accomodati ad apprendere qual si voglia scienza* (Venice: Barezzi e compagni, 1600), 445-46.

Ulysses's men into pigs to Moderata Fonte's epic romance *Tredici canti del Flori-doro*, which has Circe's daughter, Circetta, prepared to do exactly the same.[88] Even a philosopher of the caliber of Pietro Pomponazzi wrote about such possibilities seriously.[89] In a novella in *Piacevoli notti*, Straparola has Galeotto's wife bear a son born in the shape of a pig. The son is loved as if he were human because he is his parents' only child, although keeping up with him is difficult, we are told, because he behaves true to his animal instincts. When he becomes an adult, he asks to get married but cannot forgive his bride for feeling disgust for him and kills her. The same happens to his second wife. It is upon marrying a third time and seeing that the new bride does not refuse him, that he acquires his true nature: no longer under the pig's skin, he becomes a handsome and kind prince, ready to rule kingdom and wife.

In general, interventions by the devil or devils were suspected in cases of unnatural human changes. Taking his cue from the *Malleus maleficarum*, Garzoni insists that only diabolical interventions can cause abnormal variations in human beings.[90] According to Sylvester Prierio's *De strigimagis*, a Renaissance book on demonology, the union of a human being and a devil generates "unnatural" beings, similar to giants.[91] Paré believes that evil spirits found in all elements—water, air, and earth—can take different shapes, enter the human

88. Moderata Fonte (1555-92), *Tredici canti del Floridoro*, ed. Valeria Finucci (1587; Modena: Mucchi, 1995).

89. On Pomponazzi's *De incantationibus*, see Bruno Nardi, *Studi su Pietro Pomponazzi* (Florence: Le Monnier, 1965).

90. "E quantunque nel Concilio Aquilegiense . . . sia chiamato infidele e peggio d'un pagano colui che crede altra creatura potersi trasformare in altra specie o similitudine da lei differente, se non dal Creatore d'ogni cosa, nondimeno si risponde che il canone parla della trasmutazione formale ed essenziale in specie perfetta e non generabile per corruzione o putrefazione, ove non si può trasmutare una sostanza nell'altra; e non ragiona altrimenti delle trasmutazioni prestigiose con le quali appaiono le cose trasmutate per illusione diabolica." See Garzoni, *La piazza universale*, 687. See also "Where children can be generated by Incubi and Succubi," in Heinrich Kramer and James Sprenger, *The "Malleus Maleficarum" of Heinrich Kramer and James Sprenger*, trans. Montague Summers (New York: Dover, 1971), I.3, pp. 21–28.

91. Sylvester Prierio (d. 1523), *De strigimagis* (Rome: n.p., 1521). The devil cannot give birth. See Paolo Grillandi (fl. 1536), *Tractatus de hereticis et sortilegiis* (Venice: Giunta, 1536); and Armando Maggi, *Satan's Rhetoric: A Study of Renaissance Demonology* (Chicago: University of Chicago Press, 2001), ch. 1.

body, and affect specifically the genitals. He gives the example of a woman who copulated one night with an evil spirit sporting a man's face. Her belly started to swell, but rather than bringing her pregnancy to fruition, she saw her entrails fall out. Garzoni recounts the case of a woman turned into a mare by a Jewish magician as a punishment for not having consented to unwelcome sexual advances.[92] In witches' trials the devil often took the shape of a donkey, as in the trial of Gostanza in Tuscany in 1594.[93]

Born of Man

Since a woman could engender and deliver all sort of things, human and not, was it possible for a man to experience pregnancy? This fantasy of escape from the maternal matrix is a stock feature of comedy but unlike female pregnancies, monstrous or self-willed, the idea of male pregnancy does not seem to have unduly preoccupied philosophers and doctors because it ran counter to cultural and biological stereotypes. But a famous story by Boccaccio, where the fool Calandrino has a joke played on him, has intriguing connotations. After a urine exam performed on the advice of three rogue friends, Bruno, Buffalmacco, and Nello, a doctor tells Calandrino that he is pregnant. Calandrino has never heard of male pregnancy, and the fact that he believes it possible is a confirmation of his stupidity, but what I find interesting in the telling is that he is sufficiently embedded in his culture to know how this could have happened. It was because his wife insisted on making love on top, he complains loudly to her ("Oimè! Tessa, questo m'hai fatto tu, che non vuogli stare altro che di sopra: io il ti diceva bene").[94] From this Calandrino proceeds to lament his lack of a sufficiently large birth canal: "chè io odo fare alle femine un sì gran romore quando son per partorire, con tutto che elle abbian cotal grande donde farlo, che io credo, se io avessi quel dolore, che io mi morrei prima che io partorissi" (9.3.561; "I think of the great hullabaloo women make when they are having babies, even though they

92. "Racconta medesimamente Antonin santo che una certa giovenetta bellissima fu da un perfido mago giudeo convertita in una cavalla a petizion d'un giovene, il quale per dispetto oprò questo, non avendo ella voluto alle sue prave e disoneste voglie consentire." In Garzoni, *Piazza universale*, 686.

93. See *Gostanza la strega di San Miniato*, ed. Franco Cardini (Bari: Laterza, 1989).

94. Boccaccio, *Decameron*, 9.3; English translation by George Henry McWilliam in *The Decameron* (New York: Penguin, 1972), 560.

have plenty of room for the purpose. If I had all that pain to contend with, I honestly think I should die before I ever produced any child").

Calandrino assumes that male pregnancy equals female pregnancy and penis equals vagina. Such is also the thinking behind the account of a creature similar to a small viper that a capuchin monk reportedly gave birth to through his urethra in 1677, after an agonizing period of thirteen months, according to Piero Camporesi; of Brother Stefano da Camerino's discharge through the same canal and in the same year of "a small animal with a head like that of a small viper"; and of a barber whose enormously extended belly carried "a long string of worms like cucumbers, all hanging together," which he expels.[95] These examples are described by doctors as births of living beings from the male organ of generation. Other strange male pregnancies, this time involving the anus, tap into homosexual liaisons. In a *facetia* by Poggio Bracciolini, "Puer gravidus," a boy accuses his master of having engendered in him during a sexual encounter *a tergo*, when a doctor examining his urine—which is in fact that of the master's pregnant daughter—reads pregnancy in the sample.[96]

Not all stories of male births necessitated replicating a woman's womb in the male physiology: male semen alone was at times sufficient to generate a child. Nicole Loraux attributes the proliferation of myths of motherless engendering in mythology to the Greeks' desire to retrace their origins from men alone.[97] Instances of such births can be traced back to the cosmic tale of ejaculation of the castrated Uranus, whose seed mixed with sea foam gave origin to Venus. Mother Nature here acts, so to speak, as an incubator in the absence of a human womb. A mythical story often retold by Renaissance writers is that of Erichthonius, a child of the god Vulcan, whose semen was spilled on the earth in his

95. Piero Camporesi, *The Incorruptible Flesh: Bodily Mutation and Mortification in Religion and Folklore*, trans. Tania Kroft-Murray (Cambridge: Cambridge University Press, 1988), 98–99, 115. Other examples of male pregnancies, usually jokes or made up to fool dimwitted characters, are in Roberto Zapperi, *L'uomo incinto* (Cosenza: Lerici, 1979).

96. Poggio Bracciolini, "Puer gravidus," in *Poggi facetiae*, 2 vols. (London: n.p., 1798), 2:178–79.

97. "By telling the story of autochthonous origins, the men rid themselves of the opposite sex and exclude all references to femininity from their discourse." See Nicole Loraux, *The Children of Athena: Athenian Ideas about Citizenship and the Division between the Sexes* (Princeton: Princeton University Press, 1993), 17.

failed attempt to rape Athena. This child, born of dust without a mother, as Ariosto elaborates in the *Furioso* in a reversed version of the "good" motherless creation of Adam ("venne / fuor de la polve senza madre in vita"), was nourished by Mother Earth but had serpentine feet.[98] Ariosto uses this myth of masculine self-sufficiency in connection with the story of Ullania and the two young women traveling with her, whose skirts have been shortened "all'ombilico" by the misogynist Marganorre, whose wish is for a world in which reproduction could bypass the need for women altogether. He is not alone. Earlier in this chivalric romance, the Saracen knight Rodomonte, equally misogynist in his views of the other sex, explicitly identifies women with the fetid and the impure and fantasizes about a spontaneous male generation whereby the new child is born the way fruit trees are propagated:

> Perché fatto non ha l'alma Natura,
> che senza te potesse nascer l'uomo,
> come s'inesta per umana cura
> l'un sopra l'altro il pero, il corbo e 'l pomo?
> Ma quella non può far sempre a misura:
> anzi, s'io vo' guardar come io la nomo,
> veggo che non può far cosa perfetta,
> poi che Natura femina vien detta. (27.120)

> Why has not fair Nature arranged for men to be born without you, just as human skill can graft one pear or sorb or apple-tree onto another? But Nature cannot always do things properly — indeed, only consider the name: Nature can do nothing perfect for she herself is a woman.

As his adventures in the *Furioso* show, for Rodomonte the fantasy that one can be "not born of woman" translates into a self-construction of manhood as bloody and strong.

---

98. *Orlando furioso*, 37.28. See also Ovid, *Metamorphoses*, 40; Apollodorus, *The Library*, 2 vols., ed. and trans. James Frazer (Cambridge: Harvard University Press, 1921); and Albert Ascoli, "Il segreto di Erittonio: Politica e poetica sessuale nel canto XXXVII dell'*Orlando furioso*," in *La rappresentazione dell'altro nei testi del Rinascimento*, ed. Sergio Zatti (Pisa: Pacini Fazzi, 1998), 53–76.

In a world where rotten seed, menstrual blood, vomit, and saliva could give rise to the most repulsive beings, theories of putrefaction naturally permeated human generation. According to Aristotle, the law that like begets like governs the reproduction of superior animals, such as man, dog, and horse; and the law of spontaneous generation applies to lower animals, such as mice, insects, and worms. Tasso repeatedly wonders why nature was constructed this way. Writing to Monsignor Scipione Gonzaga in 1579, he confesses that he does not know what is true and untrue about engendering because there appears to be no certainty in science ("mi andava accorgendo de l'incertitudine de le scienze mondane"). He wonders why some animals are generated from putrefaction and others from semen, how those whose mother is putrefaction and father the sun can generate living beings similar to themselves, and why a beneficent nature allows the birth of monsters.[99] Many animals like lizards, lice, and bedbugs, it was thought, were born by themselves, out of nowhere, helped by the sun. Cockroaches and wasps were thought to be generated from cow dung, butterflies and ants from the morning dew, toads from mud.[100] Scorpions could be engendered by crushed basil left in the sun, and snakes by decomposing human bodies. Della Porta quotes Virgil to confirm that bees were engendered from putrefied oxen and writes that many species of fish, unequipped for coitus, were generated *ex putre*. Eels did not even require rotting matter and were born straight from rain.[101] The philosopher Aldrovandi declares that worms come from putrefaction, while wasps and flies can be produced either by intercourse

99. "Nè saprei de la generazion de gli animali abbastanza ragionare; o come o perchè alcuni di materia putrida, altri di seme sian generati; e come quelli che altra madre non hanno che la putrefatta materia, o altro padre che il sole, siano poi atti a generar figliuoli a sè somiglianti; . . . o come di due bruti di diverse specie ne nasca un misto che nè a la madre nè al padre sia somigliante, o come i mostri sian generati oltre l'intenzion de la natura, ch'è sì saggia e sì potente maestra." See letter 123, April 15, 1579, in *Lettere*, 2 vols., ed. Cesare Guasti (Florence: Le Monnier, 1901), 2:21–22.

100. Moderata Fonte claimed that there were in the far north of Europe duck-like birds born of tree branches. See *The Worth of Women* (*Il merito delle donne*), ed. Virginia Cox (1600; Chicago: University of Chicago Press, 1998), 167.

101. Della Porta, *Magiae naturalis*. The same opinion is held by Fonte, *The Worth of Women*, 144. See also Piero Camporesi, *The Incorruptible Flesh*.

or by decomposition.[102] In his Discorso 13, "Degli alchimisti," while rejecting the possibility that higher species, such as bear and lion, can mutate, Garzoni writes that even imperfect metals produced by nature, like imperfect creatures, can generate. They can produce themselves, he argues, as long as there is matter, heat, and cold.[103]

But how about humans? Ariosto's Rodomonte, to return to my earlier example, has no problems in linking serpents, horseflies, and wasps — all thought to be born from putrefaction — to women ("scelerato sesso"):

Credo che t'abbia la natura e dio
produtto, o scelerato sesso, al mondo
per una soma, per un grave fio
de l'uom, che senza te saria giocondo:
come ha produtto anco il serpente rio
e il lupo e l'orso, e fa l'aer fecondo
e di mosche e di vespe e di tafani,
e loglio e avena fa nascer tra i grani. (27.119)

I believe that Nature and God brought you into the world to be a burden, you evil sex, a heavy penalty for men, who without you would be happy, just as they produced the foul snake, the wolf, the bear, and make the air teem with wasps and horseflies, and sowed tares and vetches among the wheat.

But a full implication of man in theories of fermentation and putrescence has to wait for the "scientific" investigation of Paracelsus. Thoroughly fascinated by the alchemic, fermenting, putrescent, and corrupt body, Paracelsus argues in *De natura rerum* that he has knowledge of how to create a man, whom he calls *homunculus*, through putrefied male semen without maternal seed or womb. Although he refuses to divulge much about this conception, since, in his explanation, only the *Wunderleit* (Miracle Men) have the recipe, Paracelsus nevertheless gives sufficient information on how to achieve such a result: the first step for human

102. Ulisse Aldrovandi (1522–1605?), *De animalibus insectis* (Bologna: Bellagambar, 1602), 205 and 638. See also Lynn Thorndike, *A History of Magic and Experimental Science*, 8 vols. (New York: Columbia University Press, 1941), 6:290.

103. "Possono generarsi e prodursi pur che v'intervenga la materia, il calor che gli concoce, la frigidità che gli aduna e raccoglie insieme." In Garzoni, *La piazza universale*, 1:251.

growth, he offers, is putrefaction of man's semen for forty days in a test tube at a very high temperature or in horse manure.[104] After such an amount of time, when the fetus starts to move and resembles a human being, though a transparent one, it is necessary to feed it with blood (*arcanum sanguinis hominis*) for forty weeks, while horse manure keeps it warm. At the end of this incubating period, a human baby is born similar in all its parts to that born of woman, but for its smaller size. This *homunculus* needs to be treated like a normal child, he warns, and educated until he can take care of himself. Once an adult, he has full generative capacities and can engender a wide range of offspring, from giants to pygmies.[105] Without any specific reference to Paracelsus, Garzoni reports a similar case in Italy. A friend of a known philosopher and alchemist, Giulio Camillo, he writes, tried this alchemical experiment in his studio and was successful in giving birth to a breathing boy of flesh and blood ("fanciullo di carne"), although he lived for too short a time.[106]

The possibility that a human could be generated from waste material was hardly new among the uneducated. A famous example is the one researched by Carlo Ginzburg in *The Cheese and the Worms*, which centers on the theologi-

104. Contemporary medicine believed that a male child would move within the womb forty days after conception, while a female needed sixty days.

105. Paracelsus, *De natura rerum*, in *The Life of Paracelsus*, 303. See also Paracelsus, *The Prophecies of Paracelsus: Occult Symbols and Magic Figures with Esoteric Explanations* (Blauvet: Rudolph Steiner, 1973), 147. It is unclear when this booklet was first published. The year 1572 has been suggested, although its material obviously circulated earlier. It was often reprinted, sometimes with changes. Paracelsus's paternity has also been questioned, with attribution to a disciple. See also Henry Pachter, *Paracelsus: Magic into Science* (New York: Schuman, 1951), 278; and Pagel, *Paracelsus*, 116-17.

106. "Formò per via di lambicchi un fanciullo di carne, a cui diede anco il fiato, benchè per uno istante solamente ritener lo potesse." In Garzoni, *La piazza universale*, 1:678. The reference is also in Giulio Camillo (1480-1544), *Trattato delle materie*, in *Tutte le opere di M. Giulio Camillo Delminio*, ed. Thomaso Porcacchi (Venice: Giolito de' Ferrari, 1567), treatise 1, pp. 157-58. A late return to an experiment resembling Paracelsus's creation is in a pamphlet by John Hill, titled *Concubitus sine Lucina* (1750) and signed Richard Roe. In this hoax Hill addresses the problem of why women would want to experience the pain of pregnancy without any of the pleasures of the sexual act. This was clearly the issue subtending the case of Lucina, about which he wrote earlier in *Lucina sine concubitu* (she is impregnated by seed that comes to her through the air). Now, however, he suggests an experiment that bears close resemblance to Paracelsus's creation of the homunculus. In Hill, *Lucina sine concubitu*.

cal apparatus of the miller Menocchio. Menocchio's idea of creation, which re-writes the orthodox account—by having God born from chaos, the way worms generate themselves from putrefaction—is more creative than one could have imagined, given his education, and was deemed sufficiently threatening by the Inquisition to condemn him to death.[107] Ginzburg writes that, in the lectures he gave in Bologna, Costantino Saccardino, a doctor and charlatan who was brought to trial and hanged as head of a heretic group in 1622, also expressed a belief in birth by putrefaction. Saccardino had published a pamphlet in 1621 in which he had argued for generation *ex putre* for lower animals.[108] But in the speeches he gave in the streets of Ferrara and Bologna, Ginzburg continues, he contended that man too was born from the mud, just like mice and toads. His lessons were confirmed by the testimony of listeners.[109]

Recently in a series of studies, Paola Zambelli has contested Ginzburg's sug-gestion that human generation *ex putredine* was simply the figment of unedu-cated and superstitious peasants and has argued that the idea was being dis-cussed and written about even in perhaps the most important university center in Italy at the time, Padua, and taught by Pietro Pomponazzi, Agostino Nifo, Tiberio Russiliano, Cesare Cremonini, and Andrea Cesalpino. Indeed, Paracel-sus's theories seem hardly to come out of a vacuum. Zambelli also retraces how close Della Porta came to accepting a theory of promiscuous generation that in-cluded humans, understood as "animals" in the Aristotelian sense, even though he had his own problems with the Inquisition. As Della Porta explains,

107. "In the beginning this world was nothing, and that it was thrashed by water of the sea like foam, and it curdled like a cheese, from which later great multitudes of worms were born, and these worms became men, of whom the most powerful and wisest was God, to whom the others rendered obedience." In Carlo Ginzburg, *The Cheese and the Worms* (Baltimore: Johns Hopkins University Press, 1980), 26.

108. Costantino Saccardino, *Libro nominato la verità di diverse cose, quale minutamente tratta di molte salutifere operazioni spagiriche et chimiche* (Bologna: n.p., 1621). Saccardino extended some theories of Leonardo Fioravanti, who operated in the same city, on the spontaneous generation, from mud and putridity, of men and animals such as rats.

109. See the testimony by Nicoló Stella and by Ridolfo Campeggi in Carlo Ginzburg and Marco Ferrari, "La colombara ha aperto gli occhi," *Quaderni storici* 38 (1978): 631–39. Cam-peggi says that Saccardino believed "che gli huomini, come tanti rospi o botti d'agosto, della terra grassa, con l'aiuto de' raggi solari esser nati affermava." See R. Campeggi, *Racconto degli heretici iconomiasti giustiziati* (Bologna: Golfarini, 1622), 1:88.

the earth brought forth of its own accord many living creatures of divers forms, the heat of the Sun enlivening those moistures that lay in the tumors of the earth, like fertile seeds in the belly of their mother; for heat and moisture being tempered together, causeth generation. So then, after the deluge, the earth being now moist, the Sun working upon it, divers kinds of creatures were brought forth, some like the former, and some of a new shape.[110]

Throughout the sixteenth century a controversy on the origins of indigenous Americans came to be widely debated by philosophers. How could human beings have propagated themselves so far away from the Old World, some learned minds asked? Are the American Indians children of Adam, and therefore human? If so, how could humans have reached America after the Great Flood? Maybe they did not, some proponents of spontaneous generation, among whom Paracelsus situated himself, hypothesized. Since lower animals were routinely generated *ex putre*, why could humans not have their origin that way as well? Philosophers confirmed these theories on both sides of the dividing line: on one side, there were those who believed in the monogenetic theory and adhered to Augustine's explanation in *De civitate dei* that all humans derive from Adam, otherwise they are not humans;[111] on the other side were those in favor of a polygenetic theory, who figured that generation from putrefied material and heat from the sun could give rise also to humans. Aquinas warmly embraced, for obvious reasons, Aristotle's supposition that no superior being can be born from putridity.[112] But in *De diluviis*, Avicenna revises another idea of Aristotle about what would happen to humankind in a "great year" of earthquakes and deluges and concludes that in such circumstances the human species would survive because it would reproduce by spontaneous generation, through the influence of the stars.[113] Averroes insists that there is a difference between what is produced

110. Della Porta, *Natural Magick*, 27. See also Paola Zambelli, "Topi o Topoi?" in *Cultura popolare e cultura dotta nel Seicento*, ed. Paolo Rossi et al. (Milan: Franco Angeli, 1993); and Thorndike, *History of Magic*, 6:156–60.

111. Augustine, *De civitate Dei*, trans. H. Bettenson (London: Penguin, 1972), 1.16, ch. 8.

112. Aquinas, *Summa theologiae*, ed. Timothy McDermott (London: Eyre and Spottiswoode, 1989), 1.4.3.

113. Avicenna repeated this theory in *Liber de animalibus* (Venice: Joannes et Gregorius de Gregoriis, ca. 1500).

by chance and what is produced according to natural law; he thus refutes Avicenna's theory of a possible rebirth *ex putre* of the human race in the case of a great catastrophe.

For Pietro Pomponazzi, birth from putrefaction is a principle that "contra fidem nostram non est" ("is not contrary to our faith"), as he states in a series of *questiones* between 1499 and 1509; the likelihood that humans, being the most perfect beings on earth, can be born *ex putredine*, is improbable, he argues, but that does not mean that it cannot happen. Paracelsus may have learned of Pomponazzi's polygenetic theory while he was a medical student in Ferrara between 1512 and 1516, when Pomponazzi was teaching in the nearby university centers of Padua and Bologna.[114] Paracelsus uses the concept in his theory that humans emerge from the dust of the earth. In *Liber de nymphis*, he distinguishes between human creatures coming from Adam's flesh and those who do not. He claims that nymphs, sylphs, and salamanders do not descend from Adam and are neither man nor animal; when they mate with human beings, human babies are the result. Giants, gnomes, and pygmies are born through the influence of stars upon matter and have no souls; when they die, they simply vanish like snow in the sun. And the aboriginal populations of America, since they are not born of the seed of Adam but by the influence of the stars upon putrid matter, bear no blood ties to European men.[115] Paracelsus also rewrites Augustine's formulation that humans were all descended from Adam by asserting elsewhere that the fact that all human beings have souls testifies only that they come from God, not that they all share the same father, Adam.[116] Juan Ginés de Sepúlveda, using Paracelsus's vocabulary, and following Pomponazzi, of whom he was a student, describes American Indians as "humunculi" unable to write and to hold laws, cowards by nature and cannibals by choice. His *Democrates* uses the Aristotelian idea of natural servitude to explain their depravity, which he argues could be

114. See Giuliano Gliozzi, *Adamo e il nuovo mondo: La nascita dell'antropologia come ideologia coloniale. Dalle genealogie bibliche alle teorie razziali, 1500-1700* (Florence: La Nuova Italia, 1977), 313-16; and Bruno Nardi, *Studi su Pietro Pomponazzi* (Florence: Le Monnier, 1965), ch. 1.

115. Paracelsus, *Liber de nymphis, sylphis, pygmaeis et salamandris, et de ceteris spiritibus* in *Operum*, 9:35-37; Paracelsus, *Explicatio totius astronomiae*, in *Operum*, 9:18-19; Charles Webster, "Paracelsus and Demons: Science as a Synthesis of Popular Belief," in *Scienze, credenze occulte, livelli di cultura*, ed. various authors (Florence: Olschki, 1982), 3-20; Gliozzi, *Adamo e il nuovo mondo*, 307-14; and Pagel, *Paracelsus*, 335.

116. Paracelsus, *Liber de generatione rerum sensibilium in ratione* (1520), in *Operum*, 1:253.

overcome by teaching them the Christian faith.[117] Tiberio Russiliano makes a similar point about the redeemability of American natives, in arguing that they must be part of the human race, since once civilized by law ("le nostre leggi") they live like men.[118]

Other philosophers weighed in with their version of spontaneous generation. Gerolamo Cardano makes no distinction between superior animals, like humans, and inferior ones, born from putrefaction, and thus sees humans as being able to be born from spontaneous generation, given the right amount of heat.[119] Andrea Cesalpino suggests that Ethiopians can be born from putrefaction, because that land is the closest to the sun, and heat is the major element in bringing life about from putrefying matter. His problem is not with the possibility that people can be born from putrefaction but that the "radical" soul cannot be produced following this process.[120] In *Spaccio della bestia trionfante* Giordano Bruno writes that it does not make sense to think that the Hebrew-Christian myth of humankind's descent from Adam and Noah after the Flood cannot be reconciled with the presence of humans in the New World.[121] Rejecting the theory that humans could have traveled somehow from the Old World to the New, he asserts that there can be different generations of human beings in

117. Juan Ginés de Sepúlveda (1490–1573), *Democrates secundus de justis belli causis*, ed. Angel Losada (Madrid: Consejo Superior de Investigaciones Cientificas, 1951), 33–36. The work was composed perhaps in 1545 and not published until 1892. The Spanish monarch ordered the manuscript destroyed. See Gliozzi, *Adamo e il nuovo mondo*, 295–300; and Robert Quirk, "Some Notes on a Controversial Controversy: Juan Ginés de Sepúlveda and Natural Servitude," *Hispanic American Historical Review* 34 (1954): 357–64.

118. See Paola Zambelli, *Una reincarnazione di Pico ai tempi di Pomponazzi con l'edizione critica di Tiberio Russiliano Sesto Calabrese, Apologeticus adversus cucullatos* (1519; Milan: Polifilo, 1994), 89. Had the inquisitors been as organized earlier in the century as they were later, Zambelli suggests, Russiliano would have hardly escaped burning for his ideas (92). See also *Il Rinascimento nelle corti padane: Società e cultura*, ed. Paolo Rossi et al. (Bari: De Donato, 1977), 494–528.

119. Gerolamo Cardano, *De subtilitate libri XXI: De hominis natura et temperamento* (Basel: Lucium, 1547), 1.2.

120. Andrea Cesalpino (Caesalpinus, 1524–1603), *Peripateticarum quaestionum* (Venice: Giunta, 1571). See also Thorndike, *History of Magic*, 6:327; and Gliozzi, *Adamo e il nuovo mondo*, 319.

121. Giordano Bruno (1548–1600), *Spaccio de la bestia trionfante*, in *Dialoghi italiani: Dialoghi metafisici e dialoghi morali*, ed. Giovanni Aquilecchia (1584; Florence: Sansoni, 1958), 797.

different continents. In *De immenso* he says that wherever nature is alive, living species can be produced with no need of a first and only father. He includes humans in the list that comprises both the higher animal species, such as the bear and the lion, and lower ones born of putrefaction, such as the serpent, the mouse, and the frog.[122] Bruno does not explicitly speak of generation *ex putre*, preferring to speak of spontaneous generation, but his argument, and the more specific one that stars are suns with their own galaxies, made the Inquisition first excommunicate him and then condemn him to be burned at the stake.

How is all this thought on spontaneous generation or generation from putrefaction and fermentation reflected in Italian literature? Dante writes of generation involving "vermi" twice. In *Inferno* 3, he tells of sinners whose punishment is to be stung by insects; the blood thus produced, mixed with tears, is a kind of excreta that trickles down to their feet, where it is gathered by worms supposedly generated by putridity:

> Questi sciaurati, che mai non fur vivi,
>> erano ignudi e stimolati molto
>> da mosconi e da vespe ch'eran vivi.
> Elle rigavan lor di sangue il volto,
>> che, mischiato di lagrine, a' lor piedi
>> da fastidiosi vermi era ricolto. (64–69)

> These wretches, who never were alive, were naked and were much stung
> by gadflies and wasps there, which were streaking their faces with blood
> that mingled with their tears and was gathered by loathsome worms at
> their feet.

In *Purgatorio* 10, worms "produce" the angelic butterfly: "non v'accorgete voi che noi siam vermi / nati a formar l'angelica farfalla" (124–25; "Are you not aware that we are worms, born to form the angelic butterfly").[123]

In *Il mondo creato*, Tasso makes Egypt the land where horrible monsters are produced through spontaneous generation from dead limbs or are brought forth by Mother Earth out of putrid matter without semen or father:

122. Giordano Bruno, *De immenso et innumerabilibus* (Frankfurt: Wechel and Fischer, 1591). See also Gliozzi, *Adamo e il nuovo mondo*, 4.18, pp. 340–43.

123. Dante Alighieri, *Inferno* and *Purgatorio*, in *The Divine Comedy*, 3 vols., ed. and trans. Charles Singleton (Princeton: Princeton University Press, 1970–73).

orridi mostri . . .

che da putride membra estinto corpo
produsse; o senza seme e senza padre
l'antica madre ancor produce e figlia
dal riscaldato e 'nsieme umido grembo. (6:1241-56)

> fearful monsters . . . born of the foul corruption of dead limbs or gener-
> ated with no parent's seed from the old mother's warm and humid womb.
> (6.1219-24)

Still, what Tasso sees engendered are monsters, not human beings. Tommaso
Campanella, who narrowly escaped death in his repeated encounters with the
Inquisition, is circumspect in his opinion but comes back to the issue more than
once. He writes that because he does not personally know of any case of a human
birth *ex putre*, he doubts it.[124] But then he finds it difficult to explain the birth of
savages or of people in the New World. In *La città del sole* he describes a world
made like a big animal in which humans occupy a space just as worms have
their space in the human body. The men and women of his utopian city think
that the sun is their father and the earth their mother, that the fire comes from
the sun, and that the sea is the sweat of the earth liquefied by the sun.[125] This
theory comes from Avicenna and Pomponazzi, that is, the sun is like a man, with
semen that actively generates, while the humid earth, like a mother, provides
menstrual nourishment. These beings are not born of Adam, and thus have no
original sin. In his belief that it is not necessary that all humankind descend
from Adam, Campanella corrects Augustine and benignly reads his "error" as
a lack of scientific knowledge and not of faith.[126]

---

124. "Possibile è al mago, come fa nascere le piante dove li pare, far nascere anco animali;
ma solamente quelli che di putrefazione si fanno, come sorci, pidocchi, mosche e serpi, ma non
cavalli, elefanti e uomini. . . . Dunque Dio provvide la generazione alli perfetti; all'imperfetti
l'una e l'altra perchè con poco magistero si finiscono. Avicenna contende che possan nascere
e così Epicuro e altri, come nel Nilo allagato superbi animali si fanno dall'umido terreno.
Delli uomini selvaggi si può pensare, e di quei del mondo nuovo, che non si sa come andarono
là. Io non voglio contendere, perchè può la natura forze tali in qualche luogo usar di far cose
sì nobili, come fa nell'utero. Nondimeno non so istoria sicura e penso essere impossibile."
In Campanella, *Del senso delle cose e della magia*, 4.18, pp. 310-11.

125. Campanella, *La città del sole*, 94-95.

126. Tommaso Campanella, *Apologia pro Galileo*, trans. Richard Blackwell (1616; Notre

As the excursus above shows, the work of scientists such as Francesco Redi that cast doubt on old ideas about the possibility of spontaneous generation or generation from decaying matter, could not have provided a swift corrective to the proliferation of theories on generation because they were too ingrained in culture and were thoroughly supported by the writings of many competent academics. In a universe where flesh was teeming with vermin, where dried-up human flesh ("mummia") reduced to powder was a healing medicine, and the cure for debilitation was an electuary made of putrefied capons kept in a glass immersed in horse manure; where a head wound was healed by placing butchered dogs and pigeons on it—in such a world, survival depended on decay.[127] Sweet and sour, honey and vinegar were the foremost condiments of the time. Eating habits reflected this universal perception of bodily mechanisms, so that a person whose inside proliferated with worms, semiaborted fetuses, and parasites—and whose outside was attacked by pus and leeches—could well develop a taste for the "olla podrida," a Spanish stew of putrid meat and vegetables that appeared all over Italy at the end of the sixteenth century "at the most lavish banquets."[128]

Was this fascination for putrefaction and nongenealogical birth a way of decentering the subject? Or was it a fantasy of birth without alterity? Was the abolishing of mother and of father, the setting aside of the mirror stage, and the abandonment of Oedipus a way of fulfilling a dream of no origins? Or were the rotting tissue, the flatulence, the flabbiness, and the stench that permeated everybody's life—the nose was to become the most important sense organ in the baroque period—the means by which people could indulge in a fascination with death as a return to worminess?[129] The alliteration of words such as *Homo*

Dame, Ind.: University of Notre Dame Press, 1994). See also Stelio Cro, "Italian Humanism and the Myth of the Noble Savage," *Annali d'Italianistica* 10 (1992): 48–68, 64–65.

127. Such a cure to the head was practiced by Baldissaro Cristiani, a physician at the Sforza court, at the end of the fifteenth century. See P. D. Pasolini, "Introduzione" to *Experimenti della Ex.ma S.ra Caterina da Furlj Matre de lo Inlux.mo Signor Giovanni de Medici*, ed. P. D. Pasolini (Imola: Tipografica Galeati, 1894), 4. For other examples, see Piero Camporesi, *Bread of Dreams: Food and Fantasy in Early Modern Europe* (Chicago: University of Chicago Press, 1989), 31.

128. See Camporesi, *The Incorruptible Flesh*, 143.

129. Writing about cloning, Jean Baudrillard wonders along the same lines: "Is there a death drive that pushes beings toward a form of reproduction anterior to their acquisition

and *humus* invites disquieting associations. In the final analysis, the answer to the neurosis that unmothered and unfathered human beings could exist at a time when scientific knowledge was inadequate to explain it any better, may simply rest in the naturalness of that etymological pairing.

---

of sexual identities . . . and that simultaneously pushes them to deny all alterity so that they need no longer to strive for anything but the perpetuation of an identity, the transparency of a genetic code all the more dedicated to procreation?" See Baudrillard, *Seduction* (New York: St. Martin's Press, 1990), 168–69.

CHAPTER 2

The Masquerade of Paternity:

Cuckoldry and Baby M[ale] in Machiavelli's

La mandragola

The status of manhood, on the other hand, is achieved
only by the stress of thought and much technical exertion.
—FRIEDRICH HEGEL, *Philosophy of Right*

The tarantula of Puglia is a certain sort of spider, that
brings all kinds of luck to those he bites.
—GABRIELE D'ANNUNZIO, *Francesca da Rimini*

The terms "paternity" and "maternity," although semantic mirrors of each other, are hardly invested with the same power in Western culture. "The meaning of paternity," Carol Delaney writes, "is not . . . primarily physiological; instead, the bio-physical elements are utilised for expressing social meaning, for example, gender, authority and kinship. . . . Maternity has meant giving nurture and giving birth. Paternity has meant begetting. Paternity has meant the primary, essential and creative role."[1] In the founding myth of Christianity, physical paternity is neither necessary nor postulated, and yet the child Jesus is thought to be at one with his father. Mary receives and nurtures the seed, an important task by all means, but not equal to that of God the Father.[2]

This monogenetic theory of reproduction is not just Christian; philosophically speaking, the father's position as representative of the Law has always been of larger significance than that of the mother. Patriarchy itself is predicated upon the conviction, as seventeenth-century political theorist Robert Filmer famously claimed, that "the man . . . is the nobler and principal agent in generation."[3] But if Christian and lay scholars alike have no problem with the concept of woman as vessel and womb-for-hire, it has not yet been demonstrated incontrovertibly that the father's role in begetting a child is physically unnecessary, although theories of generation out of putrefaction have occasionally extended to humans, as I discussed in chapter 1. Before modern genetics there were problems, of course, in linking a biological father and a legal one; still no father, apart from God, ever claimed physiological paternity by refusing to have sexual congress with the mother of his child. Until, that is, surrogate parenthood became a possibility. Hence, in his opinion in the famous Baby M case, Judge Harvey Sorkow elaborated creatively on the meaning of paternity. "It must be reasoned,"

1. Carol Delaney, "The Meaning of Paternity and the Virgin Birth Debate," *Man* 21 (1986): 494–513, 495.

2. For a recent reading of the debate on Jesus's father, see Elizabeth Clark, "Generation, Degeneration, Regeneration: Original Sin and the Conception of Jesus in the Polemic between Augustine and Julian of Eclanum," in *Generation and Degeneration: Tropes of Reproduction in Literature and History from Antiquity to Early Modern Europe,* ed. Valeria Finucci and Kevin Brownlee (Durham, N.C.: Duke University Press, 2001), 17–40.

3. Robert Filmer (d. 1653) *Patriarcha and Other Political Works,* ed. Peter Laslett (Oxford: Blackwell, 1949), 245.

he wrote, "that if one has a right to reproduce coitally, one has the right to re-produce non-coitally."[4] He then proceeded to assign custody of Baby M not to the biological mother nor to the biological father, but to the father's wife, who was at this point the farthest away in this family romance from embodying the principle of maternity as delineated above by Delaney. It was her inability to conceive, we were told in court, which put into motion the Baby M saga.[5]

The Baby M case has proved the battling ground for a heated controversy over procreative rights, with maternity and paternity seen at times as biologi-cally grounded and at others as culturally constructed. Those in favor of sur-rogacy have argued, for example, that certain body parts are equal in men and women, and thus equally for sale: men should be able to sell their sperm and women their uterus. Appropriate banks should be established for such pur-poses. Those against surrogacy have recoiled at the exploitative use of female bodies, since poor women are often employed to guarantee legitimate issue to moneyed fathers or are contracted to avoid bodily contact. More recently, Dr. Cecil Jacobson, an infertility doctor in suburban Alexandria, Virginia, cre-ated quite a personal sperm bank of which he was the main (or only) donor. Bragging that he, not God, could give babies to his female patients, Jacobson donated his sperm not because he wanted to be a father, nor because he wanted to create an occasion to enjoy sex, and perhaps not even for money, but because it made scientific sense: genetically speaking his contribution was better than that of other donors because it was—literally—fresher.

In the following pages I will bring these issues of patrilineal transmission back to the Renaissance by concentrating on the plot of Niccolò Machiavelli's (1469-1527) *La mandragola*, first staged in Florence in 1518.[6] Here too, it turns

4. *In re* Baby M, 525 A.2d 1128. N.J. Super. Ch. 1987, 1164 (opinion of J. Harvey Sorkow).

5. Judge Sorkow's decision was subsequently overruled, and Baby M was given in cus-tody to the genetic father, while the mother's rights were partly reinstated and she was granted visitation privileges. On the Baby M case, see Tania Modleski, "Three Men and Baby M," *Camera Obscura* 17 (1988): 69–81; Janice Doane and Devon Hodges, "Risky Business: Familial Ideology and the Case of Baby M," *differences* 1.1 (1989): 67–81; and Linda Singer, "Bodies-Pleasures-Powers," *differences* 1.1 (1989): 45–65.

6. Roberto Ridolfi's claim is well accepted, that *Mandragola* was written in 1518 and repre-sented at court in the carnival of that year and perhaps also in September on the occasion of Lorenzo de' Medici's wedding to Madeleine D'Auvergne. See "Composizione, rappresen-tazione e prima edizione della *Mandragola*," *Studi sulle commedie di Machiavelli* (Pisa: Nistri-Lischi, 1968), 17–20. Richard Andrews suggests that the play was first performed in a private

out, a lawyer, Messer Nicia Calfucci, has something at stake in presuming that any man has the right, and thus, perhaps, the choice, to reproduce both coitally and noncoitally and still be considered a biological and legal father. Therefore he enters a contract with a surrogate man, Callimaco Guadagni, with the purpose of making his wife, Lucrezia, a willing, if exploited, bearer of a child soon to be generated. The unwritten contract establishes that as a result of practices that are to take place on a specifically controlled and carefully timed occasion, a child will hopefully be engendered who will bear the patronymic of the original male contractor. In this particular case, Nicia, unlike Baby M's biological father, whose contractual counterpart refused to reveal her baby's sex following amniocentesis, is sure that the child being engendered is a baby boy; the contract is even backed by a promise of two thousand ducats if the woman finds herself unable to conceive. Like Dr. Jacobson, Nicia thinks that a father is not so much the one who provides the sperm but the one who earns this specific title daily by behaving like a responsible caretaker. Like Dr. Jacobson, Callimaco sees no psychological problems in seemingly becoming the biological father of a child whose legitimacy he could not easily prove (just as the legal father, Nicia, could not prove it, should a dispute on the subject arise). In the end, as sperm brokers would have it, this artificially commissioned family accommodates everybody's urges and desires, order returns, and inheritance worries are satisfied.

To be sure, there are other, perhaps better ways, to summarize *Mandragola*. A more usual reading would give this plot: in the year 1504, Callimaco, a young Italian student in Paris, comes back to Florence because he has heard of the astonishing beauty of Lucrezia Calfucci and has fallen in love with her, sight unseen. But Lucrezia is the faithful wife of an aging lawyer, Nicia, and offers him no occasion to pierce her heart. Not easily resigned, Callimaco asks for the help of a friend, Ligurio, a marriage broker and social parasite. Ligurio in-

---

house a few times, in front of perhaps only a male audience. See *Scripts and Scenarios: The Performance of Comedy in Renaissance Italy* (Cambridge: Cambridge University Press, 1993), 51. Only male, nonprofessional actors were involved. The play was first printed under the title *Commedia di Callimaco e di Lucrezia* (Florence: n.p., 1518), but in the "Prologo" Machiavelli himself announces the title: "La favola *Mandragola* si chiama." Fredi Chiappelli argues that 1519 is a more probable date for the composition; see "Sulla composizione della *Mandragola*," *L'approdo letterario* 11 (1965): 79–84.

vents a thrilling joke to exploit Nicia's repeatedly stated desire for a son and has Callimaco pass for a doctor in order to promote a miraculous mandrake potion whose controlled ingestion guarantees fertility. The potion, he explains to the gullible Nicia, has a peculiar side effect, however, after it is administered to the man sexually approaching the woman: it can kill him. To avoid such an outcome and to fulfill Callimaco's sexual aims, it is decided—with Nicia's full agreement—that a street boy, a "garzonaccio," who turns out to be Callimaco, be kidnapped to make love to the woman first and draw the poison out of her body. During their rendezvous Callimaco reveals his identity and his love to Lucrezia. Surprisingly, she decides to go along with the ruse, aware that the stupidity or connivance of those who should have respected her most, including her mother, Sostrata, and her priest, Timoteo, have landed her in this situation.[7]

In this chapter I am not interested in the political stakes of *Mandragola*, a topic that has been fruitfully expounded by a number of critics through the years, but in its sexual stakes.[8] How does paternity without sperm inform the libidinal economy of this play, I ask? How does a man approach a woman in an environment in which it is believed that a womb has the power to kill the male who dares to approach it? What makes a womb the repository of life (for the new child) and of death (for the child's father), a gimmick necessary to the story but also a fear registered among the populace? And why is the woman herself unaffected by the poison she ingests? My focus is on the drama at stake: on the part of the outwitted Nicia, how to have his wife engender the son he so much desires, even though he is unwilling to risk his own life in the bargain; on the

7. A source for the trick played on Nicia is in *Gesta Romanorum: Entertaining Stories Invented by the Monks as a Fire-Side Recreation and Commonly Applied in Their Discourses from the Pulpit, Whence the Most Celebrated of Our Own Poets Have Extracted Their Plots*, trans. Charles Swan (London: Routledge, 1924).

8. For a political reading of the play, see, for example, Antonio Parronchi, "La prima rappresentazione della *Mandragola*: Il modello per l'apparato. L'allegoria," *La Bibliofilia* 64 (1962): 37–86. For Parronchi, Lucrezia is Florence the body politic; Callimaco is Lorenzo di Piero de' Medici, Duke of Urbino; Nicia—like the Athenian general Nicia, who had wisdom but was unable to make decisions—is Pier Soderini; and the friar Timoteo is the monk Savonarola. For a similar reading, see Theodore Sumberg, "La *Mandragola*: An Interpretation," *Journal of Politics* 23 (1961): 320–40. For a reading of the play following Machiavelli's political writings, see Mera Flaumenhaft, "The Comic Remedy: Machiavelli's *Mandragola*," *Interpretation* 7 (1978): 33–74.

part of Callimaco, how to have sexual access to the woman he wants by side-stepping both her consent and that of her husband in a ruse that, paradoxically, guarantees him consent from both.

I do not discount, of course, the fact that *Mandragola* is a comedy and that, as in the classic *beffe* of the period, there is a huge element of trickery enacted at the expense of the main character. Machiavelli wants the audience both to laugh at Nicia—the literary heir of the always outwitted Calandrino in Boccaccio's *Decameron*—and to expose the unscrupulous behavior of those who invent the joke about poisonous wombs at his expense and eagerly participate in it, with no respect for civic and ecclesiastical laws. The audience of the time may have believed that fertility potions were somewhat effective in furthering pregnancy but was able just as well to laugh at the gullibility of the lawyer Nicia who, although improperly educated, should have known better. Himself a specialist *de re herbaria* and creator of concoctions to cure his bodily ailments, Machiavelli may have offered this discourse on pregnancy—which I think fully reflects the medical pronouncements of his time as I outlined them in the introduction—not only to denounce its most fanciful aspects but also to underline the economic motives that presided over its expansion.

That said, it is worth examining what it means to have a womb stand for the terrifying, the repelling, and the strange—the fountain, as Hippocrates put it, of "six hundred calamities." In *Mandragola*, woman's womb is thoroughly excessive: it can easily accommodate what would kill a man; it is unnatural, in that it refuses to perform the most common female task, of conceiving; it is threatening, because from being sterile it can suddenly proliferate with life; and it is engulfing, when thought of exclusively in procreative terms. Lucrezia's womb is indeed a tomb, the desired and feared fulfillment of an irresistible death wish. If this discourse sounds uncannily familiar, well, it is familiar. Ours is, after all, the era of women used as incubators, of sperm banks, of neurotic fears of epidemics, of cleansing rituals, and of daily reminders of sexually transmitted diseases. That death can even be excusable if it falls upon a lower-class man tells us, unfortunately, nothing new about inferiors (whatever the gender) being used as sexual commodities.

Generational issues, often understood as harbingering degeneration, are central to Machiavelli's thought. In an article on Castruccio Castracani, Jeffrey Schnapp, for example, has argued for the identification of modernity in Machiavellian narrative with the figure of the foundling, a being who by definition cannot lay claim to any precise origin or identifiable maternal, let alone paternal, biological legacy.[9] Machiavelli conceives the founding of Rome itself as mono-genetic, according to Hanna Pitkin, since "despite the imagery of birth in blood, no mother appears; it seems the issue is a purely masculine generation, singular paternity."[10] In *Mandragola*, however, the mother does appear; all, in fact, hinges on her body, the functions associated with it, and her willingness to have it manipulated. We know that there is apparently nothing wrong with Lucrezia Calfucci to explain her inability to conceive: she is young, in good health, and has a good disposition. Her husband has consulted fertility doctors, and they have recommended a visit to the baths.[11] He doubts, however, that his wife will accept their advice and personally finds any move from Florence unduly fatiguing, even a short one. We also know that Lucrezia has applied prayers and alms in good measure, since when everything else failed women at the time were told to frequent places of worship and make vows to God and saints. She has even attended early morning mass daily, because she has been told that forty consecutive visits had brought pregnancy to other women. She stopped abruptly and short of the goal, however, when a friar ("fratacchione"), taken by her beauty, molested her. At this point Nicia is ready to believe any new doctor and any new cure.

Introduced by Ligurio as a physician from Paris, Callimaco reviews right away with Nicia the common reasons for woman's sterility in a speech meant to impress for its professional references and Latin scholarship: "Nam causae sterilitatis sunt: aut in semine, aut in matrice, aut in instrumentis seminariis, aut in virga, aut in causa extrinseca" ("In fact, the reasons for sterility are in the semen, the uterus, the testicles, the penis, or in some external cause").[12] He

9. Jeffrey Schnapp, "Machiavellian Foundlings: Castruccio Castracani and the Aphorism," *Renaissance Quarterly* 45 (1992): 653–76.

10. Hanna Pitkin, *Fortune Is a Woman: Gender and Politics in the Thought of Niccolò Machiavelli* (Berkeley and Los Angeles: University of California Press, 1984), 54.

11. Sulphur baths were considered particularly beneficial at the time, because of their smell, and iron-tinted waters were recommended because of their bloody color. See Jacques Gélis, *History of Childbirth: Fertility, Pregnancy and Birth in Early Modern Europe*, trans. Rosemary Morris (Boston, Mass.: Northeastern University Press, 1991), 27.

12. Niccolò Machiavelli, *La mandragola* (Milan: Rizzoli, 1980), 2.2. [Hereafter act and scene are cited in the text.] English version from *Five Italian Renaissance Comedies*, ed. and trans. Bruce Penman (London: Penguin, 1978). This passage is left in Latin in Penman's translation. Nicia is so taken by Callimaco's ease with Latin that, as Levi remarks, the "grammatica," and not the "mandragora," seem to facilitate the escapade. See Eugenio Levi, "La

then asks Nicia whether there are sexual problems on his part. Not at all, Nicia replies: "Impotente io? Oh! voi mi farete ridere! Io non credo che sia el più ferrigno ed il più rubizzo uomo in Firenze di me" (2.2; "Impotent? Me? I can't help laughing at that! I don't believe there's a harder case or a better performer in Florence than me!").

Callimaco then shifts to uroscopy. As he knows well, the most common way at the time to check why a woman would not become pregnant was to examine a urine specimen since, as in men, the same opening was thought to serve for the discharge of her semen, menses, and urine.[13] To the right onlooker, the color of a woman's urine was like an open book delivering a wealth of information on her physical status, just as excrement offered far-reaching explanations on human health. As Albertus Magnus's *De secretis mulierum* reveals, "The urine of virgins is clear and sparkling white; if it is clear and golden, the woman is still pure but won't remain so for long as the golden color indicates heat in her body and therefore a strong desire for sex. Once a girl has lost her maidenhead, her urine is turbid because of the broken membrane, and male sperm appears in the bottom of it."[14]

For Giambattista Della Porta the trick was to have the woman drink a potion

Mandragola di Machiavelli," in *Il comico di carattere da Teofrasto a Pirandello* (Turin: Einaudi, 1959), 54. That Nicia would believe Callimaco is not as strange as it sounds. There were few doctors with university degrees in circulation in that period in Italy, and those with degrees from Paris, Bologna, and Padua were particularly esteemed. According to Katharine Park, the relation of Florentine patients to their physicians during the Renaissance was on the whole one of trust. See Park, *Doctors and Medicine in Early Renaissance Florence* (Princeton: Princeton University Press, 1985), 54.

13. Hippocratic doctors distinguished the urethra from the vaginal canal, but their knowledge made no difference in conceptualizing the function of women's sexual organs.

14. Quoted in Helen Lemay, "Human Sexuality in Twelfth- through Fifteenth-Century Scientific Writings," in *Sexual Practices and the Medieval Church*, ed. Vern Bullough and James Brundage (Buffalo, N.Y.: Prometheus Books, 1982), 187–205, esp. 194. The text also offered a detailed experiment meant to discover the causes of infertility in a couple: "A urine specimen should be obtained from each of them; bran of wheat should be added to this; and the pot should then be closed up for nine days or longer. If the defect is in the man, there will be worms in his pot; if the fault is the woman's, menses will be found in hers." See Lemay, "Human Sexuality," 200–201. For an irreverent take on the wisdom of reading women's urine, see the story of Salvestro Bisdomini, written around the middle of the sixteenth century by Anton Francesco Grazzini, called il Lasca (1503–84), *Le cene* (Milan: Rizzoli, 1989), 1.1.

of black amber and wine. If she was no longer a virgin, she would need to uri-
nate immediately; a virgin would retain her urine longer than usual.[15] Antonio
Guainerio complained of men called "travantuli," who used urine to figure out
whether a woman was or had ever been pregnant, how many times she had delivered, whether she had been married, or even whether her mother and father
were alive.[16] In Savonarola's *De urinis*, we see almost the same words Callimaco
uses in *Mandragola*: "Urine mulierum sunt subcitrine ad albedinem cum turbu-
lentia quadam & notabili grossitie declinantes.... Item ad earum ingrossationem
& turbulentiam concurrunt materie que a matrice per canale urine magnum
una cum urina ad extra propellantur."[17]

Callimaco judges Lucrezia's urine sample dark because he knows that the
urine of wives is less beautiful than that of men ("minoris pulchritudinis, quam
virorum") because in sexually active wives urine is mixed with seed and both are
discharged through their vaginal canals.[18] He further inquires whether Lucrezia
is properly covered at night, since another cause for differing urine color could
come from weakness in the kidneys. Nicia replies that his wife regularly gets
chilly before climbing to bed because she spends too much time praying. Callimaco's meaning is of course ambiguous, since it hints that Nicia is failing to be
sufficiently amorous toward his wife, but his is also a legitimate medical question: chills were thought to reduce the possibility of pregnancy because they
made woman's body colder than usual.[19] Also, as I pointed out in the introduction, chills could displace a womb, a problem in need of a cure all its own.

15. Giambattista della Porta, *Magiae naturalis* (1558; reprint, Palermo: Il Vespro, 1979), 115.
On ways to fake virginity through proper response to potions, see Marjorie Garber, "The
Insincerity of Women," in *Desire in the Renaissance: Psychoanalysis and Literature*, ed. Valeria
Finucci and Regina Schwartz (Princeton: Princeton University Press, 1994), 19–38.

16. Antonio Guainerio (Anthonius Guainerius), *Tractatus de matricibus* (*Treatise on the
Womb*), in *Opera omnia* (Pavia, 1481), f.2z5va–b. On Guainerio, see also Helen Lemay, "An-
thonius Guainerius and Medieval Gynecology," in *Women of the Medieval World*, ed. Julius
Krishner and Suzanne Wemple (London: Blackwell, 1985), 317–36.

17. Giovanni Michele Savonarola, *De urinis*, in *Practica Savonarolae de febribus* (Venice:
Giunta, 1517), 96v.

18. "Nam mulieris urinae sunt semper maioris grossitiei et albedinis, et minoris pulchritudinis, quam virorum. Huius autem, inter caetera, causa est amplitudo canalium, mixtio
eorum quae ex matrice exeunt cum urina" (2.6). Passage left untranslated in the English
version.

19. Interestingly, Nicia is the character throughout the play most obsessed with sex and

Having gathered all proper information, Callimaco recommends the appropriate therapy for fertility: a potion of mandrake roots. In the early modern period when herbs, roots, juice from plants, seeds, and kernels were widely used and the form of the plant suggested the remedy (walnuts were used for headaches, for example, and scallions, fava beans, and eggplants were stimulants for men), mandrake roots were recommended as fecundity agents for women, thanks to their anthropomorphic shape.[20] Mandrakes were in such high demand at the time and the price was so steep, that often only substitutes, such as bryony and flag, could be obtained through ambulant merchants or self-proclaimed herbalists. Following standard medical advice, Callimaco asks that the mandrake remedy be drunk at night after dinner to better profit from the propitious phase of the moon: "Questa sera doppo cena, perchè la luna è ben disposta, ed el tempo non può esssere più a proposito" (2.6; "This evening after supper, for the moon's in the right quarter and the time couldn't be more suitable"). The concoction had to be followed by intercourse. As for the workings of this homeopathic remedy and for Callimaco's assurances that Lucrezia would be able to release its poisonous surrogate through coitus, they make sense according to early modern medical thought because what was taken in through the mouth would circulate down to the canal used in coitus. There it could be released through orgasmic contractions. Notice that the placebo Lucrezia is given to drink as a substitute for the mandrake, the "hypocras," was considered aphrodisiacal.[21]

---

dirty sexual expressions, especially those related to the backside: "cacastecchi," "cacasangue," "scingasi" (stickshitter, bloodshitter, let him drop his pants). See Ronald Martinez, "The Pharmacy of Machiavelli: Roman Lucretia in *Mandragola*," *Renaissance Drama* 14 (1983): 1–43, esp. 35. For Rebhorn, this anal fixation means that Nicia "wants to defecate on the world, for to excrete — to be able to excrete on others — is to manifest power." See Wayne Rebhorn, *Foxes and Lions: Machiavelli's Confidence Men* (Ithaca: Cornell University Press, 1988), 62. It could be argued, of course, that this interest in anal excretions compensates in Nicia the lack of other, more generative secretions.

20. Walnuts could also be considered the cause for headaches, as in Moderata Fonte, *The Worth of Women (Il merito delle donne)*, trans. Virginia Cox (1600; Chicago: University of Chicago Press, 1998), 174. Fonte's text is among the first to inscribe and comment on women's popular knowledge of homeopathic cures.

21. As Geoffrey Chaucer writes in "The Merchant's Tale," this potion increases man's lust ("He drynketh ypocras, claree, and vernage of spices hoote, t'encressen his corage"). See *The Canterbury Tales*, ed. Nevill Coghill (Baltimore: Penguin, 1952). For a look at medieval

There are therefore at least two reasons why Lucrezia needs to be patiently convinced by her husband, her mother, and her priest, to accept the experiment on her body: first, only by participating in the coital procedures, doctors held, would she be able to release her poison.[22] Secondly, if we assume that Nicia would also take the occasion to have a stranger impregnate his wife because of his own problems in the area, Lucrezia needed not only to have an orgasm, just like men, but also to want the act, because women who copulated in a disordered fashion were thought to be at risk of conceiving a monstrous offspring.[23] As for penis size, like most men Nicia does not follow Aristotle; when he is given the chance to survey the size and shape of Callimaco's organ he can only marvel at the other's equipment. More on this later.

The last scene of the play shows Lucrezia undergoing a rite of purification in church, following a thorough bodily cleansing, the morning after her sexual encounter with Callimaco. Daria Perocco has retraced this rite to the popular "Candelora" feast celebrating the purification after childbirth of the Virgin Mary and to the churching ("andare in santo") of all new mothers forty days after parturition, when they were deemed sufficiently cleansed to enter church (or later, if they gave birth to a female).[24] Perocco writes that Nicia's desire to have

---

and early modern theoretical bases of magiferous plants, botanical medicamenta, and pharmaceutical recommendations, see *Herbs and Herbalism in the Middle Ages and the Renaissance*, ed. Katherine Stannard and Richard Kay (Aldershot: Ashgate, 1999).

22. The same understanding appears in a novella by Bandello, in which a woman is told to engage in repeated love making to keep releasing her seed for the sake of curing a possible infection contracted through a sexual encounter with a leper: "per tre o quattro mesi, ogni giorno, quante più volte poteva, con diverse persone amorosamente si prendesse piacere; perciocché ella potrebbe di leggiero di tal maniera purgarsi, che daria il male ad altri, ed ella si sanerebbe, come dicevano anche avvenire a una donna che avesse il mal francese." In Matteo Bandello, *Tutte le novelle*, 2 vols., ed. Francesco Flora (Milan: Mondadori, 1935), 1:37.

23. A treatise attributed to Albertus Magnus intimated as much: "Above all it is necessary to particularly avoid disorderly and violent copulation . . . . . . so that the seed will not be badly attached to the womb." See Ottavia Niccoli, "*Menstruum Quasi Monstruum:* Monstrous Births and Menstrual Taboo in the Sixteenth Century," in *Sex and Gender in Historical Perspective: Selections from Quaderni Storici*, ed. Edward Muir and Guido Ruggiero (Baltimore: Johns Hopkins University Press, 1990), 1–25, esp. 7; and ch. 3.

24. Daria Perocco, "Il rito finale della *Mandragola*," *Lettere italiane* 25 (1973): 531–36. For more on the churching of new mothers, see Gail Paster, *The Body Embarrassed: Drama and the Disciplines of Shame in Early Modern England* (Ithaca: Cornell University Press, 1993). For the tradition of baptizing girls later than boys, see chapter 3.

his wife go through the rite is the result not of the fact that Lucrezia may have been impregnated but that her husband has the imagination of a far-sighted individual who visualizes and enjoys the future before it happens. Hence, Nicia has Lucrezia purified as a new mother because he knows that as a result of imbibing the mandrake potion she will become a mother. Mireille Celse goes one step further: she is not so sure that Nicia does not know that perhaps he, rather than Lucrezia, constitutes the reason for her failed pregnancy and attributes his own boasting of virility to "pure fanfaronade."[25]

I see Nicia as a true Machiavellian character who consistently adapts to circumstances: he may believe that the man making love to his wife may be killed after intercourse; he may have no hint of the ruse and of the real *garzonaccio's* identity, but there is no reason for him not to know that the young man may generate a child before he himself has a chance to do so, now that Lucrezia's womb, thanks to the mandrake and the moon, is ready for it.[26] In my mind, Machiavelli's use of the rite of purification, a ceremony unheard of for the kind of sexual activity taking place in the play, is necessary to reground woman as the site of reproduction under civic and religious laws. We know that in the Hebrew and Christian traditions a menstruating woman was considered impure and needed to cleanse herself before reentering the grace of God. But also a woman who had a sexual discharge following copulation was thought to be impure, just like man, and needed washing or bathing.[27] This is doubly true in our case, when another man has made love to a married woman and when it was believed that the mandrake's poison would be discharged through the sexual act.

In *Mandragola*, Lucrezia has been read both in a positive light, as strong and

25. Mireille Celse, "La Beffa chez Machiavel, dramaturge et conteur," in *Formes et significations de la Beffa dans la littérature italienne de la Renaissance*, ed. André Rochon (Paris: Université de la Sorbonne Nouvelle, 1972), 99–110, esp. 102.

26. In *Clizia*, Machiavelli clearly implies that the man who copulates first with a woman will be the one who makes her pregnant. The servant Pirro acknowledges the fact with a sarcastic comment when his master Nicomaco schemes to enjoy Pirro's bride before Pirro does: "Io ringrazio Dio, poichè mi ha dato una moglie in modo fatta, ch'io non arò a durare fatica nè a 'mpregnarla, nè a darli le spese." In *Mandragola/Clizia*, ed. Riccardo Bacchelli (Milan: Feltrinelli, 1995), 4.2.

27. See Shaye Cohen, "Menstruants and the Sacred in Judaism and Christianity," in *Women's History and Ancient History*, ed. Sarah Pomeroy (Chapel Hill: University of North Carolina Press, 1991), 237–99, esp. 277.

virtuous, and in a negative light, as stupid and conventional.[28] Either way, the majority of critics agree that at the end of the play she is as immoral as everybody else. In short, Lucrezia is chastised for not having behaved like her famous namesake, Livy's Lucretia, who committed suicide after being raped in order to save her own and her family's reputation.[29] And yet what alternatives does Lucrezia have? Unmasking the plot would have made her forfeit her marriage.

28. For a view of Lucrezia as active and full of wisdom with a "capacity for accepting her own corruption and transformation," see Giulio Ferroni, " 'Transformation' and 'Adaptation' in Machiavelli's *Mandragola*," in *Machiavelli and the Discourse of Literature*, ed. Albert Ascoli and Victoria Kahn (Ithaca: Cornell University Press, 1993), 81–116, esp. 109; Levi, "La *Mandragola* di Machiavelli," 48–62; Luigi Vanossi, "Situazione e sviluppo del teatro machiavelliano," in *Lingua e strutture del teatro italiano del Rinascimento*, ed. G. Folena (Padua: Liviana, 1970), 1–108; and Maristella Lorch, "Women in the Context of Machiavelli's *Mandragola*," in *Donna: Women in Italian Culture*, ed. Ada Testaferri (Toronto: Dovehouse, 1989), 253–71. For a view of Lucrezia as a fearful woman ("una povera donna, pavida e priva d'energia"), see Gennaro Sasso's introduction to the edition of *Mandragola* from which I quote, 41.

29. Machiavelli refers to Livy's Lucretia in his *Discourses*, where he discusses how women, even raped ones, can represent danger to rulers. For a lucid analysis of the correspondences between the two Lucretias, see Martinez, "The Pharmacy of Machiavelli." For Flaumenhaft, Lucrezia is a Christian version of Livy's matron with whom she shares the same concern for honor ("The Comic Remedy," 46). Padoan too compares Machiavelli's and Livy's Lucretia and finds the same words in the two Italian versions: "La volonta' é quella che pecca, non il corpo." See Giorgio Padoan, "Il tramonto di Machiavelli," *Lettere italiane* 33 (1981): 457–81, esp. 478. Nino Borsellino writes that the ending of *Mandragola* is very ambiguous, because, unlike *Clizia*, which closes with the reestablishment of the bourgeois family, here everything depends on Lucrezia's sexual satisfaction. See Nino Borsellino, "Per una storia delle commedie del Machiavelli," *Cultura e scuola* 33–34 (1970): 229–41. For Russo, Lucrezia is virtuous in all circumstances. She is "virtuosa prima e dopo; virtuosa nella via del bene, quando resiste alle balorde esortazioni della madre e ai goffi desideri del marito; virtuosa nella via del male, quando, ritrovandosi, non esita a percorrerla fino in fondo." See Luigi Russo, *Machiavelli* (Bari: Laterza, 1949), 117. Pitkin finds Lucrezia's transformation from tamed wife to bold lover difficult to accept (*Fortune Is a Woman*, 112). D'Amico argues that what Machiavelli means in keeping women under ("tener sotto") is mastery rather than rape, and Lucrezia's acceptance of Callimaco's ruse means that she understands why it is better for her interests. In this reading, Fortuna combines manly and womanly virtue: Callimaco is changed by the experience, and Lucrezia accepts the practical side of the situation. See Jack D'Amico, "The 'Virtù' of Women: Machiavelli's *Mandragola* and *Clizia*," *Interpretation* 12 (1984): 261–73, esp. 269.

Returning to the status quo would have not been a good choice either, since in order to continue enjoying her present social standing she needed to have a child, a role to which her husband seemed unsuited to contribute. Begging for civic redress would have meant losing her reputation and giving up everything she had. Asking for parental advice would have been stupid, since her mother betrays her; soliciting religious counsel would have brought the same results, because her priest uses her for money. The fact is that Lucrezia has no choice but to accept what needs to take place.

To be sure, Lucrezia is highly esteemed by critics when she is cast as chaste and with no desires of her own. Even her own concession to Nicia's desire to make love to another man is then read as normal, given that everything can be justified in terms of maternal wishes. But giving one's body away, whatever the reason, is hardly the right thing to do, as the decision in the Baby M case reveals: a mother who submits her body to sex solely for breeding purposes, the judge ruled, may be unfit to mother the child she generated. Lucrezia understands only too well that her rights to manage her persona have strong definitions: she needs to control her body for the sake of conventions, but she has also to accept her husband's desire to give it away, because only through descendants can she continue to have a "respected" body.

Mandrakes, Spiders, and the Fear of Wombs

I would like to concentrate at this point on Callimaco's "cure," the mandrake, and see how and why such a plant/root is deployed in the story.[30] It is well known that Machiavelli had an extensive knowledge of herbs, potions, and medical remedies. In a letter to his friend Guicciardini, for example, he included the recipe for a laxative; Machiavelli himself was thought to have died blurting out obscene words at his deathbed as a result of self-prescribed concoctions.[31] We know that from the fifteenth century on, there was a documented, heavy resur-

---

30. The first critic to draw attention to the importance of the mandrake in Machiavelli's play was Giovanni Aquilecchia, in "La Favola *Mandragola* si chiama," in *Collected Essays on Italian Language and Literature Presented to Kathleen Speight*, ed. Giovanni Aquilecchia (Manchester: Manchester University Press, 1971), 74–100. See also Ezio Raimondi, *Politica e commedia: Dal Beroaldo al Machiavelli* (Bologna: Mulino, 1972).

31. See Antonio Sorella, *Magia, lingua e commedia nel Machiavelli* (Florence: Olschki, 1990), 80–84.

gence of herbal medicine. The belief in the curative power of medicinal herbs was so widespread that a first professorship of simples was created in Rome in 1514 under the sponsorship of Pope Leo X. The list of remedies offered by doctors, herbalists, spice merchants, pharmacologists, midwives, peasants, charlatans, exorcists, and astrologers to cure the various epidemics of the age often reached, Piero Camporesi has said, the heights of a "toxicological delirium": "There were perfumes against deafness, anti-venereal perfumes, perfumes for 'hopeless fluxes' and 'intestinal hernias'; ointment for scabies, chronic fevers and burns; powders against gout and stones.... Then came the gallery of amulets."[32] Machiavelli's knowledge of herbals comes presumably from the pronouncements of the first-century Greek doctor Dioscorides of Anazarba, who was, with his contemporary, toxicologist Nicander of Colaphon, the uncontested authority on the topic. Both described at length the benefits and the dangers associated with the use of the mandrake. Dioscorides's text, De materia medica (77 A.D.?), recovered in the fifteenth century, was translated from Greek into Latin with a commentary by Marcello Virgilio Adriani, a colleague of Machiavelli in Florence, who could very well have allowed him to read his manuscript (it was printed the year of the Mandragola's performance, 1518).[33] Both versions of Apuleius Barbaro, the Latin Herbarium Apulei (1481) and the Italian Herbolario volgare (1522), also enjoyed wide circulation.

Today the mandrake has lost most of its reputation and is employed, like mayapple, only in gastrointestinal ailments, but it was not so in the past. Charles Thompson has found twenty-two treatises on the mandrake written between 1510 and 1850.[34] According to Charles Randolph, the mandrake (Lat. *mandragora*) had been used by Greeks and Romans in medicine and as an anesthetic

32. Piero Camporesi, *Bread of Dreams: Food and Fantasy in Early Modern Europe*, trans. David Gentilcore (Chicago: University of Chicago Press, 1989), 113. For pharmaceutical knowledge, see Richard Palmer, "Pharmacy in the Republic of Venice in the Sixteenth Century," in *The Medical Renaissance of the Sixteenth Century*, ed. Andrew Wear, Roger French, and Iain Lonie (Cambridge: Cambridge University Press, 1985), 100–117.

33. Dioscorides, *The Greek Herbal of Dioscorides*, ed. Robert Gunther (London: Hafner, 1968); Dioscorides was translated into Italian later in the century by Pietro Mattioli (1501–77). See *Dei discorsi di m. Pietro Mattioli sanese . . . nelli sei libri di Pedacio Dioscoride Anazarbeo, della materia medicinale* (Venice: Valgrisi, 1568).

34. Charles Thompson, *The Mystic Mandrake* (New York: University Books, 1968), 20. See also Joseph Crellin and Jane Philpott, *Herbal Medicine Past and Present*, 2 vols. (Durham, N.C.: Duke University Press, 1989), 1:137 and 2:183.

in surgery since the first century A.D.; the plant was known to render a patient unconscious for up to four hours in surgical practice and in cauterizing procedures.[35] The mandrake was sometimes feared because it was supposed to cause madness. Romans thought so or at least considered it highly poisonous.[36] The lore about the difficulty of digging its roots—one had to look west and make three circles around the plant with a sword—originated in the East. The mandrake could only be dug at night, it was thought, and diggers could die performing the task. Thus, by the fifth century, dogs substituted men; reportedly the animals died soon after unearthing the roots. Given the context, one can see why in *Mandragola* a street boy, a person of a lower social class, an unprivileged "dog," is made to substitute for the lawyer Nicia and die in his stead. Like many plants, the mandrake had a sex. For Dioscorides the male plant was white and had large leaves and a pleasant smell; the female was black, with narrow leaves, no stalk, and an unpleasant, heavy scent.

During the Middle Ages new details were added to the lore: the mandrake roots resembled a human body, with bifurcated legs, no arms, and no head. Pietro Mattioli wrote that Pythagoras called the mandrake *Anthropomorphos* because it had the shape of a man's face. In a much-reproduced image, Dioscorides is represented as writing a codex in the company of a goddess holding a mandrake root shaped as a man. The mandrake was supposed to have grown where the last urine of a thief wrongly condemned to death fell (a new twist of the Prometheus story), which explains the groans that the roots supposedly emitted when dug. This brought along the uncanny custom for onlookers to cover their ears while the roots were being dug up. Reduced to a poultice, the mandrake was used to cure inflammations and abscesses, Randolph writes, to provide relief for snake bites, to soothe hemorrhoids, and to help in the flux of humors. Being able to cure mental problems, it was prescribed in cases of melancholia, insanity, and neurosis.

The mandrake was usually dug on Friday, the day of Venus, because it was important in love matters. It also worked best with a rising moon. Roots were kept as fetishes: women carried them as charms against sterility; men as talismans to

35. Charles Randolph, "The Mandragora of the Ancients in Folk-lore and Medicine," *Proceedings of the American Academy of Arts and Sciences* 40 (1905): 487–537.

36. In *Metamorphoses*, bk. 10, Apuleius directly refers to the mandrake root. For the source in Apuleius and his Renaissance imitator, Francesco Vettori, see Raimondi, *Politica e commedia*, 257–58.

arouse passions.[37] Joan of Arc was accused of having mandrakes hidden in her breast in order to acquire riches; in *Turandot*, Carlo Gozzi gives the mandrake the power to make one talk when asleep.[38] Its narcotic and soporific qualities are mentioned in Genesis (30.14) and referred to by a number of authoritative writers such as Plato.[39] Shakespeare's Cleopatra asked to drink mandragora to sleep while Antony was away, but "Not poppy, nor mandragora, / Nor all the drowsy syrups of the world" were to help Othello.[40] With his own experience to support his finding, Tasso classified the root as hallucinogenic.[41]

The mandrake was also recommended as an aphrodisiac by quack herbalists; Aphrodite was called Mandragoritis, and Circe was said to have used the mandrake to seduce Ulysses' companions.[42] In the fourth chapter of *Physiologus*, a text widely read in the Middle Ages for its accounts of wonders, the mandrake is said to govern sexual arousal and to cause temptations in women: "The female seeks out the so-called mandragora plant, and partakes of it; straightway she is inflamed, and going to the male, gives him the plant; he partakes of it, and straightway is inflamed, and cohabits with the female."[43]

From aphrodisiac herb to fecundity agent the step is a short one. In Genesis 30.14–16, for example, Rachel is given mandrakes by her sister Leah to cure her

37. Thompson, *The Mystic Mandrake*, 120. The anthropomorphic shape of the mandrake is recalled in Samuel Beckett's *Waiting for Godot*, where the two main characters elaborate on the homunculus within the root of the mandrake. In *Godot* the mandrake comes from the semen rather than from the urine of a hanged man.

38. Carlo Gozzi, *Turandot* (Rome: Salerno, 1990), 134.

39. Plato, *Republic*, 488c.

40. William Shakespeare, *Othello* (Mineola: Dover, 1996), 3.8.

41. See *Il mondo creato*, ed. Giorgio Petrocchi (Florence: Le Monnier, 1951), 3:1080. For hallucinogenic and aphrodisiac recipes containing mandrakes, see Enrico Malizia, *Ricettario delle streghe: Incantesimi, prodigi sessuali e veleni* (Rome: Edizioni mediterranee, 1992), 104, 143–48, and 177.

42. For the reference to Aphrodite, see Hugo Rahner, "Moly and Mandragora in Pagan and Christian Symbolism," in *Greek Myths and Christian Mystery* (New York: Harper and Row, 1963), 179–277, esp. 229; for the reference to Circe, see Randolph, "The Mandragora of the Ancients," 502. Camporesi writes that mandrake pills were widely used as aphrodisiacs and tonics in the United States in the thirties and that the cartoon superman Mandrake was baptized with a mandrake root. See Piero Camporesi, *The Incorruptible Flesh: Bodily Mutation and Mortification in Religion and Folklore*, trans. Tania Kroft-Murray (Cambridge: Cambridge University Press, 1988), 204.

43. The citation is in Randolph, "The Mandragora of the Ancients," 502.

barrenness and win back her husband's affections. But not all women would benefit from its powers. Dioscorides recommended the root of the mandrake to purify the womb, but in conception the mandrake was useful, according to Bartholomaeus Anglicus, only in the case of women "calidas et umidas."[44] For Michele Savonarola, the cure for sterility caused by a cold matrix was "triphera magna"; for a hot one, mandragora.[45] A hot matrix could be determined by the turbid color of the urine sample. But turbidity could also come from a malfunction of the kidney ("calidità di rene"), Savonarola argued.[46] In the case of Machiavelli's play, Callimaco reads the turbid color of Lucrezia's urine as coming from the kidneys, but he also asks what makes Lucrezia cold, assuming that she is not naturally so. Thus the mandrake, a plant whose roots evoked male anatomy, could cure and kill humans at the same time: wrong dosages would poison, right dosages would further procreative aims; wrong diggings of its roots would be fatal, right diggings would make a patient reap benefits and make money. To this Machiavelli adds the notion that the mandrake could kill, through sexual intercourse, the lover of the woman who, thanks to the same act, engenders a new life.

But why are the effects of this plant so much divided along gender lines? Why is what is beneficial to the female deadly to the male? What makes a female womb so poisonous that men cannot come close to it? The Bible presents the connection between a woman's poisoning body and sexual danger with the story of Sarah, who was told not to have sex with her new husband, Tobit, for a few nights until her body had been detoxified (Tobit 6.1–22, in the Vulgate version). We know that a menstruating female was thought to have a toxic body and that contact with her was not only dangerous to humans but also to dogs, which would become mad, and to flowers, which would shrivel up and die. Women lacking their menses and postmenopausal women were especially venomous, because they no longer had a way to get rid of their humors; old women, Tommaso Campanella wrote, have offending vapors coming out of their eyes and

44. Bartholomaeus Anglicus, *De rerum proprietatibus* (1601; Frankfurt: Minerva, 1964), 17.104. For the reference to Dioscorides, see Thompson, *The Mystic Mandrake*, 77.

45. Michele Savonarola, *Practica Major* 6.21, 265r. On this, see Martinez, "The Pharmacy of Machiavelli," 37.

46. Michele Savonarola, *De regimine pregnantium et noviter natorum usque ad septennium*, in *Il trattato ginecologico-pediatrico in volgare*, ed. Luigi Belloni (Milan: Stucchi, 1952), 45.

mouth.[47] They can poison sleeping babies, Albertus Magnus asserted, just by looking at them. In short, the view that females are always somewhat poisonous was very much in tune with the philosophical necessity to biologize cultural tenets and postulate female bodies as inferior to males and positively dangerous. Woman is a putrid swamp ("La donna è una putrida palude"), Michelangelo Biondo wrote in his libelous *Angoscia, doglia e pena*.[48] Giovanni Della Casa echoed his disgust: what can be more repelling than a sick woman, he asked, if even in good health she is "inevitably so smelly" ("che cosa può esserci di più ripugnante e sconcio di una donna ammalata, se perfino da sana è inevitabilmente maleodorante?")[49]

Danielle Jacquart and Claude Thomasset have suggested that man's fear of the calamitous female was perhaps precipitated from the thirteenth century onward by epidemics as well as by the influential writings of clerics who had very little understanding of couples' problems, given their lack of practical knowledge of marital issues.[50] Readings of the female body were in fact much more negative at the time Machiavelli wrote than later in the century, when the anatomical observations of Andreas Vesalius, Gabriele Falloppio, and Realdo Colombo contributed to a better understanding of bodily functions. By the end of the sixteenth century, for example, woman's coldness was no longer seen as the mark of her imperfection compared to man, but as a functional condition of her body, in that by burning fat more slowly due to her colder nature, she was able to nourish the fetus and to lactate.[51]

Recently, Giovanni Aquilecchia has argued that Machiavelli borrowed the motif of the toxic female from the folklore legend of the poisonous girl who kills her mate with her embraces. Citing the verse remake of Brunetto Latini's *Li*

---

47. Tommaso Campanella, *Del senso delle cose e della magia*, ed. Antonio Bruers (Bari: Laterza, 1925), 4.14, p. 285.

48. Michelangelo Biondo (1497–1565), *Angoscia, Doglia e Pena* (Venice, 1546), in *Trattati del Cinquecento sulla donna*, ed. Giuseppe Zonta (Bari: Laterza, 1913), 128.

49. Giovanni Della Casa (1503–56), *Una questione piacevolissima: Se si debba prendere moglie*, in *Prose di Giovanni Della Casa e altri trattatisti cinquecenteschi del comportamento*, ed. Arnaldo Di Benedetto (Turin: UTET, 1970), 48–133, 77.

50. Danielle Jacquart and Claude Thomasset, *Sexuality and Medicine in the Middle Ages*, trans. Matthew Adamson (Princeton: Princeton University Press, 1988), 129.

51. Ian Maclean, *The Renaissance Notion of Woman: A Study in the Fortunes of Scholasticism and Medical Science in European Intellectual Life* (Cambridge: Cambridge University Press, 1980), 34.

tresor, Aquilecchia refers to the legend of the virgin fed on snakes since infancy, who had a venomous body and with whom Alexander was warned not to sleep, for if he did, he would die ("Questa pulcella era di veleno nutricata, / Sì che Alessandro quando co'llei coisse / Immantanente morisse"). Alexander's tutor, Aristotle, sees this woman as a serpent ("Io veggo e conosco in questa creatura / Atto e reggimento di serpente").[52] The connection of women and snakes is ingrained in our cultural imaginary: in describing the various mutations of the uterus, Plato says, for example, that it can convert into a snake; likewise, the hair of a menstruating female placed for a time under a dung heap will engender a snake, according to Albertus Magnus.[53] Hair from a woman's pubis mixed with menstrual blood also makes her breasts venomous. Galen cites a woman in Athens who ingested increasing amounts of hemlock without sustaining any health damage, although she could kill others through her breath; she was deadly even as a corpse. Freud makes explicit the connection between woman's snaky hair and her pubis and relates it to man's horror of castration.[54]

Lorenzo Gioberti considers the mandrake a "cold poison" like hemlock and poppy; they are supposed not to cause death when ingested. He then elaborates on the specific use of such herbs in situations similar to the one Machiavelli presents in the play. Where would a woman lodge the poison, he writes? If she put it too deep inside her womb, it would not come out at the right time, and although women's bodies were made to resist poison "seeping to the heart and other noble parts," the womb itself would be inflamed. If she put the poison at the neck of her womb, there wouldn't be enough to come in contact with a man's member and cause his poisoning. Moreover, given the unpredictability of men's readiness for sex, a woman runs the risk of harming her internal organs without getting the chance of damaging his. If she soaked a cloth with poison and put that inside her parts, he reasons, other organs in her body could be damaged by the fumes. Moreover, the poison could be smelled in her breath, since women's "two mouths" were known to communicate with each other. Unless, of course,

---

52. See Aquilecchia, "La favola *Mandragola* si chiama," 83. On the legend of the poisonous virgin and its sources, see Wilhelm Hertz, "Die Sage von Giftmädchen," in *Gesammelte Abhandlungen* (Stuttgart-Berlin: Cotta, 1905), 156–277.

53. See Jacquart and Thomasset, *Sexuality and Medicine*, 76.

54. Sigmund Freud, "Medusa's Head," in *The Standard Edition of the Complete Works of Sigmund Freud* [hereafter *SE*], 24 vols., ed. and trans. James Strachey (London: Hogarth Press, 1953–74), 18:273–74 (1955).

women could be made poisonous by repeatedly ingesting poison, and this poison was not, all considered, as harmful to females as to males, given women's colder nature and the "wider and dilated opening" of their genitalia. Despite his many circumscriptions of the subject, Gioberti too ends up embracing Galen and constructs woman as venomous.[55] In Machiavelli's play the effects of the mandrake are postulated along the same lines: the encounter with this "fecundating" poison in woman's genitals is said to be able to kill man but does woman no harm.

Not only serpents but deadly spiders also are frequently associated with females. Albertus Magnus describes the case of a three-year-old girl who fed herself poisonous spiders and acquired a body utterly resistant to poison.[56] Ralph Little traces identical stories in China and Japan, where spiders change into young girls and trap men with their silken cords.[57] The female black widow spider, which kills and eats her mate after copulation, is well known, as is the female Australian redback, which starts to chew its mate while sperm is being deposited.[58] In sum, in both Western and Eastern culture, woman is deadly to others but is herself immune to harm. Machiavelli was himself authoritatively cited as an expert on spider poisons in two Renaissance treatises that appeared

55. Lorenzo Gioberti, *La prima parte degli errori popolari. Nella quale si contiene l'eccellenza della medicina e de medici, della concettione e generatione, della gravidanza, del parto, e delle donne di parto, e del latte, e del nutrire i bambini* (Florence: Giunta, 1582), 2.13. In the English translation of the original French text, the chapter from which I am citing is titled: "Whether It Is Possible for a Woman to Poison a Man through the Venereal Act." See *Popular Errors*, trans. Gregory David de Rocher (Tuscaloosa: University of Alabama Press, 1989). The reference to the mandrake as a cold poison was present in the original French version, *Erreurs populaires* (Bordeaux, 1579), 2.13, and subsequently dropped. Gioberti also did not think that a woman could poison a man by making love when menstruating.

56. Albertus Magnus, *De animalibus*, 7.2.5. See Jacquart and Thomasset, *Sexuality and Medicine*, 192; Claude Thomasset, "La Femme au moyen age: Les composantes fondamentales de sa réprésentation: immunité-impunité," *Ornicar?* 22–23 (1981): 223–38, esp. 234–36; and Ottavia Niccoli, "Il corpo femminile nei trattati del Cinquecento," in *Il corpo delle donne*, ed. Gisela Boch and Giuliana Nobili (Bologna: Transeuropa, 1988), 35–36.

57. Ralph Little, "Oral Agression in Spider Legends," *American Imago* 23 (1966): 169–79.

58. An article in *Science* by Maydianne Andrade documents the eagerness with which the male allows itself to be devoured in order to deposit the maximum amount of sperm and genes into the female. One could call it paternal sacrifice. For a review, see *Time*, Jan. 15, 1996, 60.

later in the century: Girolamo Mercuriale's text on venoms and toxic diseases and Pietro Mattioli's commentary in Italian on Dioscorides, where "il Niccolò" is mentioned in connection with a case of poisoning in a monastery in Florence, following the fall of a black spider into the communal soup pot.[59]

Fear of spiders (tarantism) reached epidemic proportions in the late Middle Ages and lasted well into the seventeenth century. In an article on the mass-hysterical reaction to spider bites in those times, Howard Gloyne writes that in the Apulia region in southern Italy, around the city of Taranto (Tarantum), the bite of the *Lycosa tarantula*, which was venomous, created hyperbolic, morbid reactions: subjects bitten by the tarantula (both men and women, but more often women) danced manically, had recurrences of the ailment during the summer months for up to thirty years, and at times committed suicide.[60] In another study, Ernesto De Martino points out that victims regularly reported that the first bite of the tarantula occurred during adolescence and immediately after puberty and that it was often located at the foot, the hand, or the sexual organ.[61] Thus the spider bite comes to be connected to castration in the psychoanalytical sense. Tarantism would occur whether or not one had seen the insect, and it would make victims jump up and down, laugh or cry, undress, or become drunk. Victims lost all their modesty, and women "called for mirrors, sighed and howled while making indecent motions."[62] In 1491 Giovanni Pontano had argued in *Antonius* that women became licentious when bitten by the tarantula.[63] Savonarola felt that it took a great deal of sexual energy, equivalent to that possessed by sparrows (in popular lore lascivious birds), to cure women's lasciviousness after they were bitten by the tarantula.[64] The only relief from tarantism was

59. Girolamo Mercuriale, *De venenis, et morbis venenosis* (Venice: Meietum, 1584). Mattioli writes: "Imperochè (come recita il Niccolò Fiorentino famoso moderno) s'avelenò in Fiorenza tutto un convento di frati, per essere cascato un ragno molto nero nella pignatta della minestra lor" (1464). See also Raimondi, *Politica e commedia*, 257; and Roberto Ridolfi, *Life of Niccolò Machiavelli*, trans. Cecil Grayson (Chicago: University of Chicago Press, 1963), 30–33.

60. Howard Gloyne, "Tarantism: Mass-Hysterical Reaction to Spider Bite in the Middle Ages," *American Imago* 7 (1950): 29–42.

61. Ernesto De Martino, *La terra del rimorso: Contributo a una storia religiosa del sud* (Milan: Saggiatore, 1961).

62. Gloyne, "Tarantism," 31.

63. See also De Martino, *La terra del rimorso*, 49 and 54.

64. "chi avesse tanta possanza bon medico sarebbe a quelle che piagate sono in Puglia da

thought to come from music, often with a sexual content. The highly energetic, erotic dance that accompanied it, usually performed with swords, has come to be known as the "tarantella." By dancing for days on end, sufferers would distribute the poison through their body and eventually expel it through the skin. Castiglione, in the *Cortegiano*, mentions the musical remedy for this kind of agitation ("agitazion").[65]

Many contemporaries felt that the rise of tarantism was a sign from heaven; others made connections to orgiastic Dionysian dances. Today we do not know what caused this outbreak of compulsive behavior; yet we know that this anxiety, directed toward an insect endowed with good and bad qualities, became at a certain point in history highly sexualized. We also know that following the outbreak of syphilis in the Italian peninsula at the time of the French invasion in the 1490s, fear of heterosexual contact, and therefore fear of toxic wombs, suddenly skyrocketed: the "morbus gallicus," first described in 1495, reached epidemic proportions within a few months and raged out of control in Europe two years later. Women came to be cast not only in the role of contaminators but as sufficiently powerful to contaminate men without themselves showing visible signs of the disease. Leprosy also, which affected men more than women, was transmitted during intercourse, it was thought, but women were held largely immune from the disease, because their bodily coldness, by constricting pores, impeded infection.[66] Contact with women whose sexual habits could not be guaranteed was to be curtailed, Doctor Corradino Gilino of Ferrara wrote in 1497. Con-

---

la tarantola lussuriosa," in *Trattato utilissimo di molte regole, per conservare la sanità, dichiarando qual cose siano utili da mangiare, e quali tristi, e medesimamente di quelle che si bevono in Italia* (Venice: Eredi di Gioanni Paduano, 1554), 39r. See also Piero Camporesi, *I balsami di Venere* (Milan: Garzanti, 1989), 40.

65. Cesare Gonzaga explains to his courtly friends: "in Puglia circa gli atarantati s'adoprano molti instrumenti di musica" (1.8.40). See also Campanella, *Del senso*, 4.14, p. 260. Tarantism abated during the following centuries but is still present. See Gabriele Mina, *Il morso della differenza: Antologia del dibattito sul tarantismo fra il 14 e il 16 secolo* (Nardò: Besa, 2000). The Italian movie director Edoardo Winspeare has made a documentary on tarantism and, in his 1998 film, *La pizzicata*, featured the "pizzica" love dance of festivities and the "tarantata" mad dance of grief and desire.

66. Gonococcal infections also could be detected much earlier in men than in women, it was thought, although vaginal examinations were rare at the time. See Jacquart and Thomasset, *Sexuality and Medicine*, 180; and Thomasset, "La femme au moyen age," 226. I have already referred to Bandello's tale on the subject, 1.37.

necting once more woman and poison, Niccolò Massa resolutely advised against intercourse with a woman suspected of being infected by the pox at a specific calendar time: the end of her menses, precisely the period in which the female body was at the time considered most fertile.[67]

In psychoanalysis the spider is a symbol of the bad, masculine, angry mother who, according to Karl Abraham, possesses a male organ, and whose embraces can engulf and kill. In male patients' fantasies, the spider "represents the penis embedded in the female genitals, which is attributed to the mother" and the mother is "formed in the shape of a man, of whose male organ and masculine pleasure in attack the boy is afraid.... The patient's feeling towards spiders can be best described by the word 'uncanny.'"[68] Freud too noticed that the female spider is larger in size than the male and that during copulation the male runs the risk of being killed and devoured by her. Abraham cited the unconscious fantasy of a terrified man examined by one of his colleagues, Dr. Nunberg, in which reference is made to the fact that the spider kills by sucking blood and that this sucking is tied to the fear of castration and of losing one's penis during intercourse.[69]

There are many ways in which the fantasy of the female spider with its castrating and incorporating elements connects to Machiavelli's Lucrezia/

67. Niccolò Massa, *Liber de morbo gallico* (Venice: Bindori ac Pasini socii, 1536). For both points, see Claude Quétel, *History of Syphilis,* trans. Judith Braddock and Brian Pike (Cambridge: Polity Press, 1990), 22 and 58. For another look at syphilis, see chapter 3 below.

68. Karl Abraham, *Selected Papers of Karl Abraham,* trans. Douglas Bryan and Alix Strachey (London: Hogarth Press, 1927), 326–32, esp. 329–30.

69. Abraham, *Selected Papers,* 332. Studying a virilized woman with hermaphroditic organs, Lawrence Newman and Robert Stoller argue that the spider is associated with both genitals: "To the patient's eye, the phallus-like clitoris (the male element) is the body of the spider, while the hairy legs of the spider are formed by the surrounding genital elements." See Newman and Stoller, "Spider Symbolism and Bisexuality," *Journal of the American Psychoanalytic Association* 17 (1969): 869. See also Richard Sterba, "On Spiders, Hanging and Oral Sadism," *American Imago* 7 (1950): 21–28. In women, fear of spiders is associated with oral sadism (penis envy and breast envy), dislike of the mother, bisexuality, the primal scene, and oedipal conflict. Melitta Sperling writes that "the spider symbol indicates a fixation to the pregenital and in particular to the anal-sadistic phase in a very ambivalent and predominantly hostile relationship to the mother." See Sperling, "Spider Phobias and Spider Fantasies: A Clinical Contribution to the Study of Symbol and Symptom Choice," *Journal of the American Psychoanalytic Association* 19.3 (1971): 472–98, esp. 494.

Callimaco story. We know that female spiders are more powerful than their mates, and in *Mandragola* Lucrezia is definitely more powerful than Callimaco, not only because he has made her such through idealization but also because she is said to be competent in smoothly running a household. We know that female spiders kill by sucking their mates dry, and in the play Lucrezia, who believes she has ingested the mandrake, will need to suck Callimaco dry to expel her poison. This can be done, the text makes clear, through his drawing her "sgocciolatura," as the friar flatly puts it, by way of intercourse: "tiri, standosi seco una notte, a sè tutta quella infezione della mandragola" (2.6; "He stays one whole night with her, and draws all the poison of the mandragora out of her into his own body").[70] The "matrix" had already been described by Andreas Vesalius as greedily want-

---

70. Concentrating on the figure of the deadly spider, Antonio Sorella has argued that *Mandragola* is a revised version of a play called *Falargho*, of which there is a reference, although in a mispelled form as *Falangio*, in a letter by Alfonsina Orsini de' Medici, mother of Lorenzo, to the Florentine ambassador to the papal court. Sorella thinks that this play was an earlier version of *Mandragola* and that the author is Machiavelli. He puts the representation of *Mandragola* on September 7 and that of *Falargo (o Commedia in versi)* the night after, September 8. Parronchi (in "La prima rappresentazione") attributes the untitled comedy played that night to Lorenzo Strozzi (76). For a case against this dating, see Andrea Gareffi, *La scrittura e la festa: Teatro, festa e letteratura nella Firenze del Rinascimento* (Bologna: Mulino, 1991), 120–22. Sorella traces the origin of the word "falangio" to a poisonous spider, the *phalangium*, and to an herb of the same name used as an antidote to the spider's bite. In his reading, Lucrezia is the spider woman, the "falangia," who has consumed a poisonous mandrake, and Callimaco is the male spider, the "falangio," who has to risk his life in order to copulate with the spider woman and impregnate her. What saves the *falangio* from death is an antidote. For Sorella there are two poisons in the story: the mandrake, which facilitates impregnation and which is given to Nicia probably by Fra Timoteo at the cost of twenty-five ducats (paid for by Ligurio with Nicia's money), and a glass of hypocras prepared by Callimaco, which would constitute the antidote to the toxic *pharmakon*. Connecting this story to the fear of the poisonous woman or of the killing woman in arachnophobic legends, Sorella argues for a plot along these lines: Callimaco is the madman in love who will have sex with the poisonous woman, absorb in the act her surrogate, and then save himself by ingesting the other potion, the hypocras, that in the extant version of the text is given to Lucrezia as a substitute for the mandrake. Sorella's reasoning is intriguing, but his documentation is insufficient to support his hypothesis. Moreover, the linguistic connections between *falargho* and *falangio* are hard to justify as causing both a misspelling and a miswriting. The title *Falangio*, whatever its possible meaning, is not present in any context in Italian literature. I thank one of Duke Press' anonymous readers for this insight.

ing to swallow men's semen, a spider-like, vampiresque mouth made to attract and catch the seed ("quando desidera il seme virile [questa bocca] con moto spontaneo lo attrae").[71] What interests me most in these arachnid fantasies is the fact that a powerful female in the stated need of reaching orgasm creates in man a fear of dismemberment, castration, poisoning, and loss of one's sex, for as Machiavelli puts it, getting out of Lucrezia's bed is for Callimaco like being uprooted from a prison ("é cavono fuora el prigione," 5.1).

Let me pause at this point to tie these issues together and historicize my approach. My argument goes along these lines: if in *Mandragola* Lucrezia is the spider woman and in psychoanalysis the spider woman is feared as having male organs inside her, what does this mean in a period in which physiologically females were thought to possess — literally — inner male sexual organs and in which there was a well-documented, hysterical fear of spiders? Moreover, if mandrakes were kept as fetishes because of their association with the shape of male sexual organs, what does it mean to have woman, literally, ingest this fetish? Finally, if female bodies are poisonous to others, what is the importance of having woman doubly poison her lover: first, through emission of what's left over from the mandrake, and second, through contamination of his body as a result of releasing her own seed?[72]

71. Andreas Vesalius, "De utero," in *De humani corporis fabrica* (Venice, 1543), 5.15.

72. Female sperm could pollute male bodies, it was believed, and Savonarola had specifically argued against the position of woman on top in coitus because her sperm would have fallen on the penis (*Practica Major*, 6.20.28). See also Jacquart and Thomasset, *Sexuality and Medicine*, 134. Poisoning humors needed to be expelled ("evomit") to avoid suffocation of the vagina, Guainerio held. The prescription was rough intercourse in the missionary position for married women and manual stimulation of the neck of the womb ("matricis collum") by a midwife for virgins (fol. x4rb). Thus, although the clitoris was not yet defined as an organ, its capacity for giving women sexual enjoyment was known. In Castiglione's *Cortegiano* Gasparo Pallavicino claims that women remain attached to the men who make love to them first, because they receive perfection from the sexual act; men, on the other hand, have a different reaction to the encounter, because their own perfection is diminished by this encounter with the imperfect other (3.15.221). But when Pallavicino wistfully asserts that every woman wants to be a man for the sake of perfection, the Magnifico retorts that what proves appealing to women is the male gender rather than the male sex: women do not want to be men but they rather desire the freedom that comes so naturally to men in culture: "per aver libertà e fuggir quel dominio che gli omini si hanno vendicato sopra esse per sua propria autorità" (3.16.222).

As I pointed out in the introduction, until the seventeenth century many doctors considered female sexual organs similar to those of the male, even if they visually did not appear so, according to the theory that heat made the difference: heat makes male organs protrude, lack of heat keeps female organs inside.[73] Giovanni Valverde, for example, elaborating in a chapter on women's testicles, lamented that he had to write on the subject, because of the danger of making women more arrogant than ever at the knowledge that they had testicles, just like men.[74] But if the difference is only in heat, then sexes are not sufficiently distinct and there is always the danger of one's changing, willy-nilly, into the other.[75] Thus, behind the campaign in the early eighteenth century to find more anatomical differences between man and woman, a drive that for a time moved away from sexual organs to concentrate on bones and skeletons, there was the uneasy feeling that there was not adequate separation. The Renaissance interest in twins, hermaphrodites, transvestites, androgynes, dwarfs, monsters, prodigies, and freaks may very well have come, in part, from the fear of what is connected to the sexual fluidity implied by a narcissistic, same-sex mirroring physiology. And, in the same vein, the ceaseless explanations of why such oddities happen may rest, in part, on the desire to find a providential sense of order in a natural world in continuous, unexplainable flux. In other words, the Renaissance may have been the moment of discovery of subjectivity, as Pico della Mirandola famously claimed, but this subjectivity was grounded upon a shaky sense of sexual differences—for as Castiglione wrote, any man has woman in him and vice versa: "non si dee chiamar maschio che non ha la femina, secondo la diffinizione dell'uno e dell'altro; nè femina quella che non ha maschio" (3.14.221;

73. The clitoris that would change this figuration by giving women their own little penis or—since women already had an inverted one in their body—a second penis (but then according to Laqueur did not) was not in play at the time Machiavelli wrote, because its recovery (by Falloppio and Colombo) took place only in the middle of the sixteenth century. See Thomas Laqueur, "Amor Veneris, Vel Dulcedo Appelletur," in *Fragments for a History of the Human Body*, 3 vols., ed. Michael Feher (New York: Zone, 1989), 1:90–131, esp. 119. Although there was no name for it, doctors who could see female cadavers knew where the clitoris was. See note 43 in the introduction.

74. "Havrei voluto con mio honore poter lasciare questo capitolo accioché non diventassero le donne più superbe di quel che sono, sapendo, che elleno hanno ancora i testicoli, come gli huomini." In Giovanni Valverde, *Anatomia del corpo umano*, quoted in Felice La Torre, *L'utero attraverso i secoli: da Erofilo ai giorni nostri* (Città di Castello: Unione Arti Grafiche, 1917), 301.

75. For a brief excursus on such cases, see chapter 5.

"we cannot call anything male unless there is the female in him, or anything female if there is no male in her" [trans. modified]).

Such a lack of precise sexual boundaries came, in turn, to be compensated for by a strict social regulation of gender differences. That is, since both sexes have a penis, the phallus, it has been suggested, rather than the penis, became in the Renaissance the mark of difference: a man is a man because he behaves as such.[76] Laws made sure that boundaries were not crossed easily; sumptuary legislation, for example, although aimed mostly at regulating class behavior, often regulated gender; when prostitutes in Venice started to dress like men, moralistic reproaches from pulpits and courts increased dramatically.[77] In treatises, plenty of room was given to censure men dressed in unmasculine ways, their bodies adorned "a guisa di femmina," with hair and beard curled with a hot iron, face and throat continuously smoothed by massages, as Bartolomeo Della Casa wrote.[78] Men also were discouraged from getting interested in what women did because they could become feminized as a result.[79] In short, to be manly, a man needed to put himself in a position of power and show himself virile, for just to appear like a man physically was not sufficient to qualify for a full manly status. Man had to "become" one according to the laws of gender.

I would go further and argue that what really makes a man such is not just that he strives to look like one but that he is able to confirm his manhood through off-

76. See Thomas Laqueur, *Making Sex: Body and Gender from the Greeks to Freud* (Cambridge: Harvard University Press, 1990).

77. For example, the Consiglio dei Dieci, the highest body politic in Venice, complained that the city's prostitutes had started to dress in masculine clothes ("con habito de homo") to better lead astray young men ("per prender et illaguear i gioveni"). July 14, 1589, register 33, 167v. See also Cathy Santore, "Julia Lombardo, 'Somtuosa Meretrize': A Portrait by Property," *Renaissance Quarterly* 41.1 (1988): 44–83.

78. "I capelli e la barba inanellata col ferro caldo, e'l viso e la gola cotanto strebbiate e cotanto stropicciate che si disdirebbe ad ogni femminetta, anzi ad ogni meretrice." See Giovanni Della Casa, *Galateo* (1558; Milan: Garzanti, 1988), 79–80. Castiglione brought up the same issue about some of his courtiers: "non solamente si crespano i capegli e spelano le ciglia, ma si strisciano con tutti que' modi che si faccian le più lascive e disoneste femine del mondo" (*Cortegiano*, 1.19.54–55).

79. As Leon Battista Alberti thundered, "questi scioperati i quali si stanno il dì tutto tra le feminelle, o che si pigliano ad animo tali simili pensieruzzi femminili, certo non hanno il cuore maschio nè magnifico; . . . [e] facilmente dimostra non fuggire d'essere reputato femminile." See Alberti, *Il padre di famiglia* (1444; Florence: Cenniniana, 1871), 94–95.

spring. It is in a sense the possession of testicles in full working order and able to generate, as I will claim in chapter 6, that guarantees men power, while overuse of sex only feminizes them, as in the episode of Astolfo and Jocondo that I examine in chapter 4. As for women, since there was only one organ that sexually distinguishes them from men — their uterus (the "matter," as Paracelsus wrote) — quite naturally that organ became the guarantor of women's gender in culture. To be a woman physically was the first step in the process of "becoming" one, through motherhood, the defining mark of womanhood in society — a point that Lucrezia in *Mandragola* knows only too well. Her own mother Sostrata articulates it: "Non vedi tu che una donna, che non ha figliuoli, non ha casa? Muorsi el marito, resta com'una bestia, abandonata da ognuno" (3.11; "Don't you know that a woman without children can't call her home her own? If her husband dies, she's left like a brute beast, abandoned by everyone"). No wonder that the uterus became in the following centuries the preferred subject of inquiries into the mystery that is woman.

The Threat of Castration

What then does intercourse with the same mean? What does it mean to make love to a woman in a culture in which women have penises hidden in their "matrix" and large testicles?[80] Even the (perhaps pseudo-) Aristotelian book 10 of *Historia animalium* suggests that the uterus not only sucks in matter but ejaculates during orgasm through the cervix into the vagina.[81] For Avicenna, desire makes a woman's cervix engorged like man's penis and brings it closer to the mouth of the uterus, to better draw in the sperm.[82] Like men, thus, and for the

80. In Niccolò Massa's words, "The matrix is said to be a male member inverted and diminished." See Massa, *Book of Anatomy*, 206. In *Chirurgia* (1476), Guglielmo da Saliceto (1210–80) added that "la matrice ha testicoli pioli e largi." Quoted in Maria Luisa Altieri Biagi, ed., *Guglielmo Volgare: Studio sul lessico della medicina medioevale* (Bologna: Forni, 1970), 128.

81. "For the woman emits not into the womb but in the place where the man's emission also falls." See *Historia animalium* [hereafter *HA*], in *The Complete Works of Aristotle*, 2 vols., ed. Jonathan Barnes (Princeton: Princeton University Press, 1984), 10.4.636a. The point is controversial, and this is one of the reasons why the Aristotelian provenance of book 10 has been questioned, since Aristotle has elsewhere written that woman does not emit seed. See *HA* 7.3.583a; and *GA* 2.4.739b.

82. Avicenna, *Canon* (*Liber canonis*) (Venice, 1507; facsimile, Hildesheim: Olms, 1964), 3.20.1.3.

sake of sexual homology, women get an erect penis inside themselves during coitus. This means, as Thomas Laqueur astutely suggests, that women have a penis (*kaulos*, that is, the cervix) that enters the vagina from the inside, while man's penis enters the vagina from the outside during the sexual act.[83] Thus there is in copulation an encounter between man's penis and woman's inner penis, which must be stimulated in order to "spermatize," — a task that in *Mandragola* Lucrezia thinks can only kill her mate. But contact with the same as other, that is with a woman who is a man, although an improperly "baked" one, can at the very least unleash fears of incorporation and turn the immature man into a feminized other, a being whose member can become, to cite from Massa again, not only "diminished" but actually "inverted," from the outside to the inside, from perfect to imperfect. Even today in Italy *invertito* stands for homosexual.

Let us be clear that Lucrezia is represented in the text in one function only: that of a mother. She is a failed mother, perhaps, a would-be mother, an unlikely mother, but there is no other characterization fitting her that is not connected with engendering. For Nicia she is no more than a breeding machine, a uterus. But for Callimaco Lucrezia owns the world. She both allures him with her beauty and nurtures him in fantasy with her reticence. She promises pre-Oedipal unity, and thus satisfies his solipsistic drives, and post-Oedipal gratification, in that she makes her own body available to the desiring son, no matter that in order to possess it he has to face in fantasy the possibility of his own destruction. As pre-Oedipal mother Lucrezia fosters identification, and as radical Other she invites investigation (all we know about her is told to us by others, and she is the obsessive subject of the plot and of all men's actions). Most of all, she is a phallic mother in the literal sense, her difference deleted by the belief—as Renaissance biological discourses would have it—that she has a penis within her body. In fact, a penis and its enhancer, for the mandrake that is inside her in fantasy came to be fetishized in her culture precisely for its phallus-like shape. The threat of the symbolic, punitive father is recuperated at this point by representing the father/husband as foolish, unmasculine, and unable to father. Like the individuals in the tales related by Gloyne and De Martino who were sexually excited at the encounter (or possibility of an encounter) with a spider, Callimaco cannot find rest anywhere after meeting Lucrezia and has suicidal

83. Laqueur, *Making Sex*, 34.

fantasies and orgasmic reactions.[84] He feels victimized by his desire, unable to concentrate on anything else, incomplete, lacking.[85]

For Callimaco to get into Lucrezia's bed is just part of the story; his problem is that he needs to convince her to invite him there again. In order to do that, he has to tell her during sex that she has been duped and has to cope with her possible anger. The embrace of the spider woman may indeed turn up to be deadly. To be sure, Machiavelli gives Callimaco two choices: he can blackmail Lucrezia, following Ligurio's advice, thus turning his sexual escapade into rape, or can reassure her of his love, hence problematically changing a momentary desire for a sexually unapproachable woman into a lasting commitment to take care of her, and possibly of her child, a commitment for which he may, however, be psychologically unprepared. Either way he has to deal with the perception that he is committing incest with a mother-defined wife after having taken the place of the father/husband Nicia in their bed.

But Callimaco needs more than sexual gratification, for he has to be acknowledged by the woman he desires in a way narcissistically gratifying to him: that is, Lucrezia has to recognize/misrecognize him in the way he wants to be seen, as a caring, skilled lover. Only through this mirroring effect, Lacan writes, can one become a subject. Thus, in Callimaco's mind, Lucrezia has to want to choose him over her husband, which means that he needs to reveal his identity to her,

84. "Oimé, che io non truovo requie in alcuno loco! . . . [D]ico meco—Che fai tu? Se' tu impazzato? . . . [I]o mi sento, dalle piante de' piè al capo, tutto alterare; le gambe triemono, le viscere si commuovono, il core mi si sbarba del petto, le braccia s'abandonano, la lingua diventa muta, gli occhi abbarbagliono, el cervello mi gira. . . . [O] io mi gitterò in Arno, o io mi appiccherò, o io mi gitterò da quelle finestre, o io mi darò d'un coltello in sullo uscio suo" (4.1; 4.4; "Alas, there's no more peace for me anywhere! . . . What do you think you are doing?—I say to myself—Are you out of your mind? . . . My whole body's affected by it, from head to toe. My legs tremble, my bowels turn over, I feel my heart uprooted from my breast, my arms dangle uselessly, my tongue loses the power of speech, my eyes dazzle, my head swims. . . . I'll drown myself in the river, or hang myself, or throw myself out of one of those windows, or stab myself on her doorstep").

85. Reflecting on the spider's bite, Leonardo da Vinci argued that the bite fixes the individual on the same thought that he had when he was bitten ("Il morso della taranta mantiene l'omo nel suo proponimento, cioè quel che pensava quando fu morso"). Quoted in De Martino, *La terra del rimorso,* 173. The same argument is made by Gerolamo Mercuriale in *De venenis.*

no matter how unwelcome her reaction may be. Unsurprisingly, in the very act of having his admiring, voyeuristic look for an inaccessible, idealized woman transformed into her admiring look for him, Callimaco is able to take care of his own lack. She has filled it. As he confesses to Ligurio the morning after, he is now the happiest man in the world, ecstasy incarnated: the unified subject ("io mi truovo el più felice e contento uomo che fussi mai nel mondo," 5.4).

Hence, Callimaco could have not taken up Ligurio's suggestion to slander Lucrezia as a way to silence her because this would have Oedipalized their encounter.[86] She could have rebelled and denounced him to her husband, a gesture that would have reestablished the Law of the Father and his injunction against access to the mother. By choosing the imaginary over the symbolic instead, Callimaco finds total satisfaction in his object of desire; in reconstituting unity with the desiring mother, the *objet a* as pure desire, he actualizes the original fantasy that made him come back to Italy in the first place. The encounter with the danger of the penis in the woman's matrix has been taken care of by taking pleasure in the protection of the maternal phallus. Callimaco will not be feminized by the encounter with Lucrezia because he can still play the child in fantasy and impishly feel, in his own words, more blessed than the blest, more sainted than the saints ("più beato ch'e' beati, più santo che e' santi," 5.4).[87]

But if Callimaco can lose himself in the imaginary, even if only for the moment, and leave Lucrezia the phallus (Nicia will compare his wife to a rooster the next morning), Machiavelli has still to make sure that Lucrezia, our prototypical middle-class wife, is safely ensconced within the social order. In the symbolic, woman does not offer blissful wholeness and is cast, at best, as different. The usual way of controlling a post-Oedipal woman is to make her bear the burden of castration so that she can hide the lack in the other. How does one construct a castrated Lucrezia in psychoanalytical terms?[88] It can be done, first

---

86. In this sense Callimaco acts as a true Machiavellian hero, for, like the prince, he prefers fraud to force. See *The Prince and the Discourses*, trans. Luigi Ricci (New York: Modern Library, 1940), sec. 18.

87. No matter how maternal Lucrezia is constructed to be and how childishly Callimaco behaves, she still is younger than he by a good number of years. Given the customary age of marriage for Italian women in the period, Lucrezia should be, more or less, twenty-two years old. Callimaco, we know, is thirty. Nicia is at least in his mid-forties.

88. I use the psychoanalytical construction of the castrated woman, well aware of the fact that—as I will argue in chapter 6—Freud substituted the historical understanding of

of all, I submit, by endowing her with exceptional beauty: as Callimaco's friend Cammillo Calfucci asserts, Lucrezia is the most beautiful woman not only in Florence but also in Paris, that is, by Italian standards, in the whole civilized world.[89] If woman needs to be cast as the embodiment of man's lack, then a beautiful woman is, as Lacan wrote, the perfect incarnation of man's castration.[90] Castration, moreover, can be imposed on woman by using her body, even if this means violating it. This is what Ligurio advises Callimaco to do. Castration can take the shape of a burden imposed on woman by dangling the specter of death in front of her. In *Mandragola*, Lucrezia is told that there is no danger to her in ingesting the mandrake, but she is not so sure: "non credo esser mai viva domattina" (3.11; "I'm sure you won't find me alive tomorrow morning"). Castration is a threat imposed on woman by making her own self a threat. In the play we have the assurance that Lucrezia kills through copulation, a circumstance that she gloomily laments: "Ma di tutte le cose che si son trattate, questa mi pare la più strana, di avere a sottomettere el corpo mio a questo vituperio, ad essere cagione che un uomo muoia per vituperarmi" (3.10; "But of all the suggestions I've heard, this seems to me to be the strangest—that I should have to subject my body to this shame and disgrace, and to be the death of the man who shames me and disgraces me").

This female menace needs to be recuperated for order to be reestablished. Thus, not only is Lucrezia made to accept Callimaco—perhaps not thanks to his superior lying ("iacitura"), as he claims (5.4), but because a scandal would hardly do her any good—but she also presumably engenders the baby that allows her to have a place in society. And not just any baby, for, at least in Nicia's mind, she will have a male child. In psychoanalytic terms, the desire for a son connects woman to penis envy and Oedipal logic. Freud writes that the little girl,

castration centered on the testicles to one centered on the penis, and then made woman bear the brunt of it, since she is so visibly lacking.

89. The motif of the man who falls in love with an unknown woman upon hearing of her beauty is not only present in Livy, in the figure of Tarquinius Sextus wanting to have Lucretia because her husband, Collatinus, had boasted of her beauty and virtue, but also in Giovanni Boccaccio, *Decameron* (Milan: Mursia, 1974), 1.5 and 4.7. In 3.6, as in this case, Ricciardo Minutolo has to trick Catella into desiring what he desires. For the influence of Boccaccio on Machiavelli, see Vanossi, "Situazione e sviluppo del teatro machiavelliano," 35–38.

90. See Slavoj Žižek, *The Sublime Object of Ideology* (London: Verso, 1989), 172.

upon surmounting Oedipus, gives up her desire for the father by wishing for a male child that she will engender through a phallic substitute. Once she has been reinscribed as the castrated woman/mother, Lucrezia is made to opt for her new lover not as a husband (he offers himself as such when she eventually becomes a widow) but as a father, a master, and a guide. In short, as the law: "io ti prendo per signore, padrone, guida; tu mio padre, tu mio defensore, e tu voglio che sia ogni mio bene" (5.4; "So I take you as my lord, my master and my guide, my father and my natural defender. I want you to be the whole world to me").

Why not as a husband? This omission has been treated by Theodore Sumberg as having political overtones: Callimaco is in this instance the father of Florence, the *pater patriae,* and Lucrezia, unable even in political terms to escape her bodily presence, is the body politic.[91] I do not question here the easiness, or even the inevitability, with which paternal and political right are brought together in culture, but I would argue that Machiavelli uses this instance to inscribe instead a seemingly free Lucrezia into an Oedipal, and thus controllable, story of feminine desire. He does so by making Lucrezia's first desire (she was granted none before) the desire for a father, by way of not being the child but of having a child from him. Hence, in the only instance in which woman's desire could have not been specifically connected to maternity (presumably Lucrezia wants Callimaco to fulfill, in accepting further encounters, her sexual rather than procreative desires), Machiavelli reimposes the Law of the Father and hints at penis envy (Lucrezia has no father and may have never known one, since there is a sense in the play that her mother was promiscuous).

If Lucrezia needs to be constructed as a mastered female, who like Fortuna will accept being beaten or pushed away, as Machiavelli famously declared in *The Prince,* Callimaco needs to be reconstructed as manly, no matter how childish his behavior has been when he was despairing of surviving without her. The magnification of Callimaco's manhood starts in earnest as soon as he gets ready to fulfill his desire. Although unrecognizable on the night of the ruse, thanks to his dressing like a lower-class *innamorato,* Callimaco still comes to be defined in the scene by an appropriate phallic symbol, a fake nose that Ligurio, who owns it, advises him to wear (4.2). It turns out to be a more appropriate accouterment than the ridiculous sword ("spadaccino") Nicia chooses for himself for the same

91. Sumberg, "La *Mandragola,*" 325.

occasion.[92] That night Nicia also takes some time to appraise the young man's genitalia after he has him undressed. His look is not simply pseudomedical, in that he screens what he takes to be a street boy in order to detect a possible history of sexual diseases, but also erotic, for he marvels at the whiteness of his competitor's flesh and at the size of his organ. It is at the same time a mercantile look for, being a Florentine lawyer, Nicia may also want to check his merchandise to see that the stranger is as manly as he should be, given his task:

> io lo menai in una dispensa che ho in sulla sala, dove era un certo lume annacquato, che gittava un poco d'albore, in modo ch'è non mi poteva vedere in viso. . . . Io lo feci spogliare; è nicchiava. . . . Egli è brutto di viso. Egli aveva un nasaccio, una bocca torta; ma tu non vedesti mai le più belle carni: bianco, morbido, pastoso. E dell'altre cose non ne domandate. (5.1)

> I took him into a little room that I've got next door to the parlour, where there's a faint sort of lamp, that gave a poor sort of light, so that he couldn't see my face properly. . . . I made him strip off. He protested . . . . He's got an ugly face, with a great clumsy nose and a crooked mouth; but you never saw such skin and flesh as he's got on him — white . . . soft . . . firm . . . — and other things that you needn't ask me about!

There is another well-documented instance in Machiavelli's writings in which a not-too-bright light is used by the author to check on his merchandise, the notorious occasion of his encounter with a prostitute, recounted in a letter to Luigi Guicciardini: "Venendomi pure voglia di vedere questa mercatanzia, tolsi un tizzone di fuoco d'un focolare, che v'era, ed accesi una lucerna, che vi era sopra. . . . Omè fu' per cadere in terra morto, tanto era brutta quella femina" ("Having the urge to see this merchandise, I took a brand from the fireplace near me and lit a lamp that was above it. . . . My God, the woman was so ugly that I almost dropped dead").[93] Here too, as with Callimaco, who had distorted his facial features to better cover his identity, there is emphasis on the nose twisted into

92. On the connections between the genitals and the nose, see, for example, S. Weissenberg, "Spermageruch des Nasenschleims," *Zeitschrift für Sexualwissenschaft* 12 (1925): 258.

93. Niccolò Machiavelli, "Spectabili viro L. Guicciardini in Mantova tanquam fratri carissimo," in *Lettere*, ed Giuseppe Lesca (Florence: Rinascimento del libro, 1929), 25–28. My translation.

a strange shape and on the mouth contorted on the side. Machiavelli is stunned at this monstrous surrogate of femininity ("questo mostro") and vomits over her, in a reiteration of badly spent money ("io le recé addosso"). Wayne Rebhorn has read Machiavelli's final gesture sympathetically. In identifying with a humiliated author who, disgusted at himself, heaps disgust on woman, he sees his vomiting on her as "an act of personal purgation."[94] Reading on the side of women instead, Juliana Schiesari and Barbara Spackman have linked this grotesque representation of a toothless female to male fear of castration and of the "vagina dentata," and to anxiety about an encounter in which masculinity and femininity, and the link between power and sex, are continuously shifting.[95]

But if the hag cures Machiavelli of any desire for women, in *Mandragola* Nicia's encounter with Callimaco results instead in narcissistic identification, as his libido draws him to the young man who resembles his (better) self in order to counter his deep feelings of anxiety toward sex. Indeed, just before catching Callimaco in the streets, Nicia sees himself younger and thinner than before, ready to play, just like the other man, the desired lover in a woman's bed (4.8). Later, in a last, satirical gesture, Machiavelli makes him identify completely with Callimaco as virile lover and control with his own hand how the "misterio," in Friar Timoteo's mystifying words, proceeds between him and his wife: "al buio lo menai in camera, messilo a letto; e, innanzi mi partissi, volli toccare con mano come la cosa andava" (5.2; "I led him by the hand into the room, all in the dark, and put him to bed. And before I left them, I felt round to see how things were going").

No wonder that Nicia refers to Callimaco as the stick ("bastone") for his aging self. In fact, it appears that, as Ligurio had ironically told him at the very beginning, Callimaco has been sent by God precisely to satisfy Nicia's desire: "io credo che Dio ci abbi mandato costui, perchè voi adempiate el desiderio vostro" (2.1; "I think God must have sent this man here specially to grant your wishes"). Nicia's wish for children is also narcissistic, for, as Tasso was to put it in his trea-

94. Rebhorn, *Foxes and Lions,* 243.

95. Juliana Schiesari, "Libidinal Economies: Machiavelli and Fortune's Rape," in *Desire in the Renaissance,* ed. Valeria Finucci and Regina Schwartz (Princeton: Princeton University Press, 1994), 169–83; and Barbara Spackman, "Inter musam et ursam moritur: Folengo and the Gaping 'Other' Mouth," in *Refiguring Woman: Perspectives on Gender and the Italian Renaissance,* ed. Juliana Schiesari and Barbara Spackman (Ithaca: Cornell University Press, 1991), 19–34.

tise, *Il messaggero*, the father desires children because he loves himself.[96] As usual, Nicia's narcissistic male self-mirroring in Callimaco excludes woman: there is no reference to Lucrezia's feelings.

For his part, experiencing, unlike Nicia, heterosexual mimetic rivalry with Callimaco, Ligurio the procurer wants no identification with the pseudodoctor.[97] When Nicia recounts him the story of the street boy's undressing, he sharply dismisses it all: "E' non è bene ragionarne. Che bisognava vederlo tutto?" (5.1; "It's best not to discuss those matters. Why did you have to examine him all over like that?"). Early in the play Ligurio had situated himself as the third man in a triangular relationship by professing to share Callimaco's desire for the escapade with Lucrezia ("desidero che tu adempia questo tuo desiderio, presso a quanto tu," "I want you to get your heart's desire almost as much as you do yourself"; 1.3); now he tells the "garzonaccio" that if he divulges what happened that night, he will behead/castrate him: "S'i' ti sento favellare, io ti taglierò el collo!" (5.2; "If there's another word out of you, I'll cut your throat!").

In chapter 5, on Bernardo Bibbiena, I will examine how complicated the taking up of masculinity is for men and in chapter 6, on castrati, I will return to the issue of how much maleness is based on generation rather than on possession of male genitalia. Here, a man finds that the ideal of manhood embodied in the figure of the *pater familias* that he should represent on account of his social status does not reflect his inner reality. In order to father, physicians and philosophers were writing at the time, a man must sexually satisfy his partner, not because a woman needs (or even wants) sexual fulfillment, however, but because she needs to have an orgasm if she is to engender an heir to vouchsafe her husband's potency. No wonder that when age differences become a factor and the stakes grow too high, withdrawal from sex comes to represent for men a cherished alternative. Thus, Nicia unbashfully finds the pleasure he was not

96. See Torquato Tasso, *Il messaggiero*, in *I dialoghi* (1580; Milan: Mursia, 1991), 76.

97. In Tommaso Garzoni, *La piazza universale di tutte le professioni del mondo*, ed. Paolo Cherchi and Beatrice Collina (1585; Turin: Einaudi, 1996), the entry "De' Ruffiani et delle ruffiane" offers this scheme: "Et Licurgo quel savio legislator della Grecia a gli Lacedemonii fece una legge, da ruffiano perfetto, permettendo, che in occorrenza, che un'huomo attempato, e per debolezza di forze, poco atto al consorzio coniugale havesse tolto per moglie una fanciulla di prima età, potesse eleggere a suo piacere qualche giovane più poderoso, e di miglior nervo di lui, il quale pigliasse cura d'ingravidarla, pur che il parto, che nascesse fosse tenuto del marito." See Garzoni, "Discorso LXXV," 445.

sure he could provide through a fantasy-engendered identification with a virile male. In the end, he makes a spectacle of himself, not so much because he gives away his patriarchal right of exclusive access to his wife's body and is duped into cuckoldry, but because he is glad that someone else does the job for him. Ligurio, on the other hand, feeling that he can still play the sexual game, is embarrassed at such a failure of maleness, and carefully sets his distance from the old fool.

This brings me back to the present. What surrogate fathers often give away today is contact with woman. Discounting any need to show their manhood in action or even any heterosexual desire, contractual fathers can now rely on science to assert their paternal right while, like James Joyce's God, paring their fingernails. Nicia's waiting near the fireplace for his child to be engendered while pretending not to be concerned with the possibility that he will be conceived without his participation, demonstrates once more, in Judge Sorkow's eloquent words, that a father, like God, can reproduce himself any way he wants, even noncoitally, as long as he can enforce a contract. In the Baby M case, the lawyer for Mr. Stern, the baby's biological father, argued that Mr. Stern had a right to the baby, not because he paid for her (a patriarchal no-no) but because he saw her mother's body as a vessel hired for the purpose of generating his child. Merging Aristotle and Marx, the lawyer asserted, in short, that Mr. Stern had a right to take ownership of the goods generated by the commodity (the uterus) in which he had invested and for which he had contracted.

Likewise, in *Mandragola*, it could be argued that Nicia had a right to his baby boy, not (or not just) because he could be his biological father, nor because, in an era with no genetic science, he would be anyhow his legal father, but because, he, as a husband, had a legal right to his wife's body or parts thereof, and therefore could hire it to somebody else to fecundate it, or, in his own version, to be killed in his stead. As Tasso put it later in *Il padre di famiglia*, women should obey men not because they are servants to their masters but because in society citizens are asked to obey laws and judges.[98] Nicia patiently convinces his wife to make love to another man, not because he could not have enforced the act, but because only through a regular sexual encounter could she engender the healthy baby he wants; only by desiring the act herself, moreover, could she have sufficiently raised her body temperature to mother a male child. In a telling, sar-

---

98. "Virtù dunque della donna è il sapere ubbidire all'uomo non in quel modo che 'l servo al signore e 'l corpo all'animo ubbidisce, ma civilmente in quel modo che nelle città ben ordinate i cittadini ubbidiscono alle leggi e a' magistrati" (128–29).

castic twist that parodies the embedded medical lore of this play, this fictitious paternity is guaranteed in *Mandragola* by no less than a representative of religion, Friar Timoteo: "se l'autorità mia varrà, noi concludereno questo parentado questa sera" (3.8; "If my authority's worth anything, this match [kinship, marriage, descent] will be concluded this evening"). To him, as for sperm brokers in surrogacy contracts, a fee will be paid.

Yet, strange as it may sound, Nicia's espousal of noncoital reproduction represents a negligible achievement when we take a look at the towering advantages subtending the model of filiation that Machiavelli puts forward in *La vita di Castruccio Castracani,* written two years later. In reading creatively the meteoric career of a Renaissance strongman, Machiavelli argues that the foundling Castruccio, offspring of no recognized parent and therefore, potentially, of any parent, overcomes any disadvantage connected to his genetic ignorance and makes himself powerful, a founder, thanks to the sheer force of his "virtù."[99] Hence for Machiavelli the individual with no recognizable genetic beginning and no legitimate name, like Moses, Oedipus, Romulus (and Christ?), is best posited to become the mythical *auctor* of a new dynasty, generator of new institutions. Doubly and inescapably inscribed with his original lack, Castruccio ("Little Castrator") Castracani ("Castrator of Dogs"), man with no father, adopted by a father who could not biologically father because of his church ties, and himself unwilling to father any legitimate issue (although he had illegitimate children), grows into the father of all citizens, the absolute *pater patriae.* The Machiavellian rewriting of paternity has reached its extreme. From this point of view, Lucrezia's child already has two fathers too many.

99. Niccolò Machiavelli, *La vita di Castruccio Castracani da Lucca,* ed. Fortunato Bellonzi (1520; Rome: Stefano de Luca, 1969).

CHAPTER 3

Performing Maternity: Female Imagination,
Paternal Erasure, and Monstrous Birth in Tasso's
Gerusalemme liberata

Nera sì, ma sì bella, o di natura
fra le belle d'amor leggiadro mostro.
—G. MARINO, "Amore"

Can the Ethiopian change his skin or the leopard his spots?
—JEREMIAH 14.23

Desolate Afric! thou art lovely yet! . . .
What though thy maidens are a blackish brown,
Does virtue dwell in whiter breasts alone?
—W. MAKEPEACE THACKERAY,
"Timbuctoo"

"Pater semper incertus est, mater est certissima," Freud wrote, repeating a well-known saying.[1] For centuries, before the onset of embryology and genetics, fathers could indeed only hope they engendered the fetuses their companions were carrying. Yet when sometime in the middle of the sixteenth century property began no longer to be divided among brothers (*in fraterna*), according to the model of a divisible patrilinear succession, but followed more frequently the rules of primogeniture, men started to have plenty at stake in wanting to know which children precisely they fathered.[2] Resemblance played a key role in linking them to the babies for whose physical and social well-being they were legally responsible, and resemblance became an organizing "biological" principle that, as Michel Foucault has argued, constructed knowledge and made it representable.[3] Even today in Italian law the man who declares himself the begetter of a

1. An earlier version of this chapter, titled "Maternal Imagination and Monstrous Birth: Tasso's *Gerusalemme liberata*," appeared in *Generation and Degeneration: Tropes of Reproduction in Literature and History from Antiquity to Early Modern Europe*, ed. Valeria Finucci and Kevin Brownlee (Durham, N.C.: Duke University Press, 2001), 41–77. The quote is from Sigmund Freud, "Family Romances," *The Standard Edition of the Complete Psychological Works of Sigmund Freud* (hereafter *SE*), 24 vols., ed. and trans. James Strachey (1909; London: Hogarth Press, 1953–74), 9:239.

2. The shift in inheritance practices from fraternal to "patrilinear indivisible," and therefore from a family asset classifiable as "horizontal multiple" to "vertical multiple," was pushed aside gradually only in the second half of the eighteenth century with the new system of "bilateral divisible," in which brothers and sisters took their fair share. The movement to primogeniture, in any case, was neither swift nor uniform throughout Italy. In Venice the custom was to entail the estate or to allow only one son to marry. For a study of how agnatic legislation impacted on women, see Thomas Kuen, *Law, Family, and Women: Toward a Legal Anthropology of Renaissance Italy* (Chicago: University of Chicago Press, 1991); and Stanley Chojnacki, *Women and Men in Renaissance Venice: Twelve Essays on Patrician Society* (Baltimore: Johns Hopkins University Press, 2000). For a general look at family structures, see Marzio Barbagli, *Sotto lo stesso tetto: Mutamenti della famiglia in Italia dal XV al XX secolo* (Bologna: Mulino, 1984), ch. 4.

3. "Up to the end of the sixteenth century, resemblance played a constructive role in the knowledge of Western culture. It was resemblance that largely guided exegesis and the interpretation of texts; it was resemblance that organized the play of symbols, made possible knowledge of things visible and invisible, and controlled the art of representing them." In Michel Foucault, *The Order of Things: An Archeology of the Human Sciences* (New York: Ran-

child born out of wedlock needs to recognize it ("riconoscere"), to see a similarity between himself and the child he claims to have fathered.[4] For many, a baby in whom the parental stamp was effaced was not just a bastard—newborns not bearing a somatic identity with their fathers were at times cast away together with their supposedly prodigal mothers—but a monster. Aristotle asserted that much: "Monstrosities come under the class of offspring which is unlike its parents."[5] Torquato Tasso (1544–95) felt this way too in *Il mondo creato*:

> E chiunque traligna, al propio padre
> ed a la stirpe de' maggior antica
> dissimil fatto, è quasi al mondo un mostro.
>
> . . . .
>
> Ned uomo è più, ma d'odioso aspetto
> del male sparso e mal concetto seme
> un mal nato animal ci nasce e vive
> ch'è detto mostro. E la natura istessa
> lo schiva ed odia, e disdegnando abborre.

And man can often so degenerate from his illustrious [lineage] as to resemble none in all mankind. A man no longer, he's an ill-born beast, the fruit of an ill-scattered, hateful seed, and therefore as a living monster's known. Nature herself abhors and dreads his sight.[6]

In *Gerusalemme liberata*, Tasso had also repeatedly called a child not resembling either parent a monster. Such was the case of Clorinda, a Saracen female knight, born white of black Ethiopian parents. Her own mother was horrified when she first saw the baby, a "novo mostro," and decided to cast the child away for fear of being accused of adultery. I will use this well-known story in the *Libe-*

---

dom House, 1970), 17. The other principles Foucault selected were convenience, emulation, analogy, and sympathy.

4. The same applies to French law. See Marie-Hélène Huet, *Monstrous Imagination* (Cambridge: Harvard University Press, 1993).

5. Aristotle, *Generation of Animals* [hereafter *GA*], trans. A. L. Peck (Cambridge: Harvard University Press, 1990), 4.4.770b.

6. Torquato Tasso, *Il mondo creato*, in *Le opere*, 5 vols., ed. Bruno Maier (Milan: Rizzoli, 1964), 4:6.1344–54. Translation by Joseph Tusiani here and subsequently in Torquato Tasso, *Creation of the World* (Binghamton: State University of New York, Medieval and Early Renaissance Texts and Studies, 1982), 6.1322–28.

rata to focus on the historical and cultural tradition behind the construction of maternal and filial monstrosity in the Renaissance. I will chronicle in broad strokes how monsters were thought to be engendered and what the mother's imagination supposedly had to do with it, why Ethiopians were considered monstrous, what the role of Saint George was in the birth of an Ethiopian baby, and finally, why characters with undefined gender alignments were cast in culture as monstrous. As in the previous chapter, I will study the female body not as the customary place of erotic investment but as a site obsessively checked and medicalized in order to manage presumed pathologies. Fantasies of what pregnant mothers could do as months of pregnancy go by—and fathers feared they were becoming less and less relevant in the gestating process—color my recreation of this emblematic tale.

Tasso provides very little information about Clorinda until the day she dies. We know that she is beautiful and strong and that the Christian hero Tancredi has fallen in love with her at first sight. Then, one evening, just before engaging in what will turn out to be her last act of bravery, Clorinda hears from her eunuch Arsete (who in nurturing and protecting her has played the role of a father) the true story of her origins. She was born in Ethiopia, Arsete tells her, the daughter of the black Christian king, Senapo, and a black queen of that land, whom Tasso does not name.[7] Her father's jealousy kept her beautiful mother a virtual recluse in a tower with the limited company of a few maids and a trusted servant, Arsete himself. With nothing else to do, the queen spent her days looking at a picture hanging on the wall, that of Saint George saving a virginal princess from a monster:

> D'una pietosa istoria e di devote
> figure la sua stanza era dipinta.
> Vergine, bianca il bel volto e le gote

7. "Black but beautiful" is how Tasso describes the queen, echoing words from the Song of Solomon 1:5 ("bruna è sì, ma il bruno il bel non toglie," 12.21). The father, Senapo, was renamed David in the *Gerusalemme conquistata* (1593). We do not know anything about the father's physical characteristics, but in "Il forno overo de la nobiltà," Tasso wrote that Ethiopian kings were often the most handsome among the citizens because Ethiopians correlated nobility and virtue with physical appearance and gave the reign to the most handsome: "Quando io lessi che gli Etiopi concedevano il regno al più bello, giudicai ch'essi il facessero credendo che la bellezza fosse argomento di nobiltà e di virtù." See *Dialoghi*, in *Le opere*, 4:4.439.

vermiglia, è quivi presso un drago avinta.
Con l'asta il mostro un cavalier percote:
giace la fera nel suo sangue estinta. (12.23)

Her room was painted with a tale of piety and with figures of devotion. A virgin—her lovely face white and her cheeks crimson—is bound there, close by a dragon. A knight-at-arms is striking the monster with his lance; the beast lies slain in his own blood.[8]

In the course of time the queen became pregnant, and throughout the pregnancy, she observed the painting. The influence of the queen's imagination on the baby she was carrying was so strong that it erased her blackness and that of the king (and thus any role of the father in the engendering): her child was as white as the princess in the picture:

Ingravida fra tanto, ed espon fuori
(e tu fosti costei) candida figlia.
Si turba; e de gli insoliti colori,
quasi d'un novo mostro ha meraviglia.
Ma perché il re conosce e i suoi furori,
celargli il parto alfin si riconsiglia,
ch'egli avria dal candor che in te si vede
argomentato in lei non bianca fede.

      E in tua vece una fanciulla nera
pensa mostrargli, poco inanzi nata.
E perché fu la torre, ove chius'era,
da le donne e da me solo abitata,
a me, che le fui servo e con sincera
mente l'amai, ti diè non battezzata;
né già poteva allor battesmo darti,
che l'uso no 'l sostien di quelle parti. (12.24-25)

Meanwhile she becomes pregnant, and brings forth a fair-complexioned daughter (and you were she). She is distraught, and marvels as much at the

8. Torquato Tasso, *Gerusalemme liberata* (finished 1575, published 1581), ed. Anna Maria Carini (Milan: Feltrinelli, 1961), 12.24 [hereafter cited parenthetically in the text]. I use Ralph Nash's translation in Torquato Tasso, *Jerusalem Delivered* (Detroit: Wayne State University Press, 1987), unless I specifically note than I am modifying it.

unusual color as if at a hitherto-unseen prodigy. But because she knows the king and his rages, at last she decides to conceal the birth from him: for he from the whiteness that is seen in you would have argued no pure-white faith in her.

And in your place she plans to show him a black child born a little before. And because the tower where she was shut in was inhabited only by her women and by me (who was her servant and loved her with sincere mind), to me she gave you, unbaptized; nor did she indeed have power to give you baptism at that time, for the custom of those regions does not permit it. (trans. mod.)[9]

Arsete, an Egyptian by birth, brought Clorinda back to Egypt and raised her, but did not christen her, although he was reminded of his promise on more than one occasion by Saint George, appearing to him in dreams. Arsete also came to realize that Clorinda was protected by this father figure. Once, for instance, a wild animal that should have attacked her, suckled her instead, a monstrous sight by all means ("io miro timido e confuso, / come uom farìa nuovi prodigi orrendi," "I am all agaze, fearful and uncertain, as a man would be, seeing strange and chilling prodigies"; 12.31); on another occasion, she was miraculously saved from death while crossing a river. Just a few hours earlier that same night Saint George had appeared to Arsete to request his charge's baptism and to make him understand that Clorinda's life was coming to a close.

Clorinda listens to Arsete's story and shrugs it off. She gives no thought to her newly found parents and simply answers that she prefers to keep the Muslim religion of her childhood and adult life. That same night, after having burned in a momentous exploit the Christian tower menacing the safety of Jerusalem, she finds herself shut out of the city. She meets Tancredi, who is looking for enemies

9. According to the tradition of the Ethiopian church, female babies were baptized later than boys, forty days after birth, a custom that Tasso learned from the travel relations of Francisco Alvarez, *Voyage in Ethiopia* (ch. 22), as he writes in his *Dubbi e risposte intorno ad alcune cose e parole concernenti alla Gerusalemme liberata*, in *Appendice alle opere in prosa di Torquato Tasso*, ed. Angelo Solerti (Florence: Successori Le Monnier, 1892), 164–65. Probably the custom comes from the notion that girls rendered the mother impure for a longer time, according to levitical law. See also David Quint, *Epic and Empire: Politics and Generic Form from Virgil to Milton* (Princeton: Princeton University Press, 1993), 237. Nash translates "mostro" as monster, but I have modified his translation to emphasize the other meaning of "monster" in Tasso as an astonishing event, a prodigy.

to show off his valor, is not recognized in the new armor she is wearing, and is fatally wounded in a duel. Feeling that the end is close, she unexpectedly asks him to baptize her. Upon removing her helmet to perform the ceremony, Tancredi recognizes his beloved and despairs: he has managed to eliminate the only enemy he wanted to save and have. Clorinda later appears to him in a dream when he is at his most melancholic and morose, forgives him for having killed her, and pronounces herself happy in heaven.

A white child born of black parents, a citizen of a part of the world often described by missionaries and travelers as inhabited by monstrous people, a baby brought up defiantly against the "laws" of nature and sex ("vincesti il sesso e la natura assai," 12.38) by a father figure without a sex—literally—and a woman warrior with manly abilities and castrating desires: can all this make Clorinda less than a "monster"? To be sure, there is nothing in Clorinda's physical description that would brand her as not normal, if we take white as the standard of normality. Following the literary tradition of the time (specifically, Ariosto, who had written race out of the description of the astounding beauty of his oriental Angelica in *Orlando furioso*), Tasso gives seemingly no importance to the fact that Clorinda is by birth black. As beauty goes, Clorinda is the best example, in fact, of white female perfection. If Armida, the other major female character in the *Liberata,* had consistently to construct her outward appearance, Clorinda's looks are instead natural: she has lovely blond hair and is tall and slender. Her very name, Clorinda, etymologically echoes her whiteness (as in "pale," "yellow," "greenish-yellow") and metaphorically reiterates her being "fresh," "living," "young." Tancredi cannot keep her image out of his mind; and the Saracen hero Argante appears to be in love with her as well. Of course, Clorinda is totally unconscious of the effect she creates on others, for in making her white, Tasso puts aside the usual association of blacks in culture with excessive sexuality and promiscuity.[10] It is also true that Clorinda is hardly the personi-

10. An example along these lines, beyond the obvious case of Shakespeare's *Othello*, is Ariosto. In the *Furioso* he has Judge Anselmo tempted by a black homosexual Ethiopian, thus coding male sexual "perversion" as other and black. See Ludovico Ariosto, *Orlando furioso,* ed. Marcello Turchi (Milan: Garzanti, 1974). The tradition is an old one. Epiphanius (fourth century) tells a story about Origen almost being forced to have sex with a black Ethiopian male. In the *Liberata*, there is an Ethiopian Saracen, Assimiro of Meroe, who will be killed and symbolically castrated in the last canto, when Rinaldo cuts off his black neck ("nero collo," 20.54).

fication of femininity. While growing up, we are told, she prefers the outdoors to closed spaces, and mastering beasts to embroidery. She even takes particular care in making her body and face strong and masculine ("armò d'orgoglio il volto, e si compiacque / rigido farlo," 2.39) and eventually appears so strange that men take her for a beast, and beasts take her for a man ("fèra a gli uomini parve, uomo a le belve," 2.40).[11]

Unlike Bradamante in Ariosto, Clorinda actively looks in the *Liberata* for occasions in which to show her worth in the battlefield. Dressed in white armor, a typical color for women warriors (it was also Bradamante's color), and with a tiger in her crest, Clorinda is easily recognized and feared by her enemies. Her appearance in the field, or even at a distance as an archer, means continuous wounding, slicing, decapitating, and maiming of any enemy coming close to her: she kills Guglielmo, heir to the English throne, with an arrow (11.42), and does the same to Stefano and Roberto (11.43); the bishop Ademaro is wounded on the forehead (11.44); Berlinghiero is stabbed from front to back (9.68); Albin is pierced in the stomach (9.68); Gerniero's right hand is cut off (9.69); Achilles' head is severed (9.70); and the chief Christian warrior, Goffredo, receives a leg wound. Again unlike Bradamante, Clorinda is constructed as a woman warrior with no other self-made purpose than that of showing that she is as good or better than all other male warriors of either camp. We know that she has feelings too, but they do not seem to take the upper hand: she cries upon hearing the story of the doomed pair, Sofronia and Olindo, at her entrance in the *Liberata* in canto 2 and actively works to save them from the stake, but we are also

11. For Tasso's characterization of Clorinda as Amazon, drawn from the Greek Penthesilea and the Latin Camilla, see Quint, *Epic and Empire*, 238–39. Especially close are the Virgilian connections (*Aeneid*, bk. 2). Clorinda and Camilla's life stories and even their death by wounds to their breasts, Amazon-like, are similar. Virginia had Latona protect Camilla; Tasso has Saint George look over Clorinda. The two babies are raised away from civilization, by men (her father, Metabus, in the case of Camilla; a father figure in that of Clorinda); both are fed on animal milk (a mare in Virgil; a tiger in Tasso); both are recommended to their protectors when they have to cross a river to escape enemies; both grow up to be invincible warriors. In what perhaps is his most autobiographical writing, "Canzone al Metauro" (also called "O del grand'Apenino," 1578), Tasso compares his own forced exile from his mother, Porzia de' Rossi, to that of Camilla: "e seguii con mal sicure piante, / qual Ascanio o Camilla il padre errante." See Angelo Solerti, *Le rime di Torquato Tasso*, 4 vols. (Bologna: Romagnoli dall'Acqua, 1900), 3:104–5.

repeatedly told that she is unresponsive to the love pangs of the Christian hero Tancredi.

To be sure, the woman warrior figure and the androgynous female were very much in vogue in Renaissance literature, but unlike Bradamante, whose posited androgyny rests only in her choice of clothes, given her engulfment in a fully sexualized career as future wife and mother of the state, Clorinda is described as sexually and psychologically unresponsive. She may be unconsciously masquerading as white, but she is consciously masquerading as male. She is monstrous, combining in her persona two antithetical views of women: very feminine in her beauty and very unfeminine in her chosen warrior role. No wonder that she does not seem to fit anywhere.

What can Tasso do with a woman who for narrative purposes cannot be made to behave like one? A happy ending for a lady warrior who wounds and maims Christian heroes with gusto is hardly acceptable. A happy ending for a white Ethiopian princess is also out of the question, because it could breed fears of miscegenation, since Tasso's outward purpose in the *Liberata* is to create a heroic genealogy for his patron, the duke of Este. Were Clorinda just a Saracen, the problem could be easily solved: like Marfisa and Ruggiero in the *Furioso*, we know that Saracen heroes turn out to be Christian the very moment in which their destiny becomes important to the ideological purposes of the epic. But as a freakish white and violent lady knight Clorinda has no chance to be absorbed into the system; born without the marks of a properly stamped paternal identity, she has to remain utterly different. Her incorrect, out-of-bound breeding, marked by her black/not-black background, effectively precludes a happy ending.

We are all aware, of course, that the only way for an unredeemed woman warrior to fit in is to die, more so in the work of an author such as Tasso, who had problems of his own in granting women—any woman, in fact—a meaningful continuous role in his romance epic.[12] That Clorinda has to be not only ritualistically killed (as Argante will say, "Ella morì di fatal morte," 12.103) but also normalized, both before and after her death, through a process of feminization

12. For Paul Larivaille, "ogni tentativo delle donne o di equipararsi all'uomo, o di invertire o intaccare in qualche modo il rapporto da inferiori a superiori intercorrente fra loro e gli uomini è considerato una trasgressione della natura femminile e immancabilmente destinato a fallire." See *Poesia e ideologia* (Naples: Liguori, 1987), 209.

and Oedipalization, should not surprise us either, given the social constraints attending the representation of women in narrative. Here, however, I would like to focus on why Clorinda is monstrous and what the stakes—cultural, historical, and literary—are for creating such a genealogy.

Monstrosity and Maternal Imagination

Let us begin at the beginning, with conception itself. As I elaborated in the introduction, for the different doctors in antiquity whose collected work has been passed down to us as the Hippocratic corpus, for Pliny, Soranus, Galen, and most everybody who wrote on the subject—apart from Aristotle—until the discovery of the woman's ovum in the seventeenth century, for conception to occur the male seed needed to mix with female seed.[13] Given men's "stronger" semen and "hotter" nature, children were supposed to resemble their fathers more than their mothers, especially, of course, boys, because like supposedly generates like. The superior paternal imagination was also an advantage in forming "perfect" offspring. As Tasso wrote in "Il messaggiero," thanks to the high quality of men's fantasy, children tend to reproduce the virtue and the beauty conveyed in their father's mind at the time of copulation.[14] In this reading the mother's role is both unrecognized and unrecognizable: she may provide her body for the child to develop, but she does not know how to control either herself or the fetus growing inside her. The father rules: from the most biological element (a "proper" seed) to the most aesthetic or philosophical one (a "proper" mind), a normal fetus bears everywhere the imprint of the one whose presence at the time of engendering could, however, never be proved after the fact.

The view that fathers provided more than mothers did not go uncontested. Isidore of Seville wrote in *Aetymologiae* that a very strong maternal seed caused the child to resemble its mother, a view that comes from Lucretius's *De rerum*

13. As I pointed out in the introduction, for Aristotle women do not contribute semen to generation, because there is no creature that produces two seminal secretions at once, thus semen in males equals menstrual fluid in females. See *GA* 1.19.727a.

14. "[P]erchè la virtù de la fantasia è grandissima, quando gli uomini vengono a gli abbracciamenti d'amore, venendoci pieni di sì alta imaginazione, i figliuoli che poi son prodotti soglion nascer simili a quell'eccellente idea di valore e di bellezza ch'i padri ne la mente avean conceputa." See Tasso, "Il messaggiero," in *Dialoghi,* ed. Bruno Basile (Milan: Mursia, 1991), 86.

naturae and influenced many Renaissance writers.[15] In his *Quaderni d'anatomia,* Leonardo da Vinci noted that the offspring of an Italian woman and of an Ethiopian man strongly resembled the mother, a demonstration, he concluded, that the "seed of the female was as potent as that of the male in generation."[16] For Tommaso Campanella, resemblance varied according to circumstances: a child was similar to the mother if her spirit and affection were predominant, he wrote, and resembled the father if his strength and imagination prevailed. But the newborn could also resemble relatives if the parents thought of them, or even strange people, when there were similarities of disposition. The parents' yearning for a certain food, their longings, the places they inhabited, or the influence of planets also had plenty of relevance.[17] Campanella's opinion can be traced as far back as Aristotle for whom a "relapse of male seed" meant that a baby would take after its grandfather, while a mastery of some male faculty on the part of the female plus a relapse of the male seed would make it look like its grandmother or some other ancestor.[18]

A weak male seed, whether it came from a father too young or one too old, constituted a problem in all cases, not only since it was held responsible for engendering female babies, because the matter was insufficiently shaped, or no babies at all—but also because it could generate a monster. Too much seed could have the same results. Aristotle postulated no clear theoretical distinction between those two categories, woman and monster. As he stated,

> Anyone who does not take after his parents is really in a way a monstrosity, since in these cases Nature has in a way strayed from the generic type. The first beginning of this deviation is when a female is formed instead of a male, though (a) this indeed is a necessity required by Nature, since the race of creatures which are separated into male and female has got to

---

15. See Jane Bestor, "Ideas about Procreation and Their Influence on Ancient and Medieval Views of Kinship," in *The Family in Italy from Antiquity to the Present,* ed. David Kerzner and Richard Saller (New Haven: Yale University Press, 1991), 150–67, esp. 157.

16. In Joseph Needham, *A History of Embryology,* 3 vols. (New York: Abelard-Schuman, 1959), 3:96.

17. In his words: "dalla disposizione insolita dei genitori per varii cibi, affetti, luoghi e stelle." See Tommaso Campanella, "Magia della generazione," in *Del senso delle cose e della magia,* ed. Antonio Bruers (Bari: Laterza, 1925), 4.18, p. 308. The text was written in Latin in the early 1590s and subsequently lost; the Italian version is probably from 1604.

18. GA 4.3.768b.

be kept in being; and (b) since it is possible for the male sometimes not to gain the mastery either on account of youth or age or some other such cause.[19]

For the Greek philosopher, monstrosity is the result of deviation from male perfection. The monster is not only the newborn who fails to resemble its makers, but woman herself, the *mas occasionatus* of Aquinas, the only difference between the two monstrosities being that the female is necessary to the human race, while the physically defective child is not. Given this line of argument, a woman unlike her parents must have appeared doubly freakish. Tasso was well aware of the problem and put it in verse in *Il mondo creato*:

> E s'adivien giamai che 'l maschio seme
> debole e raro sia del veglio stanco
> o sparso dal fanciul, nè vincer possa
> con quella sua virtù ch'informa e move
> ne' chiostri occulti del femineo ventre
> l'indigesta materia umida e informe,
> femina nasce; e ch'ella nasca è d'uopo,
> e se non caro, è necessario il parto.
> Ma d'uopo già non è che sia prodotto
> orrido mostro al mondo. (6:1324–33)

If the male semen of a weak old man, or of an adolescent, fails to win and fecundate, to rouse and therefore shape in the dark corners of a woman's womb its matter, shapeless, wet, and still impure, a female's born—a necessary birth if not a happy one. But it is not necessity that brings monstrosities to this our world. (6:1299–1307)

Choices made during the sexual act could also be dangerous to the wellbeing of a fetus. In *De secretis mulierum*, Albertus Magnus warned that violent coitus and coitus while standing were conducive to monstrosities because the seed would have been unable to properly attach itself to the womb.[20] Other doctors recommended against coitus with menstruating women to avoid birth

---

19. *GA* 4.3.767b. Later Aristotle repeated it: "[W]e should look upon the female state as being as it were a deformity, though one which occurs in the ordinary course of nature" (*GA* 4.6.775a).

20. Albertus Magnus, *De secretis mulierum* (Lyons: A. De Marsy, 1595).

defects, an interdiction already present in the Bible.[21] Acts against nature, such as sodomy and coitus with women on top, also were thought to produce monsters. A rebellious female seed was just as problematic as a weak male one, because at best it would be responsible for engendering a female child and at worst a monster, Antonio Guainerio wrote.[22] Too much seed, stated Ambroise Paré, could engender twins in the best cases and a monstrous child with too many organs in the worst ones, while too little seed could breed a child with missing body parts. Paré cited as causes for fetal malformations a narrow maternal womb, bestiality, problematic pregnancy, and hereditary diseases. Strange or even habitual positions of the maternal body could have horrifying effects as well: seamstresses who crossed their legs while working or women wearing clothes that were too tight could give birth to "hunchbacked and misshapen" children, Paré warned, to say nothing of the problems resulting from a pregnant woman's fall or illness.[23] Monstrous sex, that is, a monstrous behavior on the part of the mother—anything too active, too unconventional, or too lacking in caution—produced monstrous beings. This view, of course, is hardly new: women have often been accused of being responsible for whatever men would rather not be held accountable themselves.

21. Leviticus 18.19. Only in the second half of the sixteenth century and with the Counter-Reformation's stress on morality and female purity, did the belief that menstruating women could produce monsters become, as Ottavia Niccoli puts it, "a precise historical fact." See " 'Menstruum quasi monstruum': Monstrous Births and Menstrual Taboo in the Sixteenth Century," in *Sex and Gender in Historical Perspective: Selections from "Quaderni storici,"* ed. Edward Muir and Guido Ruggiero (Baltimore: Johns Hopkins University Press, 1990), 1–25, esp. 19. For more on the turn from the positive view of menstruation to a negative one, see Gianna Pomata, "Menstruating Men: Similarity and Difference between the Sexes in Early Modern Europe," in Finucci and Brownlee, *Generation and Degeneration,* 109–50. Corrupt menstrual blood was also held responsible for pregnant women's longings. See Patricia Crawford, "Attitudes to Menstruation in Seventeenth-Century England," *Past and Present* 91 (1981): 47–73, esp. 52.

22. Antonio Guainerio, *Tractatus de matricibus (Treatise on the Womb),* in *Opera Omnia* (Pavia, 1481), fol. 2z6vb.

23. Ambroise Paré, *On Monsters and Marvels,* trans. Janis Pallister (Chicago: University of Chicago Press, 1982), chs. 4, 8, 10, 11, 13. Paré also mentioned a category, that of artifices, which covers the case of pretenders or of children mutilated by their parents for the sake of getting more money from begging. Like many other doctors and philosophers of the time, Paré attributed monstrous birth to God's will and wrath and to the intervention of demons, but he also took steps to naturalize monstrosity.

The fate of monstrous children in history has been a dire one. The Romans used to drown or expose them; their act was not considered murderous. Early Christianity, however, followed the Jewish custom of repudiating the killing of weak and deformed infants, and by 374 infanticide had officially become a crime.[24] This is not to say that it did not still happen. From the Middle Ages on malformed newborns were at times murdered in the delivery room by the very midwife who delivered them; if they survived, their crippled, displaced, excrescent bodies could be shown for money at fairs and freak shows.[25] The church considered monsters human beings and legislated on the circumstances in which they should be baptized. How should Siamese twins be christened, for example? Were they supposed to be one body and one soul, and thus be baptized once, or did they constitute two bodies and two souls? Realdo Colombo found that one twin in a joined Siamese pair had no brain and no heart. Did he have a soul? The conclusion to which he came, together with the Platonist philosopher Marco Antonio Genua, was that the deformation did not allow consideration of this monster as a human being.[26] Midwives were repeatedly instructed on the procedures to follow in such peculiar instances because a sacrament, baptism, was at stake.[27]

24. See Uta Ranke-Heinemann, *Eunuchs for the Kingdom of Heaven: Women, Sexuality and the Catholic Church* (New York: Doubleday, 1990), 68.

25. The spice merchant Luca Landucci, for example, described in his diary the showing in Florence in 1513 of a Spanish man having another creature coming out of his body, with legs and genitals protruding, but no head. See *Diario Fiorentino: A Florentine Diary from 1450 to 1516* (New York: Dutton, 1927). Celio Malespini recollected a similar case in Rome late in the sixteenth century when a man with two heads, one of which was coming out of his stomach, was being shown for money. See Malespini, *Giardino di fiori curiosi* (Venice: Ciotti, 1597), 1.16. The book is a translation of a Spanish text by Antonio Torquemada, which came out originally in 1590.

26. Realdo Colombo, *De re anatomica* (Venice: Bevilacqua, 1559). On Genua (1491–1563) and the issue of the soul, see Eckhard Kessler, "The Intellective Soul," in *The Cambridge History of Renaissance Philosophy,* ed. Charles Schmitt, Quentin Skinner, Eckhard Kessler, and Jill Kraye (Cambridge: Cambridge University Press, 1988), 485–534, esp. 515.

27. Niccoli reports the case of a midwife who baptized a deformed baby even before its full emergence from the birth canal (" 'Menstruum,' " 21, n. 12). Extremely deformed babies were, however, judged nonhumans and were not baptized. Also christened immediately upon delivery were children born by cesarean section or those whose mother died during delivery. See Renate Blumenfeld-Kosinski, *Not of Woman Born: Representations of Caesarian Birth in Medieval and Renaissance Culture* (Ithaca: Cornell University Press, 1991), ch. 1.

All in all, Christian thought followed Augustine. In *De civitate Dei* he had argued that monsters are not errors but prodigies of nature because they plainly show God's will. His tripartite argument was that there may be races of monsters that actually do not exist, that if they exist they may not be human, and that if they are human they are all children of Adam, therefore people have no business in second-guessing God's intentions.[28] Following him, Isidore of Seville too saw monsters as signs from heaven: they tended to die soon after seeing the light, he explained, because their birth was sufficient to fulfill their purposes.[29] The birth of a monster in Ravenna in 1512 was taken as a premonitory sign of the forthcoming devastation of Italy on the part of the French troops of Louis XII; that of the monstrous pope-ass left to die in the Tiber in Rome in 1496 became for Philip Melanchton a demonstration that God was fed up with the corruption of the Church of Rome. The same conclusion was reached by Martin Luther in his examination of a monstrous baby born in Freiburg in 1522.[30]

In time, monstrosity was no longer read as supernatural manifestation and the subject was secularized through a number of philosophical, scientific, and literary pronouncements. No longer explained as precursors of things to come, as Cicero had argued in *De divinatione*, nor as signs of God's intervention in human affairs, monsters became the field of inquiry of anatomists, geneticists, and pathologists.[31] One result of this shift is evident in the obsessive compilation of

28. Augustine, *De civitate Dei*, ed. J. E. C. Welldon (London: Macmillan, 1924), 21.8.

29. Isidore of Seville, *Aetymologiae*, 1.11.3, *Patrologia latina* [hereafer *PL*], ed. Jacques Paul Migne (Alexandria, Va.: Chadwick-Healey, 1995), 82.420. See also Niccoli, "Menstruum," 3; and Jean Céard, *La Nature et les prodiges: L'insolite au XVIe siècle en France* (Geneva: Droz, 1977), 21-33. Pietro Pomponazzi will later attribute monstrosity to cosmographic influences. See *De naturalium effectuum admirandorum causis, seu de incantationibus liber, item de fato, libero arbitrio, praedestinatione, prouidentia Dei* (Basel: Henricpetri, 1567).

30. Martin Luther and Phillip Melanchton, "Deuttung der czwo grewlichen Figuren, Bapstesels czu Rom und Munchkalbs zu Freijberg ijnn Meijsszen funden," in Martin Luther, *Werke*, 58 vols. (Weimar, 1883-1948), 11:370-85. Fanciful nicknames often described these repugnant bodies. On the political use of monsters and the anxieties their appearance fed, see Ottavia Niccoli, *Prophecy and People in Renaissance Italy* (Princeton: Princeton University Press, 1990), ch. 2.

31. Marcus Tullius Cicero, *De divinatione*, ed. Arthur Pease (Urbana: University of Illinois Press, 1920-23), 1.42. For a late-sixteenth-century text that examines all that can go right or wrong in generation, see Giuseppe Liceti (d. ca. 1599), *Il ceva overo dell'eccellenza et uso de' genitali. Dialogo di Gioseppe Liceti Medico Chirurgo genovese. Nel quale si tratta dell'essenza, et*

manuals on teratology, the classification of monsters, that became fashionable after 1550.[32] Descriptions of monstrosity in the period were often enhanced by fantasy, as in reports of newborns with the head or body of cows, cats, dogs, and frogs. At other times the account was given in a matter-of-fact style. Benedetto Varchi, for example, described the case of two girls with one head joined at the chest and belly button. They had blue eyes and white teeth in one face, and two ears in what would have been a second face. Upon dissection the monster showed two hearts, two livers, two lungs, but one windpipe. The girls were born in Prato, he recalled, twelve years before his disquisition on the subject, that is, in 1536.[33]

A second result of the shift is that women—in particular women's imagination—became even more the cause of newborns' deficiencies. Many doctors, such as Marsilio Ficino, Paré, and Paracelsus, remarked that the maternal imagination at the time of conception, be it influenced by something the mother dreamt or saw, had a peculiar importance in shaping the fetus. To start with, female imagination was stronger than male imagination, it was thought, because

generatione del seme humano; delle somiglianze dell'Huomo, e lor cagioni; della differenza del sesso; della generatione de' mostri, e d'altre cose non meno utili; che dilettevoli (Bologna: Heredi di Gio. Rossi, 1598). On Renaissance monstrosity, see Katharine Park and Lorraine Daston, "Unnatural Conceptions: The Study of Monsters in Sixteenth- and Seventeenth-Century France and England," *Past and Present* 91 (1981): 21–54, esp. 23–24; and Jacques Gélis, *History of Childbirth, Fertility, Pregnancy and Birth in Early Modern Europe*, trans. Rosemary Morris (Boston: Northeastern University Press, 1991), 267.

32. The Flemish doctor Levinus Lemnius's (Lievin Lemnes) text on "miracles of nature" was translated into Italian as *De gli occulti miracoli, et varii ammaestramenti delle cose della natura* and published in Venice in 1560; Sebastian Munster issued *Cosmographia universalis* in 1544 in German, soon translated into Italian; and Jacob Rueff wrote *De conceptu et generatione hominis* in 1554. A few years later Benedetto Sinibaldi published in Rome a much researched and scholarly text of more than a thousand folio columns titled *Geneanthopeiae sive de hominis generatione decatheuchon*; Tommaso Garzoni wrote *Serraglio degli stupori del mondo* in the 1580s, although it was not printed until 1613; Fortunio Liceti's contribution, *De monstrorum caussis, natura et differentiis*, appeared in Padua in 1616, and Ulisse Aldrovandi's *Monstrorum historia* was printed almost forty years after his death in Bologna in 1642. For a most comprehensive study of teratology in five volumes, see Cesare Taruffi, *Storia della teratologia* (Bologna: Regia Tipografia, 1881); and Ernest Martin, *Histoire des monstres depuis l'antiquité jusqu'à nos jours* (Paris: Reinwald, 1880).

33. Benedetto Varchi, *Lezzione . . . sopra la generazione de' mostri, e se sono intesi dalla natura, o no*, in *Lezzioni di M. Benedetto Varchi* (1548; Florence: Giunti, 1590), 85–132.

of women's cold and humid nature, and it was known that cold objects were subject to metamorphosis.[34] Since Empedocles' remark that statues and paintings seen during pregnancy could bring changes to a fetus's bodily features, maternal imagination had constituted one of the inscrutable, uncontrollable incursions into one's yet unborn life. Galen advised hanging a picture of a handsome man or of a beautiful doll on the ceiling of the expectant mother's bedroom or at her bedpost to assure pleasant-looking features for the newborn, each choice coded around the preferred sex.[35] The custom became so common by the middle of the sixteenth century that Lodovico Domenichi declared it fashionable among Venetian nobles.[36]

Problems were always lurking. A story often reported was that of a baby girl covered with hair as the result of her mother having gazed at a portrait of Saint John in a bearskin hanging over her bed. Then there was the case of a baby girl born in 1517 with a frog-like face because her mother had held a frog for the sake of curing a fever and kept holding it during coitus.[37] For Paracelsus it was crucial to cheer up melancholic and angry pregnant women because their unbridled imagination could have bad effects. A woman dying in childbirth may wish the whole world to die with her, he wrote, and this volition could convert into a spirit that "by means of the ('menstrual') birth discharge . . . can generate an epidemic." A pregnant woman with lascivious imagination, likewise, by offending Venus, produced "the semen of contagion, notably plague." In fact, whenever there was no complete concordance between man, woman, and heaven, the woman produced monsters, Paracelsus concluded.[38] Benedetto

34. See Ian Maclean, *The Renaissance Notion of Woman* (Cambridge: Cambridge University Press, 1980), 42.

35. See Gélis, *History of Childbirth*, 55. Francesco da Barberino (1264–1348) also told pregnant women to look at good images in order not to generate monsters. See *Del reggimento e costumi di donna*, ed. Giuseppe Sansone (Rome: Zauli, 1995).

36. "Par che hoggi sia nato il costume fra gran Signori di tener per le camere quadri nobilissimi di pitture perchè da simili oggetti le donne prendano imaginazione bellissima." In Lodovico Domenichi, *Historia naturale di G. Plinio Secondo, . . . tradotta per m. L. Domenichi con le addittioni in margine* (1561; Venice: G. Bizzardo, 1612), 156.

37. See Paré, *On Monsters*, ch. 9. Holding frogs in one's hand was the cure for an array of problems. Falloppio recommends it for women with heavy menstruation. See Gabriele Falloppio, *Secreti diversi e miracolosi* (Venice: Bonfad, 1658), 1.120.

38. Paracelsus, *De virtute imaginativa*, in Walter Pagel, *Paracelsus: An Introduction to Philosophical Medicine in the Era of the Renaissance* (New York: Karger, 1958), 122 and 124.

Varchi strongly lamented the effect of the mother's imagination on the fetus, as Ulisse Aldrovandi and Benedetto Sinibaldi did later on.[39] Likewise, in his treatise on sacred and profane images, Gabriele Paleotti argued that it is a theory commonly accepted by both philosophers and doctors that bodies can show the signs of what we fantasize.[40]

Many cases of monstrosity dealt with racial intermixing. A white woman, a story went, delivered a nonwhite child because she often gazed at the picture of a dark-skinned man in the bedchamber during her pregnancy. Juan Huarte categorically denied that a child with a different skin color than the father or the mother could be engendered.[41] Yet the jurist Andrea Alciati defended a woman accused of adultery following her delivery of a black child, although she and her husband were white, because there was a painting of an Ethiopian in her bedroom.[42] Some believed that women themselves were to blame for staining with black the race born of Adam. The dark color of skin came about, Agostino Tornielli claimed, because maternal imagination focused on something very black that could not be satisfied during pregnancy and in due course a black baby was born.[43] Joseph-François Lafitau made a similar statement on the power of maternal introjection as late as 1724. Originally there was one color for all mankind,

39. Varchi, *Lezzione*; Ulisse Aldrovandi, *Avvertimenti del Dottore Aldrovandi sopra le pitture mostrifiche e religiose* (1581), reprinted in *Osservazione della natura e raffigurazione in Ulisse Aldrovandi*, ed. G. Olmi, special issue *of Annali dell'Istituto Storico Italo-Germanico di Trento* 3 (1977): 177–80; Giovanni Benedetto Sinibaldi (1594–1658), *Geneanthropeiae sivi de hominis generatione decatheuchon, ubi ex ordine quaecumque ad humanae Gegnerationis liturgiam, ejusdem principia, organa, tempus, usum, modum, occasionem, voluptatem . . . adjecta est historia foetus mussipontani* (1642; Frankfurt: Petri Zubrodt, 1669).

40. "Secondo i varii concetti che apprende la nostra fantasia delle cose, si fanno in essa così salde impressioni, che da quelle ne derivano alterazioni e segni notabili nei corpi, di che chiaro testimonio ci rende l'esperienza stessa." Gabriele Paleotti (1522–97), *Discorsi intorno alle immagini sacre e profane* (Bologna: Alessandro Benacci, 1582), reprinted in *Trattati d'arte del Cinquecento fra Manierismo e Controriforma*, ed. Paola Barocchi, 3 vols. (Bari: Laterza, 1961), 2:230.

41. Juan Huarte, *Essamina de gl'ingegni de gli huomini accomodati ad apprendere qual si voglia scienza* (Venice: Barezzi e' compagni, 1600), 432–33 and 445.

42. Andrea Alciati (1492–1550), *De verborum et rerum significatione*, in *Opera omnia* (Basel: Thomas Guarinum, 1582), 2.1196.

43. Agostino Tornielli (1543–1622), *Annales sacri, et ex profanis praecipui, ad orbe condito ad eumdem Christi passione redemptum* (Antwerp: Moretum, 1620), 2 vols. See also Giuliano Gliozzi, *Le teorie della razza nell'età moderna* (Turin: Einaudi, 1986), 131–32; and Massimo

he argued, but some men painted themselves black or red and this left a remarkable impression on the imagination of pregnant women, with perceivable racial results.[44] Even after James Blondel published not one but two treatises (1727, 1729) denying in detail the possibility of any role for maternal imagination in the generative process, beliefs in its power went unabated.[45] More than thirty years later, in his treatise on skin color, Nicolas Le Cat gave an example of a white German woman who gave birth to a black infant because she had seen a black servant during her pregnancy.[46] Friedrich Hegel too kept fearing the mother's imagination. In *Philosophy of the Mind*, he wrote "of children being born with an injured arm because the mother had actually broken an arm or at least had knocked it so severely that she feared it was broken, or, again, because she had been frightened by the sight of someone's else broken arm."[47] In more modern times, the so-called Elephant Man got his name not from his misshapen head, we are told, but from the fact that before his birth his mother had witnessed a circus elephant gone mad and was extraordinarily impressed by the elephant's trunk.[48]

At the time Tasso wrote, mothers could not only determine the features of

---

Angelini, "Il potere plastico dell'immaginazione nelle gestanti tra XVI e XVIII secolo: La fortuna d'una idea," *Intersezioni* 14 (1994): 53–69, esp. 57.

44. Joseph-François Lafitau, *Moeurs des sauvages amériquains* (Paris: Saugrain, 1724), 67. On this, see also Pierre Darmon, *Le Mythe de la procréation à l'âge baroque* (Paris: Seuil, 1979), 161.

45. James Blondel, *The Strength of Imagination in Pregnant Women Examin'd and the Opinion that Marks and Deformities in Children Arise from thence Demonstrated to be a Vulgar Error* (London: Peele, 1727), and *The Power of the Mother's Imagination over the Foetus Examin'd* (London: Brotherton, 1729).

46. Nicolas Le Cat, *Traité de la couleur de la peau humaine en général, de celle des nègres en particulier et de la métamorphose d'une de ces couleurs en l'autre, soit de naissance, soit accidentellement* (Amsterdam: n.p., 1765), 1.2, p. 20. In *The Enchantments of Love* (1637), Maria De Zayas elaborated on a lady from Seville who gave birth to a black infant because her black maid's baby was lying on her bed while she was engaged in coitus. See Marina Scordilis Brownlee, "Contexted Genealogies: Maria De Zayas," in Finucci and Brownlee, *Generation and Degeneration*, 189–208.

47. Friedrich Hegel, *Hegel's Philosophy of Subjective Spirit*, ed. and trans. M. J. Petry, 3 vols. (Dordrecht: Reidel, 1978), 2:237.

48. See Arnold Davidson, "The Horror of Monsters," in *The Boundaries of Humanity: Humans, Animals, Machines*, ed. James Sheehan and Morton Sosna (Berkeley and Los Angeles: University of California Press, 1991), 36–67, esp. 53.

the fetus through their imagination and have phantom pregnancies that they would later abort (*molae*); they could also determine skin pigmentation. Birth-marks ("*voglie*" in Italian, or "envies" in French, that is, wants, desires) could take many shapes; usually they were thought to be fruits that the mother longed to taste during pregnancy, reminders of another fruit perhaps, the apple that the mother of all mankind desired, thus dooming all her children to a life of toil.[49] When the use of coffee became common, a number of newborns started to show coffee-colored pigment stains. Women were recommended not to touch them-selves or only to touch parts of the body hidden to sight, so that a mark would not disfigure the newborn.[50] In Matteo Maria Boiardo's chivalric romance *Orlando innamorato* (1492), Fiordespina is described as having a birthmark because of her mother's wandering mind. Children, in short, bore the mark of their mother's hysterical or promiscuous desires. Thus, in the case of a newborn resembling a dog, the resemblance did not mean, Ulisse Aldrovandi wrote, that the child was the fruit of bestial copulation, because for him an animal cannot reproduce itself in a human being. Rather, it showed that the mother must have been so much obsessed by her transgression and bestiality during coitus that she engendered a child resembling what she was thinking at the time.[51] In short, the monstrous child needs to be born as a witness to a mother's monstrous nature.

There is therefore a palpable difference between paternal and maternal imagi-nation vis-à-vis the formation of a fetus's features. The father, as we saw with Tasso, needs simply to think of something in order for the child to be a perfect or perfected image of what he thinks; the mother, however, can only manage a poor reproduction of what she is desiring or seeing and can be influenced by

---

49. See Alain Grosrichard, "Le Cas polyphème: Un monstre et sa mère," *Ornicar?* 11–12 (Sept.–Dec. 1977): 19–35, 45–57.

50. It was also thought that birthmarks could be produced by excess menstrual discharge, although Lorenzo Gioberti denies it. Moreover, some women, he stated, specifically Brazil-ian women, never menstruate. See Lorenzo Gioberti, *La prima parte degli errori popolari: Nella quale si contiene l'eccellenza della medicina e de medici, della concettione, e generatione, della gravidanza, del parto, e delle donne di parto, e del latte, e del nutrire i bambini* (Florence: Giunta, 1592). In En-glish see *Popular Errors*, trans. Gregory David de Rocher (Tuscaloosa: University of Alabama Press, 1989). See also Thomas Laqueur, *Making Sex: Body and Gender from the Greeks to Freud* (Cambridge: Harvard University Press, 1990), 104.

51. Aldrovandi, *Monstrorum historia*, fol. 1642. Popular thinking and even some learned minds, such as Pliny, thought that interbreeding could be possible. I gave examples of such births in chapter 1.

circumstances to do things properly or to botch them. The father's imagination can improve on a child's genetic baggage; the mother, by not controlling herself and letting biology rather than fantasy work, can make a seemingly normal fetus monstrous.[52]

The implications of maternal imagination were far-reaching. If a fetus is imprinted with the image of something that its mother saw, or desired or was frightened by, that confers on the pregnant mother only a passive role in the shaping of her offspring. Some doctors and philosophers, however, felt that the imaginative mother could actually shape the child she was carrying into whatever she wanted. Giambattista Della Porta reported the case of a woman who had a marble reproduction made of her imagined offspring in order to conceive the exact copy of the son she desired. She kept looking at it during intercourse and throughout pregnancy, and the son was born with the wanted features.[53] Years later Campanella too was sure that women impress on children the image of what they desire, as long as they desire to engender a child with human and not bestial features.[54]

52. On having pregnant women desire something of a shape and color that will be apparent upon delivery, see Campanella, Del senso, 4.8, p. 309. For Thomas Lupton, A Thousand Notable Things (1579; London: White, 1586), and Thomas Fienus (Thomas Feyens), De viribus imaginationis tractatus (Louvain: Officina Gerardi Rivii, 1608), the power of maternal imagination was so great that a single bad thought was sufficient to imprint a malformation on the child. For more examples of maternal power through fantasy, see Darmon, Le Mythe de la procréation, 158–62. Only in the eighteenth century did doctors dismiss the view that maternal imagination was responsible for monstrosity. See Paul Gabriel Bouché, "Imagination, Pregnant Women, and Monsters in Eighteenth-Century England and France," in Sexual Underworlds of the Enlightenment, ed. G. S. Rousseau and Roy Porter (Chapel Hill: University of North Carolina Press, 1988), 86–100. For an analysis centered on Italy, see Angelini, "Il potere plastico." Even today in Italy pregnant women's cravings are very much accomodated to avoid birthmarks. The idea that women's imagination could mark the fetus was still alive scientifically well into the nineteenth century. See, for example, F. Viparelli, Sulla influenza che ha sul germe la fantasia d'una pregnante (Naples: n.p., 1842). More generally, see Claudia Pancino, Voglie materne: Storia di una credenza (Bologna: Cluebb, 1966).

53. He was "as pale and as white, as if he had been very marble indeed." In Giambattista Della Porta, Natural Magick (Magiae naturalis) (1558; New York: Basic Books, 1957), 53–54.

54. "le donne incinte esprimono nei loro parti l'imagine di quello che bramano, perchè il loro spirito così affetto si comunica al feto e esprime facilmente nel corpo tenero del bambino l'oggetto dell'immaginazione. Le cose tuttavia agiscono come sono disposte: perciò lo spirito del cane organizza un corpo canino, e lo spirito dell'uomo un corpo umano giacchè è legato

To ensure that a child looked like his/her father, the Hippocratics and Soranus suggested that during coitus and especially before having an orgasm (the
sine qua non for conception to occur, as I wrote in the introductory chapter), the
mother concentrate on evoking in her mind a picture of her husband. This guaranteed that the newborn would resemble him.[55] A number of medical treatises
also carried information on how women committing adultery could try to make
the child engendered from the affair look like their legal husbands. For Antonio
Persio, for example, an illegitimate child could resemble the mother's husband
because she may have been so afraid of having her adulterous encounter discovered that she impressed in the child the feature of the man paramount in her
imagination at the time of conception, not the actual father but the legal one,
and not because she loved him but because she did not.[56] The doctors Giovanni
Marinello and Paré argued along the same lines.[57]

While alternately enhancing or canceling maternal contribution, what these
doctors argue—uncannily so—is interesting: the mother carries a fetus that will
look like her husband not because he is the genetic father of the baby but because
she chooses, among a number of possibilities, to have her child look like what
she finds desirable for herself—like the husband this time, like somebody else in
the future. But this means that the engendering of a physically similar child has
suddenly been put outside the reach of fathers. A man was still needed for gen-

---

a tale figura." In Tommaso Campanella, *De homine* (Rome: Centro internazionale di studi
umanistici, 1960-61), 159.

55. See Ann Hanson, "The Medical Writers' Woman," in *Before Sexuality: The Construction of Erotic Experience in the Ancient Greek World*, ed. David Halperin, John Winkler, and
Froma Zeitlin (Princeton: Princeton University Press, 1990), 309-37.

56. Antonio Persio (1542-1612), *Dell'ingegno dell'huomo* (Venice: Manuzio, 1576), 97. Alain
Grosrichard, "Le Cas polyphème," sees a double identification at play on the part of the child:
one with the mother, since the child desires what she desires, and one with the father, or at
least with the father as he is imagined by the mother, in that he/she desires to be what the
mother desires for the child to be (48).

57. "per aventura ne viene che i bastardi più somigliano coloro che non sono padri veri,
ma imaginati, percioché le moglie essendo in adulterio e temendo de' lor mariti, di continuo
mentre dura quello atto gli hanno nella mente." In Giovanni Marinello, *Le medicine partenenti
alle infermità delle donne* (Venice: G. Francesco de' Franceschi, 1563), 3.3. Abridged version in
Medicina per le donne nel Cinquecento: Testi di Giovanni Marinello e di Girolamo Mercurio, ed. Maria
Luisa Altieri Biagi et al. (Turin: UTET, 1992). See also Ambroise Paré, *Toutes les oeuvres* (1585),
24.1, 925-26; and Darmon, *Le Mythe de la procréation*, 159.

eration to occur, but any man would do. All that a legal husband could hope for in matters of paternity was that his pregnant wife would not make him a laughing stock by choosing to have a child not resembling him, whether or not he was the child's biological father. Philosophically minded intellectuals were most in danger of having a child not similar to them, but to their wives' lovers, doctor Girolamo Mercurio wrote, for intellectuals tended to be too much distracted by their thoughts during coitus to keep their wives' attention focused on them. Their offspring ended up resembling those men more able to satisfy women in "the act of Venus" ("dilettando la donna nell'atto di Venere").[58] For Mercurio, educated men are often melancholic, a condition that women hate. This may push them to imagine making love to a joyous, and perhaps stupid, man with strange consequences for the embryo.[59] The same opinion is expressed by Persio, who asserts that because men of letters and businessmen tend to make love with their minds elsewhere, they generate stupid and uncouth children ("certi figlioli balordi, zotichi, et istupiditi").[60]

Thus, at the very moment in which woman performs her most clear-cut role in society, and her most recommended one biologically — that of reproducing — she manages to set herself free from patriarchy. To mother turns out to be a pose because woman can perform maternity as she can perform femininity: all for the sake of what is expected of her. If the mask of femininity in which a woman willingly appears as men would want her to appear (especially before marriage) is what keeps her desirable in her younger years, the performance of maternity requires an equal intervention in the reproductive process to keep her stock high after marriage. One way or the other, she has learned to play to her own advantage the games she needs to play.[61]

It is clear that a mother with the power to put paternity under erasure is too

---

58. Girolamo Mercurio (Scipion Mercurii), *La commare o riccoglitrice* (Venice: Ciotti, 1596), 1:12. Abridged version in *Medicina per le donne*.

59. Mercurio, *Commare*, 3.12.

60. Persio, *Dell'ingegno*, 93. For an extended discussion of the dangers encountered by intelligent fathers insufficiently diligent in matters of engendering to generate similarly intelligent children, see Huarte, *Essamina de gl'ingegni*, ch. 15.

61. For a study of the masquerade of femininity, see Valeria Finucci, "The Female Masquerade: Ariosto and the Game of Desire," in *Desire in the Renaissance: Psychoanalysis and Literature*, ed. Valeria Finucci and Regina Schwartz (Princeton: Princeton University Press, 1994), 61–88.

dangerous. To punish her, her behavior is pathologized: the impostor she produces is called a monster, monstrous because the mother is monstrous or monstrous because the child is unstamped, that is, illegitimate, unfathered, unfinished, mismatched, misrelated, and misgenated. For some critics, the popularity in the sixteenth and seventeenth centuries of stories of monstrosity coming from maternal imagination and desire can be read as the outcome of the repression of maternity and concomitant reinscription of paternal law that followed the Reformation.[62] Be that as it may, even today the fear of the possible cancellation of the father's signature is behind the emphasis on control of pregnancy and manipulation of mothering on the part of science and law. In our age of in vitro fertilization paternal participation has turned out to be not only highly controllable but also suitable to be chosen at random, deferred in time, achieved, even, without any heterosexual or paternal desire on the part of man. Woman at the same time has been freed from the law of reproduction with her access to contraception and safe abortion on demand.

It comes as no surprise then that the New Right and the pro-life movements have rushed to defend not just the fetus but also the embryo. In our age of sexual epidemics women are constantly reminded of the value of abstinence and safe sex, and made to understand that the fetus they carry is not their property, because it has the right to be born (against their wishes if needs be) or to receive ag-

---

62. Julia Kristeva argues that in the Middle Ages maternity was not repressed: "Christianity celebrates maternal fecundity and offsets the morbid and murderous filial love of paternal reason with mother/son incest." See "The Father Love and Banishment," in *Literature and Psychoanalysis,* ed. Edith Kurzweil and William Phillips (New York: Columbia University Press, 1983), 396. For Marie-Hélène Huet the widespread presence of Mary in fourteenth- and fifteenth-century art and culture, is part of a move to "defeminize" the Church and deemphasize maternal power, a move that took Mary as a specific target for disempowerment. The punishment of the mother's idolatry of an image (e.g., painting) at the expense of her husband through the birth of a monstrous child thus reinstated the importance of the father in procreation, just as the Reformation revived the role of God as Father and forbade adoration of Christ's mother in church worship. See Huet, *Monstrous Imagination,* 28–29. But this construction took time to hold. Queen Elizabeth I, for example, used the construction of the Virgin Queen to further her political agenda. For a reading of the reinscription of the father's law in political terms in the Renaissance from Castiglione's *Il libro del cortegiano* (1528) to Tasso's *Il Malpiglio, overo della corte* (1585), see Valeria Finucci, "In the Name of the Brother: Male Rivalry and Social Order in B. Castiglione's *Il libro del cortegiano,*" *Exemplaria* 9.1 (1997): 91–116.

gressive medical interventions aimed to bringing it to maturity. The new interest on different ways to mother—by donating an egg (ovarian mothers), by providing the uterus (uterine mothers), and by raising the child (social mothers)—has also demythified the lore of motherhood as a unique, irreplaceable activity, one that instead needs to be monitored, poked, timed, and controlled by science. Woman once more becomes the container, the vessel, as Aristotle famously put it, of a life that is not only better understood by science than by her, but which she could easily endanger. Her womb is once more a feared tomb.[63]

Aethiopian Roots

In *Gerusalemme liberata*, Tasso makes Clorinda not only unlike her father but also unlike her mother, since she is said to resemble not her, but the white virgin Sabra in the painting of Saint George. What the mother's imagination cancels from the reproductive process is thus race: seeing the "white monster" she has given birth to, the black queen reacts with "maraviglia."[64] For Tasso and the people of his time, however, the Ethiopians themselves were monstrous. Writing in those years, for example, Tommaso Campanella argued that children of beautiful women could be born not only monstrous or bestial, thanks to their mother's imagination, but also as Ethiopians ("mostri et etiopi").[65] It was common knowledge, Isidore of Seville had written in *Etymologiae*, that an entire

63. Thus the appeal of the aptly named Operation Rescue, whose members block abortion clinics. For the womb as an "inhospitable waste land at war with the 'innocent' person within," see Carol Stabile, "Shooting the Mother: Fetal Photography and the Politics of Disappearance," *Camera Obscura* 28 (1992): 179–205, esp. 179; and Valerie Hartouni "Containing Women: Reproductive Discourse in the 1980s," in *Technoculture*, ed. Constance Penley and Andrew Ross (Minneapolis: University of Minnesota Press, 1991), 27–56, esp. 43.

64. What constitutes the marvelous? Tasso asked in a letter to Father Marco da Ferrara in 1581. Are there things that are always marvelous, or do marvelous things cease to be such once we know the reason for their happening? Are marvelous things only the impossible ones or the most miraculous? (*Lettere*, 2:158–60).

65. Campanella, *Del senso*, 4.10, p. 272, and 4.18, p. 305. Fortunio Liceti attributed the drive toward interspecies coupling to the African heat. See *De Monstrorum caussis natura et differentiis*, in *De la nature, des causes, des différences de monstres*, ed. François Houssay (1616; Paris: Editions Hippocrate, 1937). See also Zayika Hanafi, *The Monster in the Machine: Magic, Medicine, and the Marvelous in the Time of the Scientific Revolution* (Durham, N.C.: Duke University Press, 2000), 35.

people could be monstrous; such monstrosities were in fact often illustrated in the same books that catalogued malformed individuals. Monstrous races were those living at the edge of the known world: the Indians in the east, for example, and the Ethiopians in the south, unless of course they were civilized by Christian faith. In the *Liberata*, the geographic space between the Nile and the Hercules' Columns is said specifically to be the one most inhabited by monsters ("Ciò che di mostruoso e di feroce / erra fra 'l Nilo e i termini d'Atlante," "Whatever of montrous or of fierce roams between Nile and the boundaries of Atlas," 15.51).[66] In a sermon once attributed to Saint Augustine, the narrator, visiting Ethiopia to spread the Word, tells of having seen monsters of both sexes without a head, others with eyes in their chest or with a single foot so large that it functioned as an umbrella to shield the individual from the scorching African sun (*sciapodes*); in the south there were men with one eye in their foreheads. Aside from these peculiarities of nature, the narrator continues, these people were similar to all others. Thus, since they were humans, they could be Christianized.[67]

Monstrous representations of Ethiopians can be found in church sculptures in twelfth-century France, Céard writes, where an Ethiopian is represented next to a martikhora (an animal with human head), a liocorn, a faun, a chimera, a camel, a lion, a bear, and a monkey.[68] Monstrous races are also portrayed in the mosaic pavements of the medieval cathedral of Casale Monferrato in northern

66. Tasso's geographical knowledge was in tune with the travel literature of his time: he seemed to know quite precisely the configuration of Italy, Greece, and the territory around Jerusalem, for instance, but had foggy ideas about northern Europe, the Far East, and the West. His understanding of the heart of Africa came from the travel accounts of Portuguese explorers such as Francisco Alvarez's *Ho Prest Joam das Indias: Verdadera informaçam das terra do Presto Joam* (Lisbon, 1540). This book was translated from Portuguese into Italian and printed ten years later. See Giovanni Battista Ramusio, *Navigazioni e viaggi*, ed. Marica Milanesi, 6 vols. (Turin: Einaudi, 1978–1988), 2:79–385; and Quint, *Epic and Empire*, 234–36. Tasso also made annotations on Ethiopia in the margins of a book on cosmography, Giovanni Lorenzo d'Anania's *L'universale fabbrica del mondo*, which he owned. His edition was published in Venice in 1582, but the book itself came out in 1573 and was published again in 1576, that is, before Tasso finished the *Liberata*. See Bruno Basile, *Poeta melancholicus: Tradizione classica e follia nell'ultimo Tasso* (Pisa: Pacini, 1984), 356–58. Tasso refers to monstrous animals, and to monkeys and baboons, which he links to the Gorgons.

67. "Ad frates in Eremo, sermo XXXVII," PL 40.1304.

68. Céard, *La Nature et les prodiges*, 48–49.

Italy and in bas-reliefs of the cathedrals of Modena and Ferrara.[69] The mythical figure of Prester John (Prete Gianni) is said to have seen men with eyes in the front and back of their heads during his missions in Africa, and others with one eye only. He also believed in the existence of Amazons, living, properly enough, in the land of Femmenie.[70] The tradition is extensive and consistent with the fact that in the teratological geography of the time Ethiopians were seen as subhumans, as cannibals.[71]

In tune with this tradition, Ethiopians were also thought to be sexually overendowed and overactive, so much so in fact that they would even tempt hermits. Hence, Saint Anthony was lured by an ugly black youngster in the desert; and in the *Vitae patrum* there is the story of a young, smelly, and ugly Ethiopian woman engaged in seducing a hermit.[72] Ethiopian women were considered immune from venereal diseases, and some Venetians believed that the use of their bodies by men affected by gonorrhea provided an instant and definitive cure. True, a cure for gonorrhea was also achievable by sleeping with a virgin, Ercole Sassonia wrote, but only in the case of "mulier Aethiope" would the woman resist the infection.[73] Ethiopian women were in principle so lustful that clitoridectomy had to be practiced on them. The custom of female circumcision

69. Rudolph Wittkower, "Marvels of the East: A Study in the History of Monsters," *Journal of the Warburg and Courtauld Institutes* 5 (1942): 159–97, esp.177; Dario Franchini et al., eds., "Mostri e immagine," in *La scienza a corte: Collezionismo eclettico, natura e immagine a Mantova fra Rinascimento e Manierismo* (Rome: Bulzoni, 1979), 101–14, esp.102; and John Friedman, *The Monstrous Races in Medieval Art and Thought* (Cambridge: Harvard University Press, 1981).

70. From *Lettres du Prestes Jehans*, quoted in Céard, *La Nature et les prodiges*, 56. See also Renato Lefevre, *L'Etiopia nella stampa del primo Cinquecento* (Como: Cairoli, 1966).

71. For the link of Ethiopians with cannibalism in the Middle Ages, see David Williams, *Deformed Discourse: The Function of the Monster in Mediaeval Thought and Literature* (Montreal: McGill-Queens's University Press, 1996), 149.

72. *Vitae patrum*, 5.23, PL 73.879.

73. Ercole Sassonia (1551–1607), *Luis venerae perfectissimus tractatus:* "Sciendum autem est. quod habui a quibusdam expertis Venetis: Dicunt se a Gonorrhaea statim curatos usu Veneris cum mulier Aethiope. . . . Haec quoque scio, si tamen literis consignam licet antiqua gonorrhaea plures fuisse liberatos, qui cum uxore Virgine rem habuerunt, sed tunc mulier inficitur" (ch. 37, fol. 40), quoted in Wilfred Schleiner, "Infection and Cure through Women: Renaissance Constructions of Syphilis," *Journal of Medieval and Renaissance Studies* 24. 3 (1994): 499–517, at 508–9.

is well recorded: "[In] Ethiopia, especially in the Dominions of Prester John, they Circumcise women. These Abassines have added errour upon errour, and sin upon sin, for they cause their Females to be circumcised."[74] Aristotle, like the Hippocratics, had argued that Egyptian women (intended here in a large sense as comprising also Libyans, for example, in the west and, one may assume, Ethiopians in the south) were too prolific and therefore more prone to engender monsters: "The occurrence of monstrosities is more common in those regions where the women are prolific—in Egypt, for instance."[75] Possession by devils— in the shape of foul-smelling black Ethiopian men—was also common, as in the case of a woman helped by Beata Bridget to get rid of the incubus destroying her psychospiritual health: when the devil was expelled, she saw a dirty Ethiopian coming out of her breasts.[76] Blacks, in short, had limited possibilities for recuperation or assimilation within the white, "civilized" world. In both Greece and Rome a useless task was described as an attempt "to wash an Ethiop white": no matter how much a black is scrubbed, he remains black to the core.[77]

Although they were often referred to as Moors, Ethiopians were Christians. In fact, the process of conversion was very successful in Ethiopia, even though that success came to be soon marred by fears that Ethiopians furthered Ana-

74. John Bulwer, *Anthropometamorphoses: Man Transformed, or The Artificial Changeling* (London: Hunt, 1653). See also Thomas Laqueur, "Amor Veneris, Vel Dulcedo Appeletur," in *Fragments for a History of the Human Body,* ed. Michel Feher (New York: Zone, 1989), 115.

75. *GA* 4.4.770a. Aristotle considered Ethiopian men cowards and identified frizzy hair with lack of manly worth: "Those with very wooly hair are cowardly; this applies to the Ethiopians." See Aristotle, *Minor Works,* ed. and trans. W. S. Hett (Cambridge: Harvard University Press, 1936), 131. Hairy men had also abundant seed and desired intercourse more often (*GA* 4.5.774b). But then Aristotle found this true also of light-skinned people like the Germans. For Aldrovandi too Egypt had more monsters than other countries because there men were more fertile and prone to intercourse, just like cats, dogs, pigs, birds, chickens, and doves; where there was too much matter, monsters could result. See "Appendice," in *Avvertimenti del Dottore Alchovandi,* 179.

76. See Isak Collijn, *Acta et processus canonizacionis beatae Birgittae* (Upsala: Almquist and Wiksells, 1924–1931), 513; and Michael Goodich, "Sexuality, Family, and the Supernatural in the Fourteenth Century," *Journal of the History of Sexuality* 4 (1994): 493–516, esp. 512.

77. In the sixteenth century, the terms "Moor," "Negro," and "Ethiopian" were used more or less interchangeably. See Charles Lyons, *To Wash an Aethiop White: British Ideas about Black African Educability* (New York: Columbia University, Teachers College, 1975), 3.

baptist practices (e.g., adult rebaptism).[78] Churches in Ethiopia abounded in portrayals of saints. The saint most ubiquitously represented from the fifteenth century onward, second only to Mary, was Saint George, according to Stanley Chojnacki.[79] Saint George was the saint in the painting Clorinda's mother gazed at in her many solitary hours during pregnancy. He is usually portrayed as a Christ figure defeating the dragon. Although for Catholics he stood as a tortured martyr, in paintings Saint George is usually depicted as a victorious knight on a white horse, spearing a monstrous animal, either a dragon or a snake. In the earliest paintings, the Virgin is present, holding the baby Jesus and a flower. Saint George is portrayed as a young man killing a serpent; the dragon was introduced later on, along with the rescued maiden.[80] The story of Saint George and the dragon had been well known in the Middle East since the Middle Ages. Pilgrimages to the spot near Beirut where the dragon was slain and the virgin Birutawit, later called Sabra, was chained were also common.[81] Sabra is usually dressed in the paintings, but is occasionally portrayed unclothed; in later representations, she is depicted perched on a tree or clinging to branches.

Saint George's rescue of a fearful virgin princess from a monster is, of course, only the Christianized version of another mythical rescue favored in the pagan world, that of Andromeda in chains, being saved by the winged Perseus from a marine monster bent on eating her. Interestingly enough, the tradition had it that Andromeda was Ethiopian. Thus, it is not surprising to find a story such as that of Heliodorus in book 4 of *Aethiopica*, which enjoyed wide circulation in the Renaissance after it was discovered in 1526, in which the black queen of

78. See Quint, *Epic and Empire*, 242–43. In assessing Clorinda's double personality, white and Ethiopian, Quint offers interesting historical sources.

79. Stanley Chojnacki, "The Iconography of Saint George in Ethiopia," *Journal of Ethiopian Studies* 11.1 (1973): 57–73; 11.2 (1973): 51–92; and 12.1 (1974): 71–132.

80. The artist responsible for the addition was Venetian, Nicolao Brancaleone, who was also called Märquoryos the Foreigner, according to Francisco Alvarez who wrote the history of the first Portuguese embassy in Ethiopia (1520–23). See Chojnacki, "Iconography of Saint George," 11.1 (1973): 58; and Charles Fraser Beckingham and G. W. B. Huntingford, eds., *The Prester John of the Indies* (Cambridge: Hakluyt Society at Cambridge University Press, 1961), 332. Francisco Alvarez too mentions the popularity of Saint George in Ethiopia. See Ramusio, *Navigazioni*, 2:146. For a study of Saint George in Italy, see Paolo Toschi, *La leggenda di San Giorgio nei canti popolari italiani* (Florence: Olschki, 1964).

81. Chojnacki, "Iconography of Saint George," 11.2 (1973): 57.

Ethiopia, Persinna, wife of king Hydustes, gives birth to a child, Chariclea, very much unlike herself and her husband: she resembles Andromeda, whose portrait Persinna had before her eyes during copulation. Like Clorinda's mother in the *Liberata*, also an Ethiopian queen, Chariclea's mother had looked at the representation of Andromeda being saved from the monster by Perseus.[82] Persinna tells her husband that the baby has died, but she has been sent away, in a basket. An old man rescues her, has shepherds take care of her and raise her as a woman warrior priestess of Apollo.[83] In commenting on the Heliodorus story, Dante Della Terza notices that there is no mention in Heliodorus of the princess's color; we know that in Ariosto she—in the shape first of Angelica and then of Olimpia, the two women who replay the Andromeda story in the *Furioso*—is white and blond, just like Clorinda.

In a previous study, I read the Andromeda story as a myth of domestication of femininity: saved by Perseus after her mother's foolishness put her life in jeopardy, Andromeda gladly accepts his offer of marriage. The myth tells us that a woman will always be rewarded if she remains passively in her place.[84] A white Christian princess is also clearly better qualified to embody the story of female submission than a black pagan from a faraway land. As if to underline the point, the princess rescued by Saint George is often represented in the tradition not naked, as Andromeda is in the classical rendering, but dressed in a white wedding dress, the perfectly subjugated daughter of Western patriarchy. The monster, be it the viscid serpentine one with which Orlando and Ruggiero fight in the *Furioso* or the serpent portrayed in representations of Saint George, represents uncontrollable sexuality and also paradoxically, given the fact that it

82. Heliodorus of Emesa, *An Aethiopian Romance* (*Aethiopica*), ed. F. A. Wright (London: Routledge, 1923). As Dante Della Terza remarks, the story was discovered in the library of Matthias Corvinus, translated in Latin, and printed in Basel in 1534 ("History and the Epic Discourse: Remarks on the Narrative Structure of Tasso's *Gerusalemme Liberata*," *Quaderni d'italianistica* 1.1 [1980]: 30–45, 45 n. 5). Walter Stephens argues that Tasso may have read the story in Italian in the translation of Leonardo Ghini, which was first published in 1556. See "Tasso's Heliodorus and the World of Romance," in *The Search for the Ancient Novel*, ed. James Tatum (Baltimore: Johns Hopkins University Press, 1994), 67–87, esp. 67.

83. For sources of this episode, see Salvatore Martineddu, *Le fonti della Gerusalemme liberata* (Turin: Clausen, 1895), 128–30.

84. See Valeria Finucci, *The Lady Vanishes: Subjectivity and Representation in Castiglione and Ariosto* (Stanford: Stanford University Press, 1992), ch. 5.

is not usually gendered, undifferentiated sexuality.[85] Thus the story of the virgin Andromeda/Sabra achieves two purposes: to punish woman's surplus sexuality by displacing it onto the monster who will be killed by a patriarchal father figure, and to reward woman's passivity by having the patient virgin marry her savior after he has rescued her from danger, a move that allows her to enter the social order. The killing of the monster establishes, in short, the importance of a properly gendered man and a properly gendered woman in social relations and the value of controlling the anticipated disruptions generated by female sexuality.

The problem with Clorinda is that she can be thought of as monstrous in yet another way: her mother's *vis imaginativa* created her not only unlike her husband and unlike herself but also, it turns out, unlike the image of the Caucasian woman she was thought to be copying, because she got the color right, but not the personality. Like Sabra, Clorinda is white; unlike Sabra, she is far from the picture of femininity and submissiveness that her model purportedly represents. The mother, in short, has been able to reproduce in her uncanny offspring the image but not the meaning: the daughter is a living lie, a fraud. Thus, although seemingly feminine, Clorinda is made to fret at the limitations imposed on women: "Dunque sol tanto a donna e più non lice?" (12.3; "Is then a woman allowed to do only this much and no more?"). When Belzebú creates a simulacrum of Clorinda, he appropriately opts to make it in the shape of a man, a marvelous monster, as Tasso parenthetically interjects:

> Questi di cava nube ombra leggiera
> (mirabil mostro) in forma d'uom compose;
> e la sembianza di Clorinda altera
> gli finse. (7.99)

85. In this sense Arsete too is a monster, neither male nor female, as eunuchs were thought to be. When he dreams of Saint George reproaching him for not having baptized Clorinda, he is, as Migiel notices, in the position of the dragon ("vidi in sogno un guerrier che minacciando / a me su 'l volto il ferro ignudo pose," 12.36). See Marilyn Migiel, "Clorinda's Father," *Stanford Italian Review* 10 (1991): 93–121, esp. 106. On the coincidence of dragon and virgin in this scene, see Paolo Braghieri, *Il testo come soluzione rituale: Gerusalemme liberata* (Bologna: Patron, 1978), 131. On the myth of Andromeda, see Adrienne Munich, *Andromeda's Chains: Gender and Interpretation in Victorian Literature and Art* (New York: Columbia University Press, 1989). For another take on this story, see the rendering of Redcross knight (Saint George) killing the monster Errour in Spenser's *Fairie Queene*.

He from a hollow cloud composed an insubstantial shade (marvellous monster) in a human shape; and counterfeited for it the face of the proud Clorinda.

Years later Aphra Behn celebrates Clorinda as both woman and man, a "fair lovely lady" and a "lovely charming youth" about whom to fantasize in a lesbian relationship.[86] It will take a life of exile from the "correct" religion and civilization for Clorinda to become, in death, what she could have been in life—passive, meek, and properly gendered—if the process of mirroring like and like had not run amok. No wonder that the story of Saint George resurfaces at the end. The mother's imagination had indeed canceled the signature of the biological father from her pale, non-Ethiopian child, as I have argued, but another father, Saint George, whose picture was hanging on the expectant queen's bedroom, was present from the beginning in the baby girl's features as her ideal father. In the mythical story, the saint who saved Sabra from the monster was none other than a patriarchal father killing the monster in woman so that she could be reunited with her true, more feminine self. In Tasso's rewriting, the new incarnation of the Law of the Father is Tancredi, who kills that uncivilized, castrating, manly, and unresponsive woman that is the pagan Clorinda. Like Saint George, he next proceeds to recuperate her to his world through baptism, although, given the author's preferences, Clorinda can be present only as an uncorporeal, angelical form, coming in a dream to thank her savior for having saved her, when, paradoxically, he has killed her.

In the end, the figure of this woman warrior sadistically pierced and killed and ultimately projected as an angel becomes the personification of the image of orthodox femininity that Renaissance culture liked to foster. Only then does Tasso mark Clorinda as nonmonstrous: feminine (she is described as seductively revealing a golden and embroidered vest), virginal and Christian, an image, as Giovanni Getto put it, of immaculate luminosity ("immacolata luminosità").[87] Only after death does Tasso make Clorinda project a newly found feminine identity: she is beautiful, she tells Tancredi in a dream, and happy ("Mira come son bella e come lieta," "Mark how happy I am and how well"; 12.91). She even

86. Aphra Behn, "To the Fair Clarinda, Who Made Love to Me, Imagined More than Woman" (1688), in *The Norton Anthology of Literature by Women*, ed. Sandra Gilbert and Susan Gubar (New York: Norton, 1985), 94.

87. Giovanni Getto, *Nel mondo della Gerusalemme* (Florence: Vallecchi, 1968), 142.

invites him to admire her beauty in heaven, together with that of God ("vagheg-gerai le sue bellezze e mie," "you shall gaze upon [his] loveliness and mine"; 12.92). Having become perfectly beautiful and perfectly feminine, the *femme* as Lacan would say, Clorinda can now hide her castration and become an object of adoration rather than aggression. To put it another way, to cancel the fantasy figure that Tancredi had created for himself, it was necessary that Woman be made, narratively speaking, into a woman (that is, feminine) and impossible to have (that is, dead and not-white). Clorinda's narrative recuperation through elimination of her improperly feminized body is now complete.

Yet why not think of maternal imagination in more powerful terms? Why would the lonely queen immerse herself in the fantasy scenario of virgin, saint, and monster? Why would she desire her baby to be what she should not be? "If . . . day-dreams are carefully examined," Freud wrote, "they are found to serve as the fulfillment of wishes and as a correction of actual life. They have two principal aims, an erotic and an ambitious one—though an erotic aim is usually concealed behind the latter too."[88] What ambitious and erotic dreams would the Ethiopian wife want gratified along the lines of the wildly imagi-native women of Persio, Paré, Marinello, and Huarte, who were able to efface their husband's presence in the reproductive process? A reading of the scene shows that by staging the fantasy of being loved as an event in which she takes the place of a virgin sufficiently valuable to be saved, Clorinda's mother makes herself worthy of consideration as an object of desire. The man who "desires" her is, after all, a knight worshiped by all and a recognized redresser of wrong-doings. And so Saint George's seedless paternity gets imprinted over Clorinda's virago-like body and determines her career.

But the queen also wants to hide the wish to be Sabra, who was perhaps only desired as white or because she was white, by displacing that wish onto her daughter, whom she would like to be desired and white, like Sabra. This desire is, however, transgressive, hence the punishment through what she ends believing is both a prodigious event, the fulfillment of her desire to be desired by a white knight, and a monstrous event, the result of the deletion of the biologi-cal father's physiognomic imprint from her offspring, for Clorinda embodies both meanings of the word "monster" in Tasso's imagination. Lynda Boose has argued that the sexual relationship of a black male and white female could be culturally accommodated in the early modern period because the resulting black

88. Sigmund Freud, "Family Romances," *SE* 238.

offspring, by canceling once more maternal input, would reinforce paternal primacy in generation; a white male–black female union, on the other hand, remained utterly unrepresentable.[89] In Tasso such a representation can only be cast as a fantasy to be punished in due time. In fact, the queen pays with her life for such disobedience against the Law of the Father, since Tasso makes her killed by her own daughter, in that she suffers either a social death—in which, by keeping Clorinda, she may be cast away—or a physical one—in which, by not keeping her, she may not outlive the pain and quasi-suicidally die of what was then called constriction of the heart: "Qui tacque; e 'l cor si rinchiuse e strinse / e di pallida morte si dipinse" (12.28; "Here she fell silent; and her heart closed up and shrank within itself, and she was the color of pale death").[90]

It is worth noticing that there is another mother of a baby girl who dies soon after her daughter's birth in Tasso. Such is the case of Armida's mother:

> Costei co'l suo morire quasi prevenne
> il nascer mio, ch'in tempo estinta giacque
> ch'io fuori uscia de l'alvo, e fu il fatale
> giorno ch'a lei dié morte, a me natale. (4.43)

> She with her death almost anticipated my birth, for she lay dead at the moment I issued from the womb, and the fatal day that brought her death was the day of my birth.[91]

Armida's mother is called Carichia, that is, she has the name of the baby girl resembling Andromeda, whose birth story, as I have shown, Clorinda mirrors. (Tasso drops the mother's name in the *Conquistata*.) Armida, like Clorinda, is "monstrous," and explicitly described as such, as in her celebrated Medusan transformation in front of Rinaldo: "ma colei si trasmuta (oh novi mostri!),"

89. Lynda Boose, "The Getting of a 'Lawful Race': Racial Discourse in Early Modern England and the Unrepresentable Black Woman," in *Women, 'Race,' and Writing in the Early Modern Period*, ed. Margo Hendricks and Patricia Parker (New York: Routledge, 1994), 35–54. Boose refers to England, but the same could be argued about Italy.

90. For some critics it is unclear whether the mother dies or simply swoons. For the monster as scapegoat, see René Girard, *Violence and the Sacred* (Baltimore: Johns Hopkins University Press, 1977), 143–68.

91. Erminia, the other major female figure in the *Liberata*, has a mother who dies just before the action begins. She is, therefore, newly orphaned (6.59).

(18.35; "she is transformed [oh, new monstrosities!]"). For both women, conversion to Christianity is the way out of monstrosity. Armida will turn into a maternal and disempowered Virgin Mary at the end (" 'Ecco l'ancilla tua; d'essa a tuo senno / dispon,' gli disse 'e le fia legge il cenno,' " "Behold your handmaid; dispose of her at your discretion [she said], and your command shall be her law"; 20.136); as for Clorinda, having abjected her mother for good, she is made to embrace the symbolic order by asking for baptism. In finding the One, the Law, and the no longer "incertus" father, she also ceases to be monstrous, because it was said that Ethiopians were monstrous only until civilized by religion.

To be sure, Clorinda is unaware that she has lost her mother and thus cannot restage this loss through self-victimization or even by adopting a melancholic attitude as a way of retaining her identification with the lost object of love.[92] The only mother she wishes to claim is not her birth mother, Tasso makes her tell Arsete, but the social mother who gave her milk and faith at the same time. Arsete, a eunuch, a man-made not-man, cannot function as a mother (or a father, for that matter) because he is unable to either feed Clorinda or save her from drowning, although he can cry abundantly for her. He is therefore incapable of being protective in the two places that are most connected to the maternal in these octaves: the woods and the whirling waters. On the first occasion, the maternal womb comes close to becoming a tomb for Clorinda, as a tiger appears from nowhere and Arsete abandons her. The animal turns into an unexpected savior and feeds the baby (12.31).[93] On the second occasion, a father

92. But on the personal level such was Tasso's response to the loss of his mother, Porzia, when he had to leave her at nine. For a reading of this autobiographical event inscribed in the poem "Canzone al Metauro," see Juliana Schiesari, "The Victim's Discourse: Torquato Tasso's 'Canzone al Metauro,' " *Stanford Italian Review* 5 (1985): 189–203. See also her *The Gendering of Melancholia: Feminism, Psychoanalysis, and the Symbolics of Loss in Renaissance Literature* (Ithaca: Cornell University Press, 1992). Margaret Ferguson writes that Clorinda could be associated to Tasso's mother, she too lost "in part on the 'confusion' of his father's political career." See *Trials of Desire: Renaissance Defenses of Poetry* (New Haven: Yale University Press, 1983), 62.

93. Tasso too in "Canzone al Metauro" went back to the woods for maternal protection, to a tall oak tree inside which he hoped to hide. See Solerti, *Le rime*, 3:104–5. Tigers are animals with strong maternal connotations, but when Armida attempts to define Rinaldo as monstrous, she accuses him of having been fed by tigers: "e le mamme allattar di tigre ircana" (16.57). Goffredo too, when he shows himself unmoved by Armida, gets the same

figure, Saint George, substitutes for the ineffective Arsete and makes the water keep the toddler afloat. Clorinda is at this point sixteen months old and starting to talk ("tu con lingua di latte anco snodavi / voci indistinte," "You with your baby speech were as yet pronouncing indistinct words"; 12.32).

Entry into language is entry into desire, and therefore into lack. Thus, at the moment of symbolic castration, which marks the male or female's first coming to terms with lack, a paternal figure saves a female child from being lost in maternal flux. That this figure stands for the law is clear; and it is because he is not seen but heard in a later dream in which he is cast as a warrior, a sword in his hand, that Saint George in fact becomes the phallus.[94] The subsequent ushering in of the Oedipus complex, in which the female child identifies with the mother and takes the father as a love object (Freud's argument in "Femininity"), does not lead Clorinda, who never had a chance to experience more than passing unity with her mother or even to register the other's self-devaluation, to assume the other's lack and thus experience melancholia.[95]

Instead, Tasso makes Clorinda incorporate the pre-Oedipal mother and feel no real attachment to any parent. Bound to no law, Clorinda makes her own laws. Born as doubly lacking and cast away because of her nonmarking mark— the absence of an identifying skin color that would give her an identity and an origin—she is slowly constructed into a character that lacks nothing. To play with this illusion, which is fundamental to her fictional being, Clorinda is given a monstrous mask for herself and is made to challenge aggressively every purported enemy. Her inability to acknowledge the other without immediately

---

treatment from his companions: "ben fu rabbiosa a lui nutrice" (4.77). Animal milk was considered unhealthy for babies; moreover, it was inappropriate, since there could be some beastly transmigrations from the animal to the human being.

94. As Kaja Silverman remarks on the male voice-over in film, "We could say that the male subject finds his most ideal realization when he is heard but not seen; when the body . . . drops away, leaving the phallus in unchallenged possession of the scene. Thus, . . . the disembodied voice can be seen as 'exemplary' for male subjectivity, attesting to an achieved invisibility, omniscience, and discursive power." See *The Acoustic Mirror: The Female Voice in Psychoanalysis and Cinema* (Bloomington: Indiana University Press, 1988), 163–64.

95. Sigmund Freud, "Femininity," SE 22 (1964), 112–35. In the *Liberata*, the mother (but not the daughter) seems to personify the melancholic subject as described by Freud: "The patient represents [her] ego to us as worthless, incapable of any achievement and morally despicable; [she] reproaches [herself], vilifies [herself] and expects to be cast out and punished." See "Mourning and Melancholia," SE 14 (1957), 242–58, at 246.

wanting to cancel him out to prove that she does not lack (does not need any-body) and her description as tall and impenetrable, constantly seen from below, towerlike, make clear that Tasso wants to show her as self-centered.[96] Clorinda kills and wounds, especially aiming, it seems, at father figures. Since the father she knows, Arsete, is hardly a figure of desire, rather than loving the father, as in the classic version of the passage through Oedipus, Clorinda is made to want to "be" the father, hence her masculine behavior.

The manly mask she constructs for her body ("vincesti il sesso e la natura assai," "in palestra indurò i membri," "allenogli al corso"), the trenchant word that defines her ("feroce"), and the boastful and insulting ways with which Clo-rinda is made to address her enemies are ways intended to dominate "the identi-fications through which refusals of love are resolved," as Lacan suggests in "The Meaning of the Phallus."[97] Unloved, Clorinda is unloving; unsure of her origins, she is made to refuse all possible lineage, African or other. In fact, she enters the narrative as Persian: "Viene or costei da le contrade perse" (2.41; "She is come now from the Persian regions").[98] Not surprisingly, it is only in the con-text of Christianity that Clorinda will appear feminine and beautiful, that is, after death. As Saracen, she is other, strange, nonwomanly, and linked mostly to animals.[99]

96. On Clorinda's linkage with towers, see Georges Güntert, *L'epos dell'ideologia regnante e il romanzo delle passioni: Saggio sulla Gerusalemme liberata* (Pisa: Pacini, 1989), 150–52. Elisa-beth Bellamy has suggested that what Tancredi loves in Clorinda is not her feminine side, but her aggressive one, because it better reflects his narcissistic investment in himself. See *Translations of Power: Narcissism and the Unconscious in Epic History* (Ithaca: Cornell University Press, 1992), 160.

97. Jacques Lacan, "The Meaning of the Phallus," in *Feminine Sexuality: Jacques Lacan and the Ecole Freudienne*, ed. Juliet Mitchell and Jacqueline Rose (New York: Norton, 1982), 74–85.

98. According to Taviani, Asia was for Tasso a disturbance ("perturbamento") of gender, nature, race, nationality, and parentage: "Sembra, infatti, che Tasso associasse all'Asia l'idea di una fragile armonia di principi opposti: una delicatezza guerriera, una femminilità feroce, un turbamento della natura, della razza. La perdita d'una sicura appartenenza a un paese, ad un sesso ed a una casa." See Ferdinando Taviani, "Bella d'Asia: Torquato Tasso, gli attori e l'immortalità," *Paragone* 408–10 (1984): 5–76, esp. 55.

99. In chivalric romances, the Christian hero is traditionally handsome, while the pagan, his specular other, is ugly; if a pagan hero happens to be handsome, he either is made Chris-tian (as Ruggiero and Marfisa in the *Furioso*) or is killed, since his handsomeness is out of place. This will be Clorinda's fate. See Hans Robert Jauss, "Giustificazione del brutto," in

Thus Tasso's imposing of Christianity on Clorinda — which he frames as her own request to Tancredi — can be read as a way of belonging, a thirst for legitimization. This desire to have an authorized, legitimate self is endemic in the author. Feeling often, in some way, an outcast, Tasso displayed it in his own repeated requests to have the theological apparatus of the *Liberata* checked by the Inquisitors; even more clearly he showed it in his autobiographical work, such as "O magnanimo figlio" in which he asked the father as ruler, Duke Alfonso as symbolic father, to protect and author(ize) him. Like Tasso, Clorinda too is made to look at the end for paternal authorization. Julia Kristeva describes this desire, which could hardly be labeled as feminine, in a stream-of-consciousness style: "The impossibility of existing without repeated legitimation (without books, map, family). Impossibility — depressing possibility — of 'transgression.' . . . Or this murmur of emptiness, this open wound in my heart which means that I exist only in purgatory. I desire the law. And since it is not made for me alone, I run the risk of desiring outside the law."[100]

For Clorinda, desiring outside the law ends the moment she wears her new black armor, which substitutes the white one stolen by Erminia. Her black armor does not embody for me her self-destructive ways and loss of identity, to reread Sergio Zatti, but precisely her discovery of an identity — Clorinda as black Ethiopian princess — that proves her own only the moment that she is bound to lose her life.[101] Since this is an identity that denies the one constructed previously, the Clorinda who came into the epic by declaring her name (" 'Io son Clorinda': disse 'hai forse intesa talor nomarmi,' " "I am Clorinda [she said]: you have perhaps heard my name some time"; 2.46) can only exit it by refusing to give herself an origin ("Indarno chiedi / quel ch'ho per uso di non far palese," "Vainly you ask what I by custom do not make known; 12.61). In the passage from Clorinda the foundling to Clorinda the docile Christian, a father is found, and a daughter is finally recognized and welcomed "home."

Alterità e modernità della letteratura medievale (Turin: Bollati Beringhieri, 1989), 285. Even as a Saracen, in any case, Clorinda is other: too magnanimous, for example, if we consider the behavior of her companions, Argante and Solimano, and too chivalric.

100. Julia Kristeva, "Stabat Mater," in *The Female Body in Western Culture: Contemporary Perspectives*, ed. Susan Rubin Suleiman (Cambridge: Harvard University Press, 1986), 99–118, 109.

101. Sergio Zatti, *L'uniforme cristiano e il multiforme pagano: Saggio sulla Gerusalemme liberata* (Milan: Saggiatore, 1983), 111.

As for Tancredi, Tasso's choice of keeping him enthralled in a vision of Clorinda as the sublime, impossible object of his desire is fraught with problems because if, on the one hand, it allows him to have her the only way he can—in fantasy—on the other, it makes him lose his place in the order of the epic. This place will be filled now by his fellow knight Rinaldo, who, having accepted the losses of the real through the usual diminishment/renunciation of woman after his departure from Armida, is ready to become the true hero of the *Liberata* and true follower of the other father, the earthly, but no less serene, and no less *certus*, Goffredo.

CHAPTER 4

The Masquerade of Masculinity:

Erotomania in Ariosto's

Orlando furioso

Mirror, mirror on the wall,
Who's the fairest of them all?
—J. GRIMM, "Snow White"

Madamina, il catalogo è questo
Delle belle che amò il padron mio,
Un catalogo egli è che ho fatt'io,
Osservate, leggete con me.
—L. PONTE, *Don Giovanni*

Stories are written to be read.[1] So what do we make of an author who urges his readers to skip the very tale he is proposing for their attention in canto 28? "Donne, e voi che le donne avete in pregio," Ludovico Ariosto pleads in *Orlando furioso,*

> per Dio, non date a questa istoria orecchia,
> a questa che l'ostier dire in dispregio
> e in vostra infamia e biasmo s'apparecchia; . . .
> . . . Lasciate questo canto, che senza esso
> può star l'istoria e non sarà men chiara. (28.1–2)

> Ladies — and ladies' devotees — by all means disregard this tale which the innkeeper is preparing to relate to the disparagement, to the ignominy and censure of your sex. . . . Skip this canto: it is not essential — my story is no less clear without it.[2]

To be sure, such modesty is often employed as a device: in *Metamorphoses* 10, Ovid uses the same tactics before he embarks on the story of Mirrha:

> Terrible my tale will be!
> Away, daughters! Away, parents! Away!
> Or, if my singing charms you, hold this tale
> In disbelief; suppose the deed not done;
> Or, with belief, believe the punishment.[3]

Ovid had some ethical reasons for his warning, since Mirrha's tale is one of incest and unlawful daughterly desire. But what Ariosto is planning to retell, almost two-thirds of the way through his chivalric romance, is a bawdy story of male sexual prowess, one that his readers would hardly find culturally demanding or difficult to condone. In fact, he did not even invent his subject matter, for this

---

1. An earlier version of this chapter, titled "The Masquerade of Masculinity: Astolfo and Jocondo in *Orlando furioso,* Canto 28," appeared in *Renaissance Transactions: Ariosto and Tasso,* ed. Valeria Finucci (Durham, N.C.: Duke University Press, 1999), 215–45.

2. Ludovico Ariosto, *Orlando furioso,* ed. Marcello Turchi (Milan: Garzanti, 1978). Numbers refer to book and octave. English translation by Guido Waldman in *Orlando furioso* (Oxford: Oxford University Press, 1983).

3. Ovid, *Metamorphoses,* trans A. D. Melville (Oxford: Oxford University Press, 1986).

novella had been widely circulated in print, under the title "Historia del re di Pavia."[4] That Ariosto included this authorial disclaimer for reasons of morality appears unlikely.

Could this repudiation then constitute a rhetorical ruse, one that Ariosto— often accused of being logorrheic—might have invented to tantalize his readers? The convoluted plot of love and war, which constitutes the main thrust of *Orlando furioso* (first published in 1516, revised in 1521, with six additional cantos added in 1532), is spiced here and there with set pieces from the novella tradition. Some of these pieces are ribald, others are not; but salaciousness is not usually a trigger for authorial restraint. It may well be that Ariosto knew that the best way to catch his readers' attention was to advise them to pass over what he was writing. One has simply to recall how successful, narratively speaking, this and other frustrating interruptions of action in the text are to realize that he knows how to create suspense in preparation for a climactic ending.[5]

To take Ariosto at his word—and his argument makes him an advocate of women's rights *ante literam*—the tale of King Astolfo and of the nobleman Jocondo is not worth reading because women do not fare well in it. Ariosto then rushes to offer the one reason he is constrained to include such a story in his *Furioso*: it is there for its historicity, because the piece comes to him from his master, Turpino, whose (questionable) authority guarantees the "truthfulness" of his other sources, at least in matters of war. But finding the novella politically incorrect for his mixed audience, he distances himself from its ostensible

4. See Marina Beer, *Romanzi di cavalleria: Il Furioso e il romanzo italiano del primo Cinquecento* (Rome: Bulzoni, 1987), 239 and 255 n. 86. Ariosto's novella constitutes the core of Giovanni Sercambi's "De ingenio mulieris adultera" and displays an array of Boccaccian elements that the audience of the time might have easily recalled. For connections with Boccaccio, see Pio Rajna, *Le fonti dell'Orlando Furioso* (Florence: Sansoni, 1900), 36–55; and Giorgio Barbirato, "Elementi decameroniani in alcune novelle ariostesche," *Studi sul Boccaccio* 16 (1987): 329–60, esp. 331. Barbirato retraces points in common with the *Decameron*'s stories of King Agilulf, 3.2; Madonna Filippa, 6.7; and Pinuccio, 9.6. This novella also bears an intriguing resemblance to the frame story of *One Thousand and One Nights*, where Shahryar and his brother decide to have the women they enjoyed during the night killed at dawn. To avoid such a fate Scheherazade spins her one thousand and one tales. See Aldo Scaglione, "Shahryar, Giocondo, Koterviky: Three Versions of the Motif of the Faithless Woman," *Oriens* 11 (1958): 151–61.

5. For a reading of this rhetorical tactic, see Daniel Javitch, "*Cantus Interruptus* in the *Orlando Furioso*," *Modern Language Notes* 95 (1980): 66–80.

narrator, an innkeeper. This narrator, however—himself a new historicist *ante literam*—knows how to avoid being dismissed: his story is true, he claims, and his source is the nobleman Gian Francesco Valerio, a historical figure of Ariosto's time.[6] Whether the novella recounts actual events or not is beside the point, for even at his most cogent moments Ariosto is unreliable; as for the innkeeper, he gives his story about women's inconstancy and sexual hunger a misogynistic spin because he needs to entertain an irascible knight, the Saracen Rodomonte. Rodomonte has hated women ever since he was scorned by his fiancée, Doralice; he had seized the occasion for a lengthy, vituperative curse on the female sex just a few octaves earlier (27.117–21).

Before offering my own hypothesis on Ariosto's motives for his disclaimer, let me summarize the novella. In two key details Ariosto revises the tale of the Lombard king who travels from country to country following his discovery of the queen's infidelity: he adds the theme of King Astolfo's handsomeness and accompanying narcissism, which seems out of place in an account of men cuckolded by women, and he shrinks the entourage of traveling companions to one, Jocondo. The story begins with the presentation of Astolfo as the most handsome man in the world: "fu ne la giovinezza sua sì bello, / che mai poch'altri giunsero a quel segno" (28.4; "[he] was so handsome in his youth that seldom had anyone matched him for beauty"). When, in this masculine version of the "Snow White" fairy tale, the king is told that there is a better looking man than himself residing in Rome, he summons the rival, Jocondo, to his court to see if the claim is true. He is warned, however, that his invitation may be refused, for this knight is too much in love with his wife ever to leave her. Eventually Jocondo undertakes the journey to Lombardy, but he has immediate reasons to regret this decision: turning back to retrieve a neck chain given him by his wife as a good-bye present and pledge of faithfulness, he finds her in bed with a stable boy. Needless to say, by the time he arrives in Pavia his vaunted beauty is lost. It takes some time for Jocondo to discover a way out of his melancholic moroseness and become once more true to his name. The occasion that affords him this recovery is the chance witnessing through a hole in the wall of King Astolfo's wife, dallying with a dwarf. Feeling equal or even superior to the king now, for at least his own wife had the decency to choose a better-looking man

6. In the 1516 and 1521 versions of *Orlando furioso* there is an octave in which the innkeeper asserts that his story is true. See *Orlando furioso*, ed. Filippo Ermini, 3 vols. (Rome: Società Filologica Romana, 1911), 2:26.75.

with whom to commit adultery, he divulges the matter to Astolfo. Since the king had promised not to harm the queen, no matter what was revealed about her, the two men decide to take their anger elsewhere.[7] They leave Lombardy on a winding journey across Europe with the avowed purpose of inflicting on one thousand men what has been inflicted on them. This task turns out to be easy, since no woman resists their sexual advances, whether because of their handsomeness or because of the money they generously bestow.

Pleasure soon disappears from this arrangement, however, because the repetitive nature of their enterprise and the need to continuously exercise their prowess make a chore of what started out as a sexual adventure: when every desire is satisfied, what is the point of desiring more? To curtail this useless libidinal expenditure, the two friends resort to a new arrangement. They buy a young Spanish woman, Fiammetta, from her father and pledge to share her sexually on an equal basis on the understanding that a woman may remain faithful if two men, rather than one, take turns in satisfying her.[8] But even this movement from polygyny to polyandry proves inadequate, failing as it does to take into account female agency: one night Fiammetta, exercising for the first time her desire to desire, to give the story a female-friendly reading—or, to give it a misogynistic one, letting her own sexual hunger dictate her actions, as do all the women in our novella—allows a former acquaintance, a Greek, to make love to her while she lies in bed between her two owners. Astolfo and Jocondo will take no more: acknowledging that women have minds and sexual needs of their own, they choose monogamy and return to their wives. "Così fan tutte!"

No wonder that this novella, with its abundance of erotic offerings, touched a nerve in people's imagination. Among the many set pieces of the *Furioso*, the story of Astolfo and Jocondo was the most successful from the very beginning: influential imitations were written not only in Italy but also in France (by Jean de La Fontaine) and Spain (by Maria de Zayas and the picaresque writers);

7. In cantos 42–43, in a similar story of a wife's betrayal, the reaction is more primitive: when Anselmo is told of his wife's unfaithfulness, he decides to kill her, although he eventually changes his mind.

8. Unfortunately, even though Astolfo and Jocondo's sexual record is nothing short of outstanding (including the Spanish girl Fiammetta and their wives, they seduce one thousand and three women), they are still unable to match the record set by Da Ponte and Mozart's Don Giovanni, who reached the same number in Spain alone ("e in Spagna son già mille e tre").

even today it stands among the best Renaissance novellas.[9] True, better than the main storyline, the novellas could nonchalantly offer some sexual *frisson* or give a polemical reading of gender frictions, thanks in part to their "disposable" nature: for, since the protagonists were not the main ones, Ariosto could eliminate—with no apparent damage to the structure of his work—whatever proved too controversial during readings at court. But I would prefer to link the success of this story to the obsession with erotica that swept Italy during the first half of the sixteenth century and reached its apex in the middle 1520s. The papal court itself under Alexander VI and Leo X was a notoriously licentious place. The publication of Pietro Aretino's *I sedici modi* (*The Sixteen Ways*), which coupled Giulio Romano's illustrations of human sexual acrobatics and Aretino's verbal nimbleness, took place in 1524; and painfully hilarious treatises on the goodness of prostitution, such as Aretino's *Ragionamenti* (1534), come out of the same obsession. Titian's *Venus of Urbino*, the great masterpiece of erotic painting (1538), was still to be executed of course, yet its commission, made years earlier, was fostered by the contemporary interest in the representation of the nude and eroticized body.[10] Voyeuristic and virtuosistic sex, in short—narrated, versified, played, or illustrated—sold.

The moral of the Astolfo and Jocondo story is that it is pointless for men to try to keep up with the desires of sex-crazed females.[11] By renouncing all women in the end, our two men seem to suggest that the reason for cuckoldry is not

9. See, for example, Marziano Guglielminetti, "Introduzione," in *Novellieri del Cinquecento*, ed. Marziano Guglielminetti (Milan: Ricciardi, 1972), 14. On Ariosto's embedded novellas, see Antonio Franceschetti, "La novella nei poemi del Boiardo e dell'Ariosto," in *La novella italiana: Atti del convegno di Caprarola, 14-24 sett. 1988*, ed. Enrico Malato (Rome: Salerno, 1989), 805-41.

10. Another contemporary case of illustrated erotics is Jacopo Caraglio's text, *The Loves of the God*, which, like Aretino's *Modi*, used an apparatus of verses. On "Venus" and eroticism in art, see Mary Pardo, "Artifice as Seduction in Titian," in *Sexuality and Gender in Early Modern Europe: Institutions, Texts, Images*, ed. James Grantham Turner (Cambridge: Cambridge University Press, 1993), 55-89; and Carlo Ginzburg, "Tiziano, Ovidio e i codici della figurazione erotica nel '500," in *Tiziano e Venezia: Atti del convegno internazionale di studi*, ed. Carlo Ginzburg et al. (Vicenza: Neri Pozza, 1980), 125-35.

11. Barbirato argues that while men leave women for love in the *Furioso*, women leave men because they are moody (Doralice), oversexed (Gabrina), or greedy (Argia) ("Elementi decameroniani," 345-47). In short, women are incapable of true love and keep their own interests in mind at all times.

that men are insufficiently potent, but that they somehow have been caught up in a definition of manhood that is linked, wrongly (as can be expected), to women's needs. No matter how often virility is staged, it must be endlessly restaged, they discover, when maleness is tied to a genital sexuality that requires women's faithfulness for confirmation of its adequacy. In this sense, the "wise" knight Rinaldo, with Orlando the most powerful Christian paladin, is right, unlike our two men, in refusing to learn whether his wife has been faithful:

> Ben sarebbe folle
> chi quel che non vorria trovar, cercasse.
> Mia donna è donna, ed ogni donna è molle:
> lascian star mia credenza come stasse. (43.6)

He would be an utter fool who sought for what he had no wish to find. My wife is a woman, and every woman is pliant. Let my faith remain undisturbed.

Whatever Rinaldo's preference, the story of Astolfo and Jocondo was understood and rewritten by a host of writers throughout Europe as the two men's Don Juanesque revenge for their wives' infidelity; the fact that the king and his companion break faith with the one thousand other women in the process never became a point of interest. Ariosto, as I mentioned, urges his readers to skip over this story because it disparages women. But I would like to propose a different reason for his disclaimer. What I read in canto 28 is not so much a sustained reflection on the perils for men of female sexuality but rather the perplexing working through of the notion that masculinity may be other than what it is made to stand for in culture, and that virility—notwithstanding the satyriasis displayed—does not *per se* guarantee male power. That this insight is embedded in the most unlikely setting for the questioning of masculinity, given the collection of "manly" acts breathlessly recorded in the story, may be less strange than it appears, for this chivalric epic probes, after all, the tattered illusions and phantasmic progresses of romances of old. And what a success the *Furioso* was at it: the text was an incredibly popular one, read, sung, recited, memorized, even staged throughout most of the sixteenth century, and with sales handily surpassing those of the Bible.[12]

---

12. For an account of the spectacular success of the *Furioso*, see Daniel Javitch, *Proclaiming a Classic: The Canonization of the Orlando Furioso* (Princeton: Princeton University Press, 1991),

Surprisingly, Ariosto portrays man in the Astolfo and Jocondo story as just as feminized and narcissistically centered on physical attributes as woman is traditionally made to be. In short, masculinity is a construct, a masquerade, a display, a performance, just like femininity.[13] It has often been said that the early modern period was obsessed with the notion of female promiscuity and the consequences that the lack of chastity among females had for men, given the then overriding preoccupation with issues of honor and the inheritance mechanisms in place.[14] By juxtaposing a plot centered on men's revenge for this penchant in women, a revenge that requires the display of some forms of macho sexuality, with a characterization of maleness that is constructed as shifting, Ariosto underscores the neurosis behind the cultural construction of masculinity as the defining trait of what a man is. I do not intend to link effeminacy directly with a discourse on homoeroticism, because for me effeminacy is central to any discourse on sexuality, be it heterosexual or homosexual. This is especially true when we focus on a period in which new, ideologically inflected definitions of

---

ch. 1; and Beer, *Romanzi di cavalleria*. Although Matteo Maria Boiardo's *Orlando innamorato*, of which the *Furioso* is a "continuation," was technically the first book published in Italian to reach beyond the rich and educated, only the *Furioso* sold by the thousands. For a reading of gender in the *Furioso*, see Valeria Finucci, *The Lady Vanishes: Subjectivity and Representation in Castiglione and Ariosto* (Stanford: Stanford University Press, 1992). See also Deanna Shemek, "Of Women, Knights, Arms, and Love: The *Querelle des Femmes* in Ariosto's Poem," *Modern Language Notes* 104 (1989): 68–97; Pamela Benson, *The Invention of the Renaissance Woman* (University Park: Penn State University Press, 1992); and John McLucas, "Ariosto and the Androgyne: Symmetries of Sex in the *Orlando Furioso*," Ph.D. diss., Yale University, 1983.

13. For femininity as a masquerade, see Jacques Lacan, "The Meaning of the Phallus," in *Feminine Sexuality: Jacques Lacan and the Ecole Freudienne*, ed. Juliet Mitchell and Jacqueline Rose (New York: Norton, 1982); and Joan Rivière, "Womanliness as a Masquerade," in *Formations of Fantasy*, ed. Victor Burgin, James Donald, and Cora Kaplan (London: Methuen, 1986), 35–44. For a companion piece to this essay, see the study of the masquerade of femininity played out in Ariosto's Dalinda and Gabrina episodes by Valeria Finucci, "The Masquerade of Femininity: Ariosto and the Game of Desire," in *Desire in the Renaissance: Psychoanalysis and Literature*, ed. Valeria Finucci and Regina Schwartz (Princeton: Princeton University Press, 1994), 65–85.

14. Though this concern is reflected in many stories of the *Furioso*, the compulsive examination of sexual indiscretions and paranoid fears of cuckoldry better fits, I think, another genre, theater, and is associated with such names as Machiavelli, Bibbiena, and Aretino, as well as Ariosto. For the case of Machiavelli, see chapter 2; for that of Bibbiena, see chapter 5.

male subjectivity were being explored and when what constituted socially legible homosexual behavior is different from our contemporary view.[15] At the same time, I do not read effeminacy as a sure sign of disorder and demise of the Law of the Father. A feminized, or potentially unstable, masculinity should not be pathologized in an era in which male homosocial ties clearly had their place within a heterosocial/sexual symbolic. My tools in examining this story come mostly from psychoanalysis, because Freudian, and, to a lesser extent, Lacanian analyses allow me more fully, I hope, to probe the inner life of characters offered as ambiguous and to concentrate on their confused articulations of identity. I will also make use, as I have done throughout this book, of medical pronouncements on sexuality in the Renaissance.

The Compulsion to Repeat

Don Juan–style sexual gratification has dependably come across in culture as manly. But does the possession of hundreds of women make men heterosexual in their object choice? More to the point, are our two fetishists of the penis, Astolfo and Jocondo, more masculine because they dispense their sexual favors widely? Lacan suggests that this is hardly so: "virile display in the human being

15. Valerie Traub has argued for such delinking in the context of Shakesperean drama in *Desire and Anxiety: Circulations of Desire in Shakespearean Drama* (New York: Routledge, 1992), 136. See also the essays in *Queering the Renaissance*, ed. Jonathan Goldberg (Durham, N.C.: Duke University Press, 1994). In the popular view, Lombards were the people who most practiced and exported the crime of sodomy, as the Englishman, Sir Edward Coke (1552– 1634), complained: "*Bugeria* is an Italian word, . . . and it was complained of in parliament, that the Lumbards brought into the realm the shameful sin of sodomy, that it is not to be named, as there it is said." See *The Third Part of the Institutes of the Laws in England* (London: Brooke, 1797); and Ed Cohen, "Legislating the Norm: From Sodomy to Gross Indecency," *South Atlantic Quarterly* 88.1 (1989): 181–217, esp. 188. In the *Decameron*, Boccaccio makes the protagonist of his only transparently homosexual story, Pietro, a man from Lombardy. See Giovanni Boccaccio, *Decameron*, trans. Guido Waldman (Oxford: Oxford University Press, 1993), 5.1. But also keep in mind that, for Germans, sodomizers were specifically Florentines, not Lombards. See Michael Rocke, *Forbidden Friendships: Homosexuality and Male Culture in Renaissance Florence* (New York: Oxford University Press, 1996). Many in Europe, on the other hand, considered Venice the "depraved" city *par excellence* of the period, given its close ties to the East and its reception of unorthodox customs. See Guido Ruggiero, *The Boundaries of Eros: Sex Crime and Sexuality in Renaissance Venice* (New York: Oxford University Press, 1985).

itself appears as feminine."[16] In the early modern period, too, excessive sexual expenditure was linked to emasculation, because overconcentration on sexual, bodily matters showed lack of manly restraint and practicality, and thus made man resemble woman. A case in point is that of Antony, whose love for Cleopatra rendered him womanish in Shakespeare's play. In *Timaeus* Plato described sexual incontinence as a mental disease caused by the overflowing of the marrow, which then flooded the body (86d). Early modern medical treatises stressed the same principle: moderation made a man manly; too much or too little sex was unhealthy, turned the individual morose, was detrimental to the brain, and could lead to an early death. Lorenzo Gioberti recommended "to abstain from what, by consuming and taxing our natural moisture, quickly dissolves or dissipates our natural heat, such as excessive work, spices, staying up at night, worries, and diverse emotions, but above all, excessive carnal copulation, especially at improper times."[17] Men who used up too much seed, Aretaeus of Cappadocia wrote, "become old in constitution, torpid, relaxed, spiritless, timid, stupid, enfeebled, shriveled, inactive, pale, whitish, effeminate."[18] But also men who used too little seed experienced health problems like melancholia and nausea. Galen noticed that such was the case in a man who had abstained from sex after his wife died, and argued that retention of sperm in man's body is harmful, just as retention of menses is in a woman's.[19] Other doctors routinely prescribed therapeutic intercourse to avoid psychosomatic problems, even weight loss, although the Church disagreed with the practice by prohibiting as early as 1215 at the Fourth Lateran Council fornication for pseudomedical purposes.[20] Temperate passions alone were healthful, Benedetto Reguardati wrote, since

> for the preservation of health we should strive most resolutely for moderate pleasures and for gladdening solaces, so that as much as possible we may live happily in temperate gaiety. That condition expands the *spiritus*

16. See Lacan, "The Meaning of the Phallus," 85.

17. Lorenzo Gioberti, *La prima parte de gli errori popolari* (Florence: Giunta, 1592). The English translation from the original French text, *Erreurs populaires*, is by Gregory David de Rocher, in *Popular Errors* (Tuscaloosa: University of Alabama Press, 1989), 42.

18. Cited in E. F. Hirsch, "A Historical Survey of Gonorrhea," *Annuals of Medical History* 2 (1930): 416.

19. Galen, *On the Affected Parts*, trans. Rudolph E. Siegel (New York: Karger, 1976), 6.5.

20. See Danielle Jacquart and Claude Thomasset, *Sexuality and Medicine in the Middle Ages*, trans. Matthew Adamson (Princeton: Princeton University Press, 1988), 196.

and natural heat to the outer parts of the body and makes the blood purer; it sharpens one's wit and makes the understanding more capable; it promotes a healthy complexion and a pleasing appearance; it stimulates the energies throughout the whole body and makes them more vigorous in their activity.[21]

Even erotic manuals tended to emphasize the quality, variety, originality, and theatricality of the heterosexual encounter, not repetition.[22]

Ariosto has Astolfo and Jocondo start their debauching errantry not because they are sexually unfulfilled or wanton themselves but because they want to cuckold other men for the sake of reestablishing some sexual worth for themselves after their respective conjugal betrayals. Thus their motive for hypersexuality is political. The mistake of conflating penis and phallus, however, makes these two friends forget where power lies; as a result, their journey toward the consolations of romance is full of pitfalls, founded as it is on the vagaries of sex: not sex as suicide, as in the case of Callimaco in Machiavelli's *La mandragola*, not sex as self-discovery, as we will see in Bibbiena's *La calandria*, but sex as social competition. Astolfo and Jocondo's search is also misplaced because their aim is to recoup a loss brought upon them by their wives. But this loss exists only in their unconscious—their sexual misadventure at home undermined their feelings of wholeness and narcissistic omnipotence—because they never truly possessed what they now mourn as lost.

This journey into sexual one-upmanship reveals more homoerotic frisson than heterosexual curiosity, a fact that is evident not only when Astolfo and Jo-

---

21. Benedetto Reguardati (Benedetto da Norcia), *Pulcherrimum et utilissimum opus ad sanitatis conservationem* (1477), in Glending Olson, *Literature as Recreation in the Later Middle Ages* (Ithaca: Cornell University Press, 1982), 50. On the advantages of a regulated life, see also Alvise Cornaro (1475-1566), *Trattato de la vita sobria: Elogi e lettere*, a popular, often reprinted book on longevity, which he wrote at seventy, now available in *Scritti sulla vita sobria*, ed. Marisa Milani (1588; Venice: Corbo e Fiore, 1983), 75-105. For reasons given in late ancient times against indulgence and in favor of sexual control—the same reasons repeated more or less in the early modern period—see Dale Martin, "Contradictions of Masculinity: Ascetic Inseminators and Menstruating Men in Greco-Roman Culture," in *Generation and Degeneration: Tropes of Reproduction in Literature and History from Antiquity to Early Modern Europe*, ed. Valeria Finucci and Kevin Brownlee (Durham, N.C.: Duke University Press, 2001), 81-108.

22. See, for example, Pietro Aretino (1492-1556), *Sonetti lussuriosi (I modi) e Dubbi amorosi* (Milan: Newton, 1993).

condo competitively share more or less the same women in sequence, but also when they perversely require one female to lie in bed between them, in a triangulation of desire à la Girard, so that each is present when the other is sexually engaged.[23] Their agenda is homosocial rather than sexual; it is directed at men and addresses male fears about sexual inadequacy. But it has nothing to do with women, whose only task is to provide the body. In this sense I would like to revise the formulation posited originally by Eve Kosofsky Sedgwick, in which homosociality is presented to prevent homosexuality.[24] In my view, this homosocial state of being does not necessarily exclude homoeroticism. Thus the apparently heterosexual triangle with Fiammetta somehow enacts the Freudian insight that in triangular situations a man can sublimate his feelings for another man by claiming that he does not love him, for she is the one who ostensibly does.

Central to this male/male sharing is the circulation and exchange of women, who are bought, used, and then released for further sexual consumption. No actual female face or name is supplied to the reader in this story, apart from Fiammetta's, since the point for Astolfo and Jocondo is not to think of any woman as a subject, but to act out an exhibitionistic need to be seen by other men as manly through the possession of their anonymous wives. Hypermasculinity is a masquerade theatrically staged for the sake of other men; what drives our two companions is after all collectomania, not erotomania. As Luce Irigaray argues, "reigning everywhere, although prohibited in practice, hom(m)osexuality is played out through the bodies of women, matter, or sign, and heterosexuality has been up to now just an alibi for the smooth workings of man's relation with himself, of relations among men."[25] Even the two men's final settling on the prostitute Fiammetta confirms that the prostitute has worth precisely because she has been used, that is, she has been thoroughly objectified and rendered passively available.[26] As the narrator explains, Fiammetta is chosen because it is

---

23. See René Girard, *Deceit, Desire and the Novel: Self and Other in Literary Structure*, trans. Yvonne Freccero (Baltimore: Johns Hopkins University Press, 1965).

24. See Eve Kosofsky Sedgwick, *Between Men: English Literature and Male Homosocial Desire* (New York: Columbia University Press, 1985).

25. Luce Irigaray, *This Sex Which Is Not One*, trans. Catherine Porter (Ithaca: Cornell University Press, 1985), 172.

26. "The more it [the body] has served," Irigaray writes, "the more it is worth. Not because its natural assets have been put to use their way, but, on the contrary, because its nature

easy to have her, for she provides the "furnace" in which to satisfy unproblematic sexual needs:

Pigliano la fanciulla, e piacer n'hanno
or l'un or l'altro in caritade e in pace,
come a vicenda i mantici che danno,
or l'uno or l'altro fiato alla fornace. (28.54)

[They] took their pleasure with her in turns, in peace and charity, like two bellows each blowing alternately upon the furnace.[27]

The ambiguous masculinity of Astolfo and Jocondo is not all that undermines the prevalent reading of this story as one of male hyperbolic sexual prowess, for Ariosto adds a trait to his characterization of the two men that does not usually sit well with hypermanhood: male beauty. If beauty is what turns women into objects of desire, why would an author strip men of their customary position of power as subjects and emphasize a physical attribute that turns them into objects? And why write so fulsomely of male beauty in a story in which women seem to be taken the least by the handsomeness of their counterparts? But here is how Astolfo is introduced by the innkeeper:

Bello era, ed a ciascun così parea:
ma di molto egli ancor più si tenea.
        Non stimava egli tanto per l'altezza
del grado suo, d'avere ognun minore;
né tanto, che di genti e di ricchezza,
di tutti i re vicini era il maggiore;
quanto che di presenza e di bellezza
avea per tutto 'l mondo il primo onore. (28.5)

Yes, he was handsome, and everyone recognized it, but he was far and away his own greatest admirer for this. He valued less the eminence of his station, which set him over everybody else; or the magnitude of his wealth

---

has been 'used up,' and has become once again no more than a vehicle for relations among men" (186).

27. On the choice of Fiammetta because of the "comodità" she offers, see Giorgio Barberi-Squarotti, *Prospettive sul Furioso* (Turin: Tirrenia, 1988), 41.

and nation, which made him greater than all the neighbouring kings; what he valued most of all was the pre-eminence he enjoyed throughout the world for his beautiful physique.

Although the issue of male handsomeness has not been tackled with the frequency with which female beauty has been on a variety of fronts in the early modern period, Vitruvian parameters of ideal proportions did indeed center on the male body. Unlike female beauty, which was associated with ornaments, following a more or less standard Petrarchan catalogue of parts, male beauty was linked to measurements. Moreover, given that beauty is the good of all exertions on the part, say, of the visual artist, and culturally and biologically the male body was considered more functionally perfect than the female, the artist, it was thought, could realize the perfect idea of beauty precisely by representing the male body.[28] Even treatises dedicated solely to women, such as Agnolo Firenzuola's *On the Beauty of Women* (*Discorsi delle bellezze delle donne*), made clear that female and male beauty are complementary: every woman should have something of the male in her and vice versa.[29]

For the Neoplatonists male handsomeness was of course a visualization of inner virtues: good external features were thought to reflect an internal moral goodness, or, as Bembo states in Baldassarre Castiglione's *Il libro del cortegiano*, the handsome are good ("e li belli boni").[30] In this sense, Astolfo would, by virtue of being handsome, be a better king than most, and Jocondo, a good nobleman. But such is hardly the case: Astolfo gives little thought to political matters and even leaves his kingdom unattended for reasons that are hardly pressing; and Jocondo proves incapable of or uninterested in improving his father's fortune ("la roba di che 'l padre il lasciò erede, / nè mai cresciuta avea nè minuita," "the inheritance bequeathed him by his father had neither grown nor shrunk in

28. See, for example, how Benedetto Varchi works through this concept in Michelangelo's art in *Il libro della beltà e grazia* (published in the 1540s but written earlier), in *Trattati d'arte del Cinquecento*, ed. Paolo Barcchi (Bari: Laterza, 1960–62).

29. Agnolo Firenzuola, *On the Beauty of Women*, ed. and trans. Konrad Eisenbichler and Jacqueline Murray (1541; Philadelphia: University of Pennsylvania Press, 1992).

30. Baldassarre Castiglione, *Il libro del cortegiano*, ed. Ettore Bonora (Milan: Mursia, 1984), 4:58. On this connection, see Eric Haywood, "Would You Believe It? A Tall Story from Ariosto," in *Italian Storytellers: Essays on Italian Narrative Literature*, ed. Eric Haywood and Cormac O'Cuilleanain (Dublin: Irish Academy Press, 1989), 113–49, esp. 131.

value"; 28.9). Both men, in fact, although born into a position of wealth, power, and authority, are described as emasculated on these fronts; their masculinity in this respect is given as problematic as if to parallel some hypothesized disarray of the paternal function.[31] Politically speaking, the two men would then reflect the historical failure of contemporary Italian princes and dukes to further a nation-building process, a goal that eluded Italy for centuries to come. This inability, Machiavelli teaches, had its roots in the opportunism, disinterest, and narcissism of those in charge: real-life, mindless, self-centered, unproductive, and ungenerative Astolfo figures.

Let me note that the politics of spectatorship are not necessarily the same when handsome men, rather than women, are displayed. Astolfo might have been a worthy subject for a painting by Apelles and Zeuxis, the narrator emphasizes. But the women that Zeuxis painted had their individualities canceled out in the representation, because Zeuxis seized whatever parts of five female bodies he saw as perfect and painted them to reflect his idea of a single beautiful woman as his mind constructed her.[32] Here, by contrast, Astolfo is shown as in control of his representation, as he lavishly praises the parts of his own body that are well formed: "essendosi lodato / or del bel viso o de la bella mano" ("[he] often flattered himself, one moment on his beautiful face, the next, on his exquisite hand"; 28.6). Earlier he had presented himself to his courtier Fausto as sure of his superior physique: "avendolo un giorno domandato / se mai veduto avea, presso e lontano, altro uom di forma così ben composto" (28.4; "he asked Fausto whether he had ever, anywhere, set eyes on a man as well built as himself"). Jocondo too, for his part, knows what he needs to improve his physical goods and acts on this knowledge, as when he orders rich clothes for himself before leaving Rome to meet Astolfo: "vesti fe' far per comparire adorno, / che talor cresce una beltà un bel manto" (28.12; "[he] ordered new clothing, to make

---

31. Compare this behavior to that of the emperor Augustus, who chose not to have sex for one year to show that he had the control needed in a ruler. See Martin, "Contradictions of Masculinity," in Finucci and Brownlee, *Generation and Degeneration*, 88.

32. For a reading of the Zeuxis story in these terms, see Castiglione, *Il libro del Cortegiano*, 1.52. See also Finucci, *The Lady Vanishes*, ch. 2. According to Pliny, Zeuxis's women were chosen following an intriguing scheme: first the most handsome men of Croton were identified, then their sisters were chosen. Thus male beauty prefigured and confirmed female beauty. I would like to thank Mary Pardo for reminding me of this connection.

his appearance suitably dressed—for a handsome cloak will enhance a man's looks").[33] Emphasis on handsomeness then is empowering and not objectifying when one is in charge of the representation.[34] In no instance, however, no matter how much masculinity is deessentialized, is the handsome male body directly appreciated by another man, for heterosexual boundaries must remain in place at all costs. Any unrepressed form of erotic contemplation would inevitably be understood as homosexually voyeuristic. Fausto, for one, although he listens politely, is unimpressed by Astolfo's body.

Of course, if beauty does not make men powerless, it makes them woman-ish. Interestingly, the feminization of men does not entail here, as is often the case, the masculinization of women, because the narrative's motor is erotics and not power. Femininity is cast as disruptive and at odds with social relations no matter who embodies it, woman or man. When men are represented as femi-nized, the apprehension that this gender-related anxiety generates is displaced onto the other sex, and the result is the representation of women as out of con-trol, devouring. Such a movement is clearly mapped in our tale. Women do not simply make love: their erotic pursuits make them betray their well-endowed husbands, choose lewd men, and forget all laws of decency and status-connected self-restraint. Jocondo's wife is unwilling to wait more than an hour after her husband's departure to betray him; the queen gives herself to a dwarf even after he rebuffs her. The two women's lovemaking is shown to have animal conno-tations: the first lover chosen is dirty; the second, grotesquely shortened. By contrast, Fiammetta is cast as less of a threat to the two men than their wives because she is unmarried and functions as a servant. Once it is settled that she will be equally shared, the level of erotic competition between the two men di-minishes, since she will—by contract—betray, but only with the other person in the triangle.

33. More than today, clothing stood for status and class in the sixteenth century. Sumptu-ous display was not necessarily linked to effeminacy, if done with taste and no garish excess. In the *Cortegiano*, for example, Castiglione spends considerable time examining the appropriate color, shape, and material of clothes befitting sophisticated courtiers on the rise.

34. Note, in this context, Mulvey's insights on pleasure in looking, where the visual rep-resentation of men stands for castration: "according to the principles of ruling ideology and the psychical structures that back it up, the male figure cannot bear the burden of sexual ob-jectification." See Laura Mulvey, *Visual and Other Pleasures* (Bloomington: Indiana University Press, 1989), 20.

The characterization of masculinity in this novella as problematic is further visualized through the rendering of the two men's narcissism, again a feature at odds in a story that apparently means to poke fun at women.[35] In "On Narcissism," Freud hypothesizes that the individual's route toward outgrowing narcissism is through outgrowing self-centeredness and loving another. Men give up their narcissism with time, but women, he argues, often retain it.[36] The men in our story have clearly not followed the path outlined above, despite their age. Astolfo and Jocondo have a specular relationship, in that each identifies with the other by desiring the same object. A characteristic of the narcissist is, notoriously, an exhibitionistic desire to be admired. Such is the case of Astolfo. He constitutes his own love object and, although married, not only loves himself alone, but even solicits admiration from his subjects — until he is told that there is another man as handsome as he. Rather than try to eliminate his rival, like the queen in "Snow White," he decides to check out the competition. His desire to see his purported double is partly a desire to dominate the other by the superiority of his physical attributes and partly a desire to recognize himself in the other. When he is reassured that Jocondo is not superior to him in beauty, he begins to "love" him because the other, handsome and of the same sex, constitutes his mirrored image.[37]

Although seemingly less narcissistically self-centered than Astolfo, Jocondo displays many of the same traits. I have already remarked on his desire for sartorial style. His love for his wife is narcissistic in that he finds gratification in seeing himself exclusively loved, in reflecting himself in the eye of an other from whom he dreads to be separated. He is so fused with her that he neglects his chivalric obligation to obey the king's command without question or delay. Like Astolfo,

35. Bellamy has called narcissism "the dominant neurosis of the *Furioso*." See Elizabeth Bellamy, *Translations of Power: Narcissims and the Unconscious in Epic History* (Ithaca: Cornell University Press, 1992), 87. For a study of female narcissism in the *Furioso*, see Finucci, *The Lady Vanishes*, ch. 4.

36. Sigmund Freud, "On Narcissism: An Introduction," *The Standard Edition of the Complete Psychological Works of Sigmund Freud*, ed. and trans. James Strachey, 24 vols. (London: Hogarth Press, 1953–74 [hereafter *SE*]) 14:69–102 (1957).

37. On the mirroring of the subject onto the object, see Mikkel Borch-Jacobsen, *The Freudian Subject*, trans. Catherine Porter (Stanford: Stanford University Press, 1988), 86.

he sees the other not as his alter ego but as his alterity. His wife functions more as a mother for him than the queen does for Astolfo, in that separation from her, because she is necessary for his selfhood and socialization, can only bring self-fragmentation and loss. This is why his narcissistic wound at discovering himself cuckolded is not only deeper than Astolfo's, but gets inscribed in his face, which loses its appeal:

> e la faccia, che dianzi era sì bella,
> si cangia sì, che più non sembra quella.
>> Par che gli occhi se ascondin ne la testa;
> cresciuto il naso par nel viso scarno;
> de la beltà sì poca gli ne resta,
> che ne potrà far paragone indarno. (28.26–27)

> His face, once so handsome, changed beyond recognition. His eyes seemed to have sunk into his head, his nose seemed bigger on his gaunt face; so little remained of his good looks that there was no further point in matching him with others.

The loss of facial beauty is a mask of hysteria, for disfigurement, Freud argues, can be the physical equivalent of "a slap in the face."[38]

Refusing to take vengeance first, Jocondo runs away from home, falls into melancholia, and withdraws from company. The melancholic state, often caused by an imbalance of humors, was frequently examined by early modern doctors who cured it prevalently with herbal potions such as infusions of rosemary and verbena. Arnaldus de Villanova highly recommended saffron wine to snap out of it.[39] Florian Canale preferred pills made of pimpernel, myrrh, aloes, saffron, and mandragora oil to "delay old age and hoary looks, make you merry and excite the intellect, cleanse the heart, stomach and intestines of all superfluities."[40] No

---

38. Sigmund Freud, "Medusa's Head," *SE* 18:273–74 (1955).

39. Arnaldus de Villanova (d. 1311), *De conservatione jouventutis et retardatione senectutis* (*The Conservation of Youth and Defense of Age*), trans. Jonas Drummond (1544; Woodstock, Vt.: Elm Tree Press, 1912).

40. Florian Canale (fl. 1612), *De' secreti universali raccolti, et esperimentati trattati nove. Ne' quali si hanno rimedii per tutta l'infermità de' corpi humani, come anco de' cavalli, bovi e cani. Con molti secreti appertinenti all'arte chemica, agricoltura, e caccie* (Brescia: Fontara, 1613); English translation in Piero Camporesi, *The Incorruptible Flesh: Bodily Mutation and Mortification in Religion and Folklore* (Cambridge: Cambridge University Press, 1988), 230.

cure is eventually necessary for Jocondo, because his problem is solved following his discovery of the queen's betrayal of her husband. In making Astolfo catch his wife *in flagrante delicto*, Jocondo finds himself vindicated, since the king is his superior and the queen shows herself to be anything but queenly in her sexual life. Having abjected the "mother" (the queen is a mother figure *par excellence*), he can now fully identify with an ideal phallic image, a substitutive paternal ego in the person of the king; Astolfo helps him regain a sense of fullness of the self.[41] Interestingly Jocondo recovers his beauty then and there:

Allegro torna e grasso e rubicondo,
che sembra un cherubin del paradiso;
che 'l re, il fratello, e tutta la famiglia
di tal mutazion si maraviglia. (28.39)

He became happy again, filled out, took on colour, looked once more like
a cherub from paradise — a transformation which astonished his brother
and the king and the entire household.

Such a turn of events, however, brings no end to the hysteria, which, in mimetic sympathy, now infects Astolfo. Hysteria appears in the figural rendering of the two men as constantly phallicized figures, their journey reduced to a series of erections as they give spur, through fantasies of omnipotence, to their narcissistic rage for having been "diminished":

Travestiti cercaro Italia, Francia,
le terre de' Fiamminghi e de l'Inglesi;
e quante ne vedean di bella guancia,
trovavan tutte ai prieghi lor cortesi.
Davano, e dato loro era la mancia;
e spesso rimetteano i denari spesi.
Da loro pregate foro molte, e foro
anch'altretante che pregaron loro. (28.48)

In disguise they scoured Italy, France, Flanders, and England, and as many
fair-cheeked ladies as they saw, they found responsive to their prayers.

41. For this movement from the abjected mother to the imaginary father, see Julia Kristeva, *Tales of Love*, trans. Leon Roudiez (New York: Columbia University Press, 1987), 41–42.

They would give money, and they would receive payments—indeed often they recovered their disbursements. Many ladies received their addresses, and as many more made advances to them.

Hysteria is evident in their choice of Fiammetta as a psychotic defense against their fear of being sexually upstaged by the other, so that she is made to exist as a welcoming vagina in a *ménage à trois*, on duty at all hours:

> sempre in mezzo a duo la notte giaccio
> e meco or l'uno or l'altro si trastulla,
> e sempre a l'un di lor mi trovo in braccio. (28.61)

> I always sleep between the two of them. There is always one or the other making love to me—I'm always in the arms of one of them.

That Ariosto makes Fiammetta throw the arrangement over in the end, allowing her to cast off a masochistic acceptance of the erotics of power in favor of a parodic sexual *presa di coscienza*, testifies not so much to the fact that where there is a will there is a way but that the stakes of Astolfo and Jocondo's picaresque search have become paranoiac.

It is not by chance that all this lovemaking is sterile. Neither the two wives nor any of the one thousand women Astolfo and Jocondo make love to ever gets pregnant. One could conclude that in tandem with their characterization as effeminate, the two men are constructed as unable to father. But this is the case only in the final, 1532, version of the *Furioso*, and the revision is significant. In the first and second editions, the narrator gave Astolfo a son; in fact, the story starts by naming Astolfo the father of the man who is king of Lombardy at the time when the story is being told: "Astolfo Re di Longobardi: quello / che costui che regna hor tenne per padre" (26.4; "Astolfo, king of the Lombards, the one who was the father of the present king," my translation). This reference is eliminated in the third version, where the king is introduced not as a father but as a brother—of a monk—also without issue, from whom he inherited the kingdom: "Astolfo, re de' Longobardi, quello / a cui lasciò il fratel monaco il regno" (28.4; "Astolfo, the King of the Lombards who was left his kingdom by his monastic brother"). The choice is telling, for in removing the anxiety over reproduction that fueled many of these early modern stories of cuckoldry, like the one by Machiavelli that I examined in chapter 2, Ariosto is able not only to explore at length and with intriguing results the vagaries of a phallic desire separated from a patriarchal injunction to secure name and property through generation; he is also able to present the work of emulation/competition between men as disruptive when it leaves no space for sublimation.

Making a series of women bear the weight of the two men's loss of self does not lead to a solution; repetition, if necessary to control feelings of bereavement or to restage lack as a way of mastering it, hardly solves their original problem or brings them closure. No matter how much the mother seems to be abjected, she returns to haunt the two men; trying to figure out what she desires — and why she does not desire them — Astolfo and Jocondo can only scatter their environment with female bodies. Still, it is only through compulsive repetition that they can rehearse the momentous scenes that eventually drew both away from their homes. And that these scenes are traumatic is onomastically suggested by the only woman named in the story, Fiammetta. Such a name is both Ariosto's literary nod to the master of the Italian novella, Boccaccio, who made of Fiammetta a household name, and an acknowledgment that love and flame are thematically linked. Jean Laplanche has argued that fire is a figure that paradigmatically allows the subject to perceive a traumatic event.[42] In the *Furioso*, more than standing as a flame of passion, Fiammetta stands, diminutively, as the emblem of a trauma that will not be healed.

Let us take the case of Jocondo. This knight seems at the beginning of the story to have a well-adjusted, heterosexual libido. But his object libido is redirected toward the ego (ego libido) following two traumatic scenes of seduction: of his wife and of the queen. Both scenes play all three of the original fantasies described by Laplanche and Pontalis: the primal scene, the seduction, and castration.[43] These scenes are fantasies in that they are framed (the first by a veil, the second by a tiny hole in the wall) and Oedipal in their figuration. Jocondo is the "child" in both the first scene, through identification with the stable boy ("'l ragazzo," 28.36) making love to an older woman, and in the second, through identification with a dwarf (a shorter man, and thus in fantasy a younger man),

42. Jean Laplanche, *Problématiques*, 4 vols. (Paris: Presses universitaires de France, 1980–81), 3:194–96.
43. Jean Laplanche and Jean-Bertrand Pontalis, "Fantasy and the Origins of Sexuality," in *Formations of Fantasy*, ed. Victor Burgin, James Donald, and Cora Kaplan (London: Methuen, 1986), 5–34.

making love to the queen.[44] The difference in the second scene is that in the movement from mother to Mother, female sexual desire has been made grotesque: the queen not only makes love to an inferior being but is insatiable and irreverent: "non si fa festa giorno" (28.37; "they had no rest-day"). Moreover, if in the first scene Jocondo is the unwilling and startled onlooker, in the second he is in control and thus reenacts, and tries to master in the repetition, the original trauma of castration in the Freudian understanding of it.

Both scenes have something *unheimlich* about them. In the first scene Jocondo is returning home in a hurry to retrieve the necklace given him by his wife, which he had left under the pillow. Seeing his wife asleep on the conjugal bed with a servant in postcoital *somnolentia,* he experiences a sort of Medusan castration and cannot react:

> La cortina levò senza far motto,
> e vide quel che men veder credea:
> che la sua casta e fedel moglie, sotto
> la coltre, in braccio a un giovene giacea. . . .
>
>   S'attonito restasse e malcontento,
> meglio è pensarlo e farne fede altrui,
> ch'esserne mai per far l'esperimento
> che con suo gran dolor ne fe' costui.
> Da lo sdegno assalito, ebbe talento
> di trar la spada e uccidergli ambedui:
> ma da l'amor che porta, al suo dispetto,
> all'ingrata moglier, gli fu interdetto.
> . . . Quanto potè più tacito uscì fuore,
> scese le scale, e rimontò a cavallo. (28.21, 22, 23)

He lifted the curtains without a word—and was no little surprised by what he saw: his chaste and loyal wife under the covers in a young man's arms! . . . Was he dumbstruck and dismayed? You had better take another's word for this than undergo the experience at first hand, as did Jocondo to his great chagrin. In a fit of fury he made to draw his sword and slay the pair of them; what stopped him was the love which despite himself he

---

44. For an examination of the primal scene, see Sigmund Freud, "From the History of an Infantile Neurosis," *Collected Papers,* 5 vols. (New York: Basic Books, 1959), 2:232–40.

bore his thankless wife. . . . So he crept out of the room as silently as he could, descended the stairs, [and] mounted his horse.

The reaction that is not staged, the scream that does not come out, shows that Jocondo is unable to separate himself as yet from his too close other and embrace the law.[45] No wonder that he plunges into melancholia. The innkeeper implicates his male listeners in his retelling, just as much as the author implicates his male readers, by deflecting paranoia on them as well: better to be told about such a fact than to experience it, better to hear than to see.

In the second scene, of the queen and her dwarf, Jocondo cannot believe the strange spectacle ("sì strano spettacolo," 28.39) that is taking place, and has to look at it again and again, for at first he thinks he is dreaming. This salacious, voyeuristic look provokes in him a feeling of disgust.[46] The dwarf, in his grotesquely shortened form and hunchback shape, moreover, is a figure of both castration and the uncanny ("uno sgrignuto mostro e contrafatto," 28.35; "vil sergente," 28.42; "il bruttissimo omiciuolo," 28.43). This time Jocondo's reaction is voiced and vindictive, for misery loves company; by calling Astolfo to witness his own debasement and thus somehow symbolically castrating him, he finds a way out of his self-imposed quarantine, recovers a sense of selfhood, and becomes a man of the world.

Astolfo at first has the identical reaction that Jocondo had in seeing his wife's adultery: he is unable to take in all this ocular proof at once. In his case, too, the scream cannot be voiced:

Se parve al re vituperoso l'atto,
lo crederete ben, senza ch'io 'l giuri.
Ne fu per arrabbiar, per venir matto;

45. As Žižek puts it, "the silent scream attests to the subject's clinging to enjoyment, to his/her unreadiness to exchange enjoyment (i.e., the object which gives body to it) for the Other, for the Law, for the paternal metaphor." See Slavoj Žižek, *Enjoy Your Symptom: Jacques Lacan in Hollywood and Out* (New York: Routledge, 1992), 118. Jocondo will stage his reaction later in the form of copulation with the one thousand other women.

46. The ability to override disgust is precisely what for Freud promotes scopophilia in the pervert: "this pleasure in looking (scopophilia) becomes a perversion (a) if it is restricted exclusively to the genitals or (b) if it is connected with the overriding of disgust (as in the case of voyeurs)." See Sigmund Freud, "Three Essays on the Theory of Sexuality," *SE* 7:122–243, esp. 157 (1953).

ne fu per dar del capo in tutti i muri;
fu per gridar, fu per non stare al patto:
ma forza è che la bocca al fin si turi. (28.44)

> That this struck the king as outrageous you will accept without my having
> to swear to it. He was ready to explode, to run amuck; he was ready to
> ram his head against every wall, to scream; he was ready to break his oath.
> But in the end he had perforce to plug his mouth.

But then, unlike Jocondo, who gets stuck in melancholia as a response to narcissistic injury, Astolfo proceeds straight to mania, and the picaresque journey
begins.

What follows, in its outer search for revenge on other men and its inner
search for a woman—a mother—who will not betray, is predicated on fantasy.
In fantasy, individuals can identify across gender and even with inanimate elements in the scene of fantasy. Astolfo can thus identify with Jocondo, and vice
versa, and possess through him and with him any woman, also available to the
other, but whose enjoyment can be magnified by seeing another person desiring
her. Each can identify with all women in their being able, at least as they are
imagined, to be utterly possessed and passive. Given the desire to be observed
while copulating, as in the arrangement with Fiammetta, each can identify also
with the men who took their place in their wives' beds. Each can identify with
Fiammetta as well and fantasize being loved/possessed by an object of homoerotic desire without actually acting out this fantasy. Finally, each can identify
with the whole scene and repeat ad infinitum his own primal scene with the
other as the silent onlooker. But although Astolfo or Jocondo can assume at
will both a feminine and a masculine position, as subject each can only look on,
excluded. Knowledge brings powerlessness.

This hysterical doubling/mutual emulation is in any case difficult to hold
down. If doubling, in its link to castration anxiety, is beneficial because it allows
the individual to cancel the female threat by getting reassurance through the
image of the other as the same ("E perchè [dicea il re] vo' che mi spiaccia / aver
più te ch'un altro in compagnia?" "Why—exclaimed the king—should I object
to sharing a woman with you more than with another?" 28.50), it can on the
other hand give rise to hostility, because the quasi-similar other is too similar.[47]

47. In Fineman's words, emulation is "that paradoxical labor of envy that seeks to find difference in imitation." See Joel Fineman, "Fratricide and Cuckoldry: Shakespeare's Doubles,"

Such a feeling does not necessarily arise out of a competition for the same object, nor is the result of wanting to act out the same desire. Freud notes, for example, that normal jealousy can be many times "experienced bisexually," that is, the jealous subject wishes to be in the place not only of the rival but also of the beloved.[48] Thus identification across gender can be sustained by jealousy just as it is by fantasy.

The way out of narcissistic rage, mimetic repetition, and duplicate selfhood presents itself when Astolfo and Jocondo recognize that they do not know what the other desires and that no woman can be wholly owned. Had they been willing to learn from Fiammetta's choice, or had they asked themselves, "What does woman want?" rather than putting their conceits on center stage, they would have understood that what matters for women in sex is neither repetition nor at least two men per night, but perhaps the chance to decide for themselves. Outwitting her two lovers, Fiammetta got herself not so much a man who did not "dismount once all night long" ("scender non ne vuol per tutta notte," 28.64), as Ariosto puts it, but the one she wanted. True, the grammatical referent for "non ne vuol" is the Greek lover rather than Fiammetta, and thus his desire rather than hers may once more be represented. Yet Fiammetta had reassured him earlier of the extent of her desire ("Credi (dicea) che men di te nol bramo," "I want this no less than you do"; 28.60), and also had to be, at the very least, inventive and precise in her directions to him, for the location in bed where she was lying was crucial to their sexual satisfaction:

> Il Greco, sì come ella gli disegna,
>
> . . . .
>
> va brancolando infin che 'l letto trova:
> e di là dove gli altri avean le piante,
> tacito si cacciò col capo inante.
>
> Fra l'una e l'altra gamba di Fiammetta,
> che supina giacea, diritto venne;

---

in *Representing Shakespeare: New Psychoanalytic Essays*, ed. Murray Schwartz and Coppélia Kahn (Baltimore: Johns Hopkins University Press, 1980), 70–109, esp. 74.

48. See Sigmund Freud, "Certain Neurotic Mechanisms in Jealousy, Paranoia, and Homosexuality," in *Collected Papers*, 2:232–40. See also Katharine Maus, "Horns of Silence: Jealousy, Gender and Spectatorship in English Renaissance Drama," *English Literary History* 54 (1987): 561–83.

e quando le fu a par, l'abbracciò stretta,
e sopra lei sin presso al dì si tenne. (28.62–64)

> The boy, following her instructions, . . . groped his way till he found the
> bed—into which, at the point where the sleepers had their feet, he quietly
> intruded head first. He slipped between the legs of Fiammetta, who was
> lying on her back, and slid up her until they were face to face, when he
> hugged her tightly. He straddled her till daybreak.

It is at this point, filled with a veritable sexual nausea, that Astolfo and Jocondo remove themselves from active heterosexual desire altogether and start
to live where they have always wanted: in fantasy. The sudden end of their erotic
quest and their return home, the resolution of the "errore"/ "errare" paradigm,
does not constitute for me a smart, bourgeois choice, as in the case of Bibbiena's
twins, which I will examine next; I read it as a way to cancel out the other by
remaining involved in the narcissistic story of selves as ideal selves.[49] In doing
so Ariosto's characters can disavow difference. Still, their choice does mark a
change. True, nothing has changed in the domestic situation that made the two
men leave their wives in the first place; moreover, desire has not been erased,
nor has concupiscence been conquered. But what has changed is that women
have been removed from the equation. They are eliminated, not to erase the
trauma, but because they in a sense were in the equation under false pretences,
for they never existed *per se*. The one thousand and three women were always
and only, to take it once more from Lacan, "symptoms" of men's subjectivity.[50]

To be sure, the two friends could have found a degree of pleasure in shifting
to some form of feminine masochism after they were apprised of Fiammetta's
adventure with her Greek lover. Or they might have responded with melancholic withdrawal, as Jocondo did following his wife's betrayal. But by now their

49. Zatti reads in the story a wisdom-bound madness ("un giocondo errore"). See
Sergio Zatti, *Il Furioso fra epos e romanzo* (Lucca: Pacini Fazzi, 1990), 50. For Gareffi, the conclusion of the novella shows that while men tell stories, women make them ("Rimangono gli
uomini a raccontarsi le storie, le donne le fanno"). See Andrea Gareffi, *Figure dell'immaginario
nell'Orlando Furioso* (Rome: Bulzoni, 1984), 91.

50. Interesting, in this context, is the observation made by Franceschetti, that there is
one element of the traditional novella completely absent in Ariosto, unlike Boccaccio: the
"beffa," in which women show—through their wit, cunning, or *savoir faire*—the stupidity
and gullibility of their mates ("La novella nei poemi," 835–36).

errantry has become shabby, and the women they share are of lower and lower social status. So they opt to show their phallic power by marking the successful exorcism of their fears with a Gargantuan, hysteric, orgasmic laughter:

> Poi scoppiaro ugualmente in tanto riso,
> che con la bocca aperta e gli occhi chiusi,
> potendo a pena il fiato aver del petto,
> a dietro si lasciar cader sul letto.
> . . . ebbon tanto riso, che dolere
> se ne sentiano il petto, e pianger gli occhi. (28.71-72)

> Then they burst into fits of laughter, their mouths open and their eyes shut till, practically breathless, they fell backwards onto the bed. . . . [T]hey had laughed so much that their ribs ached and their eyes streamed.

This also puts an end to their adventures in the never-never land of unbound sexual gratifications; before leaving, they allow Fiammetta to wed her lover and thus sanction the institutionalization of desire through marriage, the end of romance through an astute reading of the economics of loving.

At home, Astolfo and Jocondo will be, as before, and as they like it, once more alone and on center stage. Surprisingly, at the very moment in which they decline to judge, and let themselves be judged, as manly men, they are rendered as fully masculinized, for their masculinity is tied now not to sex—the flesh after all cannot signify, Lacan teaches—but to the power of the phallus. In the final version of this tale Ariosto omits an octave, present in the two earlier editions, that refers to a son born from the union between the queen and the dwarf and aptly named Strange Desire ("Stranodesiderio"). This name was later shortened to "Desire" to avoid improper allusions to the queen's sexual tastes.[51] Had he kept this bastard son in the text, Ariosto would have left Astolfo still living through the story of his sexual and Oedipal demise, still trapped in the tensions and pleasures of the family romance. By deleting the illegitimate son, Ariosto brings the novella full circle, for we are told that neither Jocondo nor Astolfo will let themselves now be contaminated anew by their wives' aberrancies: "di ch'affanno mai più non si pigliaro" (28.74; "who never occasioned them another

---

51. "Il Re il primo figliuol che poi gli nacque / nomo a battesmo Stranodesiderio / ma poi crescendo Strano se gli tacque / che pel Nano alla madre era improperio" (2.26.75 of the Ermini edition). We do not know whether the child was a dwarf like his father.

moment's distress"). Erotic politics are pushed aside to make room for gender politics. There is no doubt that, once back in power, the king and the knight will restart their love affair with the mirror. Again this excludes the possibility that they will have offspring, quite a failure not only in the case of Astolfo, because he has an institutional duty to guarantee a legitimate succession to his kingdom, but also in the case of Jocondo, who should be concerned as a nobleman with transmitting his title and status.

So what does this story tell us about the representation of masculinity in *Orlando furioso* and the chivalric romance, and about gender relations in the sixteenth century in general? Should the reader skip the canto because women are portrayed dismissively, as Ariosto suggests, or because men are represented as masquerading masculinity, even when they aggressively test its most praised attribute, virility? Is there a real difference, all things considered, between the kind of manhood impersonated by the paladin Orlando, whose desire thrives on postponement until he realizes that he has arrived too late at his dreamed sexual banquet and goes mad, and the kind of manhood impersonated by Astolfo and Jocondo, whose desires are gratified to the point of disenchantment? In both cases what constitutes masculinity is very much at stake; if, as the Saracen knight Mandricardo hints, the end of Orlando's search for love leads him to a metaphoric self-castration ("E dicea ch'imitato avea il castore, / il qual si strappa i genitali sui," "The count had imitated the beaver, he explained, who rips off his genitals"; 27.57), then Astolfo and Jocondo's return to reality neither brings them closer to understanding the secret of women nor makes them better equipped to put an end to their self-mystification. In any case, whether in Orlando's world of romance or in the cynical, commodified realm of Astolfo and Jocondo, the confrontation with otherness leaves women out of the equation. But while for Orlando the endless search for armor or for Angelica is a post-Oedipal longing for a lost or perhaps never fully developed selfhood, for Astolfo and Jocondo, I would argue, the search for a mother who will not betray them is a search for a pre-Oedipal, primal, Edenic world, uncontaminated by the confrontations and the urgencies of the symbolic. Thus, for Orlando the end of his story in the *Furioso* means his return to, and total embrace of, the paternal order, while for Astolfo and Jocondo the end of their search is a reimmersion in the narcissism with which their story started out, the return to sameness.

The trials of masculinity in Ariosto show how unstable the articulations of identity — masculine as well as feminine — were in the period in which he wrote, and how deeply the emergent definitions of what was private and what was public influenced the social construction of gender. The boundaries between normal, normative, and deviant behavior were in many ways just as permeable in the secularized world of Ariosto testing the illusions of a bygone era of romance adventures as they are in our postmodern times. In the end, if gender is, in the Lacanian sense, a masquerade, a form of fetishistic transvestism, then the labyrinthine, ironic narrative of the *Furioso* clearly lends itself to an examination of undecidability. For here identity is mimicry, and fantasy—or its extreme, madness—is endlessly employed to protect impassioned and neurotic characters from a death drive that demands attention but allows delays now and then, *petites mortes* indeed.

The authorial feint at the beginning, Ariosto's plea to his readers not to pay attention to him because the social conventions he is representing are not his credo but belong to a spurious father, Master Turpino—who has throughout been unable to signify any truth—was just a gambit. One cannot in fact read the story's surface and not its depth, and laugh at women no matter how reproachable the business may be, not because it is too dangerous—or too bewildering— to laugh at men, but because the story has a coda. The innkeeper's tale is met with the strongly registered disagreement of an old man, one full of shrewdness and courage, says Ariosto, who calls the storyteller's account of women's wiles a bag of lies and points out that in fact men have a far worse record than women, not only in matters of chastity but also in those of theft, murder, and fraud. He ends his diatribe by proposing a law to be applied equally to man and woman because it follows universal Christian principles:

> Saria la legge, ch'ogni donna colta
> in adulterio, fosse messa a morte,
> se provar non potesse ch'una volta
> avesse adulterato il suo consorte:
> se provar lo potesse andrebbe asciolta,
> né temeria il marito né la corte.
> Cristo ha lasciato nei precetti suoi:
> non far altrui quel che patir non vuoi. (28. 82)

> Every woman caught in adultery would be put to death unless she could prove that her husband had once done so too. If she could prove it, she would be absolved—she would need fear neither her husband nor the court. Christ left us among his precepts: Do not do to others what you would not endure yourself.

The old man is silenced by a fierce look from Rodomonte, whose misogyny has just been affirmed by the tale of Astolfo and Jocondo and will stand no contradiction. But throughout this romance Rodomonte's story only confirms that the man who is unable to "listen" to women has plenty to lose figuratively: his manhood, for one, as well as his social standing and, finally, his place in the narrative.

CHAPTER 5

Androgynous Doubling
and Hermaphroditic Anxieties:
Bibbiena's *La calandria*

Women are more changeable.

—BOCCACCIO, *Decameron*

Doctors promote themselves shamelessly,
making exorbitant claims about their competence.

—PETRARCH, "Letter"

Servants in Renaissance comedy are witty and mischievous; Fannio in Bernardo Bibbiena's *La calandria* (*The Comedy of Calandro*) could even teach a trick or two to his peers and superiors.[1] Yet even Fannio has problems in explaining how his "master" Santilla, who is dressed like a man and calls herself with a masculine name, Lidio, is going to satisfy sexually Fulvia, a Roman matron in love with Santilla's fraternal twin brother, also called Lidio, who goes to her lodgings dressed not as a man—after all he was one—but as a woman. Eventually Fannio devises a linguistic explanation for a sexual lack: his master—whose female identity is unknown to everybody but two servants—is a hermaphrodite, he tells the necromancer Ruffo, matchmaker for the day. Unsure of the full meaning of what he has heard, Ruffo asks more specifically: does he have a woman's sex and a man's "root" ("E ha il sesso della donna e la radice dell'uomo")?[2] As things go, at their meeting Fulvia finds Santilla lacking in what she wants most ("per me privo si trova di quel che più si brama," 4.2) and begs Ruffo to send her the person she desires, one in the clothes of a woman but in possession of the sine qua non for her sexual satisfaction, the dagger for my sheath ("coltel della guaina mia," 4.2), as she puts it. What Ruffo has to do is simply to reverse his magic, Fulvia argues, because he must have understood her earlier request wrong, when he sent her a person feminine in gender and female in sex. She wants Lidio feminine in gender and male in sex, so that he, passing for a woman, can enter her household inconspicuously. Ruffo teases Fulvia's ingenuity because her reasoning implies that sex is a prosthesis that can be put on and off:

1. Bernardo Dovizi (1470–1520), called Bibbiena after his native town, Bibbiena in Tuscany, was a recognized master politician at the Medici court and became a cardinal when a Medici pope, Leo X, was elected. He is represented as a facetious character and polished courtier at the Urbino court in Baldassarre Castiglione's *Il libro del cortegiano*. *La calandria* (or *Calandra*) is his only play. For an interesting insight into Bibbiena's literary and diplomatic life, see Carlo Dionisotti, "Ricordo del Bibbiena," in *Machiavellerie* (Turin: Einaudi, 1980), 135–72.

2. Bibbiena, *La calandria*, ed. Paolo Fossati (Turin: Einaudi, 1967), 3.17. Subsequent citations referring to act and scene will appear directly in the text. The English translation is mine. A useful, albeit partial English version of the play by Oliver Evans, under the title *The Follies of Calandro*, is in *The Genius of the Italian Theater*, ed. Eric Bentley (New York: New American Library, 1964).

Costei è per amore accecata sì ch'ella s'avvisa che uno spirito possa fare una persona femina e maschio a posta sua: come se altro fare non bisognasse che tagliare la radice de l'uomo e farvi un fesso, e così formare una donna; e ricucire la bocca da basso e appiccare un bischero, e così fare un maschio. (4.2)

This woman is so blinded by love that she believes a spirit can make a person male or female at will, as if to make a woman one only needs to pull out the root and replace it with a crack, and to make a man one needs to sew up the mouth down there and replace it with a peg.

The audience is made to agree with him: one can put on gender at ease, but sex is stable. Or is it in *La calandria*?

This chapter examines the negotiations that sexual and gender categories undergo for the sake of producing heterosexual desire in a story of similar-looking, late-adolescent twins of different sex. As a result of having lost their parents and country and of having been separated in childhood, at an age in which they liked to mirror each other, Santilla and Lidio (still apart) keep experimenting with gender in their everyday life by cross-dressing and calling themselves by each other's name. Their sartorial shuffle is part of a general mismatch of clothes in the play, whereby almost every character, male or female, changes attire and gender with such frequency that Bibbiena himself, apparently losing control of his own play, gives us a scene of gratuitous cross-dressing, he too caught in the game of exchangeable identities.[3] Soon, not only gender but also sexual parts are shown as independent of bodies, since thanks to a magician's prestidigitation, it becomes possible to attach and detach members at ease.

In the midst of this disorder no father is found with the authority to impose his *fiat*, for Bibbiena's world is one of missing, failed, pompous, or uncognizant

---

3. The scene occurs toward the end of the play when Santilla, dressed as a man, exchanges clothes with her servant Fannio, also dressed as a man, and ends up with an identity that she already has. It could be argued, of course, that in exchanging clothes with her servant, Santilla is crossing social classes, an intriguing addition, to which Bibbiena, however, seems to attach little importance. And yet, if we give credit to the repeated suggestion on the part of critics that the servant Fessenio, who is hired by Calandro but actually works to foster Lidio's amorous desires, is a stand-in for the author, we cannot avoid noticing that Fessenio never cross-dresses. Had Bibbiena been present at the first representation of his play, he would perhaps have caught the gratuitousness of the last exchange of clothes.

fathers. Santilla's adoptive father does not know the true sex of his adoptee; as for Lidio, his father's substitute, Momo di Polinico, who should teach the orphan boy everything in life, is called a vile hypocrite and characterized as an inveterate, feminized pedant. Only the male servants of both brother and sister, Fessenio and Fannio, can stand as paternal figures, and even then Fannio is too ready to play the game of gender bending to usefully restrain his charge, Santilla, and become a positive father substitute. As for the simpleton Calandro, nobody would mistake him for a father, given his unrivaled stupidity ("che castrone è," 1.3), although we are told that he is one. In focusing on the negotiations that adolescents in crisis undergo in order to bridge their need for truth and knowledge, Bibbiena literalizes the ease with which those who do not know who they are cross sexual boundaries, stumble across piquant situations, and live in a hybrid state. Hence his use of fetishistic structures to allay psychic anxieties, as his main characters look for the absolute, which they identify with the recovery of their lost or "stolen" self. Once they find the complementary part of themselves, Santilla and Lidio discard their cross-dressing, name each other, put in place a procreative agenda (Bibbiena doubles at the end the comedic device of marriage), and harmony is restored.

In tune with the action of the play, which emphasizes at the start the androgynous appearance of the two main characters, I will first concentrate on the use of cross-dressed boy actors to play young women's parts on stage. Then, as *Calandria* offers an array of surgical jokes to foreground male trouble, I will examine the issue of castration in its psychoanalytical implications and look at the options posited by newly available and anatomically correct prostheses to substitute for missing body parts. Finally, as the play, at Fulvia's urgent request, shifts its emphasis from the gender played by the twins to their actual, verifiable sex, I will focus on some cases of supposed or real hermaphroditism that came to the attention of Renaissance doctors.

Let me offer first a summary of the complicated plot of *La calandria*: Lidio and his sister Santilla (also called Lidio and Lidio femina) are two eighteen-year-old Greek orphan twins separated at the age of six when the Turks seized their native Modon and burned it. They are currently in Rome in search of each other; in fact, they live in the same neighborhood without realizing it. Santilla dresses as a man and has hidden her identity from everybody, thanks to the complicity of Fannio. Lidio, meanwhile, is busy with a married noblewoman, Fulvia, whom he visits dressed as a woman in order not to arouse suspicions in her husband, Calandro. For his part, thinking Lidio is a young woman, Calandro too wants a dalliance with him and arranges for a meeting. Lidio is eventually substituted with a prostitute in Calandro's bed, and such is the situation Fulvia finds when, dressed as a man to have ease of movement in securing a meeting with Lidio, she catches her husband in bed with the woman.

Preoccupied by Lidio's seemingly cooling passion for her—a new development given his past assiduous frequentations of her house—Fulvia asks next the neighborhood necromancer, Ruffo, to rekindle his interest. Unaware, like everybody else, that brother and sister are being confused for each other, Ruffo arranges for Santilla, whom he takes for Lidio because she dresses as a man, to go to Fulvia's house in female clothes, just like Lidio. With her servant Fannio's acknowledgment, Santilla agrees that the only way she can explain what soon will turn out to be, upon Fulvia's scrutiny, a set of unexpected sexual attributes, is to tell Ruffo that she is a hermaphrodite. At the meeting, Fulvia despairs when she finds her lover changed into a woman and urges Ruffo to send her the usual manly one, who could so well fulfill her desire. She obtains her wish, but soon has to beg the necromancer to turn Lidio back into a female, because her brothers accuse her of lodging a man in her bedroom. Matters are eventually resolved: Lidio and Santilla recognize each other as long-lost twins, Fulvia avoids a scandal, and the play ends with two propitious marriages.

All critical accounts agree that the major innovation Bibbiena brought to the stage of his day, beyond popularizing and perfecting the new genre of Italian erudite comedy ("commedia erudita"), was the use of identical twins of opposite sex.[4] In the original play of which La calandria is a creative remake, Plautus's much-read and erudite Menaechmi, the main characters were two brothers, and one of them was already married.[5] Bibbiena lightened up the strong homo-

4. See, for example, Giulio Ferroni, Il testo e la scena: Saggi sul teatro del Cinquecento (Rome: Bulzoni, 1980), 85; Giorgio Padoan, "Introduzione," in Bernardo Bibbiena, La calandria, ed. Giorgio Padoan (Padua: Antenore, 1985); and Franco Ruffini, Commedia e festa nel Rinascimento: La calandria alla corte di Urbino (Bologna: Il Mulino, 1986), 114–19. That comedy was a Renaissance "resurrection" is now a topos. Unlike Christian tragedy, which involved the community of believers, and unlike liturgical dramas, comedy was not congenial to the Middle Ages, with its scarce penchant for irony. But with the rise of the mercantile class, which brought an ironic attention to everyday details, modern comedy was born. It is assumed that Ariosto reinvented the genre chronologically, but Bibbiena perfected it through information on the ways plays could be performed.

5. Menaechmi was represented many times in the Renaissance both in the original Latin and in Italian. See Padoan, "Introduzione," 15. The Codex Ursinianus, which contains many

sexual component of the Plautine story and gave his play a seemingly hetero-sexual, though variegated, plot. The change of one of the twin's sex also en-riched the narrative much more than could have been anticipated: the frequent cross-dressing that thus became necessary not only introduced onstage the rich motif of gender transgression but also gave women in the audience a sense of empowerment, no matter how fleeting.

Plots of courtship may have struck a chord because women and ladies of the court were almost always in the audience—they soon became *de rigueur* on the occasion of high-class weddings.[6] And although all plays ended with the impo-sition of the correct social and gendered behavior on the transgression-bound pair, the ride into double entendres and quasi-pornography must have been an exciting one. The number of female characters in Bibbiena was highly unusual at the time, especially if we consider that plays written immediately after did not follow suit. To be sure, at a time in which the stage setting was usually a town's main square, it would have been implausible to have unmarried women loitering outside their homes, thus scenes in which women had parts in Re-naissance comedy, even though they were played by male actors, were few. Yet women in *La calandria* are present in two-thirds of the fifty-nine scenes.[7] That

---

plays by Plautus and Terence, started to be closely studied by humanists after it was acquired in 1429 by Giordano Orsini. The *Codex* lay the foundations of modern Italian theater, in that close attention came to be paid to the theater as a physical space for representations and to the connections between texts and the way they could be staged. The first representa-tions in Latin of Plautus and Terence took place sometime after 1476 in Florence and Rome. Beside Plautus, another model for *La calandria* was Boccaccio's *Decameron*. On the many con-nections between these two works, see Angela Guidotti, "Il doppio gioco della *Calandria*," *Modern Language Notes* 104 (1989): 98–116; Pamela Stewart, *Retorica e mimica nel Decameron e nella commedia del Cinquecento* (Florence: Olschki, 1986), 110–14; and Anna Fontes Baratto, "Les Fêtes à Urbin en 1513 et la *Calandre* de Bernardo Dovizi da Bibbiena," in *Les Écrivains et le pouvoir en Italie a l'époque de la Renaissance*, ed. André Rochon (Paris: Université de la Sorbonne Nouvelle, 1974), 45–79, esp. 69–74.

6. For the public in Urbino, see *Codice Vaticano Urbinate 490*, 193–96, in Vito Pandolfi, *Il teatro del Rinascimento e la commedia dell'arte* (Rome: Lerici, 1969), 69. For example, five Plautine plays were staged for the marriage of Lucrezia Borgia and Alfonso d'Este in 1502; the *Man-dragola* was performed to celebrate Lorenzo de Medici's marriage. See chapter 2. The public could be vast. One to two thousand people saw the representations of Ariosto's *Cassaria* in 1508 and *I suppositi* in 1509. See Dominique Clouet, "Empirisme ou égotisme: La politique dans la *Cassaria* et les *Suppositi* de l'Arioste," in Rochon, *Les Écrivains*, 6–44, esp. 20.

7. See Laurie Detenbeck, "Women and the Management of Dramaturgy in *La Calan-*

the copious use of women proved, longer-term, a gold mine for subsequent the-atrical representations goes without saying: Bibbiena was imitated not only in Italy, as in Ariosto's Fiordispina and Ricciardetto episode in *Orlando furioso* or Alessandro Piccolomini's *L'Alessandro*, Ruzante's *La moschetta* and *L'Anconitana*, Gl'Intronati's *Gl'ingannati*, and Girolamo Parabosco's *L'hermafrodito*, but specifi-cally in Shakespeare's plays, as in *Twelfth Night*. Although in the original script Santilla and Lidio must have been played by two different actors because they appear twice onstage together, it would have been quite possible to modify the script so one actor played both parts, preserving the illusion in the audience that one could really pass for the other.[8]

There is a second innovation that Bibbiena introduced in Renaissance play-writing that is important for my analysis: he wrote with performance in mind and with an eye to the likes and dislikes of a courtly audience of some sophisti-cation, or at least pretense to it. It is widely known that until the beginning of the sixteenth century plays were not really written for the purpose of being per-formed. If they were, they enjoyed one staging, perhaps two, after which they were simply presented as readings or circulated in manuscript. Only later did they appear in print. We know that even admired Latin plays, with which Ital-ian courtiers liked to entertain themselves, were read aloud, just like chivalric romances and Petrarchan poems.[9] *La calandria*, however, contains specific stage directions, as we see in early printed editions. In the "Prologo del Bibbiena" the narrator dreams, voyeur-style, of roaming invisibly in households where women were getting ready to see the performance. He recommends his comedy to their

---

dria," in *Donna: Woman in Italian Culture*, ed. Ada Testaferri (Ottawa: Dovehouse Press, 1989), 245–52. By contrast, in Machiavelli's *Mandragola*, Lucrezia's presence is limited, and in *Clizia*, Clizia is not even seen. In Ariosto's *Lena* and *I suppositi*, female characters appear infrequently; when they do, they are old and have a dubious reputation, like Lena; such women could plausibly be walking in the streets or gossiping outdoors.

8. In Roman comedy, identical twins were played by different actors using identical masks. But already in *Gl'ingannati* the same (male) actor played both a female and a male role, which meant that brother and sister could not appear together. See Richard Andrews, "Gli Ingannati as a Text for Performance," *Italian Studies* 37 (1982): 26–48, esp. 36.

9. Giorgio Padoan, "Il senso del teatro nei secoli senza teatro," in *Concetto, storia, miti e immagini del Medio Evo*, ed. Vittore Branca (Florence: Sansoni, 1973), 325–38; and Jonas Bar-ish, "The Problem of Closet Drama in the Italian Renaissance," *Italica* 71 (1994): 4–30. The tradition of play readings ("teatro letto") continued through the sixteenth century, especially for tragedies.

generosity and professes to be afraid that men will pay little attention to the work because they will be too interested in contemplating the female beauties among them.[10] He had no need to worry. The play was an instant success when it was first performed in the ducal palace in Urbino for celebrations commissioned by its ruler, Francesco Maria della Rovere, on February 6, 1513. It was staged again in 1514. The stage was a public hall so beautiful that even Castiglione found hard to believe that it could have been readied in just four months.[11] Bibbiena was unable to attend the first performance, but a good number of local and nearby nobility and people from the mercantile class joined the duke in celebration. *La calandria* was then staged in Rome in December 1514 in the presence of Pope Leo X, on the occasion of the visit there by Isabella d'Este; and again in 1515, with scenery by Baldassarre Peruzzi.[12] It was first printed in 1521.[13]

10. This prologue may or may not have been written by Bibbiena, or may have not been written for *La calandria*. On the doubts that accompany the authorship, see Paolo Fossati's explanations in the biobibliographic note to the edition of *La calandria* I use. Giorgio Padoan's edition of this play does not use this prologue. The presence of women was also acknowledged in the prologue of Ariosto's *Lena* and Gl'Intronati's *Gl'ingannati*. Women and men often sat in separate parts of the theater. Women were not necessarily part of the public at all times, however. Contrary to what we may assume today about the tastes of theatergoers of the early modern period, women took jokes about women lightly, or at least we are told that such was the case by a Venetian censor of the second half of the sixteenth century, who wrote that some noblemen asked comedians for crude jokes and then brought their wives and daughters along: "v'erano nobili che pregavano i commedianti che dicessero le più grasse, per non dir più sporche cose che mai sapessero, et essi ci menavano poi le mogli e le figlie." See Ludovico Zorzi, *L'attore, la commedia, il drammaturgo* (Turin: Einaudi, 1990), 66.

11. Castiglione's letter in which the stage is discussed is in Mario Apollonio, *Storia del teatro italiano*, 2 vols. (Florence: Sansoni, 1938), 2:19–21. For the specific importance of the 1513 Carnival as a celebratory moment for the duke in Urbino, see Baratto, "Les fêtes à Urbin."

12. Other performances were in Mantua in 1520 and 1532; in Venice in 1521 and 1522, where the public paid for the staging in keeping with that city's practice; and in Camerino in 1549. The 1548 representation in Lyons was done in celebration of the entry in the city of Henri II and Caterina de' Medici. See Giorgio Padoan, *L'avventura della commedia rinascimentale* (Padua: Piccin, 1996), 31–33; Luigina Stefani, "Le Ottave d'Italia del Castiglione e le feste urbinati del 1513," *Panorama*, Sept. 1977, 67–83; and Maurice Scève, *The Entry of Henri II into Lyon, September 1548*, ed. Richard Cooper (Binghamton: State University of New York, Medieval and Renaissance Texts and Studies, 1997). Plays were mostly courtly affairs at the time. Only in Venice (with youth clubs such as the Compagnie della Calza) and in Florence were plays organized and performed outside the court. Squares, churches, schools, convents, aca-

At the time *La calandria* was written, only male, nonprofessional actors were recruited for court performances, although already by 1545, as theater became a medium of high entertainment, a group of actors ("fraternal compagnia") entered a contract to play professionally in Padua.[14] The major significant step toward popularizing the theater was to get rid of masks, even though the first representation of *Menaechmi* in Italian was given by masked actors.[15] The nonprofessional entertainers were often young sons of the local aristocracy; the group that recited the play *Penulo* in 1513 on the Roman capitol in Latin under the direction of Tommaso Inghirami, for example, was made up mostly of boys, with only a couple of men old enough to sport a beard.[16] Some men became famous specifically for the female roles they were called upon to play. In Rome,

---

demies, private halls, and gardens were also used for representations, some of them strictly private, others open to the public. On this, see Jack D'Amico, "Drama and the Court in *La calandria*," *Theater Journal* 43 (1991): 93–106, esp. 103. Ariosto's remarkable theater in Ferrara went up in flames during the fire of the façade of the Ducal Palace in December 1532. According to some contemporaries, the event so devastated the author that he died because of it one year later. A contemporary wrote that the stage was like a city with windows, balconies, shops, and churches. See Egidio Scoglio, *Il teatro alla corte Estense* (Lodi: Biancardi, 1965), 91.

13. The play enjoyed at least twenty-six reprints during the century, the most reissued play of the Renaissance. Machiavelli's *Mandragola* by contrast went through fifteen reprints. On *Calandria*'s fortune, see Giuseppe Lorenzo Moncallero, "Precisazioni sulle rappresentazioni della *Calandria* nel Cinquecento," *Convivium* 2 (1952): 819–51; and Richard Andrews, *Scripts and Scenarios: The Performance of Comedy in Renaissance Italy* (Cambridge: Cambridge University Press, 1993), 48.

14. The transcript of that contract is in E. Cocco, "Una compagnia comica nella prima metà del secolo XVI," *Giornale storico della letteratura italiana* 65 (1915): 57–58. The first recorded case of an actor charging a fee is Francesco Cherea (Francesco de' Nobili) in Venice in 1508. See Cesare Molinari, *La commedia dell'arte* (Milan: Mondadori, 1985), 66.

15. *I menechini,* as the vulgar version of Plautus's play was italianized, was given in Ferrara in 1486 on the occasion of the engagement of Isabella d'Este and Francesco Gonzaga. See Padoan, *L'avventura della commedia rinascimentale,* 9–10. It was also privately given, without masks and scenery, and in the presence of both men and women, at the Vatican in 1502 to celebrate the marriage of Lucrezia Borgia, daughter of pope Alexender VI, and Alfonso d'Este. See Alessandro D'Ancona, *Origini del teatro italiano,* 2 vols. (Turin: Loescher, 1891), 2:73–74.

16. "quasi tutti figliuoli delli primi gentiluomini di Roma, de aspetto belli et gratiosi, de anni teneri, imperocché in tanto numero, due soli erano barbati." See D'Ancona, *Origini,* 2:86.

for example, Inghirami was called "Fedra" for having played that part in 1486 when he was sixteen in Seneca's *Hippolytus;* in Siena, Bastiano di Francesco Linaiuolo was known for playing old women's parts.[17] In general, boys played young women; they would have sounded feminine, since the vocal cords of boys and of women are the same length.[18] Postpubertal boys, whose voices could change suddenly, posed problems at times, as shown in a decision in 1591 to substitute the young man playing Amarilli, Titiro's daughter, in Giambattista Guarini's pastoral eclogue *Pastor Fido,* because his voice had changed register in the period in which the play was being rehearsed.[19] Adult males may have used falsetto to render parts truer to life; Leone De' Sommi, for example, a theater director and author of a theatrical treatise, recommended the register of a trembling falsetto for the role of a shadow in a tragedy.[20] The quality of voice in

17. On Fedra/Inghirami and other humanist actors, see Cristina Valenti, *Comici artigiani: Mestiere e forme dello spettacolo a Siena nella prima metà del Cinquecento* (Ferrara: Panini, 1990), 14, 31, 63. Inghirami was later part of a group of learned men involved in a trial of homosexuals, as we learn from a letter of 1501 by Agostino Vespucci to Machiavelli. See Niccolò Machiavelli, *Lettere,* ed. Franco Gaeta (Milan: Feltrinelli, 1961), 62ff. Men playing old women's parts appear to have been an Italian choice. In England, documentation suggests that only boys played women, no matter the age of the character. See Stephen Orgel, *Impersonations: The Performance of Gender in Shakespeare's England* (Cambridge: Cambridge University Press, 1996), 69. Old women were usually cast as comic or witch-like figures, and bawdy female parts kept being played by men for a very long time, even after women were allowed on the stage, perhaps because it was considered indecorous to have women themselves play such parts. The character of Franceschina, for example, was assigned to a man in a cast list of "Comici uniti" in Padua in 1584. See Louis Duchartre, *The Italian Comedy,* trans. Randolph Weaver (New York: Dover, 1966), 90–93 and 320.

18. See Bruce Smith, *The Acoustic World of Early Modern England: Attending to the O-Factor* (Chicago: University of Chicago Press, 1999), 228–29.

19. "Et quel giovane che faceva l'*Amarilli,* parte lunghissima, per la mutazione della voce, si giudica del tutto inabile." This information is in a letter of November 26, 1591, by Annibale Cheppio to Duke Vincenzo Gonzaga in Mantua, relating changes in the staging of Guarini's play. The part of Amarilli proved difficult to fill because of the limited number of available substitutes, and three young men were auditioned for it ("per l'incredibile scarsezza di giovani a proposito, rispetto alla bellezza, affetto et leggiadria di quella parte"). See D'Ancona, *Origini,* 2:542–43.

20. "E se io, poniam caso, avessi a far recitare un'ombra in tragedia, cercarei una voce squillante per natura, o almeno atta con un falsetto tremante a far quello effetto che si richiede

acting male and female parts was consistently remarked upon, almost as much as acting itself.[21]

Still, although the idea of employing male and not female actors for all roles was strongly advocated for the sake of morality, the transvestite theater was not embraced by all as a good solution for staged comedies, and the powers above often attempted to get rid of it.[22] The Council of Ten in Venice, for example, outlawed theater altogether in 1508, a few years before the first staging of *La calandria*, on the grounds that cross-dressed actors incited lascivious behavior. The ban had a moralist goal in that its stated purpose was the protection of citizens through expunging ("levare de medio") whatever in city life could corrupt and deprave the youth.[23] And indeed some transvestite twists must have been

in tale rappresentazione," in Leone De' Sommi, *Quattro dialoghi in materia di rappresentazioni sceniche*, ed. Ferruccio Marotti (1556; Milan: Polifilo, 1968), dialogue 3, 39–40.

21. For example, writing to the duke of Ferrara about the first representation of Ariosto's *I suppositi* at the papal court in Rome in 1519, with scenes by Raphael and an audience of at least two thousand people, the nobleman Paolucci remarked that the play was very well pronounced ("fu molto ben pronunciata"). See "Letter," March 8, 1519, in Filippo Clementi, *Il carnevale romano nelle cronache contemporanee: Dalle origini al sec. XVIII*, 2 vols. (Città di Castello: Unione Arti Tipografiche, 1939), 1:192.

22. See Padoan, *L'avventura della commedia rinascimentale*, 39; and Eric Nicholson, "'That's How It Is': Comic Travesties of Sex and Gender in Early Sixteenth-Century Venice," in *Look Who's Laughing: Gender and Comedy*, ed. Gail Ginney (Langhorne, Pa.: Gordon and Breach, 1994), 17–34, esp. 21–22. Tracts against the use of boy actors for female parts also proliferated. A compendium of attitudes is in the text of the Jesuit Giovan Domenico Ottonelli, *Della Christiana moderatione del theatro* (1649), now reprinted in *La commedia dell'arte e la società barocca*, vol. 1: *La professione del teatro*, ed. Ferdinando Taviani (Rome: Bulzoni, 1969).

23. Archivio di Stato di Venezia, *Misti*, reg. 32, fol. 55v. To be sure, Venice was reeling at the time from the surprise defeat at Agnadello, in which it lost most of its territory inland, and the governing council was keen to enact limitations on every aspect of cultural life. The decree was not directed at punishing the prostitutes who were often seen and invited to the spectacles. The chronicler Marin Sanudo offered a political reason for the ban: the actor being wildly acclaimed in these new plays, Cherea, an outsider from Tuscany, was no longer satisfied with small, private halls, and wanted to stage comedies in public places such as the Loggia di Rialto ("tramava di aver la loza di Rialto"). Hence the ban. See Marin Sanudo, *I diarii di Marin Sanudo (1496–1533)*, ed. Rinaldo Fulin et al., 58 vols. (Venice: Visentini, 1879–1903), 7:701. The prohibition against staging was enforced in the two years following, 1509 and 1510. But by 1511 a few representations were allowed. There were about one hundred

worked into plays specifically because the audience thereby had the added pleasure of knowing that men played women's parts. In any case, the period in which such plays were allowed to be staged was itself a transgressive moment in city life, when gender and social infractions were understood or even encouraged: Carnival week. Such was the case for Machiavelli's *La mandragola* in Florence, such was the case for Ariosto's *I suppositi, Il negromante,* and *La Lena,* all represented in Ferrara during Carnival time. In Anton Francesco Grazzini's *Le cene,* the lady of the house acknowledges, as Bakhtin would have, that for Carnival anything goes: priests can be happy; friars can engage in sports, recite comedies, play instruments, and dance and sing in costume; and nuns can cross-dress without being reproached ("non si disdice").[24] *La calandria* too was first staged on the Sunday before Lent. The following Monday and Tuesday the noble audience came masked in the spirit of the week, an anonymous chronicler writes, with the duke's explicit approval.[25] Also *La calandria*'s second Roman staging in 1515 was given at Carnival time. When the play was staged in Mantua for a similar festivity in February 1520, some in the public came with "dissimulated" clothes, ready for the dance that was to follow the representation.[26]

---

plays staged in Venice in the period 1496–1533, according to Sanudo. See also Lodovico Zorzi, "Scheda per *La Venexiana,*" in Ignoto Veneto del Cinquecento, *La venexiana,* ed. Lodovico Zorzi (1533; Turin: Einaudi, 1965), 113.

24. Carnival is "il tempo . . . nel qual . . . è lecito a i religiosi di rallegrarsi; e i frati tra loro fanno al pallone, recitano commedie e, travestiti, suonano, ballano e cantano; e alle monache ancora non si disdice, nel rappresentare le feste, questi giorni vestirsi da uomini." See Anton Francesco Grazzini, *Le cene,* ed. Giorgio Barberi Squarotti (Milan: Rizzoli, 1989), 55.

25. "Li lor Signori, di Luni e Marte, ultimi giorni di Carnasciale, Francesco Maria valse che dispensassimo solo in maschera di varia et bella inventione, suoni, canti, et danze et le vaghe dame convenute ai solazzevoli balli." In *Codice Vaticano Urbinate 490,* quoted in Pandolfi, *Il teatro del Rinascimento,* 70.

26. "La notte poi che seguì, essendosi preparata un'ampia scena, si recitò la comedia dell'ingegnosissimo Bernardo Bibbiena; alla quale succedette la magnificentissima cena, dopo la quale si ballò, e molti comparvero in abito dissimulato." See Mario Equicola d'Alveto, *Dell'historia di Mantova* (Mantua: Osanna, 1608), 296, quoted in Padoan, "Introduzione," 15 n. 3.

In a play based on repeated cross-dressings, gender demarcations are hard to come by. Women and men, masters and servants, repeatedly disguise themselves across gender and class lines in *La calandria*, often with exhilarating effects. The two main characters, Santilla and Lidio, have an identity for others, as I suggested earlier, only when they put one on through clothes: "dove il vestire la differenzia non facea, non era chi l'uno dall'altro cognoscere potessi" (prologue; "they could not be distinguished except for their clothes"). Even as children, when there was no specific reason for choosing a disguise, Santilla and Lidio had exchanged clothes so often, we are told, that neither their mother nor their nurse could see a difference between the two: "a Modon, talor vestendosi Lidio da fanciulla e Santilla da maschio, non pur li forestieri, ma non essa madre, non la propria nutrice sapea discernere qual fusse Lidio o qual fusse Santilla" (1.1; "at Modon, when Lidio dressed at times like a little girl and Santilla like a little boy, their mother and their own nurse could not tell who was Lidio and who was Santilla, let alone strangers").

Since the purpose of any cross-dressing in Renaissance stories is to find a gendered identity, or as Stephen Greenblatt puts it, to find "the male trajectory of identity," for Santilla and Lidio to cross-dress is a way to retrieve the other part of themselves.[27] That is, while during their early years their dressing in the clothes of the other twin may have been done to somehow occupy the place of the other in a state of quasi-symbiosis, now in their late adolescence disguise seems to work for both Santilla and Lidio to mask the lack of, and the longing for, the other, so that their family's disintegration can be denied, following the tragic events that separated them in Modon.

Lidio and Santilla are indeed described in the play as absolutely identical adults: "amendue de un parto nati, di volto, di persona, di parlare, di modo tanto simili gli fé Natura" (1.1; "they were born twins, and Nature made them very similar in their face, appearance, way of speaking, and manners"). Given their androgynous status, they are distinguished not by gender but by sex: one is called "Lidio" and the other "Lidio femina." Even when, later on in Rome, they

---

27. Stephen Greenblatt, "Fiction and Friction," in *Shakespearean Negotiations: The Circulation of Social Energy in Renaissance England* (Berkeley and Los Angeles: University of California Press, 1988), 66–93.

need names to match their cross-dressed identities, each calls himself/herself unknowingly for the missing other: Lidio goes to Fulvia's house as Santilla, and is known as Santilla by Calandro; Santilla is called Lidio even by her adoptive father. Identical in appearance, the twins are seen in turn by Calandro, by Fessenio (Lidio's servant), and by Samia (Fulvia's servant). Samia elaborates on such a double sight—the twins coming from identical eggs—along the lines of Plautus's *Menaechmi*: "Oh Dio! oh, miraculosa maraviglia! Non è alcuno sí simile a se stesso né la neve alla neve né l'uovo a l'uovo, come è l'uno all'altro di costoro" (5.1; "My God, what a miracle! There is nobody so similar to himself nor snow to snow nor one egg to another, as one resembles the other in these two").[28]

And yet to grow, the twins have to abandon their exchangeable, insufficiently male or female condition, and find that each is a separate, different being.[29] According to Freud, the "double was originally an insurance against the destruction of the ego.... The invention of doubling as a preservation against extinction has its counterpart in the language of dreams, which is fond of representing castration by a doubling or multiplication of the genital symbol."[30] This is indeed the case in *Calandria*, as we will soon see.

In the *Menaechmi* the recovery of the lost other and the reunification of the brothers brought a narcissistic unity at the physical level, in that the two men returned to their original city, Syracuse, as well as at the psychological level, in that they eliminated everything that crowded their life: property, friends, and a wife.[31] In Bibbiena, the twins' recognition of each other leads to entry into society and to full adulthood through a marriage. Only then do Santilla and Lidio appear together dressed in the clothes of their own gender and their

28. On the fantasies, identifications, and projections that the use of twins engenders on the viewer, see Giulio Ferroni, "Il sistema comico della gemellarità," in *Il testo e la scena*, 65–84.

29. On the androgyne in the Renaissance, see Edgar Wind, "Pan and Proteus," in *Pagan Mysteries in the Renaissance* (London: Penguin, 1967), 191–217; on the androgyne in relation to this play, see Roberto Alonge, "*La Calandria* o il mito di Androgine," in *Struttura e ideologia nel teatro italiano fra '500 e '900* (Turin: Stampatori, 1978), 9–31.

30. Sigmund Freud, "The Uncanny," in *The Standard Edition of the Complete Psychological Works of Sigmund Freud* [hereafter *SE*], ed. and trans. James Strachey, 24 vols (London: Hogarth Press, 1953–74), 17:219–52, esp. 240 (1955).

31. Eric Segal is right in seeing in the *Menaechmi* a fantasy of the first twin, Surreptus, to conjure up "a surrogate self to indulge in forbidden pleasures while he himself preserves the outward respectability of every day." See "The *Menaechmi*: Roman Comedy of Errors," in *Roman Laughter: The Comedy of Plautus* (Cambridge: Harvard University Press, 1970), 43–51.

own sex (previously they were dressed both as women, both as men, or both as the other—but never as him/herself should have dressed, following customary gender demarcations). They are also symbolically reunited in the sort of maternal dark womb that is Fulvia's bedroom, while Fulvia herself is removed from the status of obsessed lover and cast into that of benign mother-in-law. Before we arrive at that point, however, it pays to examine how gender and sex become prosthetic devices in *La calandria*.

In the prologue to the anonymous play *La venexiana*, recently recovered and now considered by many to be one of the best Italian Renaissance plays, the acknowledgment that women's parts are played by men is made explicit and emphasis is given to what lies beneath the dress: "E non vi immaginate altrimenti di vedere delle donne, se non in quanto esse hanno indosso le vesti loro; spogliate le quali non sono creature da amarsi soltanto, ma amanti come voi uomini siete" ("Don't imagine that you are seeing women, although they are dressed as such, because, with those clothes taken off them, they aren't just creatures to be loved, but lovers, as you men are").[32]

The statement indicates that not only the actors in this performance but also the audience invited to it are men; more intriguingly, we are reminded that cross-dressing has somehow to always call attention to the fact that there is a real woman or man under the disguise. In chivalric romances, there are scenes where a knight is revealed as a cross-dressed woman at the moment when, in meeting the man who will fall in love with her at first sight, she loses her helmet and displays her long, blond hair. In both *Orlando furioso* and *Gerusalemme liberata* this regrounding into femininity, this castration in a psychoanalytical sense, is reinforced through a wounding: the women warriors Bradamante and Clorinda receive cuts at their necks soon after the uncovering of their identity in drag (in Bradamante's case this occasions a haircut that Ariosto uses later to full advantage). That is, hair length is inscribed in romances of chivalry metaphorically as a sign of sex (long hair equals women, short hair equals men) and not of gender.

In comedy, however, hair is a prop and is used as an inherently unreliable prosthetic device. True, voice could have grounded sexual identity and although it seems to have held no remarkable importance in romances of chivalry, it must have been of consequence in plays; hence the frequency of remarks on how the actors on stage sounded. But something even more undeniable was needed to

32. I cite from the modern Italian version by Zorzi rather than from the original Venetian dialect, which faces it. Translations here and subsequently are mine.

differentiate sexes, and this explains perhaps the insistent allusions in plays to the actors' sexual organs.

In *La calandria*, Fulvia is made to refuse Santilla, whom she thinks is Lidio, because in embracing him/her she does not find what she thought was there: "Tutto l'ho maneggiato e tocco; né altro del solito ritrovo che la presenzia in lui. Ed io non tanto la privazion del mio diletto piango quanto el danno suo; ché, per me, privo si trova di quel che piú si brama" (4.2; "I have touched him and felt him all over, and of his usual self I can only find the figure. I am not crying so much for having been deprived of my pleasure, but for his injury, because I feel he has lost that which is most prized").[33] Here, lack is referred to in detail but is not shown. But when later Fessenio fears that Lidio has been truly changed into Santilla by the necromancer, he resolves to reassure himself right there in the street (and thus onstage) about the presence of Lidio's male sexual organ: "Però chiarir me ne voglio. . . . Con man lo toccherò, se me amazzassi" (5.2; "I want to make sure. . . . I'll touch him with my hand, even if I were to die in the attempt"). Fessenio finds what he is looking for, literally in front of the audience: "Sei desso, sì; e sei anche maschio" (5.3; "Yes, you are Lidio, and you are a man too"). In both situations where characters are hoping to find a male sexual organ (this scene with Fessenio and the earlier one with Fulvia), the penis was of course always there, whatever sex the fictional characters were supposed to represent, because both Lidio and Santilla were played by boys. The public must have gotten some satisfaction at being reminded of the specificity of male

---

33. This scene has close connections to the one in *Mandragola*, where Nicia wants to ascertain himself of the sexual equipment of the young man, Callimaco, who is going to make love to his wife, Lucrezia: "volli toccar con mano" (5.2). See chapter 2. Another example is in Gl'Intronati's *Gl'ingannati*, where a young female servant is made to report in excited terms in the last act on the "weapon" that suddenly reveals a young page, thought to be a woman, to be a man instead, Lelia's long lost brother, Fabrizio. In the episode in the *Orlando furioso* modeled on Bibbiena's play, Fiordispina despairs when the cross-dressed knight with whom she has shared her bed for the night turns out to be a woman. Not believing that she can desire so much a person without the proper sexual equipment for the purpose she has in mind, Fiordispina keeps checking for changes all night long: "Si desta; e nel destar mette la mano, / e ritrova pur sempre il sogno vano!" (25.43). On what this means in the context of crossdressing in the *Furioso*, see Valeria Finucci, *The Lady Vanishes: Subjectivity and Representation in Castiglione and Ariosto* (Stanford: Stanford University Press, 1992), 202–25.

and female bodies, knowing all along that only one sex, albeit two genders, was on stage.[34]

At other times, there are references to female body parts that actors playing women's roles did not possess and yet were "shown." In *La venexiana*, to return to my earlier example, Iulio openly kisses the breasts of Angela, also played by a male actor, who remarks: "Ah, ghiottoncello, tu le baci sì. Guarda di non spremerle, ché strilleranno" (3.3; "You glutton! You kiss them so. Be careful not to squeeze them, because they will scream"). Playing along, Iulio wisely adds: "Questa pomellina la voglio per me; l'altra sia la vostra" (3.3; "This little apple I want for me; the other can be yours"). What was the audience seeing in the costumed actor?[35] And why was the author specifically drawing attention to a cleavage that was not there? Why self-consciously stage a lack? For Peter Stallybrass this fixation on visualizing specific body parts that nevertheless are missing in the boy actor demonstrates how impossible it is to fix gender, how in fact gender is a production, an addition of prosthetic parts.[36] And indeed in *La calandria*, when Santilla is dressed as a woman to meet Fulvia, Fannio—he too dressed as a woman—tells her that she looks so feminine that everybody would take her for a woman ("e sta tanto bene che non è persona che non lo pigliasse per donna," 3.21). The joke is that she is a female character, although everybody else takes her for a man, but since she was being represented on the stage by a male actor, the author's reference to the fetish that subtends the construction of gendered identities must have been put in as a specific aside for the audience. A similar joke is present in a previous scene involving the same two actors. Here

34. Genders were carefully staged among singers as well. A 1589 Florentine intermezzo provided men with papier maché breastpieces and chests ("poppe di cartone") to better appropriate a fiction of femininity. But they were given to women, too, so that we have both the creation of a gender and the inscription of a sex, according to circumstances. All performers wore masks. See Aby Warburg, "I costumi teatrali per gli intermezzi del 1589," in *Gesammelte Schriften* (Leipzig: Teubner, 1932), 431; and Alois Maria Nagler, *Theatre Festivals of the Medici, 1539–1637* (New Haven: Yale University Press, 1964), 77–79.

35. It is doubtful that *La venexiana* was ever staged. Padoan seems to think so, Franco Fido (private conversation) doubts it. As I will further elaborate in the last chapter, whenever castrati singing female parts had anything resembling a cleavage, they showed it.

36. Peter Stallybrass, "Transvestism and the 'Body Beneath': Speculating on the Boy Actor," in *Erotic Politics: Desire on the Renaissance Stage*, ed. Susan Zimmerman (New York: Routledge, 1992), 64–83.

Fannio consents to Santilla's visit to Fulvia dressed as a woman with the words "Tu donna sei; ella in forma di donna te adomanda; da lei anderai. Al provar quel che cerca, troverrà quel che non vuole" (2.4; "You are a woman; she wants you to go to her dressed like a woman, and you will go there. Feeling what she looks for, she will find what she does not want"). But then, what can one find in a woman's body, which has precisely "nothing," or at the most a crack ("fesso") as the author is at pains to repeat? Unless again the joke is for the audience, since the cross-dressed male actor playing Santilla has indeed something to be found.

Throughout *La calandria* clothes project a sex that may not be there, and characters respond according to the gendered signals given out by constructing a sex beneath it. That gender is a production can clearly be seen in the behavior of Santilla, in whom the dislocation from Modon brought a loss of identity. In passing for a man—melancholia makes her fetishize her masculine clothes—Santilla becomes assertive, in charge, manly. She, in short, reincorporates what she considers the most traumatic event of her life, the loss of her brother, by trying to be him, again and again. But even when she accepts Fannio's invitation to go to Fulvia's house in order not to be found for the day (her adoptive father is looking for her to finalize his daughter Virginia's marriage with him/her), Santilla makes clear that she would be content with her status as a woman if women were afforded the same opportunities as men in society: "Assai è manifesto quanto sia miglior la fortuna degli uomini che quella delle donne. Ed io piú che l'altre l'ho per prova cognosciuto" (2.1; "It is well known that men are more fortunate than women, and I can bear better witness to this than most women").[37] Like other unmarried female heroes of later comedies, Santilla is allowed to cross-dress and experiment with gender just before bidding adieu to her androgynous-looking adolescent years and embracing femininity with an inevitable marriage. Let us remember that at the start of the sixteenth century, Florentine girls married when they were about seventeen and Venetian girls

37. In her sharp pro-woman stance, Lucrezia Marinella adduces the same argument: "è falso, che ogni donna desideri d'essere huomo, e se lo desiderasse ciò farebbe ella per sottrahere il collo dalla tirannesca signoria del maschio." See *La nobiltà et l'eccellenza delle donne co' i diffetti e mancamenti degli uomini* (Venice: Ciotti, 1601), 124. Maggie Gunsberg also notices that unlike other crossdressed females in Renaissance comedy, Santilla does not desire anybody. See her *Gender and the Italian Stage: From the Renaissance to the Present Day* (Cambridge: Cambridge University Press, 1997), 85.

when about sixteen.[38] This was the only moment in life when women could be still under the illusion that they had a choice in selecting a partner, an illusion that the comedies of the time, perhaps not reflecting real life, liked to foster.

As a married woman in her thirties, Fulvia has a different agenda from Santilla in her cross-dressing, for her wearing of male clothes makes her not socially equal to men but a sexual opportunist. Dressing as a man has nothing to do with identity for Fulvia and matches more closely instead male cross-dressing, which is done in the play only to further sexual goals. As many stories by Boccaccio registered at the time, it was popular belief that women who had some sexual experience had a hard time doing without sex and would resort to subterfuges to get it anyway. Even doctors keenly recommended women who had been sexually active to release their seed any way they could to avoid problems down the road, the sin of fornication (or of masturbation, perhaps) being easier to accommodate than withering melancholia or the invasive use of medical props. Following Galen, Juan Huarte, for example, described cases of women who lost their hearing, motion, breathing, and sight because they became widows too young and had no access to sex.[39] Visiting Florence, the Catalan doctor Arnaldus of Villanova, himself a strong believer in the need for therapeutic coitus (to the extent that he recommended it even to monks), was shocked by the habits of local widows and wives of absentee husbands who masturbated or used an artificial phallus, "a small stuffed bag in the shape of a man's penis." A more elaborate dildo made of brass or bronze, he noticed, could be filled with aromatic rosewater.[40] As for cross-dressing, whether it was practiced in everyday life in the

38. For the age of marriage of Florentine women, between seventeen and eighteen, see Julius Kirshner and Anthony Molho, "Il monte delle doti a Firenze dalla sua fondazione nel 1425 alla metà del sedicesimo secolo: Abbozzo di una ricerca," in *Ricerche storiche*, n.s., 10 (1980): 21–47, esp. 41. For the Venetian case, see Stanley Chojnacki, *Women and Men in Renaissance Venice: Essays on Patrician Society* (Baltimore: Johns Hopkins University Press, 2000), 175 and 313. Men too at times married at eighteen, although rarely. Earlier than eighteen would not have been plausible at the time, and this is the reason why Lidio's twin, Santilla, had to be eighteen. Later plays make adolescent women a bit younger, more or less sixteen, perhaps because at that age they were more realistically played by boy actors.

39. "assaissime donne restate vedove nella gioventù loro, persero l'udito, il moto, la respirazione, e finalmente la vista." See Juan Huarte, *Essamina de gl'ingegni de gli huomini accomodati ad apprendere qual si voglia scienza* (Venice: Barezzi, 1600), 15.375.

40. Arnaldus of Villanova (Arnau de Villanova), *Breviarum practice*, in *Opera* (Lyons: Fradin, 1504), ch. 9, 222v.

sixteenth century, as this and other plays imply, is open to discussion, although we know that some women chose occasionally to travel in male apparel to escape the dangers of the road.

Cross-dressing by men is in any case more problematic than cross-dressing by women, no matter the gratifications. The wearing of female clothes makes Lidio appear womanish: Calandro falls in love with him looking like a "she" and dreams of "quelle labra vermigliuzze e quelle gote vino e ricotta" (2.6; "those red lips and those cheeks the color of wine and ricotta cheese"), and Fulvia actively pursues him. Unlike his sister, Lidio dresses as a woman not to be her, but to replace her in a way that brings him advantages; thus his cross-dressing is parodic, just like that of the servant Fannio. It also allows him in fantasy to resolve his anxiety about castration through a feminine masquerade.[41] Such a production of the body as a performance of both sex and gender has recently been visualized in a freely rendered cinematic version of *La calandria* by director Pasquale Festa Campanile (Titanus, 1972). In the movie, when Fulvia asks that Lidio be substituted with his sister in the last scene so that her own infidelity remains hidden, the substitute is not an androgynous-looking Santilla played by a boy actor, but a castrato singer. To be sure, Festa Campanile threw historical truthfulness out of the window when he put a castrato in the Rome of 1513, although it is true that castrati were often admitted to women's bedrooms in later years, when their number increased, because husbands did not feel their presence in taboo places sexually threatening. But in a sense he brought the play back to its urtext, since in Terence's *Eunuchus*, a young lover, Chaerea, pretends to be a eunuch in order to have access to his beloved Pamphila's bed.[42]

Following the carnivalesque use of ithyphallic prostheses, sex too is used as a prosthetic device in *La calandria*, especially in relation to Calandro, the play's acknowledged fool and the butt of the author's jokes — as in the case of Boccaccio's Calandrino to whom, as I wrote in the introduction, he is linked onomastically.

41. As Judith Butler asks: "Is drag the imitation of gender, or does it dramatize the signifying gestures through which gender itself is established? Does being female constitute a 'natural fact' or a cultural performance, or is 'naturalness' constituted through discursively constrained performative acts that produce the body through and within the categories of sex?" In *Gender Trouble: Feminism and the Subversion of Identity* (New York: Routledge, 1990), x.

42. In the all-male Roman stage, eunuchs also acted. See Dympna Callaghan, "The Castrator's Song: Female Impersonation on the Early Modern Stage," *Journal of Medieval and Early Modern Studies* 26 (1996): 321–53, esp. 324.

When people have to travel long distances in boats—the servant Fessenio tells Calandro—they are dismembered for space and ease of transportation only to be literally remembered upon arrival. Sometimes, in the confusion, certain body parts are attached back wrongly or exchanged with others of the wrong size:

> Poi, arrivati in porto, chi vuol si piglia e rinchiava il membro suo. E spesso anco avviene che, per inavvertenzia o per malizia, l'uno piglia el membro dell'altro e sel mette ove piú gli piace; e talvolta non gli torna bene perché toglie un membro piú grosso che non gli bisogna o una gamba più corta della sua, onde ne diventa poi zoppo o sproporzionato, intendi? (2.6)

> Upon arrival each person picks out and screws back his member. Often it happens, whether through carelessness or malice, that a man takes a member that belongs to someone else and puts it where he likes it most, and sometimes this is not advantageous because he picks a larger member than the one he needs or a leg shorter than his own, which renders him crippled and malformed.

The public clearly is asked to view the episode as one more instance of the author's use of wit at the expense of a gullible character.

But the theory of limbs "torn asunder" has a long philosophical genealogy. In explaining why a child resembles both parents and has, for example, his father's eyes and his mother's chin, Empedocles held that limbs are torn apart by some process and get united only in the womb. Aristotle criticized this argument because the combination of severed limbs meant that an extra set of parts would have to be discarded, which would have been contrary to the mechanism of nature. Likewise, Galen showed that these surplus arms, legs, fingers, and eyes were not found in women upon dissection. Moreover, to organize this disorder a third seed would have been necessary, a possibility that he rejected right away.[43]

Not that people in the early modern period did not see their share of prosthetic devices or lacked doctors' advice on how to attach them properly to the body, if needed. Ambroise Paré carefully illustrated artificial hands, legs, eyes, penises, noses, and ears in his book on surgery and noticed that the material used for organ repair or substitution could be papier maché, tin, iron, wood,

---

43. For a reading of Empedocles's fragment 63 DK and of Aristotle's and Galen's comments, see Michael Boylan, "The Galenic and Hippocratic Challenges to Aristotle's Conception Theory," *Journal of the History of Biology* 17 (1984): 83–112, esp. 87.

silver, or gold. Color was applied at the end of the procedure.[44] Leonardo Fioravanti gave a detailed description of two brothers making a nose by grafting skin after a patient happened to have his nose cut off. For the restoration of Andres Gutiero's nose, which he supervised, Fioravanti recurred to a more homely remedy: he picked up the cut off portion from the ground, urinated on it to sterilize it, patched it back on, and in eight days, he assures the reader, the man was cured.[45]

We also know that there were prosthetic sexual devices that could be carried along to use even for occasions that one might deem rare. Here is one case (from the eighteenth century but offered here because it is so precisely described). The lovely singer Teresa, alias the castrato Bellino, has a problem: she needs to pass for a castrato in order to perform in the Marches, a papal region where the presence of female singers was forbidden on the stage. As she recounts to her would-be seducer, Giacomo Casanova, the castrato Salimbeni, her former lover, rose to the challenge she presented by fitting her with a device so easy to purchase in a provincial street that we can fancy it must have been used often: "It's a sort of flabby, long tube, about as thick as a human thumb, with very soft, white skin. I laughed to myself this morning when you called it a clitoris. The tube is attached to a thin, transparent oval of skin five or six inches long and about two inches wide. This skin is then applied, with gum dragon, to the area of the female sex organ, to hide it."[46] This organ needs to be put on, Teresa explains, when she has to convince the impresarios hiring her that she is not a woman although she has breasts. So far she had to put it on only for old priests to certify her sex, and since they looked but did not touch, the falseness of the addition went undetected. As Casanova realizes, this was no simple model of a male sexual organ, because it had to be modified to fit the circumstances, considering that Teresa needed to appear not as a man, but as a castrato; her prosthesis

44. Ambroise Paré, *The Books of Surgery with the Magazine of the Instruments Necessary for It*, ed. and trans. Robert Linker and Nathan Womack (Athens: University of Georgia Press, 1969), 144, 147, 237, 242.

45. Leonardo Fioravanti, *Il tesoro della vita humana* (Venice: Sessa, 1582), bk. 2, ch. 27. See also Domenico Furfaro, *La vita e l'opera di Leonardo Fioravanti* (Bologna: Società Tipografica Editori, 1963), 101 and 108.

46. Giacomo Casanova, *The Story of My Life*, trans. Stephen Sartarelli and Sophie Hawkes (New York: Penguin, 2001), 105. Casanova was so impressed with the device that he asked Teresa to wear it again just for him.

therefore had to be reproduced without testicles. Note that Casanova is not deceived and immediately links this modified male organ not to its uncastrated look-alike, but to the clitoris, thus relieving men, and the male sex, of any link to monstrosity.[47] That is, rather than perceiving that both male and female subjects have their own identity in castration and that lack is inscribed in the male as well as in the female body, he disavows what he sees. If the fetish works in Freudian terms not to hide that women are castrated but to negate that men are, then Bellino's prosthesis is only cause for panic, were it to refer to men, as Casanova instinctively realizes.[48]

In Freudian psychoanalysis, all fantasies of screwing off arms and legs or of losing one's eye constitute the equivalent of castration.[49] In *Calandria* the scene featuring unnattached members foregrounds Calandro's fear that men with large members may be more fortunate with women than he is. And the fact that, as Bibbiena writes, the places that stick out in man's body are those to be cut off ("ove tu vedi svolgersi," 2.6) confirms that we are enmeshed in a fantasy of castration. Sex changes in any case do not stop at master-and-servant fantasies in the story. Countering a pedant's speech against women, Fessenio argues that in his world every man wants to become a woman not only in spirit but also in body, a joke perhaps addressed to the large number of "catamites" living in the papal court, which Cardinal Bibbiena knew intimately: "Non sappiam noi che le donne sono sí degne che oggi non è alcuno che non le vadi imitando e che volentieri, con l'anima e col corpo, femina non diventi?" (1.2; "Don't we know that women are so worthy that nowadays there is not a man who will not go about imitating them and who would not willingly become female in body and soul?").[50]

47. For a fuller examination of the charms of the castrato, see the last chapter.

48. As Freud writes in his description of the athletic support belt, a sort of "fig-leaf on a statue" as he puts it, since this apparel hides the genitals and therefore the difference between the sexes: "Analysis shows that it signified that women were castrated and that they were not castrated; and it also allowed of the hypothesis that men were castrated, for all these possibilities could equally well be concealed under the belt." See Sigmund Freud, "On Fetishism," in SE 21:157 (1961).

49. Sigmund Freud, "The Uncanny," in SE 17:231-32 (1955).

50. The joke of course runs counter to whatever was commonly understood to be the case, that if women could choose they would want to be men. As Gasparo Pallavicino argues in Castiglione's treatise, "universalmente ogni donna desidera essere omo, per un certo

To be sure, in the Galenic humoral system the possibility of a sex change due to variations in heat was accounted for, as I argued earlier. Following Galen, the anatomist Alessandro Benedetti put it very concisely: "The male genitals are external, the female genitals or vagina are located within the body; if they fall forward the male groin appears."[51] Tommaso Campanella insisted that cases of sudden sex changes happened in Italy more than once and many men witnessed them, because male genitals sprout ("uscire fuori"), he stated, when internal heat increases in individuals who have been born as females.[52] Juan Huarte made heat the culprit for variations in sex. To explain why some men appear effeminate and some women manly he concentrated on the temperature of the mother's womb. Sudden heat in the first two months of pregnancy, he argued, may make male organs sprout ("usciti fuora") in those who originally were female fetuses; sudden cold may produce the opposite result and push the male genital apparatus back inside ("rientrano dentro"). Although Huarte feared that his theory was difficult to prove, nonetheless he urged his readers to believe it, since it could be confirmed at least by historians, if not by doctors' opinions.[53]

Intriguing in this respect is the case of Huarte's compatriot Elena de Céspedes, a "mulatto" slave who claimed that in giving birth to a daughter in 1562, she pushed out a penis as well: "with the force that she applied in labor

<hr>

istinto di natura che le insegna la sua perfezione." See *Il libro del cortegiano* (Milan: Mursia, 1972), 3.15.222.

51. Alessandro Benedetti (1450–1512?), *The History of the Human Body* (*Historia corporis humani*, 1502), in *Studies in Pre-Vesalian Anatomy: Biography, Translations, Documents*, ed. Levi Robert Lind (Philadelphia: American Philosophical Society, 1975), 84. To be sure, doctors too often took a prolapsed uterus for a descended penis; changes in sex therefore may have been far fewer than claimed. Some of the medical literature was written expressly to educate doctors on how to recognize problems. See Evelyne Berriot-Salvadore, "The Discourse of Medicine and Science," in *A History of Women in the West: Renaissance and Enlightenment Paradoxes*, ed. Natalie Zemon Davis and Arlette Farge (Cambridge: Harvard University Press, 1993), 348–88, esp. 360. See also my introduction and chapters 1 and 6.

52. "Dopo che dall'utero erano uscite delle donne ed in stato perfetto, queste sono divenute maschi a causa del caldo interno divenuto maggiore e più robusto, che è riuscito così a far uscire fuori i genitali; e questo fatto è accaduto nelle nostre regioni e lo hanno visto molti uomini." In *Philosophia sensibus demonstrata*, ed. L. De Franco (Naples: Libreria Scientifica Editrice, 1974), 284. See also Lina Bolzoni, "Tommaso Campanella e le donne: fascino e negazione della differenza," *Annali d'Italianistica* 7 (1989): 193–216.

53. Huarte, *Essamina*, 378.

she broke the skin over the urinary canal, and a head came out, (the length) of about half a big thumb . . . in its shape it resembled the head of a male member."[54] This sexual metamorphosis motivated Elena to call himself Eleno, marry a woman, and live under this identity for the next twenty years. In the meantime, he became a soldier and surgeon. In her trial, the Inquisition did implicitly admit that, given the right combination, it is possible for a female body to metamorphose into a male, but such was not the case here because doctors could not find a clear, visible sign of manhood. Eleno was thus condemned as a female bigamist in 1588. During the trial, however, a number of witnesses, including doctors, Eleno's female lovers, and other male friends, testified that he had a well-developed penis and testicles regular in size, with a small mark under them. As it turns out, this almost unnoticeable mark was crucial to Eleno's case, because it was there, he said, that his appearing/disappearing penis was located, although some doctors disagreed that such a position was anatomically correct for a male organ.[55]

A magical intervention also was held responsible for physiological changes. As Girolamo Mercurio lamented, the "vulgar crowd" widely believed that witches could change men into beasts and themselves into cats, that they could introduce in a woman's stomach all sorts of objects—nails, knives, pens—for no reason, and could dry men's semen through enchantment.[56] Witches could also deprive men of their sexual organs. For example, in *Malleus maleficarum* a man told a Dominican father during confession that he had lost his member and gave ocular proof of the fact. The priest advised him to think of a witch who

54. The documents relative to the Inquisition trial of Elena de Céspedes are under her name in the Archivo Histórico Nacional, Madrid, legajo 234, expediente 24, sección Inquisición. I am using the translation given by Israel Burshatin in "Written on the Body: Slave or Hermaphrodite in Sixteenth-Century Spain," in *Queer Iberia: Sexualities, Cultures, and Crossings from the Middle Ages to the Renaissance,* ed. Josiah Blackmore and Gregory Hutcheson (Durham, N.C.: Duke University Press, 1999), 420–56, at 435.

55. In his defense, Eleno used humoral theories. Being himself one of those "androgynous beings or, in other words, hermaphrodites, who have both sexes," he said, when the male sex was more prevalent in his body he took his cue: "At the time I arranged to be married the masculine sex was more prevalent in me; and I was naturally a man and had all that was necessary for a man to marry a woman." Translation by Burshatin in "Written on the Body," 447–48.

56. Girolamo Mercurio, *De gli errori popolari d'Italia* (Venice: Ciotti, 1603), 4.16.211v, 212v, 213v.

could have done this to him and to soften her with words for the purpose of having his organ restituted. A few days later the man reported that things had worked satisfactorily and he had been given back his penis.[57] Searching through trial documents, Romano Canossa tells the story of a woman named Pasqua, who was told by a devil that he could perform a sex change. When she gave birth to a baby girl, he cut off her index finger and inserted it into the baby's "nature." Immediately, the girl became a boy. The Inquisition summarily condemned her.[58] In *La calandria*, when Fulvia touches Santilla's body thinking she is caressing Lidio's and notices a body part missing, the audience of the time understood the joke but knew just as well and perhaps even half-believed that such a sexual mishap could happen, although rarely and in very unclear circumstances.[59] Like Samia and Fessenio, Fulvia thinks that sex is not a given but a production, an artifice, the result of prestidigitation.

Since nature supposedly tends toward perfection even when challenged by genetic mistakes, however, sexual metamorphosis did not concern men: there were no reported cases of males changing into females. In Ariosto's *Orlando furioso*, Ricciardetto tells his credulous Fiordispina that he became a man because he desperately wanted to be one to satisfy her as a man. When a nymph sprinkled water on him he felt his sexual organs shoot up, and from female (that is, from his twin sister Bradamante, whom he had pretended to be) he turned into male (25.64). Since every organ was in place, such claimed transformations could be believed. Fiordispina has no problems in accepting the account and gladly welcomes the knight in her bed.

57. Heinrich Kramer and Jacobus Springer, *The "Malleus Maleficarum" of Heinrich Kramer and James Sprenger*, trans. Montague Summers (New York: Dover, 1971), 93 (originally published 1485). See also Walter Stephens, "Witches Who Steal Penises: Impotence and Illusion," *Journal of Medieval and Early Modern Studies* 28 (1998): 495–529.

58. See Romano Canossa, *Sessualità e inquisizione in Italia tra Cinquecento e Seicento* (Rome: Sapere, 2000, 1994), 148.

59. This scene will be repeated with a telling change in the comedy *Amore nello specchio* (1622) of Giovan Battista Andreini. The main character, Florinda, wants a woman and not a man in her bed and is surprised when Lidia turns out to be her brother-in-law. There, a lesbian scene is conveniently changed into a heterosexual one.

Agitated at the possibility of a sexual mishap when she touches Santilla's body and finds it lacking, Fulvia asks the magician Ruffo for an explanation. No problem, she is told: what is missing can be easily put back, because Santilla/Lidio is not a woman but a hermaphrodite, and hermaphrodites could use their male and their female organs equally well, according to their needs. Showing appreciation for intersexual subjects, Ruffo asks the "hermaphrodite" Santilla next to use a different organ—the male one—in visiting Fulvia: "Fa che il barbafiorito usi or con Fulvia il pestello, non il mortaro" (4.3; "See that our 'Flowerbeard' use his pestle instead of his mortar with Fulvia"). He then reiterates in the letter he sends Fulvia to reassure her that sex can be bestowed: "ma sta sicura che allo amante tuo rimetterà presto il ramo" (4.6; "but rest assured that he will soon restore to your lover the missing branch"). Indeed, Fulvia has no problem in believing that the dismembered can be re-membered ("faccia e disfaccia," 2.3). As if this dizzying taking off and putting back the male organ in males, females, and hermaphrodites is not enough, Fulvia later asks that Ruffo change Lidio into Santilla, thus having him perform a reverse sex change—from having to not having, from penis to "nothing," from transgendered to woman, and from intersexual to female, so that she can fool her brothers, who want to shame her because they think she has a man in bed with her (5.4).

Ruffo is unsure of what hermaphrodites are, because he keeps misnaming them as "merdafiorito" or "barbafiorito" (3.17; "Shitflower, Flowerbeard"), attributing to the hermaphrodite either the passive or the active role in a homosexual relationship. Although unaware of it, Ruffo here follows Aristotle, who in *Generation of Animals* treated hermaphroditism as a case of twinship gone wrong. The defect that causes genitalia to double in hermaphrodites, Aristotle argued, comes from the mother, who has unbalanced matter to offer: too much for one child, too little for two. When that surplus is in the groin, the result is a being with two sets of genitals. Since matter meant imperfection, and the father provided no matter to generation (semen was the vector of form and movement and was not a material), the hermaphrodite was most often a female and the redundant male genitals were considered a useless extra growth.[60] The hermaph-

---

60. "Some creatures develop in such a way that they have two generative organs [one male, the other female]. Always, when the redundancy happens, one of the two is operative and the other inoperative, since the latter, being contrary to Nature, always gets stunted so

rodite's sex was only apparently unstable in Aristotle because the temperature of the heart would confirm one sex or the other. In a work wrongly attributed to Galen, *De spermate*—itself a reelaboration of Hippocratic thought—hermaphroditism is said to be caused by both parents, since it was the result of male and female sperm mixing wrongly:

> It may even happen that from the combination of a weak male seed and a strong female seed there is born a child having both sexes. If the seed falls into the left-hand part of the womb, what is formed is female . . . and if the male seed prevails, the girl child created will be virile and strong, sometimes hairy. It may also happen in this case that as a result of the weakness of the female seed there is born a child provided with both sexes.[61]

For Avicenna, it was more a problem of sperm direction than of mechanics: sperm deposited in the right side of the womb produced males, he wrote; in the left, females; and in the middle, hermaphrodites. Albertus Magnus believed that hermaphrodites with a double set of genitals could not impregnate and be impregnated, but could have sex with both organs.[62]

The sixteenth century took its fascination for the hermaphrodite to a new level, whether pure hermaphroditism was denied, as by followers of Aristotle, or accepted, as by the school of Galen.[63] According to Ambroise Paré, there are four types of intersexuality: the male hermaphrodite, who possesses a functioning penis but inactive female organs; the female hermaphrodite, who has functioning female organs and periodic menses, but only a rudimentary penis; the hermaphrodite in which neither the male nor the female organs are functional; and the hermaphrodite in possession of functional male and female organs. The last

---

far as nourishment is concerned." In *Generation of Animals*, trans. A. L. Peck (Cambridge: Harvard University Press, 1990), 4.4.772b. Aristotle never uses the word "hermaphrodite."

61. Quoted in Danielle Jacquart and Claude Thomasset, *Sexuality and Medicine in the Middle Ages*, trans. Matthew Adamson (Princeton: Princeton University Press, 1988), 141.

62. See Joan Cadden, *The Meaning of Sex Difference in the Middle Ages: Medicine, Science and Culture* (Cambridge: Cambridge University Press, 1993), 212–13. Cadden's examples show that general beliefs on the subject did not change much from the medieval to the early modern period.

63. For this argument, see Lorraine Daston and Katharine Park, "The Hermaphrodite and the Orders of Nature: Sexual Ambiguity in Early Modern France," in *Premodern Sexualities*, ed. Louise Fradenburg and Carla Freccero (New York: Routledge, 1996), 117–36, at 117.

category is the most dangerous, because individuals with a surplus of functioning sexes can engage in promiscuous behavior; therefore laws have to make sure
that they choose "which sex organs they wish to use, and they are forbidden on
pain of death to use any but those they will have chosen, on account of the mis-
fortunes that could result from such."[64] Contemporary legislation still required
that the hermaphrodite belong to a specific sex to enter marriage and inherit
but allowed for nature to manifest itself slowly. So, for example, Andrea Ar-
naldi baptized as male the misshapen body of his daughter Giovanna Gaspara,
who was born premature.[65] If the baby reached adulthood, the parish records
and name could be changed at the appropriate time. As late as the eighteenth
century, in the registers of the bishopric of Battaglia Terme, infants with unclear sex were registered as such, without any attempt on the part of midwife,
doctor, parents, or priest to guess one way or the other.[66] When sexual identity
was absolutely undecidable, which was quite rare, the person affected could be
allowed to figure out to which gender he or she wanted to belong, following
natural inclinations. By adulthood it was necessary to wear the clothes specific to
the choice made. Lapses in behavior were punished.[67] In short, shifts in sex were

64. Ambroise Paré, *On Monsters and Marvels*, ed. and trans. James Pallister (Chicago:
Chicago University Press, 1982), 27.

65. See James Grubb, *Provincial Families of the Renaissance: Private and Public Life in the Veneto*
(Baltimore: Johns Hopkins University Press, 1996), 51.

66. As in this entry of October 7, 1752: "Un figlio di Pietro Mondin della Rivella battiz-
zato dalla comare appena nato senza nome per non sapere se fosse figlio, o figlia, e subito
morto." Or in this other entry of March 25, 1759: "Una fanciulla figlia di Antonio Gaio, non
sapendosi se fosse maschio, o femena, perché non ancora ben nata, fu battizzata senza nome
dalla Comare." I owe this information about the registers of Battaglia Terme, in the province
of Padua, to Luciano Donato, who is inventorying them.

67. This is the argument of Michel Foucault. See *Herculine Barbin, Being the Recently
Discovered Memoirs of a Nineteenth-Century Hermaphrodite*, trans. Richard McDougall (New
York: Pantheon, 1980), vii–viii. On hermaphroditism, see also Ann Rosalind Jones and
Peter Stallybrass, "Fetishizing Gender: Constructing the Hermaphrodite in Renaissance
Europe," in *Body Guards: The Cultural Politics of Gender Ambiguity*, ed. Julia Epstein and Kristina
Straub (New York: Routledge, 1991), 80–111; Greenblatt, "Fiction and Friction," 82; Julia
Epstein, "Either/Or–Neither/Both: Sexual Ambiguity and the Ideology of Gender," *Gen-
ders* 7 (1990): 99–142; Thomas Laqueur, *Making Sex: Body and Gender from the Greeks to Freud*
(Cambridge: Harvard University Press, 1990); and Daston and Park, "The Hermaphrodite
and the Orders of Nature," 117–36.

deemed possible because nature could all too easily produce deviations from the (male) norm, but shifts in gender needed to be regulated, because a rigidly structured system of binary differentiation was needed for the proper functioning of society. To be bisexed amounted to being a freak, but to be bigendered was a threat to society.

In most cases of what we call today chromosomal aberrations, the opinion followed was that of doctors, who considered in their deliberations both the shape of the genitals and the weight of humors. Paolo Zacchia recommended that the organ on the right (for hermaphrodites with organs doubled horizontally) or the organ on top (for those doubled vertically) be used to determine correct gendering.[68] Hermaphrodites with male genitals or infants born with two penises were to be treated as male and circumcised, according to Moses Maimonides, the Jewish Spanish philosopher of the Middle Ages.[69] Sometimes doctors themselves preferred not to assign and correct sex. Realdo Colombo asked himself why nature in its providential and wise ways could allow for the presence of more than one sexual organ in an individual, and considered surgery too risky for a woman who asked him to cut off her penis because the organ was an obstruction to her intercourse with a man.[70] Popular culture and poetry, meanwhile, often sidestepped the medical explanations and used the term "hermaphrodite" to refer to nonheterosexuals of either sex and males who liked the passive feminine role.[71]

In classical mythology the hermaphrodite was male. Ovid tells us that Hermaphroditus, the son of Aphrodite and Hermes, was lured by the nymph Salmacis to a pool. In embracing him, she entwined so much her body with his that, although he was unwilling to submit to her desire, the person emerging later from the pool was neither a man nor a woman, but a combination of both. Hermaphroditus mourned his loss of masculinity; the myth tells us no more

68. On this point by Zacchia, see Laqueur, *Making Sex*, 141.

69. Moses Maimonides (1135–1204), *The Guide of the Perplexed*, ed. and trans. Shlomo Pines (Chicago: University of Chicago Press, 1963). See also Cadden, *The Meaning of Sex Difference in the Middle Ages*.

70. Realdo Colombo, *De re anatomica* (Venice: Bevilacqua, 1559), 494–95.

71. See Randolph Trumbach, "The Birth of the Queen: Sodomy and the Emergence of Gender Equality in Modern Culture, 1660–1750," in *Hidden from History: Reclaiming the Gay and Lesbian Past*, ed. Martin Dauml Duberman, Martha Vicinus, and George Chauncey, Jr. (New York: New American Library, 1989), 129–40, esp. 133.

about Salmacis. Ovid followed the Roman practice of assigning hermaphrodites a masculine identity on the basis of their visible male organ. Augustine states that in his time too the preference was "assigning them to the superior sex."[72]

By the sixteenth century things had changed, and the hermaphrodite came to be considered not a man (because this clearly makes hermaphroditism a male problem) but a woman with masculine behavior and a choice of masculine clothes. The Bolognese anatomist Constantino Varolio, for example, classified hermaphrodites as females with enlarged genitals. Many cases of supposed female hermaphroditism, he wrote, may have been the result of a prolapsed or inverted uterus.[73] Paré distinguished four sexes: the male, the female, the undecidable, and that of individuals with both sets of genitalia. As he described it, the hermaphroditic woman "in addition to her vulva which is well-formed and through which she ejects seed and her monthlies, has a male member, situated above the said vulva, near the groin, without foreskin, but with a thick skin which cannot be turned over and around, and without any erection, and from this, urine and seed do not issue; and no vestige of scrotum or testicles is to be found there."[74] Women who were not hermaphroditic but exhibited an enlarged clitoris were also at times cut back by castrators, Paré tells us in his reading of Leo Africanus's explanation of the practice of clitoridectomy in Africa, but attributing it to lesbian women in Fez.[75] Infibulation, in this reading, is practiced to reduce an enlarged clitoris that may make women seek each other for sexual satisfaction. Refusing to acknowledge the importance for women of the medical rediscovery in 1559 by Realdo Colombo, of the existence of the clitoris, Andreas Vesalius explained "this new and useless part" as a malformation present only in female hermaphrodites.[76]

72. Augustine, *De civitate Dei,* trans. H. Bettenson (London: Penguin, 1972), 16.8.

73. Constantino Varolio, *Anatomicae, sive de resolutione corporis humani libri IIII* (Frankfurt: Wechel and Rischer, 1591), 99.

74. Paré, *On Monsters,* ch. 6.

75. The accounting from Leo Africanus's *Historical Description of Africa* (1556) is not in Parè's original edition of *Monsters* of 1573, but in the second of 1575. It was removed in that of 1579. See Thomas Laqueur, "Amor Veneris, Vel Dulcedo Appeletur," in *Fragment for a History of the Human Body,* ed. Michel Feher, 3 vols. (New York: Zone, 1989), 1:91–131; and Katharine Park, "The Rediscovery of the Clitoris: French Medicine and the Tribade, 1570–1620," in *The Body in Parts: Fantasies of Corporeality in Early Modern Europe,* ed. David Hillman and Carla Mazzio (New York: Routledge, 1997), 171–93, esp. 171–72.

76. "You can hardly ascribe this new and useless part, as if it were an organ, to healthy

In *La calandria*, although the reality of the situation suggests it as possible, sexual gratification of women by women is rejected as unimaginable and thus becomes recuperable to men narcissistically. When Fannio reassures Santilla that it makes sense for her to go back to Fulvia, for example, even though by doing so she will be discovered as female, because where there are men there are means ("ove omini sono, modi sono"), Santilla retorts that in the case of women, there are no "means" to get satisfaction: "Ma dove non sono se non donne, come saremo ella ed io, non vi sarà giá il modo" (4.4; "But where there are only women, like her and me, the means are lacking"). Tribadism is not acknowledged as a possibility, because in the masculine mentality that subtends the logic of the play no satisfying erotics can be imagined without penetration.[77] So even though Santilla decides to go ahead with the ruse proposed to her by Fannio and to act out a cross-gendered fantasy in which she identifies with her lost brother and takes unknowingly his position, this is done only to uncover (and this time for good) a feminine gender.[78]

But in *La venexiana*, to return one more time to my earlier example, female-female desire is represented with little trouble and no redressing. Was feminine

women. I think that such a structure appears in hermaphrodites who otherwise have well formed female genitals . . . but I have never once seen in any woman a penis . . . or even the rudiments of a tiny phallus." See Andreas Vesalius, *Observationum anatomicarum Gabrielis Fallopii examen* (Venice: Francesco de' Franceschi da Siena, 1564), 143, quoted in Park, "The Rediscovery," 177. See also Valerie Traub, "The Psychomorphology of the Clitoris; Or, the Reemergence of the *Tribade* in English Culture," in *Generation and Degeneration: Literature and Tropes of Reproduction in Literature and History from Antiquity to Early Modern Europe*, ed. Valeria Finucci and Kevin Brownlee (Durham, N.C.: Duke University Press, 2001), 153–86. Let us not forget that women were already endowed with another penis in their body, since in the physiology of the time the vagina (or the cervix) was described and illustrated as a penis that had remained inside for lack of heat. See chapter 2.

77. Institutions intervened only rarely to control female homosexuality, as in a 1574 law in Treviso in which lesbian practices could be punished with death. See L. Crompton, "The Myth of Lesbian Impunity: Capital Law from 1270 to 1792," *Journal of Homosexuality* 6 (1980–81): 18.

78. "Performance allegorizes a loss it cannot grieve," Judith Butler writes, "allegorizes the incorporative fantasy of melancholia whereby an object is phantasmatically taken in or on as a way of refusing to let it go. Gender itself might be understood in part as the 'acting out' of unresolved grief." See "Melancholy Gender / Refused Identification," in *Constructing Masculinity*, ed. Maurice Berger, Brian Wallis, and Simon Watson (New York: Routledge, 1995), 21–36, esp. 32.

desire unrepressed there because it did not mean what it could have meant, since the plot makes clear that the two women desire not each other but the man who is missing from the scene, whose behavior they are mimicking in anticipation? Was this decision to represent two women in bed inconsequential, since male actors were playing their parts? Or was this choice less threatening because roles may have been recited rather than acted? Whatever the situation, the heterosexual agenda the play espouses blinds the onlooker to the import of a lesbian scene, since rather than *fricatrices*, we have men representing, once more, unrestrained feminine desire.

Love between men also gets censured in *La calandria*, according to the principle explained above, that if a person identifies with one gender, he or she must desire the other. Unlike lesbianism, however, love between men is imagined as possible and receives representation on stage. Having fallen in love with Lidio, thinking that he has fallen for Santilla, the fool Calandro actively pursues him. In the scene in which, thanks to Fessenio, a meeting is arranged, Calandro is made to kiss Lidio before a prostitute takes Lidio's place in the bed. The scene is brushed off as necessary to the plot, and the commentary allows for no possibility of further male-male sex, but it makes such a desire understood: "bisognerà pure che Lidio si lassi baciar da costui. Ma, se gli baci sui li fianco fastidiosi, li parranno poi piú suavi quelli di Fulvia" (3.3; "I am afraid Lidio may have to let Cassandro kiss him. But if his kisses will be annoying to him, Fulvia's kisses will seem all the sweeter afterwards").[79]

The denial of possible homosexual responses through the reidealization of heterosexuality may, in *La calandria*, be the direct result of the fact that in the early sixteenth century there was a new institutional zeal in many Italian cities for the uncovering and possible exposure of nonheterosexuals. As Michael Rocke writes, sodomy started to be punished more vigorously only after the second half of the fifteenth century: thirteen men were prosecuted for sodomy in the first half of that century in Venice, four times that number in the second half.[80] The issue was a hot one at the time of the play's staging, no matter

79. Other Renaissance plays in which homosexual possibilities are explored through the veil of crossdressing and mistaken identity are Gerolamo Parabosco (1524–57), *La fantesca*; Scipione Ammirato (1531–1601), *I trasformati*; and Alessandro Piccolomini (1508–78), *Alessandro*. In Pietro Aretino's *Il marescalco* (*The Stablemaster*, 1533) there is no possibility of misunderstanding what the stablemaster desires.

80. Ten thousand cases were brought to court during the century in Florence; two thou-

the city, and became hotter in later plays. In Gl'Intronati's *Gl'ingannati*, for example, a servant makes reference to the fact that if he wanted, he could have the homosexual tutor, Messer Piero, burned at the stake.[81] A later play, Giordano Bruno's *Il candelaio*, a work probably not performed until the twentieth century and willed officially to oblivion following the author's death by public burning in Rome in 1600, has a pedophile and a bisexual in leading male roles.[82]

The blotting out of homosexuality, which has nevertheless to be evoked in order to be abandoned, confirms the usual plot of Italian comedies of the time, one in which the move toward marriage requires that the main character fully appropriate masculinity by the last scene. Thus, Lidio is shown as literally shedding his female clothes and giving them to his sister, which she alone will now wear for good. Gender gets firmly linked to sex, and Santilla no longer is called "Lidio femina." As they learn who they are by realizing how different they are—and this difference for Bibbiena is grounded in the exposure of their different sex—the twins realign erotic fantasies and erotic practices, and name each other. Santilla rhapsodizes: "Tua sorella sono; e tu mio fratel sei. . . . Or tanto maggior

---

sand resulted in penalties, mostly with fines. Although "condemnations for sodomy burgeoned in the 1540s, they dropped off sharply in the 1550s." See Michael Rocke, *Forbidden Friendships: Homosociality and Male Culture in Renaissance Florence* (New York: Oxford University Press, 1996), 235. Bruce Smith essentially supports this shift: "tolerance for homosexuality in late antiquity and the earlier Middle Ages yielded to mounting homophobia from the thirteenth century onward, reaching a climax in the sixteenth century, when homosexuals relations between men were made a capital offense under the civil law of all over Europe." See Bruce Smith, *Homosexual Desire in Shakespeare's England* (Chicago: University of Chicago Press, 1991), 42. Following Ruggiero's research, it was believed that Venice had the most cases of condemnation for sodomy from the Inquisition. But Canossa argues that Sicily held the record, for while there were 84 cases judged in Venice between 1590 and 1630, there were 181 in Palermo in the same period. Those condemned for sodomy constituted the largest number of detainees in jail in the city. See Guido Ruggiero, *The Boundaries of Eros: Sex Crime and Sexuality in Renaissance Venice* (New York: Oxford University Press, 1985); and Romano Canossa, *Sessualità e inquisizione in Italia*, 60–61. Charges against sodomy let up after 1647; there were also no more laws against homosexuals enacted in Venice after the 1580s. See Gabriele Martini, *Il "vitio nefando" nella Venezia del Seicento: Aspetti sociali e repressione di giustizia* (Rome: Jouvence, 1988).

81. Gl'Intronati, *Gl'ingannati*, ed. Ireneo Sanesi (Bari: Laterza, 1912), 4.1

82. Giordano Bruno, *Il candelaio*, ed. Augusto Guzzo (1582; Milan: Mondadori, 1994). The first staging of the play seems to have taken place in 1911; it was then turned into a musical in 1964.

letizia mi porta la salute tua quanto io manco la aspettavo" (5.12; "I am your sister, and you are my brother. Now that I find you are healthy, my joy is greater since it is unexpected"). And Lidio, whose love for Santilla, we were told in the very first page, was greater than the love of any brother for his sister ("maggior che mai fratello a sorella portassi," 1.1), chimes in: "Or son contento; or ho adempiuto il desiderio mio; or più affanno avere non posso" (5.12; "Now I am happy, now I have gained my wish, now I can no longer be anguished"). Having sealed his difference from his sister by "recognizing" her, Lidio can indeed stop worrying about his masculinity.

All talk of androgyny is discarded now, for the androgynous state was not, as it was argued most notoriously by the Neoplatonists, a way for both sexes to incorporate something of the other, but rather a passage from the indifferentiation of childhood to adulthood, and from latent, or at least functional and not yet discarded femininity in men to enforced masculinity. The hermaphroditic anxieties raised to comic effect in the second part of the play are just as well resolved at the end, by espousing a comfortable orthodoxy vis-à-vis both gender and sex. When Bibbiena next ties sex to heterosexuality, he shows that rebellion is a comedic event that takes place before adulthood, a state spelled out in the last page by a ritualistic double marriage. Paternity and genealogy are left to be played out in a nondelineated future when one can assume that Lidio, who entered the play fatherless but now gets a father in the adoptive parent of his sister, Santilla, may be able through his marriage to Santilla's promised wife (the one she was supposed to marry when she was thought to be a man) to rethread the genealogical lines broken by the Turks' invasion of his father's house ten years earlier.

Male sexual organs are lost in *Calandria* only in fantasy or only when they were supposed not to be there. Androgyny evolves in due time into full-fledged masculinity and femininity. What happens when genitalia are lost through a rational premeditated decision on the part of fathers who sign an agreement to put their preadolescent boys under the knife—and when one's desires, drives, and sublimations, rather than passing through a temporary, almost undifferentiated in-between state have to undergo permanent complex restructurings because of that "impediment"—is the subject of the next chapter.

CHAPTER 6

The Masquerade of Manhood:

The Paradox of the Castrato

I am young, Italian, and castrated
and seek my glory only through singing.
—FILIPPO BALATRI, *Frutti del mondo*

O fairies, o buggers, o eunuchs exotic! . . .
With soft little hands, with flexible bums,
Come, o castrati, unnatural ones!
—PETRONIUS, *Satyricon*

Castrati were males, mostly in Italy, whose sexual organs were surgically treated, all seemingly with consent, between the age of seven and thirteen in order to preserve the prepubescent structure of their vocal chords. Within a century of the start of this phenomenal practice, castrati became the single best known Italian commodity export on the Continent, one that wove, as the epigraph quoting the castrato Filippo Balatri registers, the construction of a prenational identity with a sexual lack. To be young, Italian, and castrated was now part of the new order of things as an erotics of feminized masculinity, a modish masochistic aesthetics, and a melancholic accommodation to reality-infected culture.[1] Only cuckolds and half-men abound in Italy, the poet and painter Salvator Rosa decried ("becchi e . . . castrati"); only betrayed husbands and crooners ("i cornuti e i cantor") infest a country decimated by plague, beset by political lassitude, and silenced by religious demagoguery.[2]

The beginning of the practice of castrating boys for musical purposes is still shrouded in secrecy. We know that by the middle of the sixteenth century a musical interest in soloists brought the virtuoso possibilities of male and female voices to the forefront.[3] Some women became successful singers, although they

1. Filippo Balatri (1676–1756), *Frutti del mondo,* ed. Karl Vossler (Naples: Remo Sandon, 1924).

2. Salvator Rosa (1615–73), *Satire, liriche, lettere,* ed. Anton Maria Salvini et al. (Milan: Sonzogno, 1892), 41.

3. In *Discorso sopra la musica dei suoi tempi* (1628), Vincenzo Giustiniani notes that a new phenomenon appeared around 1575: "L'anno santo del 1575 o poco dopo si cominciò un modo di cantare molto diverso da quello di prima, e così per alcuni anni seguenti, massime nel modo di cantare con una voce sola sopra un istrumento. . . . Nell'istesso tempo il Cardinale Ferdinando de' Medici . . . ha premuto di haver musici eccellenti e specialmente la famosa Vittoria, dalla quale ha quasi avuto origine il vero modo di cantare delle donne. . . . [Other singers] cantavano di basso e di tenore. . . . E oltre a questi molti altri soprani . . . che cantavano in voce di falsetto, e molti altri eunuchi di Cappella." See Angelo Solerti, *Le origini del melodramma* (Turin: Bocca, 1903), 106–10. We are much more knowledgeable, of course, about the end of this practice in Italy, more or less after Napoleonic laws were imposed and the pope was abducted in 1798—although already by 1730 the number of castrati had contracted, scores for them were no longer written with the same intensity, and women cross-dressed as men had taken over their parts. By 1814, Piedmont and Lombardy had banned castrati from their stages. Pope Pius X banished male sopranos from the Vatican choir in 1903, although the

were not allowed to perform in church, following Saint Paul's long-standing prohibition against the use of their voices in sacred places.[4] On the male side, falsettists trained to reach the soprano register of women appeared at first the proper response to the complex style of lavish ornamentation invading Rome and the northern Italian courts, but their voice was deemed artificial and strident. Within a few decades, "contraltini" were replaced by castrati. First employed in church choirs and as chamber or chapel singers in courts, castrati became indispensable to the operatic stage as soon as it was created. Their success as the first group of extravagantly rich, charismatic prima donnas in Europe was unprecedented. "Blessed be the knife!" ("Evviva il coltello!" "Il benedetto coltello!"), the adoring public shouted at hearing their ethereal voices, which sometimes could reach a whole octave in pitch above that of women — this was in a country that famously frowned upon circumcision of its infants and reacted with panic to rumors that Jewish doctors were plotting to circumcise Christian boys.[5]

My intention in this chapter is to focus on the figure of the castrato, and on stories of castration found mostly in the low genre of the novella, to examine how social and juridical identities and erotic and aesthetic practices were organized in Italy in the late Renaissance and baroque periods. Who liked the castrato, and what fantasies could he fulfill or titillate? Was the performance of the castrato one of masculinity, was it one of femininity, or was the castrato simply a tabula rasa on whom to project anyone's desire? Were the attachments of this man "queer," or, rather, did the men and women who ran after him have questionable fancies? Did the castrato contaminate and debauch both sexes, as it was claimed, because of his postulated inability to fit neatly into binary divisions — heterosexual and homosexual, normal and abnormal, male and female — or did his heavenly androgynous voice cleanse his audience of earthly desires? Finally, why on earth would fathers petition to have their sons castrated, and why would

---

last known castrato, Alessandro Moreschi, was allowed to finish his career there as soprano and director of the choir. Moreschi died in 1925.

4. "Mulier tacet in Ecclesia" ("Let your women keep silence in the churches," 1 Corinthians 14.34.

5. The link between circumcision and castration is emphasized most notoriously by Freud, although different parts of the male genitalia are involved. But then the ritual cutting of newborn Jewish boys is not as significant for Freud as the "real" castration of all women. Thus the male problem became a female one.

Italians promote abroad the idea that their most successful men were not-men with feminine voices and freakish bodies?

Lorenzo Bianconi has argued that Italian literature had exhausted itself by 1640, following the death of Giambattista Marino (1569-1625), and thus opera theater, the most successful Italian invention of that century, rather than literature, speaks best to the intellectual life of the times.[6] The hyperbolic and ornate verses of Marino's *L'Adone* (1623) clearly belong to the same culture that swooned over the exhibitionistic and mesmerizing thrills of the castrato; literati and academicians in great numbers, once more blurring boundaries between mediums, started to write the librettos that projected on the castrato the cultural upheavals and sexual dissidence of the period. Staged plays had progressively introduced music throughout the sixteenth century, as commedia dell'arte actors found that their twin ability to sing and recite increased revenues. Within a play, *intermedi* often generated more interest than the comedies they accompanied, given their lavish props, costumes, scenarios, and controlled political agenda. Opera was an extension of *intermedi* with a theatrical plot at the center, all set to music. Slowly but steadily it replaced comedies in the public's favor.[7]

Unlike most genres, opera did not take centuries to mature but decades. Its antecedents can be traced back to Angelo Poliziano's *Orfeo* (1480) and subsequent *rappresentazioni* and *favole pastorali*, but essentially it was "invented," and its success came quickly, when poets writing pastoral fictions and court musicians writing scores followed two sets of reasoning: that drama set to music had a precedent in the ancient Greek theater, and thus it could be revived; and that patrons could muster an appetite for a style of acting through music and declamation, following the success of the *intermedi*.[8] We know very little about

6. Lorenzo Bianconi, "Il Cinquecento e il Seicento," in *Letteratura italiana*, vol. 6: *Teatro, musica, tradizione dei classici*, ed. Alberto Asor Rosa (Turin: Einaudi, 1986), 319-64, esp. 358.

7. Such is the matter-of-fact statement of a contemporary: "Prima che s'introducessero i drammi in musica in Venezia era molto gradita la commedia. Le compagnie de' comici erano famosissime e il fine de' medesimi era d'allettare con la virtù un concorso nobile." See Cristoforo Ivanovich, *Minerva al tavolino*, 2 vols. (Venice: Pezzana, 1688), 1:393. For the political importance of early opera, see Lorenzo Bianconi and Thomas Walker, "Production, Consumption and Political Function of Seventeenth Century Italian Opera," *Early Modern Music* 4 (1984): 209-96.

8. Opera was swiftly justified. In his preface to *Euridice*, Jacopo Peri creatively argued, for example, that the recitative style, although not the same used in Greek plays, still was

the first opera, *Dafne,* by librettist Ottavio Rinuccini, a poet of the Tasso school, and composer Jacopo Peri. It was performed in Florence in 1598, but only a few fragments have survived. We know a lot more about the second opera by the same team, *Euridice,* staged in Florence two years later for the marriage of Maria de' Medici and Henry IV of France. The tenor part of Orfeo was sung by Peri himself, and the role of Euridice was given to a woman, Vittoria Archilei, called La Romanina, but the castrato Giovannino and "the castrato del Sig. Emilio de' Cavalieri" sang the parts of Tragedy, Venus, and Proserpine, thus starting an unprecedented, soon almost exclusive, and reciprocally successful, cooperation between castrati and the new art form. In just seven years, when Claudio Monteverdi's *Orfeo* was staged in Mantua in 1607 during Carnival season, with Alessandro Striggio's libretto taking its cue from Dante's *Commedia,* opera theater had its masterpiece. All the main female parts now were assigned to castrati: Girolamo Bacchini, a priest, sang perhaps the role of Euridice; and Giovanni Gualberto, a Florentine soprano, took the parts of Proserpina, La Musica, and probably La Speranza.[9] Church music had just passed its apogee, and the new

---

very much suited to Florentine speech ("nostra favella"). See Solerti, *Le origini del melodrama,* 45–49. In his *Lezioni* on the role of music in classical drama delivered in 1624, Giovanni Battista Doni contended that ancient tragedy had not only choral odes sung, as it was believed, but also soliloquies. See Frederick Hammond, *Music and Spectacle in Baroque Rome: Barberini Patronage under Urban VIII* (New Haven: Yale University Press, 1994),100–101; and Deirdre O'Grady, *The Last Troubadours: Poetic Drama in Italian Opera, 1597–1887* (London: Routledge, 1991), 6–11. Maria Galli Stampino has challenged this smooth narrative of a classical pedigree for opera by problematizing its relationship with other musical court forms of entertainment. See "Classical Antecedents and Teleological Narratives: On the Contamination between Opera and Courtly Sung Entertainment in the Early Seventeenth Century," *Italica* 77 (2000): 331–56. For the genres that influenced opera, see Nino Pirrotta and Elena Povoledo, *Music and Theatre from Poliziano to Monteverdi,* trans. Karen Eales (Cambridge: Cambridge University Press, 1982), ch. 1.

9. See Ian Fenlon, "Monteverdi's Mantuan *Orfeo:* Some New Documentation," *Early Music* 12 (1984): 163–72, esp. 165. For the stagings of these early operas, see Tim Carter, *Music in Late Renaissance and Early Baroque Italy* (Portland, Or.: Amadeus Press, 1992), 205– 18. Rome too figures in this genealogy, since the *Rappresentazione di anima et di corpo* by Emilio de' Cavalieri in 1599, performed without a stage set, constitutes for some musicologists the first opera and for others the first oratorio. This is a moot point, since at the time there was not sufficient distinction between the two genres.

medium soon invaded theaters all through Italy and Europe, which were rapidly being opened.[10]

That at the center of this "recitar cantando" style was a feminized impostor whose gender identity, sexual role, and perhaps object choice were counter to any imaginable institutional discourse on the Italian male gives reasons for pause. One can understand how a culture like the baroque, in which the ability to fantasize and marvel was highly praised — and the rituals of masquerading, impersonating, and cross-dressing were coyly practiced — could embrace the castrato. I am not arguing that a newly chic feminizing style fostered the fashion for a man with a feminized voice, but protocols of appearing can be usefully linked to protocols of hearing when studying cultural changes. On the sociopolitical level, the appeal of the castrato can be connected to a documented crisis of institutions: the new practice of refeudalization to foster absolutist regimes, the phenomenon of deindustrialization, which often resulted in economic impoverishment, and high taxation rates contributed, as did the wars, sacks, plagues, and droughts sweeping the Italian peninsula in the seventeenth century, to foster creative forms of survival among indigent families. Castration of one son must have seemed a small price to pay for some destitute fathers.[11]

10. When opera was most fashionable, there were, according to Barbier, 159 cities in Italy with at least one public theater. Since Italy did not have that many cities, one must assume that even small towns had their opera house and that the cities had several. Venice had fifteen theaters and seven opera houses, although only a few of them were active. See Patrick Barbier, *The World of the Castrati: The History of an Extraordinary Operatic Phenomenon*, trans. Margaret Crosland (London: Souvenir Press, 1996).

11. See Geoffrey Parker and Lesley M. Smith, *The General Crisis of the Seventeenth Century* (London: Routledge, 1997) on the dire economic situation of Italy — reduced by waves of plague in the 1630s in the north (Milan lost 46 percent of its inhabitants; Verona 56 percent) and in the 1650s in the south — as well as the desperate conditions in most of Europe at the time as a consequence of the Thirty Years War. For the repercussions on family structures, see Marzio Barbagli, *Sotto lo stesso tetto: Mutamenti della famiglia in Italia dal XV al XX secolo* (Bologna: Mulino, 1984), 146–77. For the repercussions in southern Italy, where 900,000 of the 4 millions living in the Kingdom of Naples died in the second wave of the plague in 1656–57, see Giovanna Da Molin, *Famiglia e matrimonio nell'Italia del Seicento* (Bari: Cacucci, 2000), 138; and Lorenzo Del Panta, *Le epidemie nella storia demografica italiana (sec. XIV–XIX)* (Turin: Einaudi, 1980). For an argument against absolute economic decline in Venice in the seventeenth century through adjustments in employment, see Richard Tilden Rapp, *Industry and Economic Decline in Seventeenth-Century Venice* (Cambridge: Harvard University Press, 1976).

Since male sopranos came to documented existence in the 1560s, we can add another cultural reason for their success. We know that women entered the stage in that decade, when contracts of acting companies started to include the names of actresses and singers, as in the case of Lucrezia da Siena (Lucretia Senensis)—perhaps an "honest courtesan," as her classical first name and generic last name would imply—who signed a contract in Rome on October 10, 1564, for performances in the Carnival of the following year together with six male professional actors.[12] These incursions by females into the traditionally male province of theater were highly criticized for supposedly loosening public morals, so much so that already in 1588 a ban was issued by Sixtus V against women performing throughout the papal state. To be sure, some female performers were said to be prostitutes. And yet the main reason for forbidding them to play or sing on stage was cultural: women were considered pliable, inherently shifty, perhaps immoral creatures; seeing or acting a certain behavior lured them to assume that behavior.[13] With femininity so labile, it was too dangerous to condone women's unchecked presence in public.[14] Once women were

12. See Mario Apollonio, *Storia della commedia dell'arte* (Rome: Augustea, 1930), 93. For general information on actresses performing on stage, see Francesco Bartoli, *Notizie istoriche de' comici italiani*, 2 vols. (Padua: Conzatti, 1781–82; reprint, Sala Bolognese: Forni, 1978), 1:50–53. For the capital importance of women in the newly formed commedia dell'arte companies, see Ferdinando Taviani, *Il segreto della commedia dell'arte: La memoria delle compagnie italiane del XVI, XVII e XVIII secolo* (Florence: Usher, 1982), 335–36.

13. See John Rosselli, *Singers of Italian Opera: The History of a Profession* (Cambridge: Cambridge University Press, 1992), 62–66; and more generally, Anthony Newcomb, "Courtesans, Muses, or Musicians? Professional Women Musicians in Sixteenth-Century Italy," in *Women Making Music: The Western Art Tradition, 1150–1950*, ed. Jane Bowers and Judith Tick (Urbana: University of Illinois Press, 1986), 90–115.

14. Sentiment against women's singing was rampant at a time in which a Counter Reformation agenda dictated a traditional view of femininity. Writing in 1602, Francisco Arias cited Augustine in arguing that it was better to hear a basilisk hiss than a woman sing, because a basilisk killed only the body, but woman the soul. See *Profitto spirituale*, cited in Ferdinando Taviani, *La commedia dell'arte e la società barocca: La fascinazione del teatro* (Rome: Bulzoni, 1969), 130. Giovanni Domenico Ottonelli (1584–1670) dedicated a whole treatise to women's dangerous "conversation." See *Della pericolosa conversatione con le donne, e poco modeste, e ritirate, e cantatrici, e accademiche . . . ove si risolvono molti casi di coscienza* (Florence: Stamperia in Luca Franceschini e Alessandro Logi, 1646). The same prejudices against women singers applied to the female audience, with different conventions working for any given city. In Rome,

excluded, actors replaced the actresses, and castrati were called from time to time to replace female singers, whose voice range they replicated.[15] Surprisingly, many roles did not have to be regendered to be assigned to a castrato rather than a woman, since in these early days of opera both were, in an uncannily hermaphroditic fashion that well expresses baroque sensibilities, almost as likely to sing male or female parts.[16]

At the time of the papal ban, "concerti di donne" were surprisingly thriving in Italian courts. *Virtuose* at the court in Ferrara, especially Tarquinia Molza, were deemed quite an asset by the Este family, although Duke Guglielmo Gonzaga of Mantua, a connoisseur of music, could not understand the reason for their acclaim when he first heard them in 1581. But his son, Vincenzo, thought the

---

women could attend musical performances only on appointed evenings and only with their husbands; unmarried ladies were unlikely to be invited. See Alessandro Ademollo, *I teatri di Roma nel secolo decimosettimo* (Rome: Pasqualucci, 1888), 26. But the "cortigiane oneste" had no such restrictions, especially in Venice, where they were assigned good seats.

15. In Florence, for example, the two pupils of composer Cavalieri, Giovanni Boccherini and Fabio Fabbri, took on roles previously sung by women and formed the first "concerto dei castrati" in 1595. See Warren Kirkendale, *The Court Musicians in Florence During the Principate of the Medici* (Florence: Olschki, 1993), 292. Jacopo Peri composed "Caro e soave legno" and "O dolce anima mia" probably for the same castrati group and accompanied them. See Tim Carter, "Jacopo Peri (1561–1633): Aspects of His Life and Works," in his *Music, Patronage and Printing in Late Renaissance Florence* (Aldershot: Ashgate, 2000), 57. As a result of the papal ban, women were not allowed on the Roman stage, whether operatic or dramatic, until the theater of Tor di Nona was opened in 1671. That theater was shut down again by Innocent XI in 1676 and reopened by Clement XIV a few years later. The prohibition against women's performance in public theaters applied throughout the papal state, with the exception of the cities of Bologna, Ferrara, Senigallia, Urbino, and towns of the Romagna region. Occasionally other cities would join the ban, such as Florence during the period of Cosimo III. See Ademollo, *I teatri*, xvii n. 1 and 137.

16. In the representation of *Pompeo* by Alessandro Scarlatti in Naples in 1684, for example, four male roles were sung by women. The castrato Senesino playing a woman's part was less of a hit than the actress Boratti in a male role. See Anton Giulio Bragaglia, *Degli "evirati cantori": Contributo alla storia del teatro* (Florence: Sansoni Antiquariato, 1959), 23. In the representation of *Il trionfo di David* in Florence (1629) not only were all the singers and actors men but there was a choir of singing and dancing virgins ("Coro di vergini che cantovono e ballavono") composed of eight men, in addition to choir of dancing maidens composed of four men. See Guido Burchi, "Vita musicale e spettacoli alla Compagnia della Scala di Firenze fra il 1560 e il 1675," *Note d'archivio per la storia musicale* 1 (1983): 9–47, esp. 29.

prima donna of Italian music of the time, Adriana Basile, indispensable for his court and was adamant in his summons, even when she came up with a series of excuses; he also brought the young Caterina Martinelli from Rome to sing in his private chamber.[17] Florence too had its own "concerto di donne," with Vittoria Archilei, Margherita Caccini, and Francesca Caccini as members. In Venice, orphaned and abandoned girls were educated to sing and play instruments in the renowned Ospedali, although they were not to be seen in public. To be sure, from the point of view of impresarios castrati made more economic sense than female singers: they had better training to develop their lungs and diaphragms; their years of employment lasted longer than women's because they could retain their remarkable treble voice indefinitely (most women stopped singing when they married); and there were no qualms about their presence on the stage.

It has been argued that we should attach no political significance to a theater's employing a castrato rather than a woman onstage, since the choice depended more on availability and timbre of voice than gender, although by the early seventeenth century roles that could have been assigned to women went to, or were written for, male sopranos. Dorothy Keiser argues that the perceived genderlessness of castrati allowed in fact for a range of theatrical guises.[18] Nevertheless, one cannot ignore the well-documented fact that castrati rose in secular music at a time when female singers had just made sizable inroads and, in fact, were better paid than men. Women kept performing, and some of them, such

17. Martinelli died suddenly, just before she was due to sing in the "tragedia in musica" *Arianna* by Rinuccini and Monteverdi, to be performed on May 28, 1608, for the wedding festivities of Francesco Gonzaga and Margherita of Savoy. The stage actress Virginia Ramponi ("Florinda") (1583–1629/30), who belonged to the commedia dell'arte troupe of the Comici Fedeli, was hurried in to substitute for her. There was no indication that Ramponi could perform on the musical stage, but at the time music was a common ingredient of most staged performances, and actors and actresses routinely trained their voices. Ramponi prepared her part in just six days, and the effect was remarkable, according to contemporary accounts. See the letter by Antonio Costantini to Vincenzo Gonzaga in Archivio di Stato di Mantova, *Gonzaga*, busta 2712, fasc. 4, lett. 7; and Alessandro Ademollo, *La bell'Adriana ed altre virtuose del suo tempo alla corte di Mantova: Contributo di documenti per la storia della musica in Italia nel primo quarto del Seicento* (Città di Castello: Lapi, 1888), 42–44 and 71–75. Ramponi sang the title role again in 1611 in another Monteverdi opera, *Il rapimento di Proserpina*.

18. Dorothy Keiser, "Cross-Sexual Casting in Baroque Opera: Musical and Theatrical Conventions," *Opera Quarterly* 5.4 (1987–88): 46–57.

as Anna Renzi and Giulietta Zuffi, basked in their success, but castrati became the rage.[19]

The history of castrated singers in Europe starts in the twelfth century in Spain, when castrati, we are told by Castil Blaze, were first used in church choirs. Italy soon followed suit.[20] We know there were two French "cantoretti" at the Ferrara court of Cardinal Ippolito II d'Este in 1555. By 1565 Duke Guglielmo Gonzaga had two French castrati and a Spanish "eunuco" priest who sang a spectacular Magnificat ("che fu cosa veramente rara"). That same year Gonzaga provided a pension for a fourth castrato, the Frenchman Guglielmo Fordos.[21] In 1571 the duke was unsuccessful in hiring a Spanish castrato because his offer was not deemed sufficiently high, but he remained so interested in castrati voices that he sent envoys to France in 1582 and to Spain in 1583 to recruit fifteen or

19. Monteverdi, for example, had lower wages than some *virtuose* when he was the "maestro della musica di camera" (1601–12) at the Gonzaga court. Male singers playing basso parts were paid the least. Only with Handel did the castrati's success and income surpass those of prima donnas. See Ellen Rosand, *Opera in Seventeenth-Century Venice* (Berkeley and Los Angeles: University of California Press, 1992), 119 n. 26. The castrati cut into men's roles as well, in that for decades fewer parts were written for tenors and basses.

20. Castil Blaze, *L'Opéra italien de 1548 à 1856* (Paris: Castil-Blaze, 1856), 30. Eunuchs were already used in Byzantium as choristers in church and as singers at court. See Kathy Ringrose, "Living in the Shadow: Eunuchs and Gender in Byzantium," in *Third Sex, Third Gender: Beyond Sexual Dimorphism in Culture and History,* ed. Gilbert Herdt (New York: Zone Books, 1994), 85–104, esp. 96; Liz James, ed., *Women, Men and Eunuchs: Gender in Byzantium* (New York: Routledge, 1997); and Peter Tompkins, *The Eunuch and the Virgin* (New York: Potter, 1962).

21. The first mention of a "soprano maschio" that I have been able to find is in Luigi Dentice, *Due dialoghi della musica* (Rome: Luchino, 1553). In the section of his treatise dedicated to interpretation, Dentice has a description of a concert held in the house of Giovanna d'Aragona, where he comments on singers, in particular a male soprano. We do not know whether the singer was a falsettist or a castrato. For Ferrara, see Anthony Newcomb, *The Madrigal at Ferrara 1579–1597* (Princeton: Princeton University Press, 1980), 30–31. For Mantua, see Pietro Canal, *Della musica in Mantova: Notizie tratte principalmente dall'Archivio Gonzaga* (1874; Geneva: Minkoff Reprint, 1978), 41; and Richard Sherr, "Guglielmo Gonzaga and the Castrati," *Renaissance Quarterly* 33 (1980): 33–56, esp. 35–36. For dates of employment of castrati in Rome and other courts, see Angus Heriot, *The Castrati in Opera* (London: Secker and Warburg, 1956). Castrati were referred to as eunuchs in the late 1580s at the papal court and were first called castrati in 1599. See John Rosselli, "The Castrati as a Professional Group and a Social Phenomenon, 1550–1850," *Acta Musicologica* 60.2 (1988): 143–79.

so of them. He got none: the best were all taken or were too expensive to con-tract.[22] Wages for castrati had inflated in a matter of years: from three scudi a month in the 1560s, the pay moved to three or four hundred scudi a year twenty years later. In Rome, the first castrati in the Sistine Chapel were from Spain: Francesco Soto had a contract by 1562; and Jacopo Spagnoletto and Mar-tino Soto had theirs by 1588.[23] The first two Italian castrati, Girolamo Rosini and Pietro Paolo Folignati, were singing by 1599. In reorganizing the Cappella Giulia in Saint Peter's Basilica in 1589, Sixtus V authorized the recruitment of four castrati out of the twelve needed singers for that choir, with the bull "Cum pro nostro pastorali munere." The Italian "Fabio puer" (Fabio Fabbri) started singing there in 1589.[24] In Florence, the pattern of employing French or Spanish castrati apparently was not followed, and the first documented "putto castrato" was a young Italian, probably Niccolò Bartolini, living in the house-hold of the Medici court's chief musician, Giulio Caccini, in 1577. We find his voice first documented for the *sacra rappresentazione* of Holy Week, 1583.[25] But already in 1565 Duke Cosimo de' Medici, looking for a young male voice to sing the role of Psyche for an *intermedio* to be performed on the arrival of Princess Joanna, asked his ambassador in Rome, Averardo Serristori, to find him a boy or a castrato of the pope's chapel ("uno Eunuco di quelli di cappella") because the young singer previously selected for the occasion had to be dismissed, his voice having changed in the meantime.[26] The castrato Onofrio Gualfreducci was a

22. See Canal, *Della musica in Mantova,* 44–45; and Sherr, "Guglielmo Gonzaga and the Castrati," 37–40.

23. It is unclear whether Francesco Soto was a castrato or a falsettist singing as soprano. As usual, the then current nomenclature does not help. Celletti seems to think he was a falsettist. See Rodolfo Celletti, "Sopranisti e contraltisti," *Musica d'oggi* 2 (1959): 245–50, esp. 246. Anthony Milner dates the first presence of castrati in the papal choirs to 1553. See "The Sacred Capons," *Musical Times* 114 (1973): 250–53.

24. For Fabbri, see Kirkendale, *The Court Musicians in Florence,* 294. In 1555, a bull by Pope Paul IV established that *cantori* had to be single. Palestrina lost his job as a result. Castrati had substituted all falsettists in Vatican choirs by 1625.

25. See Giuseppe Gerbino, "Castrati in Renaissance Italy," paper delivered at the Re-naissance Society of America Meeting, Los Angeles, March 1999. On Florentine castrati, see also John Walker Hill, "Oratory Music in Florence, I: *Recitar cantando,* 1583–1655," *Acta Musicologica* 51.1 (1979): 108–36, esp. 114.

26. "Egli harà da rappresentare un' giovane di 15. o, 16. anni, vorremmo che havessi bella voce, et buona grazia di cantare con i suoi passaggi alla napoletana, la voce fusse naturale non

performer at the wedding ceremonies of Ferdinando de' Medici and Christine of Lorraine in 1589 and figures in the payment accounts. Other castrati used for that occasion were "Pierino castrato" and Niccolò Bartolini, mentioned above.[27]

Castrati would usually start their careers in a woman's part or in an allegorical role, because their youth made them look androgynous; they usually debuted in their late teens. Some *musici* ended up playing only women's parts because their voices had insufficient power for heroic roles. The casting of castrati in more masculine roles and the return to themes of military honor and moral soundness started to come about first in Venice in the 1640s, following the conclusion of the twenty-year war in Candia, and then elsewhere by 1680, when the split between opera seria, in which castrati sang, and opera buffa was taking place. This regularization brought women singers in feminine roles and castrati in strong male roles, with a number of exceptions here and there, as in the cases of castrati who kept playing feminine parts even in musical theaters where women were allowed, or the cases of women who played heroic male parts, such as those of Achilles and Hercules, and who, again subverting gender, were called "primo uomo" and cross-dressed on stage as men.[28] Monteverdi's *L'incoronazione di Poppea* (1643) staged in Venice with the libretto written by the academician Gianfrancesco Busenello, seems to have been the first opera to coalesce these new stereotypes. Castrati were assigned parts of powerful men, such as Nero, but they were represented as emasculated, lustful tyrants. The women, such as

falsetto." The letter is dated October 11, 1565. The ambassador did not find a castrato but the young Roman musician Giulio Caccini, who soon became a star and a composer. See Tim Carter, "Giulio Caccini (1551–1618): New Facts, New Music," in his *Music, Patronage and Printing*, 6.13–31, esp. 14. Carter also mentions a castrato, the Niccolò Bartolini mentioned earlier, living in Caccini's house in 1577, and two castrati, probably Giovanni Boccherini and Fabio Fabbri, in 1578 (21 n. 23).

27. See James Saslow, *Florentine Festivals as Theatrum Mundi: The Medici Wedding of 1589* (New Haven: Yale University Press, 1996), 52 and 55.

28. Castrati were, nevertheless, not cast as kings, demonstrating that no matter how inconsequential it seemed to have a feminized man perform male heroic parts, it was not right for a ruler to be associated with one. See Rosand, *Opera*, 239 n. 60. Roles in which lack and masculinity are equated seem to have required the choice of a castrato. To give a more modern example, when Wagner was looking for a perfect singer for his Klingsor, he thought of assigning the part to the castrato Domenico Mustafà (1829–1912), in order to establish a visual correspondence between his emasculated knight and the singer performing the role. In fact, Mustafà did not sing the role.

Poppea or the lascivious and power-hungry Agrippina and Semiramis of other operas, became castrating, manipulative, and cruel. Masculine uncertainty and powerlessness were thus projected onto women, who ended up scapegoated as uncontrollable and voracious sexual predators.[29] That such choices reflected public preferences cannot be doubted, for theaters in Venice were public and the group of noblemen sponsoring operas did so not to display their power but in order to make a profit.

In Rome, on the other hand, the fate of the musical stage was with ecclesiastical patrons from ruling families, who had private theaters built in their palaces. Thus the ideological reasons behind the development of the musical stage in that city were different. The sensual and lascivious librettos popular in Venice had no way of penetrating deeply in the papal court, but the fact that in Rome male and female roles were all played by men and (mostly) for men of the nobility and clerics, must have offered its titillations.[30] A common plot would give two castrati, one dressed as a man and the other cross-dressed as a woman, declaring their passion for each other in long-lasting duets. In the lavish opera *Il palazzo incantato* (1642), based on Ariosto's *Orlando furioso*, the parts of Bradamante and Angelica went to castrati; Loreto Vittori sang the role of beautiful Angelica, and even then he complained that he was not given good "affettuoso" passages.[31]

Historical documentation on successful castrati is plentiful, but information on how and where the practice became widespread remains sketchy, since a strategy of exclusion applied to castrati everywhere. The French, for example, abhorred this "Italian" custom, although the first castrati came from northern France; the Spanish did likewise; and Germans employing large numbers of Italian sopranos overlooked the fact that they were making some of their own.[32]

29. For such castings in Monteverdi, which constitute "an anomalous moment in culture when power relationships associated with gender and rhetoric are oddly reconfigured," see Susan McClary, *Feminine Endings: Music, Gender, and Sexuality* (Minneapolis: University of Minnesota Press, 1991), 51.

30. In private stages, such as the one in Palazzo Farnese where the French embassy was located, women were, however, allowed to sing. See Ademollo, *I teatri*.

31. See Hammond, *Music and Spectacle in Baroque Rome*, 248.

32. For castrati of German origin employed at court, see Rosselli, *Singers of Italian Opera*, 147. According to Antonio Arjona Castro, the town of Verdun, France produced eunuchs in the early part of this period; a center there was run by Jews, who passed the technique from father to son. A castration center in North Africa, perhaps in the city of Lucena, was

Building on this geography of exculpation, the Italians themselves othered the practice by considering it an Eastern phenomenon that came to them from Spain, through that country's long-standing historical and cultural acquaintance with the Moors. The idea is less far-fetched than it seems, since Venice, a major cross-cultural point in the Mediterranean with ties to the Orient, could have been connected to the production of castrati, though there seem to have been no remarkable number there.[33] As I have noted, the first castrati recruited in Rome, Mantua, and Ferrara were not Italian but Spanish and French, and were hired after long searches. By the late 1570s, however, Italians started to provide their own singers; early in the next century they controlled the production and training of castrati for internal consumption and were able to supply an adequate number for export.[34]

Even within Italy, the place where the knife was plied was always elsewhere: the Venetians would name Bologna as a key location, since that city had surgeons who were called even to Germany to perform the operation, and was rumored to have reserved eight beds in a hospital for boys waiting for castration, or recovering from it; the Bolognese would place the manufacturing in Florence; and the Florentines would cite Rome, given the popes' successful use of "castratini"; the Romans would point their fingers to Naples, because of its four large musical conservatories; and the Neapolitans would argue for any point south, given the extreme indigence of the area.[35] Be that as it may, some towns were especially known in the Renaissance for the bravura of their castrators. In *La piazza universale*, Tommaso Garzoni dedicates "Discorso 132" to the castrating skills

---

also run by Jews. See "Los eunucos y la cirurgia de la castracion en la España musulmana," *Axerquia* 3 (1981): 279–82, esp. 280.

33. See Sherr, "Guglielmo Gonzaga and the Castrati." Venice, of course, used castrati singers extensively after the first of its many theaters opened in 1637.

34. Also around 1607 we have the first account by a Westerner of the presence of eunuchs in Ottoman harems. See Ottaviano Bon (1552–1623), *Descrizione del serraglio del Gransignore* (Venice: Naratovich, 1865), English trans. by Robert Withers, *The Sultan's Seraglio: An Intimate Portrait of Life at the Ottoman Court*, ed. Godfrey Goodwin (1625; London: Saqi, 1996). For a French account of the phenomenon, see Jean-Baptiste Tavernier (1605–89), *Nouvelle relation de l'intérieur du serrail du grand seigneur* (Paris: n.p., 1679).

35. Traveling in Italy in the 1770s, Charles Burney found Italians so ashamed of the practice that cities always named other cities as manufacturing points. See Charles Burney, *Present State of Music in France and Italy: Men, Music and Manners in France and Italy*, ed. Edmund Poole (1770; London: Folio Society, 1969), 128.

displayed by some in the Umbrian city of Norcia, where animals and men went indifferently under the knife. The castrator is a doctor of testicles, he wrote, or better, a barber whose intervention is a further wounding rather than a cure ("un medico da testicoli, anzi più tosto un barbiero, il quale, pien di rigore, non sa sanar la piaga se non impiaga"). In Garzoni's humorous rendering, there is enough castration around to keep these barbers occupied in their town; other places prefer their men with horns rather than without testicles.[36]

The very least one can say about castrati is that they were thought of, or often thought of themselves, as diminished males, since their lack of functioning testes implies etymologically that they were without that which "testifies" to a man's virility. We are told that they liked to be called "putti," boys, no matter their age.[37] Often they self-inscribed their disorientation in their names, which were those of their conservatory teachers in diminutive form: singers like Appianino, Nicolino, Matteuccio, Gizziello, and Senesino figure prominently in operatic historiography.[38] Castrati provoked homophobic reactions and were subject to taunts, verbal abuse, coercion, physical brutalization, and psychological intimidation. They were teased as "evirati" ("emasculated"), "non integri" ("not whole"), "coglioni" ("testicles," but also "stupid"), goats, mignons, and capons. Playing with their appellative in all its endearing forms (for their angelic voices) and pejorative connotations (for their sexual distinction), they were also called "castratini," "castratelli," and "castroni," shamed in the act of being interpellated as subjects. Their body, lacking and fragmented, was further deidealized through references to their apelike or spiderlike appearance.[39]

36. Tommaso Garzoni, *La piazza universale di tutte le professioni del mondo*, ed. Paolo Cherchi and Beatrice Collina (1585; Turin: Einaudi, 1996), 1350–51. These pseudodoctors were famous not only for cases of castration but also for curing hernia and kidney stones. I return to related medical issues later in this chapter.

37. As in this letter of Aurelio Zibramonte to Guglielmo Gonzaga about a Spanish castrato singer: "Questo putto che così vole esser nominato fu tenuto un grande valent'huomo nel principio." Quoted in Sherr, "Guglielmo Gonzaga and the Castrati," 41. No irony at the use of "putto" and "valent'huomo" in the same breath is registered.

38. See Barbier, *The World of the Castrati*, 84–85.

39. Farinelli (Carlo Broschi), the greatest castrato ever, was described as having a gigantic stature and "if he had grace, it could be only a sort envied by a penguin or a spider." Quoted in Francis Rogers, "The Male Soprano," *Musical Quarterly* 5 (1919): 413–25, at 417. Balatri wrote in his will that no woman should be called to prepare his body for burial, so that there would be no laughter at his physical deformities. See Balatri, *Frutti del mondo*, 23.

They were the abjects of society, "that which beseeches, worries, and fascinates desire…, disturbs identity, system, order,… does not respect borders, positions, rules. The in-between, the ambiguous, the composite," in Kristeva's definition.[40] Even dreaming of them was dangerous because it was a premonition that the dreamer's penis would "become diseased."[41]

Castrati were described as cowards, with "weak eyes and a weak pulse, lacked fortitude and strength of mind, and had difficulty in pronouncing the letter R."[42] They were associated with hysterical fits and moody behavior, and were described as having no strength, no willpower, and no capacity to manage their emotions. For the doctor Juan Huarte, in losing their testicles, they lost their minds, since out of one thousand eunuchs who were educated, none made much progress, he wrote, and even in music, their very profession ("loro propria professione"), they were uncouth and ignorant, because music needed heat and castrati only offered a cold and humid body.[43] Often castrati were described as having a docile and good-humored personality and were deemed maternal, even in literary renderings, as in Torquato Tasso's Gerusalemme liberata, where the eunuch Arsete is protective and solicitous toward his charge, Clorinda. Like eunuchs, castrati were thought not to get arthritis because their capacity for sexual expenditure was restrained.[44] In private life, some became female-identified, carried feminine bric-a-brac such as mirrors and rouge, and wore makeup and corsets to make their waist appear smaller. They had no Adam's apple; some had noticeable breasts; their voices were feminine; and they were referred to as

40. Julia Kristeva, *Powers of Horrors: An Essay on Abjection* (New York: Columbia University Press, 1982), 1 and 4.

41. Dreaming about eunuchs presages such an outcome, according to Artemidorus's *Onirocriticon*, 4.37. Quoted in Gary Robert Brower, "Ambivalent Bodies: Making Christian Eunuchs," Ph.D. diss., Duke University, 1996, 185.

42. See Rosselli, *Singers of Italian Opera*, 145.

43. Juan Huarte, *Essamina de gl'ingegni de gli huomini accomodati ad apprendere qual si voglia scienza* (Venice: Barezzi, 1600), bk. 15, 393. Considering that Huarte's text came out in Spain in 1575, there must have been by the middle of the sixteenth century a good number of castrati in that country for him to make such a sweeping statement, many more than in Italy in any case.

44. Michele Mercati (1541–93), *Instruttione sopra la peste: Nella quale si contengono i piu eletti e approvati rimedij, con molti nuovi e potenti secreti così da preservarsi come da curarsi* (Rome: Vincenzo Accolti, 1576), 112.

"femelle" (little females), or more properly, "signora," beside the usual "prima donna" or even "seconda donna."[45] They could easily pass, if they chose, for transvestites. Others remained male-identified. Occasionally they shifted their object choice or, following a decrease in testosterone, lost interest in sex altogether.

Women swooned at the strong and yet sweet sound of a *musico's* voice, crowded the theaters where castrati performed, and ran away with them. Giacomo Casanova, who lived at the height of the phenomenon, declared that a woman might even prefer to pass for a castrato in order to be allowed to sing in the papal state and reap the financial benefits coming from fashionable performances.[46] Men too could on occasion find it difficult to resist the appeal of a castrato, so much so that—to paraphrase Casanova—Rome, in forbidding women onstage, made all men focus erotically on male actors and singers.[47] The castrato's success was such that a male singer with a falsetto or alto voice might have wanted to pass for a castrato in order to bask in the enthusiasm of admirers, as in the case, perhaps, of the eighteenth-century prima donna singer, Giusto Tenducci, who claimed that he was a castrato with a difference. Having married and being rumored to be the father of two children, he wittily explained that his peculiar status was the result of having had the castrating surgeon leave intact a surplus, third testicle.[48]

45. In *Frutti*, Balatri writes that he was never called by his last name, but addressed as "signora," and thus from neuter he was made a hermaphrodite ("et essendo io veramente neutro, hanno reso ermaf...il mio nome col scrivere tanto sui biglietti che in capo alle liste dei conti e ricevute dattemi, *Signora*, o al più, *Sinora Philippi*," 23). The castrato Antonio Angelini advertised himself as "prima donna," and Francesco Nelli as "seconda donna." See Bragaglia, *Degli "evirati cantori*," 41.

46. Giacomo Casanova, *The Story of My Life*, trans. Stephen Sartarelli and Sophie Hawkes (New York: Penguin, 2001), 84–108.

47. Charles de Montesquieu makes a similar reference to the beauty of transvestite castrati on the Roman stage in 1728, whom he fancied very able to excite male fantasies. An Englishman, he reports, fell in love with one, thinking he was a woman, and remained enthralled for a month. See his *Viaggio in Italia*, ed. Giovanni Macchia and Massimo Colesanti (Bari: Laterza, 1995), 164. Honoré de Balzac builds his story "Sarrazine," which Barthes examines in *S/Z*, along the same lines.

48. Giusto Tenducci married the Irishwoman Dora Maunsell, and this liaison caused a scandal. We do not know who fathered those children. The marriage was later annulled. See Henry Pleasants, *The Great Singers: From Jenny Lind and Caruso to Callas and Pavarotti* (New

Today, cases of ambiguous genitalia are resolved by assigning a sex first, and then by refining it through surgery and hormonal therapies, according to a philosophy of the predominant. Gender is bestowed immediately after, hopefully for good.[49] Civil law enforces a binary sex/gender system because it allows marriage only when the sex of the person is established by medical fiat, so as to foreclose the possibility that by mistake homosexual marriage can have legal status. In the past, castrati were cast as unsexed, asexual, heterosexual, homosexual, bisexual, and "hermaphroditic,"—whatever the label, they were the taboo icons of a culture in which the link to humors and heat made biological indeterminacy a reality. The German writer and admirer of castrati, Johan Archenholtz, wrote, for example, that he was a witness to a marvel while in Naples:

> A very particular accident happened a few years ago to a singer of the name of Balani. This man was born without any visible signs of those parts which are taken out in castration, he was, therefore, looked upon as a true-born castrato; an opinion which was even confirmed by his voice. He learned music, and sung several years upon the theatre with great applause. One day, he exerted himself so uncommonly in singing an arietta, that all of a sudden those parts, which had so long been concealed by nature, dropped into their proper place. The singer from this very instant lost his voice, which became even perceptible in the same performance, and with it he lost every prospect of a future subsistence.[50]

York: Simon and Schuster, 1981). Although he was known as a castrato, Tenducci could have been a countertenor.

49. In most cases of intersexuality the sex assigned by surgery is female; hormone treatments then fix the gender. Results in fitting in the assigned sex/gender as adults vary greatly. See William Reiner, "Sex Assignment in the Neonate with Intersex of Inadequate Genitalia," *Archives of Pediatric and Adolescent Medicine* 151 (1997): 1044–45. A penis measuring less than 0.6 inches at birth is deemed insufficient for a boy, and surgeons will surgically refashion it as a clitoris. See Anne Fausto-Sterling, "How to Build a Man," in *Constructing Masculinity*, ed. Maurice Berger, Brian Wallis, and Simon Watson (New York: Routledge, 1995).

50. Johann Wilhelm von Archenholtz, *A Picture of Italy*, trans. Joseph Trapp (Dublin: W. Corbet, 1791). See also Heriot, *The Castrati in Opera*, 47. The event seems to have occurred in 1765.

This story teaches us that nature moves toward perfection, that is, an incomplete man can become complete when the humors in his body are sufficiently hot, like those in a man's body. By behaving like a man ("he exerted himself so uncommonly"), Balani becomes one; his endocrine disorder (perhaps a case of Reifenstein's syndrome, which may have given him undescended testicles) gets suddenly cured through virilization of his voice, and from nothing ("no visible sign") he ends up having something.[51]

I mentioned in the introduction the case of Marie Germain, who similarly had male sexual organs drop down from her genitals, when she leaped over a ditch while chasing a pig. Like Marie, Balani gets recuperated into normative heterosexuality by an accident involving heat, but the recovery of masculinity brings him only loss: he is a man because his new physiology and voice testify that much, but he no longer has the means to sustain himself. His phallic instrument and erotogenic zone were his powerful voice and large throat that substituted, in a symbolic inversion, for his inadequate sexual equipment. Able to give pleasure by utterance, his new pleasure by emission disempowers him, for as Zaccaria Pasqualigo, a castrator of boys by profession ("puerorum emasculator ob musicam"), elaborated, when all is said and done, a boy's throat has more intrinsic value than his testicles.[52]

The erotic correspondence between voice and virility, vocal cords and sexual cords, is well known, so much so, for example, that there have been many studies in the last decades in which tonsillectomy and circumcision have been compared as a pair in a ritual for boys.[53] A treatise on the larynx, De vocis, written

51. On this medical problem, which seems to have affected most publicly the second-century Roman Sophist Favorinus, see H. Mason, "Favorinus' Disorder: Reifenstein's Syndrome in Antiquity," *Janus* 66 (1979): 1–13. Favorinus was involved in a heated debate on whether "eunuchs" could teach eloquence to the young. Cases of undescended testicles are hardly rare in medical literature. In the United States today one boy in three hundred is born with the problem.

52. Zaccaria Pasqualigo (d. 1664), *Eunuchi, nati, facti, mystici: Ex sacra et humana literatura illustrati* (1641; Dijon: Apud Philibertum Chavance, 1655). See also Rosselli, *Singers of Italian Opera*, 151.

53. See R. P. Bolande, "Ritualistic Surgery—Circumcision and Tonsillectomy," *New England Journal of Medicine* 280 (1969): 591–96; and M. Calnan, J. W. Douglas, and H. Goldstein, "Tonsillectomy and Circumcision: Comparison of Two Cohorts," *International Journal of Epidemiology* 7 (1978): 78–85.

toward the end of the sixteenth century by the Paduan doctor Giulio Casseri connects tampering with man's voice to disrupting his social standing, for, without a good, correctly pitched and toned male voice it is not possible for a man to give orders to inferiors or to rule over a household and be respected in the public domain.[54] And yet, as Roland Barthes writes in *S/Z*, apropos of the fictional castrato Zambinella, at a certain time in history "the Italian voice was produced *a contrario* . . . by singers without sex: this inversion is *logical*, as though, by selective hypertrophy, sexual density was obliged to abandon the rest of the body and lodge in the throat. . . . Music . . . can effect orgasm."[55]

Music and genitals are assimilated in another story, where, according to the Venetian traveler Nicolò di Conti, some men advertise their newly achieved manhood by making their penises literally sing. The happy and pleasant people living along the river Ava in India, di Conti asserts, start a sexual adult life (or make known their interest in getting married) by having old women decorate their penises with gold, silver, or copper bells attached between the shaft and the prepuce. Men are proud of such well-wrought penile decorations and love the sound the bells emit when they walk.[56] Unlike the incisions performed on

54. "our speech is taken from us if the larynx and the other instruments of voice are corrupted . . . ; we cannot rejoice in the intercourse of our fellows or share our ideas with others; nor do we have the ability to give our servants and maids their orders, to rule our household or to hold a good position either in private or public life." See Julius Casserius (Giulio Casseri, 1552?–1616), *The Larynx, Organ of Voice*, trans. Malcolm Hast and Erling Holtsmark (Uppsala: Almquist and Wiksells, 1969), 14. Even for women the connection between the throat and the cervix/vagina was well established, and not just by Freud. As in the case of castrati singers, a good voice meant lack of progeny for women too, according to Aristotle, who held that female singers were sterile because they could not menstruate. See Aristotle, *History of Animals* [hereafter *HA*], in *The Complete Works of Aristotle*, ed. Jonathan Barnes, 2 vols. (Princeton: Princeton University Press, 1984), 10.5.637a. See also Anne Hanson and David Armstrong, "The Virgin's Voice and Neck: Aeschylus, *Agamemnon* 245 and Other Texts," *British Institute of Classical Studies* 33 (1986): 97–100.

55. Roland Barthes, *S/Z*, trans. Richard Howard (New York: Farrar, Straus and Giroux, 1974). As the character Eunuch puns in the Venetian opera *La finta pazza*, the fact that he had some cords cut for the benefit of other chords makes him now curse music: "Sia maledetto il dì, ch'io ti conobbi, / Musica, eterna morte, / Di chi t'adopra in Corte. / Come scoppian le corde / Che non mi scoppia il petto?" (1.6).

56. "Come l'uomo è in età di poter usare con donne, overo che si voglia maritare, gli vanno ad acconciare il membro mettendo fra carne e pelli detti sonagli . . . e posti dentro e cucita si salda [la pelle] in pochi dì. . . . Molti di loro, camminando per la strada, hanno una cosa molto

castrati, cuts in the male organ are innocuous here ("si salda in pochi dì"); they do not announce a hormonal imbalance but show off a hormonal surplus. Music advertises not only a presence but also hints at an action: it spells men's availability for another kind of music, one that puts in place a performative and procreative agenda. Such a linking is not far-fetched. In *Historia musica*, Giovanni Andrea Angelini Bontempi equates the power of making music to that of producing semen. And yet by using this Neoplatonic metaphor of generation, Angelini Bontempi, himself a castrato, seems unaware of the irony he generates, since unlike the men living along the Ava, he could produce the music but not the heat sufficient to generate.[57]

In considering what kind or kinds of genital surgery prepubescent boys underwent for musical reasons, we lack referents. Descriptions tend to be given euphemistically, since the operation per se, unless medically recommended, was illegal, following Roman, and thus Italian, law, although it was left unlegislated by canon law. Early modern texts also bundle together eunuchs (males who underwent demasculinization with ablation of all sexual organs), castrati (from the Greek *kao*, which means to take out, to pluck, to twist — males who underwent removal or disablement of testicles before puberty), *spadones* (males who either had congenital sexual defects or were treated for them and whose penis, testicles, or scrotum were damaged or cut after puberty), and hermaphrodites (individuals, at times apparently male, born with male and female organs or the genetic capacity to grow them). The operation performed in Italy never involved full ablation; in fact, often it did not even involve removal of testicles (bilateral orchiectomy). At the time of the surgery the boy was given some opium, his carotid artery was compressed to induce a coma-like state, and he was immersed in a bath of milk to soften his genitals or in frozen water to anesthetize the cut. At this point the vas deferens, which takes the sperm from the testicles to the urethra were severed, just as it is done today for vasectomy. The testicles were then scored with a three-quarter-inch-deep cut so they would atrophy. At

---

onorata che se gli senta il suono di detti sonagli che hanno addosso." In Nicolò di Conti, *Viaggio in Oriente*, written in 1430, published in 1495. Di Conti was asked many times whether he would have liked the same operation performed on himself but always demurred. Excerps of the text are in Giovanni Battista Ramusio, *Navigazioni e viaggi*, ed. Marica Milanesi, 6 vols. (Turin: Einaudi, 1978–88), 2:796.

57. Giovanni Andrea Angelini Bontempi, *Historia musica* (Perugia: Constantini, 1695), 239–40. See also Rosselli, *Singers of Italian Opera*, 174.

times, testicles were simply squeezed or twisted, but results from those procedures were uneven, thus surgery was preferred. Alternately the scrotum was
removed.[58]

Surgery meant that not only would there be no sperm in the ejaculate, as for
vasectomy, but also that hormonal production would cease altogether. The procedure must not have been unduly difficult, since the normal length of recovery
was judged to be less than two weeks, a trifle at a time when even stomach upsets
were cured with a week or so of rest. Castrati rarely acknowledged that they were
forewarned or had consented to their mutilation. Often the cause for their disablement was attributed to a fall from a horse or to bites by pigs and wild boars.
Castration was easily readable on what has been called the eunuchoid body:
lack of androgen hormone, for one, caused the penis to remain infantile and the
prostate to stay undeveloped. Castrati also lacked beards and rarely went bald,
had a female rather than a male distribution of pubic hair, were often tall, with
long limbs; their skin was markedly pale and tended to wrinkle; they perspired
abundantly and developed large torsos and fat hips.[59] Many of them reached a
very old age and must have mused at the correlation between the length of one's
life and lack of male hormones.

The effects of castration had been known since antiquity in animals of both
sexes: gelding, Aristotle wrote, stimulates fatness, diminishes sexual urges, and
makes meat tastier. Aristotle linked women and castrated male animals; he did
not state that the male becomes female following surgery but described it as

58. For Paolo Zacchia there are three ways to remove testicles: "per excisionem, per
contusionem, vel attritionem," and "per frigida quaedam pharmaca." See *Quaestiones medico-
legales* (Lyon: Huguetan and Ravaud, 1661), 2.3.7. See also Joseph Bajada, *Sexual Impotence:
The Contribution of Paolo Zacchia, 1584–1659* (Rome: Ed. Pontificia Universitaria Gregoriana,
1988), 51.

59. For a complete list of bodily changes, see Enid Rhodes Peschel and Richard E. Peschel,
"Medicine and Music: The Castrati in Opera," *Opera Quarterly* 44 (1986–87): 21–38, esp.
27. There are reports that some castrati grew a beard, and in fact they were occasionally
reminded to shave before performing on stage, but these stories may be fabricated. In Roman times masters would sometimes have their favorite young boys castrated, so the boys
would keep their youthful looks for longer. When Domitian prohibited castration of Roman
citizens, eunuchs were imported. Dietary methods were also recommended as substitutes
for surgery—eating lettuce seeds, for example. See Aline Rousselle, "Personal Status and
Sexual Practice in the Roman Empire," in *Fragments for a History of the the Human Body*, ed.
Michel Feher, 3 vols. (New York: Zone, 1989), 3:313-14.

becoming effeminate as a consequence.[60] For Galen, eunuchs—like women, boys, and light skinned men–were cold and full of phlegm.[61] The same opinion was held by Ambroise Paré, who advised mild medical remedies for curing diseases in those "of soft and delicate temperament, as women, young children, idle people living delicately, eunuchs, and others."[62] That prepubertal castration affected vocal cords had already been observed in eunuchs. Macrobius described their voice as shrill but musically enticing. Aristotle thought that the difference in the male's vocal tone was due to the fact that when "the testes are removed, the tautness of the passages is slackened ... [and] the source (or principle) which sets the voice in movement is correspondingly loosened. This then is the cause on account of which castrated animals change over to the female condition both as regards the voice and the rest of their form."[63] Galen, however, dismissed this analysis in De semine.[64] It was, in any case, a common belief that abstention from sex was salutary in maintaining a high, bright sound quality in men's voices. For this purpose, for example, and for general health some young males were infibu-

60. Aristotle, *Generation of Animals* [hereafter *GA*], trans. A. L. Peck (Cambridge: Harvard University Press, 1990), 1.2.716b. For Aristotle the fact that eunuchs retained their hair, just like women, was a negative fact and one more reason to argue for their passage from the male to the female condition. See *GA* 4.1.766a.

61. Galen, *On semen (De semine)*, in *Corpus Medicorum Graecorum*, ed. Philip de Lacy (Berlin: Akademie-Verlag, 1992), 3.1. See also Ringrose, "Living in the Shadow," nn. 7 and 28.

62. Ambroise Paré, *Ten Books of Surgery with the Magazine of the Instruments Necessary for It*, trans. Robert Linker and Nathan Womack (1564; Athens: University of Georgia Press, 1969), 130.

63. Aristotle, *GA* 5.7.788a. Aristotle believed that the voice issued from the heart. Realdo Colombo demonstrated that that was not the case in his vivisection of a dog, when he silenced the dog's voice through compression of the langyngeal nerves. See *De re anatomica* (Venice: Bevilacqua, 1559), 257. Vocal cords were anatomized for the first time at the beginning of the seventeenth century.

64. See Brower, "Ambivalent Bodies," 170. According to Barbier, "the castrato voice differed from that of the normal male singer through its lightness, flexibility and high notes, and from the female voice through its brilliance, limpidity and power. At the same time it was superior to a boy's voice through the adult nature of its musculature, its technique and expressivity" (*The World of the Castrati*, 17). A historically important version of Alessandro Moreschi's Vatican recordings, made in 1902 and 1904 — the only castrato voice ever recorded — gives a sound well past its prime, slightly "goatish" to my untrained ears and somewhat eery and uncanny.

lated in Rome according to Celsus ("Infibulare quoque adolescentulos interdum vocis interdum valetudinis causa").[65]

Castration was hardly uncommon in the Renaissance, and not so much because there were castrati singers, I would argue, but because at any given day a number of men circulated in the streets with somewhat suffering or damaged genitalia. One has just to look at medical manuals of the time to see how often cures were offered for conditions described as inflammation of the prepuce, overheating of the penis ("riscaldazione de la virga"), contraction or numbness of the member ("membro ritiratosi"), "overflowing" of semen, and congestion or swelling of testicles ("coglioni enfiati"). Timoteo Rossello's prescriptions can serve as examples of the recommended treatments. For curing an inflammation, egg whites and olive oil were to be mixed and spread on the affected part; dry figs and wheat flour mixed in oil would give the same result.[66] To stop the overflowing of semen, one should drink a mixture of mint, mummy, red coral, *agnus castus*, olive oil, and fresh egg on getting up in the morning (87r). Bathing in water steeped with an herb called "the bite of the chicken" was suggested for an itchy prepuce (53r). And for a contracted member, the remedy was to cook the fat of marten, wolf, cat, chicken, and goose in white wine, to which one added leaves of althea. The mixture had to be spread with a warm hand (32r). Poor men could cure an ulcerated penis by simply using a damp washcloth with drops of vinegar and oil in it; more refined remedies were given for rich constituents (70r). Girolamo Ruscelli too had his own detailed list to cure tumors of the penis as well as general impotence, and cold and hot abscesses of the testicles.[67]

Whatever the problem, doctors seemed hardly prepared to fix it right or even to wait for nature to cooperate. Gugliemo da Saliceto complained that some

65. Cornelius Celsus, *De medicina*, ed. and trans. W. G. Spenser (Cambridge: Harvard University Press, 1935–38), bk. 7, ch. 25. The operation was also performed to prevent masturbation or coitus.

66. Timoteo Rossello, *Della summa de i secreti universali in ogni materia sì per huomini, e donne di alto ingegno, come ancora per medici* (Venice: Miloco, 1619), 42v and 71r.

67. Girolamo Ruscelli (d. ca. 1566), *De secreti del R. D. Alessio Piemontese* (Venice: Bonsadino, 1611), pt. 4, 31r, 37r, 74r, 76r, and 80r. Another equally debilitating, although nonsurgical, reason for impotence was mumps, which suppressed the production of male hormones before adolescence; the condition is easily cured today through hormonal therapies. See Joke Dame, "Unveiled Voices: Sexual Difference and the Castrati," in *Queering the Pitch: The New Gay and Lesbian Musicology*, ed. Philip Brett, Elizabeth Wood, and Gary Thomas (New York: Routledge), 152–53 n. 26.

doctors with no expertise ("non sano niente") were too ready to cut testicles rather than allow them to descend properly.[68] Men with undescended testicles were called natural eunuchs ("eunuchs from their mother's womb"). Leonardo Fioravanti had a simple remedy for undescended testicles: chewed paper had to be put over the affected body part. The sick person would then miraculously display a fully operational sexual apparatus in just fifteen days.[69]

Many cases of castration were the result of human agency and were inflicted for criminal, political, or moral reasons. The Church had little respect for sexual organs and often authorized blood-curdling tortures, as in the case of Tommaso Campanella, who had his joints dislocated and his testicles squeezed by the Inquisitors.[70] Men condemned to death by secular courts often had their genitals cut off and put in their mouths before being pierced, hacked, hanged, quartered, and burned, whatever the sentence. Rapists and sexual offenders at times were also summarily castrated. For example, the punishment inflicted on Maso of the village of San Gueninello in Tuscany in 1414 for having impregnated his sister was to have his testicles removed, while the sentence against Muccino from the village of Rassina, also in Tuscany, for having raped his eleven-year-old grandniece, involved his penis and a more creative procedure: his penis, it was ordered, was "to be sliced in four places and then burnt in each by a red-hot iron."[71] Castration was advocated for Jews found in the company of Christian women and for deserters. Some sodomites were disciplined through castration; more rarely, even passive male partners were condemned to undergo the same mutilation.[72] Sometimes distinctions were made between different forms of cas-

68. "Lassa lo coione desender alo logo suo et per nesun muodo ardisse de taiare li coioni come fa li paci miedigi che non sano niente." See Guglielmo da Saliceto (1210–80), *Chirurgia* (Venice: Di Pietro, 1474). Quoted in Maria Luisa Altieri Biagi, *Guglielmo Volgare: Studi sul lessico della medicina medioevale* (Bologna: Forni, 1970), 66.

69. See Domenico Furfaro, *La vita e l'opera di Leonardo Fioravanti* (Bologna: Società Tipografica Editori, 1963), 77.

70. See Piero Camporesi, *Il governo del corpo* (Milan: Garzanti, 1995), 161. There were also instructional books on instruments of torture, such as that of Antonio Galloni (1577–1605), *Trattato de gli instrumenti martirio* (Rome: Donangeli, 1591).

71. See Samuel Cohn, *Women in the Streets: Essays on Sex and Power in Renaissance Italy* (Baltimore: Johns Hopkins University Press, 1996), 102 and 104.

72. Michael Rocke, *Forbidden Friendships: Homosexuality and Male Culture in Renaissance Florence* (New York: Oxford University Press, 1996), 7 and 132. For similar cases in Venice, see Guido Ruggiero, *The Boundaries of Eros: Sex Crime and Sexuality in Renaissance Venice* (New

tration as penance. In 1497, for example, Domenico Cecchi put out an agenda for the punishment of sodomites in Florence. First-time offenders were to be given a fine and a prison term; second-time offenders were to be partially castrated but could retain their generative capacity; third-time offenders were to be totally castrated; and fourth-time offenders were to be put in an asylum.[73] The connection between homosexuality and mental disease is new for the early modern period (although not for the nineteenth century), but one wonders what kinds of sexual crime a man with already debilitated sexual organs could commit to be relegated to the madhouse.

In the past a variety of medical problems were treated by surgical castration with incision or ablation of testicles (and occasionally of the penis) for an effective cure. The most typical of these disorders were those connected to the genitalia per se, such as cancer of the penis or tuberculosis of the testicles.[74] But venereal diseases were also at times cured with castration, especially syphilis. Kidney stones, elephantiasis, epilepsy, and gout required similar draconian measures. Other not so closely associated diseases, such as madness, pox, and the plague, were cured with castration as well. Fear of contracting leprosy was sufficient reason to remove the testicles, Girolamo Fracastoro writes, for it was believed that eunuchs were immune from this affliction.[75] Hernia was an enormous problem among poor adults, because of their life of hard toil, and among poor infants, because of the relative neglect and restriction of movement in which they were kept. One can easily understand how babies tightly bundled in dirty linens, tormented by mosquitoes and other insects, fed on a poor diet that caused colic, or insufficiently fed, lying in a crib and crying unattended for

York: Oxford University Press, 1995); and Gabriele Martini, *Il 'vitio nefando' nella Venezia del seicento: Aspetti sociali e repressione di giuudizia* (Rome: Jouvence, 1988).

73. See Rocke, *Forbidden Friendships*, 225.

74. Eve Sedgwick offers an anecdote about a male friend, after she herself had been diagnosed with breast cancer: "he, too, had had a pretty bad breast cancer scare several years before. But his lump had turned out to be benign–'And it was a good thing too,' he said on the phone, 'because you know what the treatment of choice is for *male* breast cancer? Castration!'" See Eve Kosofsky Sedgwick, "Gosh, Boy George, You Must Be Awfully Secure in Your Masculinity," in *Constructing Masculinity*, ed. Maurice Berger, Brian Wallis, and Simon Watson (New York: Routledge, 1995), 11–20.

75. Girolamo Fracastoro, *De contagione et contagiosis morbis et eorum curatione*, trans. Wilmer Wright (New York: Putnam's Sons, 1930), sec. 213, esp. 163.

hours would sooner or later develop hernias. Hernias were reportedly treated by castration, sometimes as a preventative, since it was believed that eunuchs did not suffer from hernias, either. Women experts with the needle were sought after as "penis menders" ("conciacazzi") to restore health to broken ("rotti"), herniated men.[76] Writing about France, Barbier finds more than five hundred cases of boys castrated because of hernia in just one parish, that of Saint Papoul, near Carcassonne, in 1676.[77]

What part or parts of the genitalia were technically removed or maimed in all these cases of castration required for curative myths is unclear, but instances of men lacking penises must have been sufficiently common for Ambroise Paré to provide an illustration of the "artificial yard," a conical instrument built of wood that men who had undergone penectomy could carry along to relieve them-

76. Piero Camporesi, *Le officine dei sensi* (Milan: Garzanti, 1985), 141. Gregory of Tours elaborates on a case reported in the sixth century: a group of rebellious nuns accused their mother superior of keeping a youth dressed as a woman in her company for her own satisfaction. The investigation into the matter led to a surprising conclusion: the person in female garb was indeed a man, but the sexual connotations of the relationship between him and the mother superior had to be discounted, since he had a "disease of the groin." The doctor who had performed the surgery, Reovalis, at the urging of the boy's mother and following the counsel of the holy Radegund, described it similar to those he had seen performed in Constantinople and deemed it a success. As a result, the mother superior was cleared of all charges. See Gregory of Tours, *The History of the Franks*, trans. Lewis Thorpe (Harmondsworth: Penguin, 1974), 570–71. The doctor's claim that he had seen this technique practiced in the East suggests that perhaps this youth had total ablation of his organs performed on him, since such soon became the requirement for guardians of Islamic harems.

77. Barbier, *The World of the Castrati*, 60. Even Fioravanti, who had a cure for everything, seems at times to doubt that hernia can be cured. Genital cutting has been used in different historical periods to cure an array of problems, as in the recommendation to circumcise boys suffering from orthopedic diseases, epilepsy, hernia, chronic mental disorders, repetitive crying, syphilis, genital herpes, tubercular meningitis, asthma, and the seemingly widespread *reflex neurosis*. Circumcision was also used by one of the pioneers of American medicine, Lewis Sayre, from 1870 through his death in 1900 to prevent masturbation. Many doctors followed the recommendation of this "Columbus of the prepuce," as he was called, and by the turn of the century millions of American boys had their foreskin ablated for reasons of health and cleanliness. The cure for "nervousness" in women was, in keeping with medical practices applied to their sex, even more drastic and highly impairing: cliteridectomy. See David Gollaher, *Circumcision* (New York: Basic Books, 2000), 73–92.

selves.[78] This prosthesis, which in Italy was also made of brass, allowed men to remain technically male when they urinated, because the attachment made them stand up, unlike women. Such a case is satirically visited by Anton Francesco Grazzini (called "Il Lasca") in a novella of *Le cene*. Here a young man of means plays a trick on his teacher as a punishment for his pedantic ways. He convinces him to insert his penis in a hole for the purpose of relieving himself and then has a companion grasp it tightly on the other side with the teeth of a dead fish. Hearing people come by, "Messer lo Precettore" becomes afraid of losing his reputation and extricates himself as best he can from the device. In the process he loses a portion of his penis. The injured penis soon becomes infected and has to be cut off. At this point he is provided with a brass "cannellino" to relieve himself.[79] The tutor is subsequently sent away from the family that employed him while his homophobic young master, unpunished, laughingly retells the episode of his castration hundreds of times.

In this story the literal loss of penis is read at the most elementary level: since the pedagogue is unmanned and his lower belly has become as flat as the palm of one's hand, we are told, he can no longer be of service to his employers. To be sure, pedagogues/pedants are always considered unmanly in literature, as if their known vocal redundancy had to translate into some form of sexual lack; the same construction employed in the case of the castrato Balani. The "cannellino," a metonymy for the lost object, reminds us that the power of the penis is in its generative capacity rather than in its urinary function and that the loss of that flesh brings social cancellation. No matter how much a man seems to be one because he urinates like one, the lesson seems to be that he is really manly only when he realizes his power through a son. But the prosthesis also shows that maleness is always constructed under the threat of castration, in the Freudian understanding of it, for the teeth of the dead fish—a *vagina dentata* figure indeed—are a constant menace to the unsuspecting intellectualized man.

78. Ambroise Paré, *The Works of that Famous Chirurgion Ambrose Parey*, trans. Thomas Johnson (London: Cotes and Young, 1634), 877.

79. "In capo di pochi giorni, o fusse la inavvertenza o la straccurataggine o il poco sapere de' medici, o fusse pure la malignità della ferita, quel poco che restato gli era di quella faccenda infradiciando, fu bisogno, se campar volle la vita, tagliar via. La qual cosa fu fatto, di corto guarì, ma rimase sotto il pettiglione, come la palma della mano; e se orinar volle, fu necessario un cannellino d'ottone." In Anton Francesco Grazzini, detto il Lasca, *Le cene* (Milan: Rizzoli, 1989), day 2, nov. 2, 72–82, at 81.

A priest in a novella by Matteo Bandello, "Uno truova la moglie con un prete," is not lucky enough to survive. As a punishment for having been found with another man's wife, he is given a knife to castrate himself. He does so, and thus he transforms himself, from cock to capon ("con un taglio, di gallo si fece cappone"). Things do not go well for him, however, and he dies soon after, without penis, testicles, or witnesses ("testes"), as the author puts it: "senza linea e perpendicoli, . . . senza testimoni se ne morì."[80] In a similar story involving a clergyman, this time by Grazzini, the punishment centers on the priest's testicles. The brothers of the woman he tried to seduce tie the "father" to a tree by his testicles, so that when he is forced to move three hours later, his scrotum tears and he faints.[81] Luckily, he outlives the painful incident and learns his lesson, no longer lusting, we are told, after women. Priesthood and castration go together also in a playful appeal by the actor and playwright Ruzante (Angelo Beolco) to Cardinal Marco Cornaro in *Prima orazione* (1521) to please authorize priests to get married for the sake of the common people, unless castrating them was an option.[82]

The presence of such an array of males with damaged sexual organs and varied sexual interests may have made the practice of castrating boys for musical reasons much more understandable in the past than could be imagined today, for every township, even a small one, must have had its share of medical victims. The 120 castrati singers in the city of Rome in 1650, when the number of castrations for musical purposes was at its highest, or the 100 in 1694, when the practice started to decline, may have been just an addition—medically unjustified to be sure—to an established practice.[83] Castration involved almost exclusively boys from indigent families in which the means of survival, let alone

80. Matteo Bandello, *Tutte le opere di Matteo Bandello*, ed. Francesco Flora, 2 vols. (Milan: Mondadori, 1934–43), 1.37, p. 449.

81. "La borsa se gli svelse, e allungogli un buon sommesso; onde sì fatta stretta ebbe a i granelli, che per la doglia grandissima si venne meno, e stette quasi un'ora tramortito" (Grazzini, *Le cene*, 2.8, 318–30, at 325).

82. See Michel Plaisance, "Città e campagna: XIII–XVII secolo," in *Letteratura italiana: Le questioni*, ed. Alberto Asor Rosa, 7 vols. (Turin: Einaudi, 1986), 5:620. Marriage for clerics was abolished at the Second Lateran Council in 1139.

83. For speculation on the number of castrati operating in Rome, see Rosselli, *Singers of Italian Opera*, 157. Pleasants raises the number considerably. He suggests that there may have been as many as four thousand Italian boys castrated each year at the height of fashion for opera in the eighteenth century (*The Great Singers*, 38).

of instruction or even of a meaningful life, were remarkably low. Cruel as it may appear, the operation afforded these boys, many of them newly orphaned as a result of the greatest plague ever to affect Italy, the chance for a passable adolescence in which they were sufficiently fed and warmly clothed. Given the dire economic situation in Italy, especially in the first half of the seventeenth century, when the practice of cutting testicles for economic survival started to become widespread, parents and tutors may have chosen to make a boy a castrato singer, just as they chose to have a girl become a nun, to assure the child's survival.[84] Paternal power, it was claimed at the time, extends to the use of sons as well as of daughters, and admits to their sexual dispossession. Giocondo, a fictional character in the treatise *Contrasto musico* by Grazioso Uberti da Cesena, published in 1630, explains that civil laws allow a father to dispose of his sons and of their earnings; he can even sell them if the decision is conducive to his survival. And he can castrate them.[85]

In Naples the institutions permitted castration of a boy when there were at least four sons in the family, on the principle that one of them could be given up to serve the church.[86] Let us not forget that entering a religious life, even an ascetic one, was not so farfetched a choice for early modern people as it would seem

84. Castrati in conservatories (there were four in Naples) were given a monthly stipend and often lost contacts with their family. Since they were unable to create a family of their own as adults, they were psychologically isolated, although of course very much courted. This must have been one of the reasons why they were at times employed as counselors, ambassadors, or spies, as in the cases of Atto Melani (1626–1714), who worked for Cardinal Mazarin in France, and of Farinelli at the court of the king of Spain.

85. "Può il padre disporre del Putto, e del suo guadagno, anzi, che poteva il padre, conforme alle leggi civili, vendere il figlio per il bisogno di vivere . . . come anco puole dare il proprio figlio per ostaggio al nemico, se bene questo è per una certa usurpatione." In Grazioso Uberti da Cesena, *Contrasto musico: Opera dilettevole* (Rome: Lodovico Grigniani, 1630), 40–41.

86. See Barbier, *The World of the Castrati*, 20. In the ancient world, too, abandoned boys were occasionally made eunuchs. See John Boswell, *The Kindness of Strangers: The Abandonment of Children in Western Europe from Late Antiquity to the Renaissance* (New York: Pantheon, 1988), 72. Abandoned children not only had an incredibly low rate of survival but also were easily victimized as adolescents, indentured to families, or sold to slavery. That a father could mutilate a son in retaliation for his wife's adultery is recorded in the life of the castrato Ottavio Cacherano d'Orasco, son of a count, who became a famous singer in 1637 in the Austrian court. See Rosselli, *Singers of Italian Opera*, 156.

today. Writing a *Defense of Eunuchs* early in the twelfth century, Theophylact of Ochrid justifies parents having their boys castrated early in their youth for the sake of serving God at the same time that he condemns adults castrating themselves because theirs is a sin against nature.[87] Just to give an idea of how much religious orders were used at the time in Italy, we know that two-thirds of male and female newborns between 1600 and 1649 and half of those between 1650 and 1699 were channeled into some form of religious life.[88] Only after castrati became successful on the stage, and especially after the middle of the seventeenth century, was the operation chosen for the sake of a prosperous life unconnected, or only partially connected, to religion. The fact that the number of castrati diminished in the eighteenth century, even though that period was their most rewarding on the stage, can be usefully correlated to the improved economic situation in Italy, when no major epidemics, such as syphilis and plague, decimated the population and new ways of distributing inheritances among brothers were devised.[89]

Following Aquinas, ecclesiastical law did not outlaw castration per se, although of course the church objected to all forms of genital mutilation, and permitted it only in cases of disease and with the child's consent. That such consent was valueless, given the boy's age and family pressure, goes without saying.

87. See *Theophylacte d'Achride, Discours, traites, poésies et letters*, ed. Paul Gautier (Thessaloniki: Association de recherches byzantines, 1980–86), 291–331. For Ringrose, this acceptance of eunuchism for religious reasons had become less anomalous than one would think at the time of Theophylact's writing. See Kathryn Ringrose, "Passing the Test of Sanctity: Denial of Sexuality and Involuntary Castration," in *Desire and Denial in Byzantium*, ed. Liz James (Aldershot: Ashgate, 1999), 123–37, esp. 131–32.

88. According to Pietro Stella, "Per tutto il '600 circa il 50% dei maschi e delle femmine risulta inserito negli ordini maschili e femminili o nel clero secolare. Più distintamente risulta che due terzi dei nati tra il 1600 e il 1649 e circa metà nel secondo cinquantennio del secolo venne inserito nel celibato sacro. Nella prima metà del '700 le figlie monacate scesero al 13%; alla fine del secolo si ridussero al 3%." See "Strategie familiari e celibato sacro in Italia tra '600 e '700," *Salesianum* 41 (1979): 73–109, at 93.

89. From the very beginning the practice of castrating even willing boys had plenty of detractors. Only Tommaso Tamburini (1591–1675), a Jesuit priest from Sicily, defended the castration of *musici*, in a treatise. See Milner, "The Sacred Capons." Eighteenth-century texts that examine the castration of boys for musical purposes come mostly from Venice; as, for example, Benedetto Marcello, *Il teatro alla moda*; Carlo Goldoni, *L'impresario di Smirne*; and Simone Sografi, *Convenienze inconvenienze teatrali*.

In principle the Church also rejected castrati as priests. In line with decisions taken on the issue by the Council of Nicaea in 325, men could enter priesthood or a monastic life, it was decreed, only if they were physically whole, although we may assume that many men with sexual dysfunctions voluntarily chose life as clerics or were ordained, whether or not they were musically trained.[90] In a satire against castrati, Salvator Rosa muses on the singer who played Filli, a nymph, on the musical stage at night and a priest at the altar the next morning.[91] A joke circulated that castrati carried their testicles in a pouch in their pocket at the time of ordination, or, in a classier context, that they had them blown inside glass cherries to meet doctrinal fiat from a technical standpoint.

Matteo Bandello relates such a case in a novella, "Un prete castrato porta a dosso i suoi testicoli." Rocco da Montepelieri, a French priest who was organ-challenged on account of some unclear disease, always carried his testicles wrapped in paper in a purse and would never celebrate mass without them.[92] One day a girl of about nine or ten living in the household that employed him, finding him asleep looked into his pockets and discovered them. Thinking that they were figs or dates, she ate them. Once awakened, the priest thought that his days of celebrating mass were over and in terror started to look for his missing parts. He was eventually reassured that — testicles or no testicles — he could remain a priest. The joke plays up the equivalence of figs and testicles and makes fun of our misnamed protagonist Rocco, who, as an unmanned man, was far from being a "rock." Wrapped and dried-up testicles give Rocco a religious and social identity, while at the subconscious level they allow him to imagine genital wholeness. The missing twinned parts constitute his perfect fetish, in that they protect him against the instability of meaning. By carrying them around

90. Council of Nicaea, *Canon* 1: "If anyone in sound health has castrated himself, such a one, if [already] enrolled among the clergy, should cease [from his ministry], and from now on, no such person should be promoted." See Brower, "Ambivalent Bodies," 20. Men whose castration was not self-inflicted but the result of violence — the case of Abelard — were, however, allowed to take the vows. On the early Christian practice of self-inflicted eunuchism, see Daniel Caner, "The Practice and Prohibition of Self-Castration in Early Christianity," *Vigiliae Christianae* 54 (1997): 396–415.

91. "Chi vide mai più la modestia offesa? Far da Filli un Castron la sera in Palco, / e la mattina il Sacerdote in Chiesa,." See Salvator Rosa, "La musica," in *Satire*, 47. In Venice priests specialized in playing old women's parts. See Barbier, *The World of the Castrati*, 140.

92. "Portava sempre in una sua borsa i suoi testicoli avvolti in un poco di carta, nè detto mai avrebbe la messa se la borsa a lato avuta non avesse" (Bandello, *Tutte le opere*, 3.30, p. 415).

in a purse, Rocco enacts each day his physical and emotional trauma, and in commemorating his original loss, he shelters his psyche from sadistic fantasies. Indeed Bandello describes him as a good-humored man, his pouches always full of little items — he who had no "pouches" left — that he would joyfully give away.

Rulers have not been implicated in manufacturing their own "puttini castratelli," although employment at their court was a motivating factor for poor boys to undergo castration. When it was politely suggested to Duke Guglielmo Gonzaga in 1565 that one way of remedying the fact that it was so difficult to find a castrato for his court was to have some Mantuan boys cut for this purpose he did not follow up on the suggestion.[93] Still, rulers often paid for castration costs when boys from indigent families petitioned them.[94] In a letter dated February 9, 1613, the agent in Rome of the duke of Mantua wrote, for example, that he found an orphan boy with a good voice who wanted help in getting himself castrated ("il puttino ha buona voce, pronto, e con buona dispositione, et ha gran desiderio di farsi castrare et a me ne fa grandissima istanza").[95] Notarized documents often spelled out that a boy be accepted at a music school with the understanding that he would be castrated in due course.[96] No matter the precision of the surgery, only 10 percent of castrati retained the kind of voice that allowed them to be successful in church singing or onstage. For those whose voice thickened, contralto parts were tried out; if this switch did not work out, they were advised to learn to play some instrument.

This leads me to a hypothesis that has never been thoroughly examined to my knowledge: could the ambiguous sexuality of the castrato, the fact that his voice was feminine as well as some of his physical features, be used not only on the musical but also on the comic and perhaps even the tragic stage to play female parts more convincingly than the boys and men who were customarily used? The documented employment of eunuchs on the Roman stage may have provided a

93. Sherr, "Guglielmo Gonzaga and the Castrati," 36.

94. These expenses were reported in a deceptive, roundabout manner. See Rosselli, *Singers of Italian Opera*, 154.

95. Antonio Bertolotti, *Musici alla corte dei Gonzaga in Mantova dal secolo XV al XVIII* (Geneva: Monkoff, 1978), 212.

96. In the case of Paolo Nannini the expense was to be paid for by his teacher, Antonio Masini. The document is dated August 3, 1671. See Gian Ludovico Masetti-Zannini, "Virtù e crudezza: Scolari di canto e famiglie tra rinascimento e barocco," *Strenna dei Romanisti* 41 (1980): 332–41, esp. 338.

historical justification for the practice. True, by the time castrati started to sing in publicly paid performances, the Italian spoken theater was no longer a transvestite theater, but Rome and surrounding cities still required male actors for all roles. And although castrati have been reproached for caring little about acting, especially at the beginning of their employment on the stage, since all their movements had to take into account the projection of their voice, we know that some of them were highly praised for their realistic performances. An anonymous booklet, *Il corago*, also advised castrati to polish their performative skills.[97] In 1639 the musicians of Cardinal Richelieu were amazed at the acting abilities of the castrati Loreto Vittori and Marc'Antonio Pasqualini performing on the Roman stage.[98] Considering that the voice of many castrati failed, it makes sense that they would look for useful employment on a stage with which they were otherwise familiar and which was never completely dominated by professional actors.[99] We know that in Ferrara the singers of the duke's private chamber both sang and acted on stage, as documented in some sacred representations.[100]

Visiting Italy, the German intellectual Volkman remarked on the advantage offered by castrati over cross-dressed actors and referred to the fact that castrati were also playing on the spoken stage because they could easily embody female parts.[101] Johan Wolfgang von Goethe, a director of the Weimar theater and thus

97. "Per esser buon recitante cantando bisognerebbe esser anche buono recitante parlando." See *Il corago o vero alcune osservazioni per metter bene in scena le composizioni drammatiche*, ed. Paolo Fabbri and Angelo Pompilio (Florence: Olschki, 1983), 91.

98. See Barbier, *The World of the Castrati*, 101. The castrati Guadagni, Crescentini, and Nicolini were also deemed good actors. See Rogers, "The Male Soprano," 424–25.

99. *Intermedi*, for example, used pages and servants of the household; sometimes the nobility recited as well. In Rome, a representation in the private theater of the noblewoman Donna Olimpia used a variety of noblemen ("tutta da Marchesi e da Duchi, li quali si compiacquero per dargli gusto di diventar Histrioni"). Another comedy was recited in 1669 in the house of Princess Rossano by her own servants and in the presence of twelve cardinals. See Ademollo, *I teatri*, 47 and 109.

100. See Mauda Bregoli Russo, *Teatro dei Gonzaga al tempo di Isabella d'Este* (New York: Lang, 1997), 16. Filippo Zorzo (that is, Filippo Angeloni) was both an actor and a singer (53).

101. "Si pensi un po,' per esempio, un attore con barba nera e voce forte nella parte di *Pamela* nella commedia di Goldoni. Egli può recitare con quanto impegno e sentimento si voglia, che la sua intera figura e il tono della voce resta sempre straordinariamente scandaloso in una parte così tenera. Coi castrati, che rappresentano nell'opere parti di femmina, la cosa è tutt'altra. La loro figura e voce è cosiffatta, che non si osserva molto la differenza e la vero-

a connoisseur of actors and playhouses, speculated that the Roman custom of using males to play male and female parts onstage was a good one: the effect was powerful, the illusion of theatricality complete, and the artistic pleasure heightened. He found that the castrati playing women's parts were very pleasing.[102] Touching on the topic, Bianconi suggests that in places like Venice itinerant commedia dell'arte groups may have mingled with court opera companies in which castrati were used, therefore encouraging acting skills in everybody.[103] It is well known that some singers, like actors, were itinerant performers; they typically moved to the provinces after the Carnival season in the major cities had ended. In the Roman operas *Sant'Alessio* and *La regina Esther* (1632), which included a number of recitative soliloquies, roles went mostly to castrati, and their acting skills were as much praised as their singing in a subsequent representation of 1634.[104] *La finta pazza*, which used to great effect the convention of several plays within a play, was a melodrama entirely sung when it was first staged in Venice, but by the time it was performed four year later in 1645 in Paris it was partly sung and partly recited by a company of an actor and three actresses summoned to France by Cardinal Mazarin.[105] In Rome, the poet Giulio Rospigliosi, who became Pope Clement IX (1667–70), had a play within an opera, *La Baldassarra o la comica del cielo* (1668), in which the actress Baldassarra renounced the stage to live as an anchorite. All female parts in the opera and in the play within it were sung and acted by castrati.[106] Giovan Battista Andreini's *La Ferinda* (1622) belonged to the commedia dell'arte genre, but it was mostly sung. When comic scenes were added to the opera *L'Egisto* or to *Chi soffre speri* (1637), inspired by

---

simiglianza per conseguenza non è offesa. Si usa anche prendere, per le parti di femmina nelle commedie, dei cattivi castrati, che non hanno buona voce pel canto." In Ademollo, *I teatri*, xix. For castrati as comic prose actors, see also Bragaglia, *Degli "evirati cantori,"* 30.

102. Johan Wolfgang von Goethe, "Frauenrollen auf dem Romischen Theater durch Manner gespielt." Quoted in Ademollo, *I teatri*, xx.

103. See Bianconi, *Music in the Seventeenth Century* (Cambridge: Cambridge University Press, 1987), 183–84 and 208–09.

104. See Murata, *Operas for the Papal Court*, 225.

105. For the Venetian performance, see Rosand, *Opera in Seventeenth-Century Venice*, 110–24; for the French performance, see Molinari, *La commedia dell'arte*, 216.

106. Baldassarra, who also played the part of Clorinda, was acted by Giuseppe Fedi, Talia by Francesco Maria Fedè, Urana by Damaso, and Beatrice, the second *comica*, by Domenico del Pane. The same castrati also played the allegorical roles of Victory and Penance. See Murata, *Operas for the Papal Court*, 169–71.

a Boccaccio novella, commedia dell'arte characters such as Coviello and Zanni were called in for long recitative sections.[107]

Sexual Persona

Although we tend to think of castrati as sexually mutilated individuals, the idea of the eunuch that has come to us though literature and culture is quite the opposite. Quintilian's maxim, "Libidinosior es quam ullus spado" ("You are more lustful than any eunuch") presents eunuchs as oversexualized satyrs.[108] The stereotype of the castrato seems at times just as sexually charged. Yet, what kind of sex, if any, could the castrato perform? The general thinking seems to have been that some castrati could have intercourse and others could not. Performance was inconsistent and depended on the status of their sexual organs: if testicles had been squeezed, they could; if testicles had been incised, they probably could not. The cases of men castrated after puberty, whatever the reason, were considered different from those of *musici*, for the capacity for sexual arousal was assumed to have been left technically untouched in them, since these men did not lack male hormones. Even if boys had no penis as adults for whatever reason, it was thought that they remained male-identified, as in the case of Abelard, who, following his punitive castration, famously managed to refashion his sexual loss into psychological empowerment. According to Peschel, having sex was not a possibility for castrati due to their hormonal insufficiency, but of course there is sex and sex, and these men could have been sought after precisely because their physical inadequacy could have enhanced creativity in the bedroom.[109] After

107. See Hammond, *Music and Spectacle in Baroque Rome*, 227.

108. Quintilian, *Institutiones oratoriae*, 6.3.64.

109. Peschel and Peschel ("Medicine and Music") do not believe that castrati could have heterosexual intercourse, but Melicow is not so sure. See Meyer Melicow, "Castrati Singers and the Lost 'Cords,' " *Bulletin of the New York Academy of Medicine* 59.8 (1983): 752. As for homosexual relations, Bullough and Bullough suggest that castrati may have found some rewards: "We can speculate that some castrati may have enjoyed playing the passive role in anal intercourse, since the prostate is an erotic and sensitive area; anal intercourse thus would have allowed them to achieve orgasm despite their castration." See Vern Bullough and Bonnie Bullough, *Crossdressing, Sex, and Gender* (Philadelphia: University of Pennsylvania Press, 1993), 85. Prepubertal castration may, however, have left the prostate undeveloped. See Peschel and Peschel, "Medicine and Music," 27. Blocked pores and a cold nature distinguish eunuchs and men called "effeminate," according to Peter of Abano (Petrus de Abano).

all, for men lacking testicles like Favorinus, a second-century Sophist described as "born double-sexed" with the shrill voice of a eunuch, sexual potency was a matter of ridicule, and yet he was tried for adultery.[110] To cite another case, Francesco, a poor man from Imola, had only daughters because he had a hernia, we are told by a fifteenth-century city chronicler. One day, with great displeasure of his wife, he chose to have himself castrated, that is, his testicles were incised for the purpose of improving his chances to father an heir. Contrary to all expectations, he became very active sexually and had four male children.[111]

Some castrati were well known for their heterosexual attachments. In 1637, the *virtuoso* Vittori, a star in the Sistine Chapel, had to run away from Rome, following a scandal caused by eloping with a married Florentine woman, Plautilla Azzolini, wife of the painter Francesco Borbone. Vittori later dismissed the episode as "a mild error of youthful desire," although he was thirty-seven at the time, and indicted her in his writings as a whore.[112] Giovanni Francesco Grossi, nicknamed Siface (1653–97), was very effeminate in his everyday comportment,

---

He claims that, because the passage through which semen flows through the penis is in their case blocked or narrow, "they cannot ejaculate through the penis, but their slight, often dry seed can be dispersed or emitted by rubbing around the anus." See Joan Cadden, *Meanings of Sex Difference in the Middle Ages: Medicine, Science, and Culture* (Cambridge: Cambridge University Press, 1993), 214. For more on Abano's naturalistic explanation on why some men prefer anal stimulation, see *Expositio Problematum Aristotelis*, ed. Stephanus Illarius (Mantua: Pualus Johannis de Puzpach, 1475), pt. 4, probl. 26.

110. Philostratus describes him as "born double-sexed, both male and female, as his appearance made plain: his face remained beardless even into old age. His voice revealed the same ambiguity, for it was penetrating, shrill, and high-pitched, the way nature tones the voice of eunuchs. Yet he was so hot-blooded when it comes to sex that he was actually charged of adultery by a man of consular rank." Cited in Maud Gleason, *Making Men: Sophists and Self-Presentation in Ancient Rome* (Princeton: Princeton University Press, 1995), 6. Cf. above, note 51, where I mention Favorinus in connection with the singer Balani.

111. "M. Francesco da Imola . . . aveva una formosa e grassa donna della quale essendo lui rotto di sotto, non aveva se non fiole femmine, et dapoi lui fattosi castrare e cavare tutti dui li cogliuni e lei di zò piangendo e lamentandosi con l'altre donne, perochè era ancora giovene, et dapoi ebbe da lui 4 fioli maschi." In Giuliano Fontaguzzi, *Caos! Cronache Cesenati del sec. XV pubblicate ora per la prima volta, di su i manoscritti con notizie e note a cura del Dott. Dino Bazzocchi* (Cesena: Tipografia Bettini, 1915), 80.

112. See "La troia rapita" (The Kidnaped Whore). See also Hammond, *Music and Spectacle in Baroque Rome*, 175–77. Vittori was forgiven by Pope Urban VIII three years later, in 1641, and admitted to sing again in his presence.

yet he too was known for an affair, with Countess Elena Forni, who was subsequently relegated by her family to a convent. Having gone to see her, Siface was killed by men hired by her family, the Marsilii, an event that led the duke of Modena to pursue the killers in retaliation. Antonio Maria Bernardi (1685–1756) too was said to have been in love with a woman called Merighi who sang in his company.[113] There were castrati whose desire for a steady relationship, and for a proper disposition of their considerable fortunes, made them also wish to get married. One of the first and most famous seventeenth-century sopranos, Domenico Cecchi (1650?–1718), called Cortona, petitioned Pope Innocent XI for permission to marry Barbara Voglia. The pope wrote back a lapidary response: "Castrate better" ("Si castri meglio"), and denied the request.[114] In *Traité des eunuques*, a tract against eunuchs and castrati bundled together, the French writer D'Ancillon argues that the reason for his intervention on the topic is to guard women against marrying castrati, once more confirming that this practice was not too unusual or was feared as being sought by women. D'Ancillon mentions the case of certain seventeenth-century Italian castrati who wanted to marry in Germany.[115] One case involved Domenico Sorlisi (1632?–72), who petitioned the elector of Saxony to wed a young woman from Dresden, Dorotea Lichtwer, and was given official permission in 1666.[116]

113. For the life of these castrati, see the biographical sections in Heriot, *The Castrati in Opera*.

114. Bragaglia, *Degli "evirati cantori,"* 34. Denials of petitions were not unusual for the conservative Pope Innocent XI, who was called Papa Minga for always saying no.

115. As in this text by Hieronymus Delphinus, pseud. (fl. 1685), *Eunuchi conjugium: die Capaunen-Heyrath, hoc est, Scripta et judicia varia de conjugio inter eunuchum et virginem juvenculam* (Jena: Bortoletti, 1730). D'Ancillon's book was published in Berlin in 1701 and then translated anonymously in English with changes and amplifications as *Eunuchism Display'd: Describing all the different Sorts of* EUNUCHS; *the esteem they have met with in the World; and how they can be made so* (London: E. Curll, 1718). D'Ancillon is a pseudonym for C. D'Ollincan.

116. Rosselli, *Singers of Italian Opera*, 176. I concentrate in this chapter on the sixteenth and seventeenth centuries, but cases of heterosexual castrati are better documented for the eighteenth. Balatri wrote in his memoirs (*Frutti del mondo*) that he fell in love with an Englishwoman, but his love was not reciprocated. He later became a monk in Germany. Gaetano Maiorano, nicknamed Caffarelli (1710–83), famous for singing women's parts, was threatened with murder by the husband of a woman with whom he carried an affair when he was eighteen. Luigi Marchesi, another castrato famous for playing women's parts, caused a scan-

It was common opinion that even if castrati could have sex they could not reproduce, because they could not emit the liquid (spermatozoa) indispensable to generation, although they could of course emit other liquids. Because of this, Roman law ("Decree of Gratian") did not allow eunuchs to legally marry or adopt, although impotence per se was not a cause for rescinding a marriage.[117] Matters were completely different in canon law, which was concerned with impotence but not with male sterility. But positions changed in June 27, 1587, when in a bull titled "Cum Frequenter," Sixtus V responded to a question of his Spanish nuncio, Cesare Spacciani, who had asked whether eunuchs and *spadones* could marry (castrati were still referred in those years as either or both).[118] There were a great number of men, the nuncio had argued in a letter dated May 30, 1586, who had married because they could have heterosexual intercourse, although they lacked both testicles and were unable to emit semen ("teste carent, et . . . ideo certum ac manifestum est eos verum semen emittere non posse"). Now he and other theologians wondered whether such a practice was legal. The pope answered that those frigid and impotent were not apt to contract marriage ("qui frigidae naturae sunt et impotentes, idem minime apti ad contrabenda matrimonia reputantur") and that those who had already married had to separate, and the marriage itself had to be annulled ("quam eos etiam, qui sic de facto matrimonium contraxerint, separari cures, et matrimonia ipsa sic de

---

dal when Maria Cosway ran away from her husband, leaving her children, to follow him around Europe for fifteen years. Giovan Maria Velluti (1781–1861) had a number of affairs in Modena and had to flee to Milan because of an affair with a noblewoman known as the marchesa Clelia G. A Russian duchess in St. Petersburg was so much in love with Velluti that she had him come to her mansion in Crimea. See note 48 for the case of Tenducci, who eloped with Dora Maunsell, whom he married in Cork. For all these cases see the biographical sections in Heriot, *The Castrati in Opera*; and Barbier, *The World of the Castrati*, 141–48.

117. A euphemistically worded law of 342 seems to prohibit marriage between two males, and a law of the year 390 "extended the death penalty from men who married eunuchs to men who had any sex at all with eunuchs." See Mathew Kuefler, *The Manly Eunuch: Masculinity, Gender Ambiguity, and Christian Ideology in Late Antiquity* (Chicago: University of Chicago Press, 2001), 102.

118. Archivum Secretum Vaticanum, Fondo Segreteria di Stato, Spagna, vol. 32, fol. 152r. Since there was no clear agreement about what the terms "castrati" and "spadones" really signified, readings of the bull were at times contradictory. See Aidan MacGrath, *A Controversy Concerning Male Impotence* (Rome: Editrice Pontificia Universitaria Gregoriana, 1988), 50–51.

facto contracta nulla, irrita et invalida esse decernas").[119] Castrati able to achieve an erection and an emission could remain married, the bull seemed to say by omission, but this was not the reading of canonists, especially the influential Tomas Sanchez, who unambiguously asked for the separation and annulment of marriage ties of all unprocreative men.[120]

Sixtus did not question the ability of these men to behave like men, that is, to have erections, but for him manly men were only those able to inseminate and procreate. Thus, he reinforced the view that masculinity needed to be associated with fertility as a foundational myth of Christian discourse. I have already discussed the link between manhood and paternity in chapter 2, where "real" men in that culture are those who father. With Sixtus's pronouncement, canon law took the same stance. The shift has historical significance because it was perhaps the first document, among many to follow, which focused on progressively analyzing, classifying, and taking apart sexuality. Sex was already part of the discourse of the Church in earlier centuries, with themes involving, for example, the desire of the flesh and the need for abstention and confession; it was already disciplined in interventions against sodomitic acts involving clerics, but ecclesiastical law had acted until then as a reactive rather than a legislative body.

For instance, a Christian marriage was understood as based on three things: men's ability to have an erection, to perform intromission, and to produce an emission. In the case of eunuchs or impotents who married, the wife could at any time petition for annulment of the marriage tie if the husband was unable to perform. But now an apparatus was created to intervene on sexuality before, and not after, a precipitating event took place.[121] As Pierre Darmon puts it, following Michel Foucault, the church's intervention on private sexual matters meant a

> leap from intellectual onanism to the most exacerbated voyeurism, from theory to practice, with a most indecent agility. The detection of an impotent individual now involved astonishing preliminary tests: from the public demonstration of "erection," "elastic tension," or "natural motion," and on occasion, the "proof of ejaculation," to the incredible "trial by con-

119. Archivum Secretum Vaticanum, Fondo Secretariatus Brevium, Spagna, vol. 129, fol. 82. The decision stood until 1965.

120. Tomas Sanchez (1550–1610), *De sancto matrimonii sacramento disputationum* (Lyon: Rigaud, 1654), 9.72.17.

121. In fact only in 1977 did the Sacred Congregation for the Doctrine of the Faith, formerly called the Inquisition, allow men lacking testicles to marry.

gress," which involved enacting the marital duties in their entirety in the presence of witnesses.[122]

The social atmosphere must have been receptive to theoretical elaborations and a papal ruling for some time, since a few months after the nuncio's letter, but before the papal pronouncement, a castrato from Parma had problems with local church authorities because he was married. Writing to Duke Guglielmo Gonzaga in December 1586 about the result of his search for singers, Ippolito Olivo explained that he had found a "castratino" willing to come to Mantua, were it not for a problem ("travaglio grande"): having married a few months earlier and having slept for a long while with his wife ("essendo dormito lungo tempo seco"), thanks to a permit issued to him by his parish priest, he was now being pursued by the local congregation because he could not take a wife, being a castrato ("per essere castrato non poteva pigliar moglie"). The priest who insufficiently policed his body, we are told, had already paid for his misunderstanding of biological mechanisms and was in prison. The ambassador's tone was matter of fact, as if it were normal for a man to be pejoratively called "castratino" and be married at the same time, or for the Church to be so intolerant of a category of men that it had willed into existence, so to speak, a few years earlier.[123]

No papal decision could be made without an understanding of the role of testicles in the then current medical view of reproduction. Renaissance practice attributed to testicles the power to determine the sex of a newborn, and at times advised the isolation of testicles for that purpose: men who wanted to

122. Pierre Darmon, *Damning the Innocent: A History of the Persecution of the Impotent in Pre-Revolutionary France*, trans. Paul Keegan (New York: Viking, 1986), 5. See also Michel Foucault, *The History of Sexuality*, vol. 1: *An Introduction* (New York: Vintage, 1980). Trials of supposed homosexuals, in Venice, for example, already often required that the accused have sex in court with a prostitute. See Ruggiero, *The Boundaries of Eros*.

123. Archivio di Stato di Mantova, *Gonzaga*, busta 1381: "Ho parlato imedimament col castratino, il qual mi a deto che al presente non puo far determinatione alcuna della persona sua per un travaglio grande che ha al presente il qual e questo che havendo preso moglie alcuno mesi sonno et essendo dormito lungo tempo seco, havendo havuto licentia da un prete parrochiano il qual per questo effetto e prigione et il papa lo travaglia cio è la congregatione, et anchor lui dicendo che per esser castrato non poteva pigliar moglie, si che fia che questo negotio non e finito non veder far rissolutione nissuna della persona ne prometter di certo a nissuno." We do not know what happened to this unnamed castrato. Canal (*Della musica in Mantova*) abridges the letter to leave out the information about the marriage. But see Sherr, "Guglielmo Gonzaga and the Castrati," 56.

have a male child were told to tie their left testicle with a string (as usual, left was connected to female or weak, right to male or strong), and men who wished to avoid reproduction could temporarily tie both testicles.[124] For Girolamo Mercurio, tying testicles to assure the proper sex of the newborn was also successful in animals, since in the Roman countryside shepherds used this technique for rams.[125] Giovanni Marinello's suggestion was creative: aware that for generation it was necessary for a woman to have an orgasm and that cold seed was less likely to engender, he recommended tying both testicles until the woman was ready to ejaculate. At the right moment, she untied the knot, and the two semens ejaculated in unison worked the magic of reproduction.[126] Men whose

124. Aristotle, GA 4.1.765a; and Michele Savonarola, Il trattato ginecologico-pediatrico in volgare, ed. Luigi Belloni (1479; Milan: Società italiana di ostetricia e ginecologia, 1952), 55–58.

125. See La commare o riccoglitrice (Venice: Ciotti, 1596), 1.13. An abridged modern edition of this text is in Medicina per le donne nel Cinquecento: Testi di Giovanni Marinello e di Girolamo Mercurio, ed. Maria Luisa Altieri Biagi et al. (Turin: UTET, 1992). The practice of playing with testicles was common among the Hottentots (Khoikhoi), according to early European anthropologists who studied their habits. Hottentots excised the left testicle of young boys to increase the chance of conceiving only males or for mothers not to conceive twins. In other accounts the practice meant that boys could run faster and hunt better. The fantasy of a castrating mother was associated with the event as well, since it was believed that some mothers castrated their own children by tearing out and eating their left testicle at birth. See Londa Schiebinger, Nature's Body: Gender in the Making of Modern Science (Boston: Beacon Press, 1993), 136.

126. Giovanni Marinello, Le medicine partenenti alle infermità delle donne (Venice: Francesco de' Franceschi, 1563), 2.1; a heavily abridged version is in Maria Luisa Altieri Biagi, Medicina per le donne nel Cinquecento. According to popular lore, concoctions of bull's testicles, prescribed to both men and women, were miraculous in guaranteeing a long life and productive sex. A typical recipe to assure potency to a sexually frigid man was to add the testicles of a two-year-old cock to the broth of an aphrodisiac mixture made of mussels cooked with salt, pepper, anise seed, laurel, cumin, thyme, and celery. The preparation had to be kept in infusion for an hour. Then wine, truffles, and pieces of mandrake root had to be added. A spoonful of the potion was enough to ensure a satisfying intercourse. See Enrico Malizia, Ricettario delle streghe: Incantesimi, prodigi sessuali e veleni (Rome: Edizioni Mediterranee, 1992), 143. Also used were testicles of ram, goat, hare, buck, mule, goose, pig, fox, and boar. To improve the chance of potency, sometimes the penis itself of these animals was added. See Malizia, Ricettario delle streghe, 254. Isabella Cortese has a recipe of testicles of quails mixed with amber and musk to guarantee an erection. See I secreti della signora Isabella Cortese (1561; Venice: Cornetti, 1584).

testicles were cold (because of continuous urination or because they passed kidney stones) were in principle sterile, Marinello stated, while those with large testicles were well suited to generate boys. Also, if a man's right testicle was turgid when he first started sexual relations, that usually meant that he was capable of generating males.[127]

For Aristotle, generation had very little to do with testicles; some animals, like serpents, in fact, he wrote, did not even have testes. Production of semen did not, according to him, take place in the testicles—the scrotum, with its weight, only provided steadiness to the movement of the seed; instead, he believed that sperm was produced in the blood vessels, since semen was perfectly concocted blood.[128] Contra Aristotle, Galen thought that testicles were important because semen was further elaborated, became foamy, and acquired its generative character only in that location.[129] Renaissance doctors, such as Gabriele Falloppio and Giovanni Bolognetti, shared the Galenic view, although they were unaware of the endocrinological function of the testicles. For Bologneti, frigid men—like eunuchs—could not generate because they were unable to produce the amount of blood needed to move from the veins to the kidneys, down to the

127. Marinello, *Le medicine partenenti alle infermità delle donne*, 2.1 and 3.3. Galen had stated that much: if the left testis was "the first to show itself at the time called puberty, . . . in this there is an indication that such an animal is a producer of a female, just as, in case the right testis remains normal and swells out first at puberty, the animal, so far as it depends on him, becomes a producer of males." See Galen, *On the Usefulness of the Parts of the Body*, ed. and trans. Margaret May, 2 vols. (Ithaca: Cornell University Press, 1982) 2:14.637. Realdo Colombo finds that women's testicles (ovaries) also produce semen, like men. He refers to his dissection of a female testicle where he found a whitish and thick seed perfectly concocted. See *De re anatomica*, 453–54.

128. Aristotle, GA 1.4.1717b. Aristotle compares the balancing act of the testicles to the stone weights that women hang on their looms when they weave. The reason why castrated animals could not engender was that in them the testes were drawn up.

129. By dissecting testicles, Galen found an intricate system of vessels (not Aristotle's straight channels) through which the blood was purified into a white fluid. See Galen, *De semine*, in *Opera Omnia*, 1.1, pp. 12 and 15; and *On the Usefulness of the Parts of the Body*, ed. and trans. Margaret May, 2 vols. (Ithaca: Cornell University Press, 1968), 2:14,.pp. 649–51. For the Hippocratics, semen was produced by the brain first; other philosophers argued for semen coming from an array of locations in the body. For a discussion of these arguments, see Herophilus, *The Art of Medicine in Alexandria*, ed. and trans. Heinrich von Staden (Cambridge: Cambridge University Press, 1989), 290–96. See note 75 in the introduction for the anatomist Jacobus Silvius's belief that semen came from all over the body.

"spermatic vases." Bolognetti, following Galen, thought that testicles did not produce semen but that they gave semen its generative quality.[130] Surprisingly, since it is difficult to understand the practical reason behind such a suggestion, Falloppio also wrote on how to stop the growth of testicles in a boy ("fantino"). His advice was to crush an herb called "malisia" and use it to anoint the testicles. They would remain forever small.[131]

In Roman law, marriage was meant to assure progeny, but the Church attributed to marriage two interrelated purposes: first, to procreate; and second, to satiate concupiscence. For Augustine marriage was based on "three goods," the sacramental bond, fidelity, and offspring. Even if the couple was childless and fidelity was at issue, the marriage was valid for him because of that bond that originally united man and wife.[132] Summarizing in 1580 the Counter-Reformation's rules that make a marriage valid, Francesco Tommasi argued that there are two types of "perfection" necessary in a Christian union: the consent of bride and groom and carnal consummation. The purpose of the last is to generate and to remedy fornication ("rimedio della fornicazione").[133] Castrati could not fulfill the first purpose (*potentia generandi*), it was thought, because of lack of semen; and most probably were insufficiently endowed for the second (*potentia coeundi*), because of their not fully developed genitalia. In fact, it was feared that

130. For Giovanni Bolognetti's (1505–75) understanding of the testicles, see his *Repetitiones* (Venice: Calegari, 1571); and McGrath, *A Controversy Concerning Male Impotence.*

131. Gabriele Falloppio, *Secreti diversi e miracolosi* (Venice: Bonfad, 1658), bk. 3, 365. The book does not shed light on why there should be a need for such a cure. This recipe is combined with another on how to make sure that maidens do not grow large breasts. A cursory look at Renaissance paintings shows that the period was not very much interested in representing women with large breasts. This fashion may originate in the fact that the middle- to high-class women who were usually portrayed in art were discouraged from breast-feeding their offspring so they could become pregnant again, and the culture, therefore, may have developed a lack of interest in large, "maternal" breasts. Why the same would be true of testicles, however, is anybody's guess.

132. Augustine, *De bono coniugali*, 32 (24), in *Corpus Scriptorum Ecclesiasticorum Latinorum* (Vienna: C. Gerodi et al., 1866–), 41.226–27.

133. Consent and union result in the following: "La causa efficiente è quella che lega il consenso degli animi con parole veramente proferite ed espresse dal sì. La causa materiale sono le persone legittime. La causa formale è la benedizione della chiesa e il dar l'anello. La causa finale è in duo modo, o per la generazione, o per il rimedio della fornicazione." See Francesco Tommasi, *Reggimento del padre di famiglia* (Florence: Marescotti, 1580), 57.

copulation with a castrato or *spadone* would achieve the opposite result: rather than satiate desire through a *copula perfecta*, it would excite it.[134] The specter of female desire disanchored from reproductive purposes and the construction of woman's physiology as yearning for man's semen could have motivated the church fathers to legislate against marriage for castrati more than perhaps their physical situation would have vouchsafed.

In siding with the fetishists of the testicles, the pope and his advisors went against current medical thought that held that men's ability to have some forms of intercourse was sufficient for the purposes of marriage. Bartolomeo Cipolla and Andrea Alciati had based their favorable opinion on cases of men lacking both testicles but also able to have erections. Entering later in the fray, the Galenist Paolo Zacchia disagreed on the merits of Sixtus's decision. For Zacchia, intercourse meant penetration but not release of "verum semen in testiculis elaboratum" in order to be technically satisfying. If the validity of marriage was based on the ability to generate, he asked, why were eunuchs and *spadones* forbidden marriage and not old men, since neither could generate?[135] Thus these men should be allowed to legally contract a marriage.

When one starts to interpret and legislate on sexuality, there is castration and castration. Women who had damaged or partially absent genital organs and lacked ovaries, called "testes" at the time, incurred technically the same limitations for which castrati were forbidden marriage. But they received different treatment. Legislation on women lacking functional reproductive organs came in those years in the form of another papal decree, *Fraternitatis*, by Pope Inno-

134. "Existimabant enim castratos copula non satiari, sed excitari," it was said of castrati. See also Sandro Gherro, "Il problema del 'verum semen' nel 'Breve' 'Cum Frequenter' di Sisto V," *Il diritto ecclesiastico* 77 (1966): 98–117; and F. Bersini, "La dibattuta questione del 'verum semen,'" *Monitor Ecclesiasticus* 101 (1976): 256–78. Today fetishism of testicles extends to neutered animals. To ease the trauma to neutered pets — or perhaps to their owners — the inventor Gregg Miller from Kansas City has recently patented implants called "neuticles" that can be outfitted in dogs, cats, and horses in a matter of minutes. These fake testicles come in two price levels: a polypropylene model that sells for $25–$32 a set, and a silicone model selling between $80 and $129. Animal owners seem to like the contraption, since "neuticles" are now sold in fourteen countries, but veterinarians interviewed on the issue still insist that the implants make no difference to the animals themselves (*New York Times*, Aug. 8, 1999).

135. Paolo Zacchia, *Questiones medico-legales* 3.1.5.30. See also Bajada, *Sexual Impotence*, 105. Zacchia believed that one testicle is sufficient to generate; removal of both renders a man like a woman ("foeminae similis") (5.3.1).

cent III, which examined a request for annulment due to an impenetrable vagina ("arctatio mulieris"). In this case the marriage was annulled, but in general it was understood that if a woman was penetrable, marriage was valid. The *mulier excisa*, that is, the woman without uterus and ovaries, was unable to emit semen and engender; thus her marriageable status could have been questioned in petitions to have nuptials rescinded. But it was deemed that, although unable to become pregnant because of her *sacca clausa*, she was still capable of having sex; moreover, since she could have pleasure in the act, she would satisfy one of the two purposes of marriage, containing lust. Therefore her marriage, although nonprocreative, was valid.[136] In a world in which both men and women were assumed to emit semen (that of men being of higher quality and greater abundance, that of women, of lower quality), lack of emission then allowed only women to attain that *una caro* that was the basis of a Christian marriage, although Aquinas had specifically stated that only the commixture of semen of wife and husband engaged in carnal copula could reach that union.[137] This contrasted with Roman law (*Decretales Gregorii IX*) in which the woman whose vagina was *inutilis* (unusable) to her husband was treated like the man whose problematic sexual apparatus rendered him *inutilis* to his wife.

The difference in ecclesiastical pronunciations between similarly "castrated" men and women is illustrative of a material reading of sex just as it is of a medical understanding of bodily functions. For a castrato to be denied marriage meant that the social construction of manhood as phallic and generative needed to be upheld, the moments of *penetratio* and *seminatio* made into one.[138] The fact that a man had a watery discharge in copulation ("quaedam aquosa materia") was no longer deemed sufficient: it was necessary that in principle this discharge could filiate. When, through some theoretical gymnastics, lack of emission be-

136. John McCarthy, "The Marriage Capacity of the *mulier excisa,*" *Ephemerides Iuris Canonici* 3.2 (1947): 261–85. See also Giacomo Santori, "La questione del *verum semen,*" *Il diritto ecclesiastico* 82 (1971): 66–78. The *mulier occlusa*, on the other hand, could not enter marriage because in her case the possibility of having intercourse was null, given her inadequate or deformed vagina.

137. "Vir et mulier efficiuntur in carnali copula una caro per commixtionem seminum." See Thomas Aquinas, *Summa Theologiae* 4, dist., 41, art. 1, qu. 4.

138. As in this recent formulation by the influential Catholic theorist John Noonan, who describes impotence as "the inability to ejaculate semen into the vagina, or inability to receive ejaculated semen." See John Noonan, *Contraception: A History of Its Treatment by the Catholic Theologians and Canonists* (Cambridge: Harvard University Press, Belknap Press, 1965), 290.

came equated with impotence—which for the Church, as I mentioned earlier, was always a cause for annulling a marriage—castrati and *spadones* were left in the lurch.[139] But for women to be denied marriage, or to have their marriage declared null when there were no other social roles assignable to them apart from a life in the nunnery—and no gender or sexual subversion in their desire to marry—could have hardly proved an illuminated paternalistic choice. Moreover, Galenic theory was clear on the relative unimportance of women's seed to generation vis-à-vis man's, so that although woman's social role was to mother, only man could activate and provide the pneuma that would make a woman carry a pregnancy and a fetus receive a soul. Women's "spermatic vessels" (the Fallopian tubes), in fact, were notoriously lacking compared to men's, Galen explained: "you will see that the male spermatic vessels are greatly superior and that they are many times as long, broad, and deep as those of the female.... The testes of women, on the other hand, are very small indeed."[140] Since women nourished but did not generate, their lack of functioning sexual organs was not as crucial as men's.[141]

139. Martin de Azpilcueta (alias Dr. Navarro; 1491-1586) gives a contrary opinion on the validity of marriage by men with one or no testicles in *Consiliorum sive Responsorum libri quinque juxta ordinem Decretalium dispositi* (Rome: n.p., 1590), 2: 154. In general theologians took a middle course: as long as there was some form of ejaculation, even though no generation could occur, the marriage was valid. See McGrath, *A Controversy Concerning Male Impotence*, 110.

140. Galen, *On the Usefulness of the Parts of the Body,* 2:14.647. Augustine had written that men transfuse ("transfundutur") children to the woman's body in the sexual act. See *Opus Imperfectum* 2.178.2, in *Corpus Scriptorum,* 85.299.

141. Let us remember that in the brief years of his papacy (1585-90), Sixtus V legislated on all the issues that I have been highlighting in this chapter and in chapter 1: he forbade castrati to marry in 1587 but in 1589 actively authorized their recruitment for the Sistine Chapel; in 1588 he banned women—actresses and singers—from the stage. He also decreed, in 1586, that death was the just punishment for sexual crimes such as defloration, incest, adultery, abortion, and making money from prostitution. See Nicholas Davidson, "Theology, Nature and the Law: Sexual Sin and Sexual Crime in Italy from the Fourteenth to the Seventeenth Century," in *Crime, Society and the Law in Renaissance Italy,* ed. Trevor Dean and Kate Lowe (Cambridge: Cambridge University Press, 1994), 74-98, esp. 90. These decrees were annulled by subsequent popes. Homosexuals were also treated harshly during his tenure. In one notable case in 1586, a priest and a boy were both burned at the stake, even though the law was usually more lenient with passive partners. See Uta Ranke-Heinemann, *Eunuchs for the Kingdom of Heaven: Women, Sexuality and the Catholic Church* (New York: Doubleday,

Is then the possibility of producing semen that which allows man to produce meaning? In Freudian and Lacanian psychoanalysis, the possession of the penis, equated to possession of the phallus as the symbolic attribute of power in the imaginary, is paramount. There is no mention of testicles or of sperm. For Luce Irigaray the reason that the sperm has never been treated as an *object-a* is that culture privileges the solid: the fantasy of castration through amputation is more threatening than a liquid emission, which, in order to be effective, to produce, cannot be dispersed and made visible.[142] This would link the sperm to the phallus, since both need to be veiled to be effective, but such a link has not been theoretically examined. Yet semen was generalized in the past as the trait of what made man manly as well as human. Devils did not emit semen, the lore went; in fact they were recognizable as devils because of this particular feature. Women who copulated with them, and did not worry about lack of a liquid emission, were condemned by the Inquisitors. Quirina Deidda, who was sentenced in 1585 as heretic, idolater, and evil-doer to three years in prison, the confiscation of her property, and one hundred lashes, confessed that the devil with whom she engaged in sex did not experience *ejaculatio* ("semenza") like normal men.[143]

1990), 250. Sixtus V treated prostitutes as he did the Jews: Roman Jews were to be closed in their "serraglio degli hebrei," and prostitutes shut in the "ortaccio" of Campo Marzio and made to wear a specific item of clothing, the "spumiglia." See Kenneth Stow, "Sisto V e il *ghet* degli Ebrei," in *Sisto V. Roma e il Lazio*, ed. Marcello Fagiolo and Maria Luisa Madonna, 2 vols. (Rome: Istituto Poligrafio e Zecca dello Stato, 1992), 1:263–76, at 269.

142. "Isn't the subjection of sperm to the imperatives of reproduction alone symptomatic of a preeminence historically allocated to the solid (product)? And if, in the dynamics of desire, the problem of castration intervenes — fantasy/reality of an amputation, of a 'crumbling' of the solid that the penis represents — a reckoning with sperm-fluid as an obstacle to the generalization of an economy restricted to solid remains in suspension." In Luce Irigaray, *This Sex Which Is Not One*, trans. Catherine Porter (Ithaca: Cornell University Press, 1985).

143. "il Maligno . . . quando raggiungeva l'orgasmo, non emetteva semenza, come facevano gli uomini normali." See Romano Canossa, *Sessualità e inquisizione tra Cinquecento e Seicento* (Rome: Sapere 2000, 1994), 153. Although the devil does not have semen of his own, he can steal it from a man. According to Heinrich Kramer and James Sprenger, the devil can take the form of a succubus and copulate with a man, then take the semen to a witch, copulate with her as an incubus, and finally inject her with the other man's semen. See *The*

Through the years there has been a persistent politicization of the grief that should have defined the psyche of men who were proscribed from the congregation of "regular" men because of a cut. Historically speaking, however, is it well known that many castrati laughed when people pitied their condition, given the obvious narcissistic and economic advantages enjoyed by the most successful among them.[144] Moreover, we tend to think of castration today mostly along Freudian lines. We know that, in putting aside all medical pronouncements on the subject, Freud single-handedly reoriented our idea of where castration takes place and fixed it on the organ of pleasure rather than on the parts in the male genitalia responsible for reproduction. As he explains, "Both male and female children form a theory that women no less than men originally had a penis, but that they have lost it by castration." But the castrati of whom I am writing had no problem with their penises, since unlike eunuchs of Islamic harems who underwent total ablation of their genitalia, they had surgery performed only on their testicles and rarely were these removed.[145]

All in all, Freud's reduction of male genitalia to the penis has gone unnoticed. More dangerously for women, his idea that women want to castrate men goes against the fact that historically men have castrated each other, whether for political, disciplinary, medical, or economic reasons, with no female involvement in the matter, unless a fantastic one. Freud's rewriting of castration as connected to the penis and not to the testicles uncannily echoes his rewriting of the origin of female orgasm, which for him is vaginal and not clitoreal.[146] In the case of women too he went against medical understandings of the vagina as the organ from which menstruation is evacuated or where the penis goes during sex, but in itself having few nerve endings. His thinking on the issue informed so much of this century's sense of female sexuality that, as Thomas Laqueur writes, when the

Malleus Maleficarum of Heinrich Kramer and James Sprenger, trans. Montague Summers (New York: Dover, 1971).

144. This seems to have been the case of the well-known castrati Carestini and Salimbeni. See Barbier, *The World of the Castrati*, 2.

145. Also, unlike the original myth of castration developed by Freud, in which Zeus castrated his father Uranus in order to steal his power, here fathers have the operation performed on their sons before they become men and can rebel.

146. Sigmund Freud, "Infantile Sexuality," in *Three Essays on the Theory of Sexuality*, trans. James Strachey (1905; New York: Avon, 1962).

report from the medical team of Masters and Johnson announced in the 1960s that female orgasm comes almost exclusively from the clitoris, the statement sounded to many like a revelation.[147] Since in the case of women the redirection goes from the organ of pleasure (the clitoris was for Freud a penis substitute) to the organ of reproduction, one does not even need to wonder at the cultural reasons subtending the opposite movement in men.

In considering castration as both a real and a symbolic event, we should keep in mind that within masculinity — as within femininity, for that matter — one can hardly speak of a norm, since there are a number of sites with which an individual can identify. We should also separate in the castrato the notion of the sex he embodies, of the gender role that he has been conditioned to assume, and of his subjective identity, since each can shift through compensatory strategies of fetishism and masquerade. According to Robert Stoller, a core gender identity in children is established when they are one year old. Most of the time, this follows anatomical sex. We can then assume that the operation castrati underwent may have not impacted tremendously on their gender identity, which is not to say that castrati automatically made an object choice of the opposite sex. Most likely, they remained aligned with men, even though later they may have modified their gender-role identity and may have balked at embracing then current views of masculinity. If their sexuality — that is, their sexual practice — was compromised by the knife, their sexual identity, modified as it was by both hormonal and culture-specific determinants, could have been heterosexual, homosexual, bisexual, or asexual.[148]

As for the way castrati could have functioned visually in culture, we can usefully employ, against gender to be sure, the famous analogies of Laura Mulvey regarding the pleasure that men get in watching women, since castrati were obviously like women according to Freud: castrated. Did they function like women then vis-à-vis an empowered, and definitely male, gaze? The pleasure of which Mulvey speaks comes from the fact that woman embodies lack; thus man, looking at her, gets the assurance by reflection that he does not lack, that is, he is not

147. Thomas Laqueur, *Making Sex: Body and Gender from the Greeks to Freud* (Cambridge: Harvard University Press, 1990), 233–34.

148. Robert Stoller, *Presentations of Gender* (New Haven: Yale University Press, 1985), 11. For a brief summary of the differences in meaning among gender identity, gender role, and gender-role identity, see Mary Hawkesworth, "Confounding Gender," *Signs* 22.3 (1997): 649–85, esp. 656.

castrated. Alternately, he can make woman the phallus, so that the apprehension her difference generates in him is displaced through a fetishization of her body.[149] The problem in transferring this analogy to castrati is that they bring men no reassurances, in that the transfer that converts anxieties about symbolic castration into anxieties about a seemingly literal female castration does not take place in their case, because the castrato is not a body-in-excess, like woman, but a body lacking otherwise. When castrati play the male part and dress as men, they remind men that they embody castration without embodying a reassuring sexual difference, thus their presence is threatening because it makes inescapable the memory of what castration means. When castrati play the female, men can temporarily fetishize their bodies, so that, like women, castrati can be made to be the phallus, and thus the desiring subjects can disavow their own homosexuality—but only as long as the onlookers choose to read gender in what they see (the castrato as feminine). Were they to read sex (the castrato as male), this feeling would need immediately to be rejected, since castrati embody lack, but, unlike women, do not embody difference. Such a turn is most threatening, because it deprives men of the reassurance that they, and not women, are whole. Since, according to Lacan, to enter desire man and woman need to acknowledge their symbolic castration, the castrato shows inescapably that both masculinity and femininity are based on castration. (I, like Mulvey, have postulated in this instance the male audience as heterosexual.)

Men have plenty of reasons for casting castrati as "non integri," hence the sense that any sexual relation between castrati and male companions may have been based on sadomasochism. Castrati can then occupy men's fantasy in two ways: as passive men and as passive masculine women. Many castrati illustrate the first option, as not-men who behave like men, in the often talked about relationships with their patrons. To return to the case of the castrato singer Cortona named earlier for his application to the pope for a marriage license: we find him a few years later as a favorite of the grand duke of Tuscany with the shocking name of Cecchino de Castris. He enjoyed such closeness to his prince that all court matters needed to pass his approval.[150] Even Casanova, for that matter, asked the woman who passed for the castrato Bellino, whose story I mentioned earlier,

149. Laura Mulvey, "Visual Pleasure and Narrative Cinema," in *Visual and Other Pleasures* (Bloomington: Indiana University Press, 1989), 14–26.

150. The story is told by D'Ancillon. Also see Francesco Ravagli, *Il Cortona, Domenico Cecchi (per nozze Furiosi-Fabbri)*, (Città di Castello: Scipione Lapi, 1896).

to wear the prosthesis she used to make her appear a castrato before making love to her, hence having drag negotiate cross-gendered identifications.[151]

As for the second option, castrati can easily be cast as masculine women, that is, as not-men who behave like women. It is known that castrati wore veils and corsets as fetishistic decorations, and their exhibitionism and feminine masochism were essential to their appeal to men, although by exaggerating femininity they may have also invited male retaliation. The appeal of the feminine castrato, the *cinaedus*, has been noticed in a number of reports. At the representation in Rome of *Il Sant'Alessio* in the Barberini palace during the Carnival of 1632, the castrati from the Sistine Chapel and the boys from the Cappella Giulia were so liked that many in the public started to sigh and a couple of cardinals invited them to sweet delights ("ad suavia invitabant"). J. J. Brouchard writes along the same lines that in Roman theaters in 1632 there were plenty of loud sighs for the young pages and the chapel castrati ("non si sentivano che ruggibondi sospiri per i giovani paggi o castrati di cappella").[152] No matter whether used as a passive, inadequate male, or as an ephebic male who can be thought of as female (after all, his cross-gendered voice gave him out as such), the castrato was a "femella," for allowing himself to be used sodomitically.[153]

Of course there is a third possibility, to cast the castrato as neither masculine nor feminine, but as a third sex rejected or lured by the other two, unthreatening

151. Casanova, *The Story of My Life:* "She got out of bed, poured some water into a cup, opened her trunk and pulled out her device and its glue. Then she melted the glue and applied the camouflage" (107–8). Teresa's story confirms that women singers went to great lengths—whether for the money or for the chance to become famous—to land the roles sung by castrati.

152. Bragaglia, *Degli "evirati cantori,"* 30. Saint Alexis's story actually lends itself to be sung by a castrato, since it tells of Saint Alexis's abandonment of the world, including his betrothed, to pursue an ascetic call. The homoerotic appeal of a thoroughly feminized *musico* on stage is fully acknowledged by Montesquieu. Writing on Roman sopranos in 1729, he noticed the uncanny temptations that castrati dressed as women offered on the stage to their audiences. See *Viaggio in Italia.*

153. When they legislated against homosexuality, Florentine and Venetian authorities usually concentrated on the active male, assuming that the passive one, the "femella," was a youth who, within a few years, would turn into an active, heterosexual male. In most visible cases, a "publicus et famosus sodomita" was condemned to burn while the younger partner was punished with just a public whipping. See Rocke, *Forbidden Friendships,* 23 passim, and Ruggiero, *The Boundaries of Eros.*

in its absolute difference. In *S/Z*, Roland Barthes sees the castrato Zambinella of the story "Sarrazine" by Honoré de Balzac as a neuter being, a "nothing," as the sculptor Sarrazine remarks, negatively neither male nor female, or positively as both, an androgynous being on whom to project anyone's desire. In a telling move, Barthes casts women as phallic and castrating, and men as positively nurturing. But this strategy of canceling sexual difference, and of appropriating positive femininity for men, not only retains a phallocentric assumption, but also cancels homoeroticism, in that Barthes conveniently forgets that the relationship highlighted by Balzac between the feminized Zambinella and his Cardinal Cicognara, the protector, was a homosexual one. No wonder that Naomi Schor feels compelled to deplore Barthes's indifference to sexual difference, since it is played, one more time, on the appropriation of women for men's purposes.[154] And, I would add, it is also played on the Freudian understanding of women as both castrated and potential castrator of male power, and of castration as centered on the penis and not on the scrotum. To be sure, one can imagine the fascination of such a fantasy of not belonging for a castrato, but we all know that "the happy limbo of a non-identity," as Foucault puts it, is only a fantasy, since—no matter how tempting—there is no sexuality before the law.[155]

As for women, they may have wanted a castrato as a hopefully active male companion for the very reason that the pope prohibited his marriage: sex with a castrato was liberating because it was without consequences. At a time when pregnancy was fraught with dangers, sex with sterile men must have offered women plenty of advantages. Already Juvenal had remarked on women's reward in such a biologically secure transaction: "There are girls who adore unmanly eunuchs—so smooth, so beardless to kiss, and no worry about abortions!"[156]

154. Naomi Schor, "Dreaming Dissymmetry: Barthes, Foucault, and Sexual Difference," in *Men in Feminism*, ed. Alice Jardine and Paul Smith (New York: Methuen, 1987), 98–110. For the reasons why Barthes refuses to signify homosexuality and is unwilling "to 'out' the cardinal," see Philip Stewart, "What Barthes Couldn't Say: On the Curious Occultation of Homoeroticism in *S/Z*," *Paragraph* 24 (2001): 1–16.

155. Michel Foucault, "Introduction," *Herculine Barbin: Being the Recently Discovered Memoirs of a Nineteenth-Century French Hermaphrodite*, trans. Richard McDougall (New York: Pantheon, 1980), xiii.

156. Juvenal, *Satura* 6.365–77. On Roman women's rumored relationships with eunuch slaves, see Walter Stevenson, "The Rise of Eunuchs in Greco-Roman Antiquity," *Journal of the History of Sexuality* 5 (1995): 495–51.

At the height of his success on stage, the castrato Senesino, a *musico* famous for playing women's parts *en travesti*, playfully versified on women's fascination for his genealogically safe exploits in a letter in which he compares his overused organ to a fruitless tree ("Abbastanza m'han distrutto / quelle caste verginelle / che sospiran poverette / l'Arbor mio, che non dà frutto") and asks forgiveness for his present tiredness ("per vogar il remo o frusto / più ne posso alzar la vela").[157] But given that an "evirato," even if able to penetrate, may not have provided much, or much consistency, toward a phallic sexual fulfillment, there might have been other reasons for women to want him. As passive male, I submit, the castrato could have offered women the chance to experiment with a sexuality that would follow the ebbs and tides of female, rather than male, desire. This must have been equally threatening to men because it disposed of their postulated indispensability in the alcove.

In his *Traité des eunuques*, D'Ancillon indicts women for creating eunuchism by following their uncontrollable desires. He cites, among others, the case of Semiramis who castrated the men she used sexually. But he also blames the eunuch/castrato for usurping male prerogatives by promising women a different sexuality. As D'Ancillon's fears amply demonstrate, the castrato could have met women's fantasies precisely because they were chameleon-like. Masquerading as active males, they could give women pleasures without consequences; masquerading as passive males, they could allow women to be sexually in charge. Like eunuchs who were employed to protect women's chastity by suppressing their desires (the most valued eunuchs in the Ottoman seraglio were the ugliest), castrati often became themselves the object of a diffuse desire. "Old Cornelia likes the scum of the limp soprano" ("Piace a Cornelia vecchia il succidume del sopran floscio"), Parini complained in "Il teatro." He took no time to elaborate why. Had he asked the ladies, Parini might have gotten other reasons for women's pursuit of the pleasures of the flaccid. What neither D'Ancillon nor Parini foresee is a third possibility, that highly effeminate, languorous castrati may have fostered a woman/woman desire thanks to their perfect falsetto voice and their preference for female clothes and female bodily preoccupations. In this construction, the feminine quasi-homo in drag throws his derided masculinity to the winds: wanted as a not-man, he is a "woman." It may not be a lesbian

---

157. See Senesino (Francesco Bernardi), "Risposta a lettera di Rolli che mi scrisse in campagna," quoted in Bragaglia, *Degli "evirati cantori,"* 74. He played in London with Farinelli.

encounter, but it may well be fantasized as such. A similar fantasy of disempowered manhood was after all behind a lady's request that the virtuoso castrato Consolino come to her house dressed only as a woman, in the voluptuous female costume he wore onstage.[158]

In his essay "On Cripples" ("Des boyteux"), Michel Montaigne makes the startling assertion that crippled women enhance erotic pleasure. To convey his point, he moves to Italy: "They say in Italy as a common proverb that he does not know Venus in her perfect sweetness who has not laid with a cripple. In that feminine commonwealth, to escape the domination of the males, they crippled them from childhood—arms, legs, and other parts that gave men an advantage over them—and made use of them only for the purpose for which we made use of women over here."[159]

In Montaigne's eroticized and feminized Italy, the appeal of the crippled woman is in her surplus: since her thighs and legs get no exercise and no nourishment from the body, the genital area becomes stronger and more lustful. By mapping power onto a disfigured body, Montaigne argues that deficiency should be construed as resistance, and that monstrosity is a libido-enhancing factor. In those very years, I argue throughout this chapter, in the very "feminine commonwealth" of which Montaigne speaks the dephallicized and deficient body of the "femella" too became the repository of frantic idolatry. His siren's voice, perceived as detached from the body, and thus not lacking, allowed the audience to fantasize possession of him as the inaccessible *object-a*. His mutilated sex incited anxiety and horror in some people; in others, all subjectivity denied, it spelled unparalleled fascination. For his part, by adapting sexual transitivity to his needs and by reinventing and unpicking the seam joining masculinity and power, the castrato ended up circulating in Europe a new, enigmatic exemplar of the Italian male, a sexually neutered anomaly created by an unnatural father motivated by vice, as the poet Parini lamented.[160]

By twists and turns, and by coupling the natural and the artificial, the quasi-man castrato came to embody the new victimized, trampled, disrespected, and

158. See Barbier, *The World of the Castrati*, 139.

159. Michel de Montaigne, *The Complete Essays of Montaigne*, trans. Donald Frame (Stanford: Stanford University Press, 1976), 791.

160. "Italo Genitore . . . / Te non error ma vizio / Spinge all'orrido ufizio." See Giuseppe Parini, "La musica," originally titled "L'evirazione," in *Il giorno e le odi* (Bologna: Zanichelli, 1817), 189.

infertile Italy, as well as the dominated and politically distributed old one. In a world that scientists had started to describe as lacking a center when new scientific discoveries began mapping the passage from a geocentric to a heliocentric universe, man — or perhaps just the Italian male — may have indeed felt that his outer dispossession, his relative unimportance in the order of things, was just a reflection of his inner, ungenerative, colonized, and mutilated self.

SELECTED BIBLIOGRAPHY

Abraham, Karl. *Selected Papers of Karl Abraham.* Translated by Douglas Bryan and Alix Strachey. London: Hogarth Press, 1927.

Adelman, Janet. "Making Defect Perfection: Shakespeare and the One-Sex Model." In *Enacting Gender on the English Renaissance Stage,* edited by Viviana Comensoli and Ann Russell. Urbana: University of Illinois Press, 1999.

Ademollo, Alessandro. *I teatri di Roma nel secolo decimosettimo.* Rome: Pasqualucci, 1888.

Alberti, Leon Battista. *Il padre di famiglia.* Florence: Cenniniana, 1871.

Albertus, Magnus. *De secretis mulierum.* Lyons: A. De Marsy, 1595.

Alciati, Andrea. *De verborum et rerum significatione.* In *Opera omnia.* Basel: Thomas Guarinum, 1582.

Aldrovandi, Ulisse. *Avvertimenti del Dottore Aldrovandi sopra le pitture mostrifiche e religiose.* In *Osservazione della natura e raffigurazione in Ulisse Aldrovandi,* edited by G. Olmi. *Annali dell'Istituto Storico Italo-Germanico di Trento* 3 (1977): 177–80.

———. *De animalibus insectis.* Bologna: Bellagambar, 1602.

Alighieri, Dante. *The Divine Comedy.* 3 vols. Translated and edited by Charles Singleton. Princeton: Princeton University Press, 1970–73.

Alonge, Roberto. "*La Calandria* o il mito di Androgine." In *Struttura e ideologia nel teatro italiano fra '500 e '900,* 9–31. Turin: Stampatori, 1978.

Altieri Biagi, Maria Luisa, ed. *Guglielmo Volgare: Studio sul lessico della medicina medioevale.* Bologna: Forni, 1970.

Alvarez, Francisco. *Ho Prest Joam das Indias: Verdadera informaçam das terra do Presto Joam.* Lisbon: n.p., 1540.

Andreski, Stanislaw. "The Syphilitic Shock: A New Explanation of the Witch-Burning." *Encounter* 58 (1982): 7–26.

Andrews, Richard. *Scripts and Scenarios: The Performance of Comedy in Renaissance Italy.* Cambridge: Cambridge University Press, 1993.

Angelini Bontempi, Giovanni Andrea. *Historia musica.* Perugia: Constantini, 1695.

Angelini, Massimo. "Il potere plastico dell'immaginazione nelle gestanti tra XVI e XVIII secolo: La fortuna di un'idea." *Intersezioni* 14 (1994): 53–69.

Anglicus, Bartholomaeus. *De rerum proprietatibus.* Frankfurt: Minerva, 1964.

Apollonio, Mario. *Storia del teatro italiano.* 2 vols. Florence: Sansoni, 1938.

Aquilecchia, Giovanni. "La Favola *Mandragola* si chiama." In *Collected Essays on Italian Language and Literature Presented to Kathleen Speight,* edited by Giovanni Aquilecchia. Manchester: Manchester University Press, 1971.

Aquinas, Thomas. *Summa theologiae.* Translated by the Fathers of the English Dominican Province. New York: Benziger Brothers, 1947.

Archenholtz, von Johann Wilhelm. *A Picture of Italy.* Translated by Joseph Trapp. Dublin: W. Corbet, 1791.

Archivium Secretum Vaticanum. Fondo Secretariatus Brevium, Spagna. Vol. 129, fol. 82.

Aretino, Pietro. *Sonetti lussuriosi (I modi) e Dubbi amorosi.* Milan: Newton, 1993.

Ariosto, Ludovico. *Orlando furioso.* 3 vols. Edited by Filippo Ermini. Rome: Società Filologica Romana, 1911.

———. *Orlando furioso.* 2 vols. Edited by Marcello Turchi. Milan: Garzanti, 1974.

———. *Orlando furioso.* Translated by Guido Waldman. Oxford: Oxford University Press, 1983.

Aristotle. *The Complete Works of Aristotle.* 2 vols. Edited by Jonathan Barnes. Translated by A. W. Thompson. Princeton: Princeton University Press, 1984.

———. *Generation of Animals.* Translated by A. L. Peck. Cambridge: Harvard University Press, 1990.

———. *Minor Works.* Translated and edited by W. S. Hett. Cambridge: Harvard University Press, 1936.

Asor Rosa, Alberto, ed. *Letteratura italiana: Le questioni.* Turin: Einaudi, 1986.

Augustine. *De civitate Dei.* Translated by H. Bettenson. London: Penguin, 1972.

———. *The Good of Marriage.* In *de bono coniugali, De sancta virginitate,* edited and translated by P. G. Walsh. Oxford: Clarendon Press, 2001.

Avicenna (ibn-Sina). *Canon (Liber Canonis).* Venice, 1507. Facsimile, Hildesheim: Olms, 1964.

———. *Liber de animalibus.* Venice: Joannes et Gregorius de Gregoriis, ca. 1500.

Bairo, Pietro. *Secreti medicinali.* Venice: Tebaldini, 1602.

Bajada, Joseph. *Sexual Impotence: The Contribution of Paolo Zacchia (1584–1659).* Rome: Pontificia Universitaria Gregoriana, 1988.

Balatri, Filippo. *Frutti del mondo.* Edited by Karl Vossler. Naples: Remo Sandon, 1924.

Bandello, Matteo. *Tutte le novelle.* 2 vols. Edited by Francesco Flora. Milan: Mondadori, 1934–43.

Baratto, Mario. *La commedia del Cinquecento: Aspetti e problemi.* Vicenza: Neri Pozza, 1975.

Barbagli, Marzio. *Sotto lo stesso tetto: Mutamenti della famiglia in Italia dal XV al XX secolo.* Bologna: Mulino, 1984.

Barberi-Squarotti, Giorgio. *Prospettive sul Furioso.* Turin: Tirrenia, 1988.

Barbier, Patrick. *The World of the Castrati: The History of an Extraordinary Operatic Phenomenon.* Translated by Margaret Crosland. London: Souvenir Press, 1996.

Barbirato, Giorgio. "Elementi decameroniani in alcune novelle ariostesche." *Studi sul Boccaccio* 16 (1987): 329–60.

Barthes, Roland. *S/Z.* Translated by Richard Howard. New York: Farrar, Straus and Giroux, 1974.

Bartoli, Francesco. *Notizie istoriche de' comici italiani.* 2 vols. Padua: Conzatti, 1781–82.

Basile, Bruno. *Poeta melancholicus: Tradizione classica e follia nell'ultimo Tasso.* Pisa: Pacini, 1984.

———. "Polemiche sulla generazione spontanea: Redi, Buonanni, Malpighi." In *L'invenzione del vero: La letteratura scientifica da Galileo a Algarotti,* edited by Bruno Basile. Rome: Salerno, 1987.

Baudrillard, Jean. *Seduction.* New York: St. Martin's Press, 1990.

Beer, Marina. *Romanzi di cavalleria: Il Furioso e il romanzo italiano del primo Cinquecento.* Rome: Bulzoni, 1987.

Bell, Rudolph. *How to Do It: Guides to Good Living for Renaissance Italians.* Chicago: University of Chicago Press, 1999.

Bellamy, Elizabeth. *Translations of Power: Narcissism and the Unconscious in Epic History.* Ithaca: Cornell University Press, 1992.

Benedetti, Alessandro. *The History of the Human Body.* In *Studies in Pre-Vesalian Anatomy: Biography, Translations, Documents,* edited by Levi Robert Lind. Philadelphia: American Philosophical Society, 1975.

Berengario da Carpi, Jacopo. *Carpi commentaria cum amplissimus additionibus super Anatomia Mundini.* Bologna: De Benedictis, 1521.

Berriot-Salvadore, Evelyne. "The Discourse of Medicine and Science." In *A History of Women in the West: Renaissance and Enlightenment Paradoxes,* edited by Natalie Zemon Davis and Arlette Farge. Cambridge: Harvard University Press, 1993.

Bersini, F. "La dibattuta questione del 'verum semen.'" *Monitor Ecclesiasticus* 101 (1976): 256–78.

Bertolotti, Antonio. *Musici alla corte dei Gonzaga in Mantova dal secolo XV al XVIII.* Geneva: Monkoff, 1978.

Bestor, Jane. "Ideas about Procreation and Their Influence on Ancient and Medieval Views of Kinship." In *The Family in Italy from Antiquity to the Present,* edited by David Kerzner and Richard Saller. New Haven: Yale University Press, 1991.

Bianconi, Lorenzo. "Il Cinquecento e il Seicento." In *Letteratura italiana: Teatro, musica, tradizione dei classici,* 7 vols., edited by Alberto Asor Rosa. Turin: Einaudi, 1986.

Bibbiena (Angelo Dovizi da Bibbiena). *La calandria.* Edited by Paolo Fossati. Turin: Einaudi, 1967.

Biondo, Michelangelo. *Angoscia, Doglia e Pena.* In *Trattati del Cinquecento sulla donna,* edited by Giuseppe Zonta. Bari: Laterza, 1913.

Blumenfeld-Kosinski, Renate. *Not of Woman Born: Representations of Caesarian Birth in Medieval and Renaissance Culture.* Ithaca: Cornell University Press, 1991.

Boccaccio, Giovanni. *Decameron.* Milan: Mursia, 1974.

———. *The Decameron.* Translated by George Henry McWilliam. New York: Penguin, 1972.

Bolande, R. P. "Ritualistic Surgery — Circumcision and Tonsillectomy." *New England Journal of Medicine* 280 (1969): 591–96.

Bolzoni, Lina. "Tommaso Campanella e le donne: fascino e negazione della differenza." *Annali d'Italianistica* 7 (1989): 193–216.

Boose, Lynda. "The Getting of a 'Lawful Race': Racial Discourse in Early Modern England and the Unrepresentable Black Woman." In *Women, 'Race,' and Writing in the Early Modern Period,* edited by Margo Hendricks and Patricia Parker. New York: Routledge, 1994.

Borch-Jacobsen, Mikkel. *The Freudian Subject.* Translated by Catherine Porter. Stanford: Stanford University Press, 1988.

Borgarucci, Prospero. *Della contemplazione anatomica, sopra tutte le parti del corpo humano.* Venice: Valgrisi, 1564.

Borsellino, Nino. "Per una storia delle commedie del Machiavelli." *Cultura e scuola* 33–34 (1970): 229–41.

Boswell, John. *The Kindness of Strangers: The Abandonment of Children in Western Europe from Late Antiquity to the Renaissance.* New York: Pantheon, 1988.

Botteri, Inge. "Ars amandi: Il galateo della procreazione responsabile." In *Educare il corpo, educare la parola nella trattatistica del Rinascimento,* edited by Giorgio Patrizi and Amedeo Quondam. Rome: Bulzoni, 1998.

Bouché, Paul Gabriel. "Imagination, Pregnant Women, and Monsters in Eighteenth-Century England and France." In *Sexual Underworlds of the Enlightenment,* edited by G. S. Rousseau and Roy Porter. Chapel Hill: University of North Carolina Press, 1988.

Boylan, Michael. "The Digestive and 'Circulatory' Systems in Aristotle's Biology." *Journal of the History of Biology* 15 (1982): 89–118.

———. "The Galenic and Hippocratic Challenges to Aristotle's Conception Theory." *Journal of the History of Biology* 17 (1984): 83–112.

Bracciolini, Poggio. "Puer gravidus." In *Poggi Facetiae,* 2 vols. London: n.p., 1798.

Bragaglia, Anton Giulio. *Degli "evirati cantori": Contributo alla storia del teatro.* Florence: Sansoni Antiquariato, 1959.

Brockbank, William. "Old Anatomical Theatres and What Took Place Therein." *Medical History* 12 (1968): 371–84.

Brower, Gary Robert. "Ambivalent Bodies: Making Christian Eunuchs." Ph.D. dissertation, Duke University, 1996.

Bruno, Giordano. *De immenso et innumerabilibus.* Frankfurt: Wechel and Fischer, 1591.

———. *Spaccio de la bestia trionfante.* In *Dialoghi italiani: dialoghi metafisici e dialoghi morali,* edited by Giovanni Aquilecchia. Florence: Sansoni, 1958.

Bullough, Vern. "Medieval Medical and Scientific Views of Women." *Viator* 4 (1973): 485–501.

Bullough, Vern, and Bonnie Bullough. *Crossdressing, Sex, and Gender.* Philadelphia: University of Pennsylvania Press, 1993.

Burney, Charles. *Present State of Music in France and Italy: Men, Music and Manners in France and Italy.* Edited by Edmund Poole. London: Folio Society, 1969.

Burshatin, Israel. "Written on the Body: Slave or Hermaphrodite in Sixteenth-Century Spain." In *Queer Iberia: Sexualities, Cultures, and Crossings from the Middle Ages to the Renaissance,* edited by Josiah Blackmore and Gregory Hutcheson. Durham, N.C.: Duke University Press, 1999.

Butler, Judith. *Gender Trouble: Feminism and the Subversion of Identity.* New York: Routledge, 1990.

Cadden, Joan. *The Meaning of Sex Difference in the Middle Ages: Medicine, Science and Culture.* Cambridge: Cambridge University Press, 1993.

Callaghan, Dympna. "The Castrator's Song: Female Impersonation on the Early Modern Stage." *Journal of Medieval and Early Modern Studies* 26 (1996): 321–53.

Calnan, M., J. W. Douglas, and H. Goldstein. "Tonsillectomy and Circumcision: Comparison of Two Cohorts." *International Journal of Epidemiology* 7 (1978): 78–85.

Camillo, Giulio. *Tutte le opere di M. Giulio Camillo Delminio.* Edited by Thomaso Porcacchi. Venice: Giolito de' Ferrari, 1567.

Campanella, Tommaso. *La città del sole e altri scritti.* Edited by Franco Mollia. Milan: Mondadori, 1991.

———. *Del senso delle cose e della magia.* Edited by Antonio Bruers. Bari: Laterza, 1925.

Campeggi, Ridolfo. *Racconto degli heretici iconomiasti giustiziati.* Bologna: Golfarini, 1622.

Camporesi, Piero. *The Anatomy of the Senses: Natural Symbols in Medieval and Early Modern Italy.* Translated by Allan Cameron. Cambridge: Polity Press, 1994.

———. *Bread of Dreams: Food and Fantasy in Early Modern Europe.* Translated by David Gentilcore. Chicago: University of Chicago Press, 1989.

———. *Il governo del corpo.* Milan: Garzanti, 1995.

———. *The Incorruptible Flesh: Bodily Mutation and Mortification in Religion and Folklore.* Translated by Tania Kroft-Murray. Cambridge: Cambridge University Press, 1988.

———. *The Land of Hunger.* Translated by Tania Croft-Murray. Oxford: Basil Blackwell, 1996.

———. *Le officine dei sensi.* Milan: Garzanti, 1985.

———. *Il paese della fame.* Bologna: Mulino, 1985.

———. *Il sugo della vita: Simbolismo e magia del sangue.* Milan: Edizioni di Comunità, 1984.

Canal, Pietro. *Della musica in Mantova: Notizie tratte principalmente dall'Archivio Gonzaga.* Geneva: Minkoff Reprint, 1978.

Canale, Florian. *De' secreti universali raccolti, et esperimentati trattati nove. Ne' quali si hanno rimedii per tutta l'infermità de' corpi humani, come anco de' cavalli, bovi e cani. Con molti secreti appertinenti all'arte chemica, agricoltura, e caccie.* Brescia: Fontara, 1613.

Caner, Daniel. "The Practice and Prohibition of Self-Castration in Early Christianity." *Vigiliae Christianae* 54 (1997): 396–415.

Canossa, Romano. *Sessualità e inquisizione in Italia tra Cinquecento e Seicento.* Rome: Sapere 2000, 1994.

Capra, Galeazzo Flavio. *Della dignità e eccellenza delle donne.* Edited by Maria Luisa Doglio. Rome: Bulzoni, 1998.

Cardano, Gerolamo. *De rerum varietate.* Avignon: M. Vincentius, 1558.

———. *De subtilitate libri XXI: De hominis natura et temperamento.* Basel: Lucium, 1547.

Carter, Tim. "Jacopo Peri (1561–1633): Aspects of His Life and Works." In *Music, Patronage and Printing in Late Renaissance Florence.* Aldershot: Ashgate, 2000.

———. *Music in Late Renaissance and Early Baroque Italy.* Portland, Or.: Amadeus Press, 1992.

Casanova, Giacomo. *The Story of My Life.* Translated by Stephen Sartarelli and Sophie Hawkes. New York: Penguin, 2001.

Casarini, Maria Pia. " 'La madrazza': Malattia o occultamento della gravidanza." In *Il corpo delle donne,* edited by Gisela Boch and Giuliana Nobili. Bologna: Transeuropa, 1988.

Casseri, Giulio. *The Larynx, Organ of Voice.* Translated by Malcolm Hast and Erling Holtsmark. Uppsala: Almquist and Wiksells, 1969.

Castiglione, Baldassarre. *The Book of the Courtier.* Edited and translated by George Bull. London: Penguin, 1976.

———. *Il libro del Cortegiano.* Edited by Ettore Bonora. Milan: Mursia, 1972.

Castro, Antonio Arjona. "Los eunucos y la cirurgia de la castracion en la España musulmana." *Axerquia* 3 (1981): 279–82.

Céard, Jean. *La Nature et les prodiges: L'insolite au XVIe siècle en France.* Geneva: Droz, 1977.

Celletti, Rodolfo. "Sopranisti e contraltisti." *Musica d'oggi* 2 (1959): 245–50.

Celse, Mireille. "La Beffa chez Machiavel, dramaturge et conteur." In *Formes et significations de la Beffa dans la littérature italienne de la Renaissance,* edited by André Rochon. Paris: Université de la Sorbonne Nouvelle, 1972.

Celsus, Aulus Cornelius. *De medicina.* Translated and edited by W. G. Spenser. Cambridge: Harvard University Press, 1935–38.

Cesalpino, Andrea (Caesalpinus). *Peripateticarum quaestionum.* Venice: Giunta, 1571.

Chojnacki, Stanley [1]. "The Iconography of Saint George in Ethiopia." *Journal of Ethiopian Studies* 11.1 (1973): 57–73; 11.2 (1973): 51–92; and 12.1 (1974): 71–132.

Chojnacki, Stanley [2]. *Women and Men in Renaissance Venice: Twelve Essays on Patrician Society.* Baltimore: Johns Hopkins University Press, 2000.

Clark, Elizabeth. "Generation, Degeneration, Regeneration: Original Sin and the Conception of Jesus in the Polemic between Augustine and Julian of Eclanum." In *Generation and Degeneration: Tropes of Reproduction in Literature and History from Antiquity to Early Modern Europe,* edited by Valeria Finucci and Kevin Brownlee. Durham, N.C.: Duke University Press, 2001.

Clementi, Filippo. *Il carnevale romano nelle cronache contemporanee: Dalle origini al sec. XVIII.* 2 vols. Città di Castello: Unione Arti Tipografiche, 1939.

Cocco, E. "Una compagnia comica nella prima metà del secolo XVI." *Giornale storico della letteratura italiana* 65 (1915): 57–58.

Codronchi, Giovan Battista. *De morbis qui Imolae.* Bologna: n.p., 1603.

———. *De morbis veneficis ac veneficijs.* Milan: Jo. Bapt. Bidellium, 1618.

Cohen, Ed. "Legislating the Norm: From Sodomy to Gross Indecency." *South Atlantic Quarterly* 88 (1989): 181–217.

Cohen, Shaye. "Menstruants and the Sacred in Judaism and Christianity." In *Women's History and Ancient History,* edited by Sarah Pomeroy. Chapel Hill: University of North Carolina Press, 1991.

Cohn, Samuel. *Women in the Streets: Essays on Sex and Power in Renaissance Italy.* Baltimore: Johns Hopkins University Press, 1996.

Colombo, Realdo. *De re anatomica.* Venice: Bevilacqua, 1559.

Contini, Gianfranco, ed. *Poeti del Duecento.* Milan: Ricciardi, 1960.

Il corago o vero alcune osservazioni per metter bene in scena le composizioni drammatiche. Edited by Paolo Fabbri and Angelo Pompilio. Florence: Olschki, 1983.

Cornaro, Alvise. *Trattato de la vita sobria.* In *Scritti sulla vita sobria,* edited by Marisa Milani. Venice: Corbo e Fiore, 1983.

Cortese, Isabella. *I secreti della signora Isabella Cortese ne' quali si contengono cose minerali, medicinali, arteficiose, e alchemiche. Et molte de l'arte profumatoria, appartenenti a ogni gran signora. Con altri bellissimi secreti aggiunti.* Venice: Cornetti, 1584.

Crawford, Patricia. "Attitudes to Menstruation in Seventeenth-Century England." *Past and Present* 91 (1981): 47–73.

Cressy, David. *Travesties and Transgressions in Tudor and Stuart England: Tales of Discord and Dissention.* Oxford: Oxford University Press, 2000.

Cro, Stelio. "Italian Humanism and the Myth of the Noble Savage." *Annali d'Italianistica* 10 (1992): 48–68, 64–65.

Da Molin, Giovanna. *Famiglia e matrimonio nell'Italia del Seicento.* Bari: Cacucci, 2000.

Dal Fiume, Antonio. "Medici, medicine e peste nel Veneto durante il secolo XVI." *Archivio veneto* 62 (1981): 33–58.

D'Amico, Jack. "Drama and the Court in *La calandria.*" *Theater Journal* 43 (1991): 93–106.

———. "The 'Virtù' of Women: Machiavelli's *Mandragola* and *Clizia.*" *Interpretation* 12 (1984): 261–73.

D'Ancillon [pseud. D'Ollincan]. *Eunuchism Display'd: Describing all the different Sorts of EUNUCHS; the esteem they have met with in the World; and how they can be made so.* London: E. Curll, 1718.

D'Ancona, Alessandro. *Origini del teatro italiano.* 2 vols. Turin: Loescher, 1891.

———. *Studi di critica e storia letteraria.* Bologna: Zanichelli, 1880.

Darmon, Pierre. *Damning the Innocent: A History of the Persecution of the Impotent in Pre-Revolutionary France.* Translated by Paul Keegan. New York: Viking, 1986.

———. *Le Mythe de la procréation à l'âge baroque.* Paris: Seuil, 1979.

Daston, Lorraine, and Katharine Park. "The Hermaphrodite and the Orders of Nature: Sexual Ambiguity in Early Modern France." In *Premodern Sexualities,* edited by Louise Fradenburg and Carla Freccero. New York: Routledge, 1996.

Davidson, Arnold. "The Horror of Monsters." In *The Boundaries of Humanity: Humans, Ani-*

mals, Machines, edited by James Sheehan and Morton Sosna. Berkeley and Los Angeles: University of California Press, 1991.

Davidson, Nicholas. "Theology, Nature and the Law: Sexual Sin and Sexual Crime in Italy from the Fourteenth to the Seventeenth Century." In *Crime, Society and the Law in Renaissance Italy,* edited by Trevor Dean and Kate Lowe. Cambridge: Cambridge University Press, 1994.

De Conches, Guglielmo. *Dialogus de substantiis physicis.* Strasbourg: Rihelius, 1567.

Delaney, Carol. "The Meaning of Paternity and the Virgin Birth Debate." *Man* 21 (1986): 494–513.

Della Casa, Giovanni. *Galateo.* Edited by Saverio Orlando. Milan: Garzanti, 1988.

Della Porta, Giambattista. *Magiae naturalis.* Naples: S. Abbati Stampatori, 1588. Reprint, Palermo: Il Vespro, 1979.

———. *Natural Magick.* Edited and translated by Derek Price. New York: Basic Books, 1957.

De Martino, Ernesto. *La terra del rimorso: Contributo a una storia religiosa del sud.* Milan: Saggiatore, 1961.

Dentice, Luigi. *Due dialoghi della musica.* Rome: Luchino, 1553.

De Sommi, Leone. *Quattro dialoghi in materia di rappresentazioni sceniche.* Edited by Ferruccio Marotti. Milan: Polifilo, 1968.

Detenbeck, Laurie. "Women and the Management of Dramaturgy in *La Calandria.*" In *Donna: Woman in Italian Culture,* edited by Ada Testaferri. Ottawa: Dovehouse Press, 1989.

De Villanova, Arnaldus. *Breviarum practice.* In *Opera.* Lyons: Fradin, 1504.

———. *The Conservation of Youth and Defense of Age.* Translated by Jonas Drummond. Woodstock, Vt.: Elm Tree Press, 1912.

De Zerbis, Gabriele. *Liber anathomie corporis humani.* Venice: Locatello, 1502.

Di Conti, Nicolò. *Viaggio di Nicolò di Conti, veneziano.* In Giovanni Battista Ramusio, *Navigazioni e viaggi,* 6 vols., edited by Marica Milanesi. Turin: Einaudi, 1978–88.

Dionisotti, Carlo. "Ricordo del Bibbiena." In *Machiavellerie.* Turin: Einaudi, 1980.

Dioscorides. *The Greek Herbal of Diosc*orides. Edited by Robert Gunther. London: Hafner, 1968.

Doane, Janice, and Devon Hodges. "Risky Business: Familial Ideology and the Case of Baby M." *differences* 1 (1989): 67–81.

Domenichi, Lodovico. *Della nobiltà delle donne.* Venice: Giolito, 1551.

———. *Historia naturale di G. Plinio Secondo . . . tradotta per m. L. Domenichi con le addittioni in margine.* Venice: G. Bizzardo, 1612.

———. *Historia varia.* Venice: Giolito, 1564.

Doni, Antonfrancesco. *Tutte le novelle.* Milan: Biblioteca rara, 1862.

Eatough, Geoffrey. *Fracastoro's Syphilis.* Liverpool: Cairns, 1984.

Epstein, Julia. "Either/Or–Neither/Both: Sexual Ambiguity and the Ideology of Gender." *Genders* 7 (1990): 99–142.

Erizzo, Sebastiano. *Le sei giornate.* Rome: Salerno, 1977.

Falloppio, Gabriele. *De morbo gallico*. Padua: Bertullus, 1564.

———. *Secreti diversi e miracolosi*. Venice: Bonfad, 1658.

Fausto-Sterling, Anne. "How to Build a Man." In *Constructing Masculinity*, edited by Maurice Berger, Brian Wallis, and Simon Watson. New York: Routledge, 1995.

Fenlon, Ian. "Monteverdi's Mantuan *Orfeo*: Some New Documentation." *Early Music* 12 (1984): 163–72.

Ferguson, Margaret. *Trials of Desire: Renaissance Defenses of Poetry*. New Haven: Yale University Press, 1983.

Ferroni, Giulio. *Il testo e la scena: Saggi sul teatro del Cinquecento*. Rome: Bulzoni, 1980.

———. " 'Transformation' and 'Adaptation' in Machiavelli's *Mandragola*." In *Machiavelli and the Discourse of Literature*, edited by Albert Ascoli and Victoria Kahn. Ithaca: Cornell University Press, 1993.

Ficino, Marsilio. *De le tre vite. A qual guisa si possono le persone letterate mantenere in sanità. Per qual guisa si possa l'huomo prolungare la vita. Con che arte, e mezzi ci possiamo questa sana, e lunga vita prolungare per via del cielo*. Venice: Tramezzino, 1548.

———. *Della religione christiana*. Florence: Giunti, 1563.

———. *Three Books on Life*. Translated and edited by Carol V. Kaske and John R. Clark. Binghamton: State University of New York, Medieval and Renaissance Texts and Studies, 1998.

Filipczaz, Zirka. *Hot Dry Men, Cold Wet Women: The Theory of Humors in Western European Art, 1575–1700*. New York: American Federation of Arts, 1997.

Filmer, Robert. *Patriarcha and Other Political Works*. Edited by Peter Laslett. Oxford: Blackwell, 1949.

Finucci, Valeria. "The Female Masquerade: Ariosto and the Game of Desire." In *Desire in the Renaissance: Psychoanalysis and Literature*, edited by Valeria Finucci and Regina Schwartz. Princeton: Princeton University Press, 1994.

———. "In the Name of the Brother: Male Rivalry and Social Order in B. Castiglione's *Il libro del Cortegiano*." *Exemplaria* 9.1 (1997): 91–116.

———. *The Lady Vanishes: Subjectivity and Representation in Castiglione and Ariosto*. Stanford: Stanford University Press, 1992.

Finucci, Valeria, ed. *Renaissance Transactions: Ariosto and Tasso*. Durham, N.C.: Duke University Press, 1999.

Finucci, Valeria, and Kevin Brownlee, eds. *Generation and Degeneration: Tropes of Reproduction in Literature and History from Antiquity to Early Modern Europe*. Durham, N.C.: Duke University Press, 2001.

Fioravanti, Leonardo. *Capricci medicinali*. Venice: Avanzi, 1568.

———. *Il tesoro della vita humana*. Venice: Sessa, 1582.

Firenzuola, Agnolo. *On the Beauty of Women*. Translated and edited by Konrad Eisenbichler and Jacqueline Murray. Philadelphia: University of Pennsylvania Press, 1992.

———. *Prose*. 2 vols. Edited by Lorenzo Scala and Lodovico Domenichi. Florence: Giunta, 1548.

Flaumenhaft, Mera. "The Comic Remedy: Machiavelli's *Mandragola*." *Interpretation* 7 (1978): 33–74.

Fonte, Moderata. *Tredici canti del Floridoro*. Edited by Valeria Finucci. Modena: Mucchi, 1995.

———. *The Worth of Women (Il merito delle donne)*. Edited by Virginia Cox. Chicago: University of Chicago Press, 1998.

Fontes Baratto. Anna. "Les fêtes à Urbin en 1513 et la *Calandre* de Bernardo Dovizi da Bibbiena." In *Les écrivains et le pouvoir en Italie a l'époque de la Renaissance*, edited by André Rochon. Paris: Université de la Sorbonne Nouvelle, 1974.

Foucault, Michel. *Herculine Barbin, Being the Recently Discovered Memoirs of a Nineteenth-Century Hermaphrodite*. Translated by Richard McDougall. New York: Pantheon, 1980.

———. *The History of Sexuality*. Vol. 1: *An Introduction*. New York: Vintage, 1980.

———. *The Order of Things: An Archeology of the Human Sciences*. New York: Random House, 1970.

Fracastoro, Girolamo. *De contagione et contagiosis morbis et eorum curatione*. Translated by Wilmer Wright. New York: Putnam's Sons, 1930.

Franceschetti, Antonio. "La novella nei poemi del Boiardo e dell'Ariosto." In *La novella italiana: Atti del convegno di Caprarola 14–24 sett. 1988*, edited by Enrico Malato. Rome: Salerno, 1989.

French, Roger. *Dissection and Vivisection in the European Renaissance*. Aldershot: Ashgate, 1999.

Freud, Sigmund. "An Autobiographical Study." In *The Standard Edition of the Complete Works of Sigmund Freud*, 24 vols., translated and edited by James Strachey. London: Hogarth Press, 1953–74 [hereafter *SE*].

———. "Certain Neurotic Mechanisms in Jealousy, Paranoia, and Homosexuality." In *Collected Papers*, 5 vols., 2:232–40. New York: Basic Books, 1959.

———. "Femininity." *SE* 22: 112–35.

———. "Fetishism."*SE* 21: 152–57.

———. "From the History of an Infantile Neurosis." In *Collected Papers*, 5 vols., 5:473–607. New York: Basic Books, 1959.

———. "Medusa's Head." *SE* 18: 273–74.

———. "Mourning and Melancholia." *SE* 14: 242–58.

———. "On Narcissism: An Introduction." *SE* 14: 69–102.

———. "Symptoms and Anxiety." *SE* 20: 87–175.

———. "Three Essays on the Theory of Sexuality." *SE* 7:122–243.

———. "The Uncanny." *SE* 17: 219–52.

Friedman, John. *The Monstrous Races in Medieval Art and Thought*. Cambridge: Harvard University Press, 1981.

Furfaro, Domenico. *La vita e l'opera di Leonardo Fioravanti*. Bologna: Società Tipografica Editori, 1963.

Galen, *On the Affected Parts*. Translated by Rudolph E. Siegel. New York: Karger, 1976.

———. *On the Usefulness of the Parts of the Body (De usu partium corporis)*. 2 vols. Translated and edited by Margaret May. Ithaca: Cornell University Press, 1968.

Galli Stampino, Maria. "Classical Antecedents and Teleological Narratives: On the Contamination between Opera and Courtly Sung Entertainment in the Early Seventeenth Century." *Italica* 77 (2000): 331–56.

Galloni, Antonio. *Trattato de gli instrumenti di martirio.* Rome: Donangeli, 1591.

Garber, Marjorie. "The Insincerity of Women." In *Desire in the Renaissance: Psychoanalysis and Literature,* edited by Valeria Finucci and Regina Schwartz. Princeton: Princeton University Press, 1994.

Gareffi, Andrea. *Figure dell'immaginario nell'Orlando Furioso.* Rome: Bulzoni, 1984.

———. *La scrittura e la festa: Teatro, festa e letteratura nella Firenze del Rinascimento.* Bologna: Mulino, 1991.

Garzoni, Tommaso. *La piazza universale di tutte le professioni del mondo.* 2 vols. Edited by Paolo Cherchi and Beatrice Collina. Turin: Einaudi, 1996.

Gélis, Jacques. *History of Childbirth, Fertility, Pregnancy and Birth in Early Modern Europe.* Translated by Rosemary Morris. Boston: Northeastern University Press, 1991.

Gelli, Giovan Battista. *La Circe.* In *Trattatisti del Cinquecento,* 2 vols., edited by Mario Pozzi. Milan: Ricciardi, 1978.

Gerbino, Giuseppe. "Castrati in Renaissance Italy." Paper delivered at the Renaissance Society of America Meeting, Los Angeles, March 1999.

Getto, Giovanni. *Nel mondo della Gerusalemme.* Florence: Vallecchi, 1968.

Gherro, Sandro. "Il problema del *verum semen* nel Breve 'Cum Frequenter' di Sisto V." *Il diritto ecclesiastico* 77 (1966): 98–117.

Ginzburg, Carlo. *The Cheese and the Worms.* Baltimore: Johns Hopkins University Press, 1980.

———. "Tiziano, Ovidio e i codici della figurazione erotica nel '500." In *Tiziano e Venezia: Atti del convegno internazionale di studi,* edited by Carlo Ginzburg et al. Vicenza: Neri Pozza, 1980.

Ginzburg, Carlo, and Marco Ferrari. "La colombara ha aperto gli occhi." *Quaderni storici* 38 (1978): 631–39.

Gioberti, Lorenzo (Laurent Joubert). *La prima parte de gli errori popolari. Nella quale si contiene l'eccellenza della medicina e de medici, della concettione, e generatione, della gravidanza, del parto, e delle donne di parto, e del latte, e del nutrire i bambini.* Florence: Giunta, 1592.

Girard, René. *Deceit, Desire and the Novel: Self and Other in Literary Structure.* Translated by Yvonne Freccero. Baltimore: Johns Hopkins University Press, 1965.

———. *Violence and the Sacred.* Translated by Patrick Gregory. Baltimore: Johns Hopkins University Press, 1977.

Gleason, Maud. *Making Men: Sophists and Self-Presentation in Ancient Rome.* Princeton: Princeton University Press, 1995.

Gl'Intronati. *Gl'ingannati.* Edited by Ireneo Sanesi. Bari: Laterza, 1912.

Gliozzi, Giuliano. *Adamo e il nuovo mondo: La nascita dell'antropologia come ideologia coloniale. Dalle genealogie bibliche alle teorie razziali, 1500–1700.* Florence: La Nuova Italia, 1977.

———. *Le teorie della razza nell'età moderna.* Turin: Einaudi, 1986.

Gloyne, Howard. "Tarantism: Mass Histerical Reaction to Spider Bite in the Middle Ages." *American Imago* 7 (1950): 29–42.

Goldberg, Jonathan, ed. *Queering the Renaissance.* Durham, N.C.: Duke University Press, 1994.

Gollaher, David. *Circumcision.* New York: Basic Books, 2000.

Goodich, Michael. "Sexuality, Family, and the Supernatural in the Fourteenth Century." *Journal of the History of Sexuality* 4 (1994): 493–516.

Grazzini, Anton Francesco (Il Lasca). *Le cene.* Edited by Giorgio Barberi Squarotti. Milan: Rizzoli, 1989.

Green, Monica. "Women's Medical Practice and Health Care in Medieval Europe." *Signs* 14 (1989): 434–73.

Greenblatt, Stephen. "Fiction and Friction." In *Shakespearean Negotiations: The Circulation of Social Energy in Renaissance England.* Berkeley and Los Angeles: University of California Press, 1988.

Grendler, Paul. *The Roman Inquisition and the Venetian Press, 1540–1605.* Princeton: Princeton University Press, 1977.

Grillandi, Paolo. *Tractatus de hereticis et sortilegiis.* Venice: Giunta, 1536.

Grosrichard, Alain. "Le Cas polyphème: Un monstre et sa mère." *Ornicar?* 11–12 (Sept.–Dec. 1977): 19–35, 45–57.

Grubb, James. *Provincial Families of the Renaissance: Private and Public Life in the Veneto.* Baltimore: Johns Hopkins University Press, 1996.

Guainerio Antonio (Anthonius Guainerius). *Tractatus de matricibus.* In *Opera Omnia.* Pavia: n.p., 1481.

Guidotti, Angela. "Il doppio gioco della *Calandria.*" *MLN* 104 (1989): 98–116.

Guinsburg, Arlene Miller. "The Counterthrust to Sixteenth-Century Mysogyny: The Work of Agrippa and Paracelsus." *Historical Reflexions/Réflexions Historiques* 8.1 (1981): 3–28.

Gunsberg, Maggie. *Gender and the Italian Stage: From the Renaissance to the Present Day.* Cambridge: Cambridge University Press, 1997.

Hammond, Frederick. *Music and Spectacle in Baroque Rome: Barberini Patronage Under Urban VIII.* New Haven: Yale University Press, 1994.

Hanson, Ann. "The Medical Writers' Woman." In *Before Sexuality: The Construction of Erotic Experience in the Ancient Greek World.* Edited by David Halperin, John Winkler, and Froma Zeitlin. Princeton: Princeton University Press, 1990.

Heliodorus. *An Aethiopian Romance (Aethiopica).* Edited by F. A. Wright. London: Routledge, 1923.

Henderson, John, Jon Arrizabalaga, and Roger French, eds. *The Great Pox: The French Disease in Renaissance Europe.* New Haven: Yale University Press, 1997.

Heriot, Angus. *The Castrati in Opera.* London: Secker and Warburg, 1956.

Herophilus. *The Art of Medicine in Alexandria.* Translated and edited by Heinrich von Staden. Cambridge: Cambridge University Press, 1989.

Horowitz, Maryanne Cline. "Aristotle and Women." *Journal of the History of Biology* 9.2 (1976): 183–213.

Huarte, Juan de San Juan. *Essamina de gl'ingegni de gli huomini accomodati ad apprendere qual si voglia scienza.* Venice: Barezzi, 1600.

Huet, Marie-Hélène. *Monstrous Imagination.* Cambridge: Harvard University Press, 1993.

Imperiale, Giovanni. *Le notti beriche overo de' quesiti, e discorsi fisici, medici, politici, historici, e sacri.* Venice: Baglioni, 1663.

[Ignoto Veneto del Cinquecento]. *La venexiana.* Edited by Lodovico Zorzi. Turin: Einaudi, 1965.

Irigaray, Luce. *This Sex Which Is Not One.* Translated by Catherine Porter. Ithaca: Cornell University Press, 1985.

Ivanovich, Cristoforo. *Minerva al tavolino.* 2 vols. Venice: Pezzana, 1688.

Jacquart, Danielle, and Claude Thomasset. *Sexuality and Medicine in the Middle Ages.* Translated by Matthew Adamson. Princeton: Princeton University Press, 1988.

James, Liz, ed. *Women, Men and Eunuchs: Gender in Byzantium.* New York: Routledge, 1997.

Javitch, Daniel. *Proclaiming a Classic: The Canonization of the Orlando Furioso.* Princeton: Princeton University Press, 1991.

Joubert, Laurent. *Popular Errors.* Translated by Gregory David de Rocher. Tuscaloosa: University of Alabama Press, 1989.

Keiser, Dorothy. "Cross-Sexual Casting in Baroque Opera: Musical and Theatrical Conventions." *Opera Quarterly* 5.4 (1987–88): 46–57.

Kessler, Eckhard. "The Intellective Soul." In *The Cambridge History of Renaissance Philosophy,* edited by Charles Schmitt, Quentin Skinner, Eckhard Kessler, and Jill Kraye. Cambridge: Cambridge University Press, 1988.

Kirkendale, Warren. *The Court Musicians in Florence During the Principate of the Medici.* Florence: Olschki, 1993.

Kirshner, Julius, and Anthony Molho. "Il monte delle doti a Firenze dalla sua fondazione nel 1425 alla metà del sedicesimo secolo: Abbozzo di una ricerca." *Ricerche storiche,* n.s., 10 (1980): 21–47.

Klapisch-Zuber, Christiane. *Women, Family, and Ritual in Renaissance Italy.* Chicago: University of Chicago Press, 1985.

Kramer, Heinrich, and James Sprenger. *The "Malleus Maleficarum" of Heinrich Kramer and James Sprenger.* Translated by Montague Summers. New York: Dover, 1971.

Krappe, A. H. "La Légende de la naissance miraculeuse d'Attila, roi des Huns." *Moyen Age* 41 (1931): 96–104.

Kristeva, Julia. *Powers of Horrors: An Essay on Abjection.* Translated by Leon Roudiez. New York: Columbia University Press, 1982.

———. "Stabat Mater." In *The Female Body in Western Culture: Contemporary Perspectives,* edited by Susan Rubin Suleiman. Cambridge: Harvard University Press, 1986.

———. *Tales of Love.* Translated by Leon Roudiez. New York: Columbia University Press, 1987.

Kuefler, Mathew. *The Manly Eunuch: Masculinity, Gender Ambiguity, and Christian Ideology in Late Antiquity.* Chicago: University of Chicago Press, 2001.

Kuen, Thomas. *Law, Family and Women: Toward a Legal Anthropology of Renaissance Italy.* Chicago: University of Chicago Press, 1991.

La Torre, Felice. *L'utero attraverso i secoli: Da Erofilo ai giorni nostri.* Città di Castello: Unione Arti Grafiche, 1917.

Lacan, Jacques. "The Meaning of the Phallus." In *Feminine Sexuality: Jacques Lacan and the Ecole Freudienne,* edited by Juliet Mitchell and Jacqueline Rose. New York: Norton, 1982.

Laplanche, Jean. *Problématiques.* 4 vols. Paris: Presses Universitaires de France, 1980–81.

Laplanche, Jean, and Jean-Bertand Pontalis. "Fantasy and the Origins of Sexuality." In *Formations of Fantasy,* edited by Victor Burgin, James Donald, and Cora Kaplan. London: Methuen, 1986.

Laqueur, Thomas. "Amor Veneris, Vel Dulcedo Appelletur." In *Fragments for a History of the Human Body,* 3 vols., edited by Michael Feher. New York: Zone, 1989.

———. *Making Sex: Body and Gender from the Greeks to Freud.* Cambridge: Harvard University Press, 1990.

Latour, Bruno. *Pandora's Hope: Essays on the Reality of Science Studies.* Cambridge: Harvard University Press, 1999.

Lavarda, Sergio. *L'anima a Dio e il corpo alla terra: Scelte testamentarie nella terraferma veneta (1575–1631).* Venice: Istituto Veneto di Scienze, Lettere ed Arti, 1998.

Le Cat, Nicolas. *Traité de la couleur de la peau humaine en général, de celle des nègres en particulier et de la métamorphose d'une de ces couleurs en l'autre, soit de naissance, soit accidentellement.* Amsterdam: n.p., 1765.

Lefevre, Renato. *L'Etiopia nella stampa del primo Cinquecento.* Como: Cairoli, 1966.

Lemay, Helen. "Anthonius Guainerius and Medieval Gynecology." In *Women of the Medieval World,* edited by Julius Krishner and Suzanne Wemple. London: Blackwell, 1985.

———. "Human Sexuality in Twelfth- through Fifteenth-Century Scientific Writings." In *Sexual Practices and the Medieval Church,* edited by Vern Bullough and James Brundage. Buffalo: Prometheus Books, 1982.

Levi, Eugenio. "La *Mandragola* di Machiavelli." *Il comico di carattere da Teofrasto a Pirandello.* Turin: Einaudi, 1959.

Levi Pisetzki, Rosita. *Storia del costume italiano.* 3 vols. Milan: Istituto Editoriale Italiano, 1964.

Lewis, Peter Allen. *The Wages of Sin: Sex and Disease, Past and Present.* Chicago: University of Chicago Press, 2000.

Liceti, Giuseppe. *Il ceva, overo dell'eccellenza, et uso de' genitali. Dialogo di Giuseppe Liceti Medico Chirurgo genovese. Nel quale si tratta dell'essenza, et generatione del seme humano; delle somiglianze dell'Huomo, e lor cagioni; della differenza del sesso; della generatione de' mostri, e d'altre cose non meno utili; che dilettevoli.* Bologna: Heredi di Gio. Rossi, 1598.

Liceti, Fortunio. *De monstrorum caussis natura et differentiis.* In *De la nature, des causes, des différences de monstres,* edited by Francois Houssay. Paris: Editions Hippocrate, 1937.

Little, Ralph. "Oral Agression in Spider Legends." *American Imago* 23 (1966): 169–79.

Loraux, Nicole. *The Children of Athena: Athenian Ideas about Citizenship and the Division between the Sexes.* Princeton: Princeton University Press, 1993.

Lorch, Maristella. "Women in the Context of Machiavelli's *Mandragola*." In *Donna: Women in Italian Culture,* edited by Ada Testaferri. Toronto: Dovehouse, 1989.

Lyons, Charles. *To Wash an Aethiop White: British Ideas about Black African Educability.* New York: Teachers College, Columbia University, 1975.

Machiavelli, Niccolò. *Lettere.* Edited by Franco Gaeta. Milan: Feltrinelli, 1961.

———. *La Mandragola.* Edited by Gennaro Sasso. Milan: Rizzoli, 1980.

———. *The Mandragola.* In *Five Italian Renaissance Comedies,* edited and translated by Bruce Penman. London: Penguin, 1978.

———. *Mandragola/Clizia.* Edited by Riccardo Bacchelli. Milan: Feltrinelli, 1995.

———. *The Prince and the Discourses.* Translated by Luigi Ricci. New York: Modern Library, 1940.

———. *La vita di Castruccio Castracani da Lucca.* Edited by Fortunato Bellonzi. Rome: Stefano de Luca, 1969.

Maclean, Ian. *The Renaissance Notion of Woman: A Study on the Fortunes of Scholasticism and Medical Science in European Intellectual Life.* Cambridge: Cambridge University Press, 1980.

Maimonides, Moses. *The Guide of the Perplexed.* Translated and edited by Shlomo Pines. Chicago: University of Chicago Press, 1963.

Malespini, Celio. *Giardino di fiori curiosi, in forma di dialogo.* Venice: Ciotti, 1597.

Malizia, Enrico. *Ricettario delle streghe: Incantesimi, prodigi sessuali e veleni.* Rome: Edizioni Mediterranee, 1992.

Malpighi, Marcello. *Opera omnia, seu thesaurus locupletissimus botanico-medico-anathomicus.* 2 vols. Leiden: Petrum van der Oa, 1687.

Marinella, Lucrezia. *La nobiltà et 'eccellenza delle donne co' i diffetti e mancamenti degli uomini.* Venice: Ciotti, 1601.

Marinello, Giovanni. *Le medicine partenenti alle infermità delle donne.* Venice: Francesco de' Franceschi, 1563. Abridged version in *Medicina per le donne nel Cinquecento: Testi di Giovanni Marinello e di Girolamo Mercurio,* edited by Maria Luisa Altieri Biagi et al. Turin: UTET, 1992.

Martin, Dale B. "Contradictions of Masculinity: Ascetic Inseminators and Menstruating Men in Greco-Roman Culture." In *Generation and Degeneration: Tropes of Reproduction in Literature and History from Antiquity to Early Modern Europe,* edited by Valeria Finucci and Kevin Brownlee. Durham, N.C.: Duke University Press, 2001.

———. *The Corinthian Body.* New Haven: Yale University Press, 1995.

Martin, Emily. "Body Narratives, Body Boundaries." In *Cultural Studies,* edited by Lawrence Grossberg, Cary Nelson, and Paula Treichler. New York: Routledge, 1992.

Martin, Ernest. *Histoire des monstres depuis l'antiquité jusqu'à nos jours.* Paris: Reinwald, 1880.

Martin, Ruth. *Witchcraft and the Inquisition in Venice, 1550–1650.* Oxford: Blackwell, 1989.

Martineddu, Salvatore. *Le fonti della Gerusalemme liberata.* Turin: Clausen, 1895.

Martinez, Ronald. "The Pharmacy of Machiavelli: Roman Lucretia in *Mandragola*." *Renaissance Drama* 14 (1983): 1–43.

Martini, Gabriele. *Il "vitio nefando" nella Venezia del Seicento: Aspetti sociali e repressione di giustizia.* Rome: Jouvence, 1988.

Masetti-Zannini, Gian Ludovico. "Virtù e crudezza: scolari di canto e famiglie tra rinascimento e barocco." *Strenna dei Romanisti* 41 (1980): 332–41.

Mason, H. "Favorinus' Disorder: Reifenstein's Syndrome in Antiquity." *Janus* 66 (1979): 1–13.

Massa, Niccolò. *Introductory Book of Anatomy (Liber introductorius anatomiae).* In *Studies in Pre-Vesalian Anatomy: Biography, Translations, Documents,* edited by Levi Robert Lind. Philadelphia: American Philosophical Society, 1975.

———. *Liber de morbo gallico.* Venice: Bindoni ac Pasini socii, 1536.

Mattioli, Pietro. *Dei discorsi di m. Pietro Mattioli sanese . . . nelli sei libri di Pedacio Dioscoride Anazarbeo, della materia medicinale.* Venice: Valgrisi, 1568.

Maus, Katharine. "Horns of Silence: Jealousy, Gender and Spectatorship in English Renaissance Drama." *English Literary History* 54 (1987): 561–83.

McClary, Susan. *Feminine Endings: Music, Gender, and Sexuality.* Minneapolis: University of Minnesota Press, 1991.

McGrath, Aidan. *A Controversy Concerning Male Impotence.* Rome: Editrice Pontificia Universitaria Gregoriana, 1988.

McLaren, Angus. *Reproductive Rituals: The Perception of Fertility in England from the Sixteenth Century to the Nineteenth Century.* London: Methuen, 1984.

Melicow, Meyer. "Castrati Singers and the Lost Cords." *Bulletin of the New York Academy of Medicine* 59 (1983): 744–64.

Mercati, Michele. *Instruttione sopra la peste: Nella quale si contengono i piu eletti e approvati rimedij, con molti nuovi e potenti secreti così da preservarsi come da curarsi.* Rome: Vincenzo Accolti, 1576.

Mercuriale, Girolamo. *De arte gymnastica.* Venice: Giunta, 1569.

———. *De venenis, et morbis venenosis.* Venice: Meietum, 1584.

Mercurio, Girolamo (Scipion Mercurii). *La commare o riccoglitrice.* Venice: Ciotti, 1596. Abridged version in *Medicina per le donne nel Cinquecento: Testi di Giovanni Marinello e di Girolamo Mercurio,* edited by Maria Luisa Altieri Biagi et al. Turin: UTET, 1992.

Migiel, Marilyn. "Clorinda's Father." *Stanford Italian Review* 10 (1991): 93–121.

Milner, Anthony. "The Sacred Capons." *Musical Times* 114 (1973): 250–53.

Mina, Gabriele. *Il morso della differenza: Antologia del dibattito sul tarantismo fra il 14 e il 16 secolo.* Nardò: Besa, 2000.

Modleski, Tania. "Three Men and Baby M." *Camera Obscura* 17 (1988): 69–81.

Molinari, Cesare. *La commedia dell'arte.* Milan: Mondadori, 1985.

Montaigne, Michel de. *The Complete Essays of Montaigne.* Translated by Donald Frame. Stanford: Stanford University Press, 1976.

Morlini, Girolamo. *Novelle e favole.* Edited by Giovanni Villani. Rome: Salerno, 1983.

Mulvey, Laura. *Visual and Other Pleasures.* Bloomington: Indiana University Press, 1989.

Mussato, Albertino. *Ecerinis*. Edited by Luigi Padrin. Munich: Wilhelm Fink Verlag, 1975.

Nagler, Alois Maria. *Theatre Festivals of the Medici, 1539–1637.* New Haven: Yale University Press, 1964.

Nardi, Bruno. *Studi su Pietro Pomponazzi.* Florence: Le Monnier, 1965.

Needham, Joseph. *A History of Embryology.* 3 vols. New York: Abelard-Schuman, 1959.

Newcomb, Anthony. "Courtesans, Muses, or Musicians? Professional Women Musicians in Sixteenth-Century Italy." In *Women Making Music: The Western Art Tradition, 1150–1950,* edited by Jane Bowers and Judith Tick. Urbana: University of Illinois Press, 1986.

Niccoli, Ottavia, "Il corpo femminile nei trattati del Cinquecento." In *Il corpo delle donne,* edited by Gisela Boch and Giuliana Nobili. Bologna: Transeuropa, 1988.

———. "*Menstruum quasi monstruum:* Monstrous Births and Menstrual Taboo in the Sixteenth Century." In *Sex and Gender in Historical Perspective: Selection from Quaderni Storici,* edited by Edward Muir and Guido Ruggiero. Baltimore: Johns Hopkins University Press, 1990.

———. *Prophecy and People in Renaissance Italy.* Princeton: Princeton University Press, 1990.

Nicholson, Eric. " 'That's How It Is': Comic Travesties of Sex and Gender in Early Sixteenth-Century Venice." In *Look Who's Laughing: Gender and Comedy,* edited by Gail Ginney. Langhorne, Pa.: Gordon and Breach, 1994.

Noonan, John. *Contraception: A History of Its Treatment by the Catholic Theologians and Canonists.* Cambridge: Harvard University Press, Belknap Press, 1965.

O'Grady, Deirdre. *The Last Troubadours: Poetic Drama in Italian Opera, 1597–1887.* London: Routledge, 1991.

Orgel, Stephen. *Impersonations: The Performance of Gender in Shakespeare's England.* Cambridge: Cambridge University Press, 1996.

Ottonelli, Domenico. *Della Christiana moderatione del theatro.* In *La commedia dell'arte e la società barocca,* vol. 1: *La professione del teatro,* edited by Ferdinando Taviani. Rome: Bulzoni, 1969.

———. *Della pericolosa conversatione con le donne, e poco modeste, e ritirate, e cantatrici, e accademiche . . . ove si risolvono molti casi di coscienza.* Florence: Franceschini e Logi, 1646.

Ovid. *Metamorphoses.* Translated by A. D. Melville. Oxford: Oxford University Press, 1986.

Pachter, Henry. *Paracelsus: Magic into Science.* New York: Schuman, 1951.

Padoan, Giorgio. *L'avventura della commedia rinascimentale.* Padua: Piccin, 1996.

———. "Il senso del teatro nei secoli senza teatro." In *Concetto, storia, miti e immagini del Medio Evo,* edited by Vittore Branca. Florence: Sansoni, 1973.

———. "Il tramonto di Machiavelli." *Lettere italiane* 33 (1981): 457–81.

Pagel, Walter. *Paracelsus: An Introduction to Philosophical Medicine in the Era of the Renaissance.* New York: Karger, 1958.

Paleotti, Gabriele. *Discorsi intorno alle immagini sacre e profane.* Bologna: Alessandro Benacci, 1582. Reprinted in *Trattati d'arte del Cinquecento fra Manierismo e Controriforma,* 2 vols., edited by Paola Barocchi. Bari: Laterza, 1961.

Pallavicino, Ferrante. *La retorica delle puttane.* Edited by Laura Coci. Parma: Guanda, 1992.

Palmer, Richard. "Pharmacy in the Republic of Venice in the Sixteenth Century." In *The*

Medical Renaissance of the Sixteenth Century, edited by Andrew Wear, Roger French, and Iain Lonie. Cambridge: Cambridge University Press, 1985.

Pancino, Claudia. *Voglie materne: Storia di una credenza.* Bologna: Cluebb, 1966.

Pandolfi, Vito. *Il teatro del Rinascimento e la commedia dell'arte.* Rome: Lerici, 1969.

Paracelsus. *De virtute imaginativa.* In *Paracelsus: An Introduction to Philosophical Medicine in the Era of the Renaissance,* edited by Walter Pagel. New York: Karger, 1958.

——. *Operum medico-chimicorum sive paradoxorum.* 11 vols. Frankfurt: Collegio Musarum Palthenianarum, 1603. Abridged English translation, *The Life of Paracelsus and the Substance of His Teachings . . . Extracted and Translated from His Rare and Extensive Works,* edited by Franz Hartman. London: Kegan Paul, 1887.

——. *The Prophecies of Paracelsus: Occult Symbols and Magic Figures with Esoteric Explanations.* Blauvet: Rudolph Steiner, 1973.

Pardo, Mary. "Artifice as Seduction in Titian." In *Sexuality and Gender in Early Modern Europe: Institutions, Texts, Images,* edited by James Grantham Turner. Cambridge: Cambridge University Press, 1993.

Paré, Ambroise. *On Monsters and Manners.* Edited and translated by Janis Pallister. Chicago: University of Chicago Press, 1982.

——. *Ten Books of Surgery with the Magazine of the Instruments Necessary for It.* Translated by Robert Linker and Nathan Womack. Athens: University of Georgia Press, 1969.

Parini, Giuseppe. *Il giorno e le odi.* Bologna: Zanichelli, 1817.

Park, Katharine. *Doctors and Medicine in Early Renaissance Florence.* Princeton: Princeton University Press, 1985.

——. "The Rediscovery of the Clitoris: French Medicine and the Tribade, 1570–1620." In *The Body in Parts: Fantasies of Corporeality in Early Modern Europe,* edited by David Hillman and Carla Mazzio. New York: Routledge, 1997.

Park, Katharine, and Lorraine Daston. "Unnatural Conceptions: The Study of Monsters in Sixteenth- and Seventeenth-Century France and England." *Past and Present* 91 (1981): 21–54.

Parker, Geoffrey, and Lesley M. Smith. *The General Crisis of the Seventeenth Century.* London: Routledge, 1997.

Parronchi, Antonio. "La prima rappresentazione della *Mandragola:* Il modello per l'apparato. L' allegoria." *La Bibliofilia* 64 (1962): 37–86.

Pasqualigo, Zaccaria. *Eunuchi, nati, facti, mystici: ex sacra et humana literatura illustrati.* Dijon: Apud Philibertum Chavance, 1655.

Paster, Gail. *The Body Embarrassed: Drama and the Disciplines of Shame in Early Modern England.* Ithaca: Cornell University Press, 1993.

Perocco, Daria. "Il rito finale della *Mandragola.*" *Lettere italiane* 25 (1973): 531–36.

Persio, Antonio. *Dell'ingegno dell'huomo.* Venice: Manuzio, 1576.

Peschel, Enid Rhodes, and Richard E. Peschel. "Medicine and Music: The Castrati in Opera." *Opera Quarterly* 44 (1986–87): 21–38.

Petronio, Alessandro. *Del vivere delli Romani et del conservare la sanità.* Rome: Basa, 1592.

Pico della Mirandola, Gianfrancesco. *Examen vanitatis doctrinae gentium et veritatis Christianae doctrinae*. Basel: Henricpetri, 1601.

Pinto-Correia, Clara. *The Ovary of Eve: Egg and Sperm and Preformation*. Chicago: University of Chicago Press, 1997.

Pirrotta, Nino, and Elena Povoledo, *Music and Theatre from Poliziano to Monteverdi*. Translated by Karen Eales. Cambridge: Cambridge University Press, 1982.

Pitkin, Hanna. *Fortune Is a Woman: Gender and Politics in the Thought of Niccolò Machiavelli*. Berkeley and Los Angeles: University of California Press, 1984.

Platina (Bartolomeo Sacchi). *On Right Pleasure and Good Health*. Edited by Mary Ella Milham. Binghamton: State University of New York, Medieval and Renaissance Texts and Studies, 1998.

Pleasants, Henry. *The Great Singers: From Jenny Lind and Caruso to Callas and Pavarotti*. New York: Simon and Schuster, 1981.

Pliny, Caius, the Elder. *Natural History: A Selection*. Edited and translated by John Healy. London: Penguin, 1991.

Pomata, Gianna. "Menstruating Men: Similarity and Difference between the Sexes in Early Modern Europe." In *Generation and Degeneration: Tropes of Reproduction in Literature and History from Antiquity to Early Modern Europe*, edited by Valeria Finucci and Kevin Brownlee. Durham, N.C.: Duke University Press, 2001.

Pomponazzi, Pietro. *De naturalium effectuum admirandorum causis, seu de incantationibus liber, item de fato, libero arbitrio, praedestinatione, prouidentia Dei*. Basel: Henricpetri, 1567.

Premuda, Loris. *Storia dell'iconografia anatomica*. Milan: Martello, 1957.

Prierio, Sylvester. *De strigimagis*. Rome: n.p., 1521.

Quétel, Claude. *History of Syphilis*. Translated by Judith Braddock and Brian Pike. Cambridge: Polity Press, 1990.

Quint, David. *Epic and Empire: Politics and Generic Form from Virgil to Milton*. Princeton: Princeton University Press, 1993.

Rahner, Hugo. "Moly and Mandragora in Pagan and Christian Symbolism." *Greek Myths and Christian Mystery*. New York: Harper and Row, 1963.

Raimondi, Ezio. *Politica e commedia: Dal Beroaldo al Machiavelli*. Bologna: Mulino, 1972.

Rajna, Pio. *Le fonti dell'Orlando Furioso*. Florence: Sansoni, 1900.

Ramazzini, Bernardino. *Le malattie dei lavoratori (De morbis artificum diatriba)*. Edited by Francesco Carnevale. Rome: La Nuova Italia Scientifica, 1982.

Randolph, Charles. "The Mandragora of the Ancients in Folk-lore and Medicine." *Proceedings of the American Academy of Arts and Sciences* 40 (1905): 487–537.

Ranke-Heinemann, Uta. *Eunuchs for the Kingdom of Heaven: Women, Sexuality, and the Catholic Church*. New York: Doubleday, 1990.

Rapp, Richard Tilden. *Industry and Economic Decline in Seventeenth-Century Venice*. Cambridge: Harvard University Press, 1976.

Rebhorn, Wayne. *Foxes and Lions: Machiavelli's Confidence Men*. Ithaca: Cornell University Press, 1988.

Redi, Francesco. *Esperienze intorno alla generazione degli insetti.* In *Scienziati del Seicento*, edited by Maria Luisa Altieri Biagi and Bruno Basile. Milan: Ricciardi, 1980.

Reiner, William. "Sex Assignment in the Neonate with Intersex of Inadequate Genitalia." *Archives of Pediatric and Adolescent Medicine* 151 (1997): 1044–45.

Renzetti, Emanuela, and Rodolfo Taiani. "Le cure dell'amore: desiderio e passione in alcuni libri dei segreti." *Sanità, scienza e storia* 2 (1986): 33–86.

Riddle, John. *Eve's Herbs: A History of Contraception and Abortion in the West.* Cambridge: Harvard University Press, 1997.

Ridolfi, Roberto. "Composizione, rappresentazione e prima edizione della *Mandragola*." In *Studi sulle commedie di Machiavelli*. Pisa: Nistri-Lischi, 1968.

Rinaldi, Rinaldo "Le novelle-pretesto di Sebastiano Erizzo ovvero un'utopia mancata." In *Metamorfosi della novella*, edited by Giorgio Barberi Squarotti. Foggia: Bastogi, 1985.

Ringrose, Kathryn. "Living in the Shadow: Eunuchs and Gender in Byzantium." In *Third Sex, Third Gender: Beyond Sexual Dimorphism in Culture and History*, edited by Gilbert Herdt. New York: Zone Books, 1994.

———. "Passing the Test of Sanctity: Denial of Sexuality and Involuntary Castration." In *Desire and Denial in Byzantium*, edited by Liz James. Aldershot: Ashgate, 1999.

Rivière, Joan. "Femininity as a Masquerade." In *Formations of Fantasy*, edited by Victor Burgin, James Donald, and Cora Kaplan. London: Methuen, 1986.

Rocke, Michael. *Forbidden Friendships: Homosexuality and Male Culture in Renaissance Florence.* New York: Oxford University Press, 1996.

Rogers, Francis. "The Male Soprano." *Musical Quarterly* 5 (1919): 413–25.

Romei, Giovanni. *Inquisitori, esorcisti e streghe nell'Italia della Controriforma.* Florence: Sansoni, 1990.

Rosa, Salvatore. *Satire, liriche, lettere.* Edited by Anton Maria Salvini et al. Milan: Sonzogno, 1892.

Rosand, Ellen. *Opera in Seventeenth-Century Venice.* Berkeley and Los Angeles: University of California Press, 1992.

Rosselli, John. *Singers of Italian Opera: The History of a Profession.* Cambridge: Cambridge University Press, 1992.

Rossello, Timoteo. *Della summa de i secreti universali in ogni materia sì per huomini e donne di alto ingegno, come ancora per medici.* Venice: Miloco, 1619.

Rousselle, Aline. "Personal Status and Sexual Practice in the Roman Empire." In *Fragments for a History of the Human Body*, 3 vols., edited by Michel Feher. New York: Zone, 1989.

Ruffini, Franco. *Commedia e festa nel Rinascimento: La Calandria alla corte di Urbino.* Bologna: Mulino, 1986.

Ruggiero, Guido. *The Boundaries of Eros: Sex Crime and Sexuality in Renaissance Venice.* New York: Oxford University Press, 1985.

Ruscelli, Girolamo. *De secreti del R. D. Alessio Piemontese.* Venice: Bonsadino, 1611.

Russo, Luigi. *Machiavelli.* Bari: Laterza, 1949.

Saccardino, Costantino. *Libro nominato la verità di diverse cose, quale minutamente tratta di molte salutifere operazioni spagiriche et chimiche.* Bologna, n.p., 1621.

Salando, Fernando. *Trattato sopra li vermi, cause, differenze, pronostico e curatione.* Verona: n.p., 1607.

Sanchez, Tomas. *De sancto matrimonii sacramento disputationum.* Lyon: Rigaud, 1654.

Sannazaro, Jacopo. *De partu virginis.* Edited by Charles Fantazzi and Alessandro Perosa. Florence: Olschki, 1988.

Santore, Cathy. "Julia Lombardo, 'Somtuosa Meretrize:' A Portrait by Property." *Renaissance Quarterly* 41.1 (1988): 44–83.

Santori, Giacomo. "La questione del *verum semen.*" *Il diritto ecclesiastico* 82 (1971): 66–78.

Sanudo, Marin. *I diarii di Marin Sanudo (1496-1533).* 58 vols. Edited by Rinaldo Fulin et al. Venice: Visentini, 1879–1903.

Saslow, James. *Florentine Festivals as Theatrum Mundi: The Medici Wedding of 1589.* New Haven: Yale University Press, 1996.

Savonarola, Michele. *De urinis.* In *Practica Savonarolae de febribus.* Venice: Giunta, 1517.

———. *Practica major Jo Michaelis Savonarolae.* Venice: Giunta, 1559.

———. *Il trattato ginecologico-pediatrico in volgare.* Edited by Luigi Belloni. Milan: Stucchi, 1952.

———. *Trattato utilissimo di molte regole, per conservare la sanità, dichiarando qual cose siano utili da mangiare, e quali tristi, e medesimamente di quelle che si bevono in Italia.* Venice: Eredi di Gianni Paduano, 1554.

Schiebinger, Londa. *The Mind Has No Sex? Women in the Origins of Modern Science.* Cambridge: Harvard University Press, 1989.

———. *Nature's Body: Gender in the Making of Modern Science.* Boston: Beacon Press, 1993.

Schiesari, Juliana. *The Gendering of Melancholia: Feminism, Psychoanalysis, and the Symbolics of Loss in Renaissance Literature.* Ithaca: Cornell University Press, 1992.

———. "Libidinal Economies: Machiavelli and Fortune's Rape." In *Desire in the Renaissance: Psychoanalysis and Literature,* edited by Valeria Finucci and Regina Schwartz. Princeton: Princeton University Press, 1994.

Schleiner, Wilfred. "Infection and Cure through Women: Renaissance Constructions of Syphilis." *Journal of Medieval and Renaissance Studies* 24.3 (1994): 499–517.

Schor, Naomi. "Dreaming Dissymmetry: Barthes, Foucault, and Sexual Difference." In *Men in Feminism,* edited by Alice Jardine and Paul Smith. New York: Methuen, 1987.

Scott, Joan. *Gender and the Politics of History.* New York: Columbia University Press, 1988.

Sedgwick, Eve Kosofsky. *Between Men: English Literature and Male Homosocial Desire.* New York: Columbia University Press, 1985.

———. "Gosh, Boy George, You Must Be Awfully Secure in Your Masculinity." In *Constructing Masculinity,* edited by Maurice Berger, Brian Wallis, and Simon Watson. New York: Routledge, 1995.

Sercambi, Giovanni. *Novelle.* 2 vols. Edited by Giovanni Sinicropi. Bari: Laterza, 1972.

Serpetro, Nicolò. *Il mercato delle meraviglie della natura: Overo istoria naturale*. Venice: Tomasini, 1653.

Sforza, Caterina. *Ricettario di bellezza di Caterina Riario Sforza*. Edited by Luigi Pescasio. Verona: Wella italiana, 1971.

Shemek, Deanna. "Of Women, Knights, Arms, and Love: The *Querelle des Femmes* in Ariosto's Poem." *Modern Language Notes* 104 (1989): 68–97.

Sherr, Richard. "Guglielmo Gonzaga and the Castrati." *Renaissance Quarterly* 33 (1980): 33–56.

Silverman, Kaja. *The Acoustic Mirror: The Female Voice in Psychoanalysis and Cinema*. Bloomington: Indiana University Press, 1988.

Singer, Linda. "Bodies-Pleasures-Powers." *differences* 1.1 (1989): 45–65.

Sinibaldi, Giovanni Benedetto. *Geneanthropeiae sivi de hominis generatione decatheuchon, ubi ex ordine quaecumque ad humanae Gegnerationis liturgiam, ejusdem principia, organa, tempus, usum, modum, occasionem, voluptatem . . . adjecta est historia foetus mussipontani*. Frankfurt: Petri Zubrodt, 1669.

Siraisi, Nancy. *Avicenna in Renaissance Italy: The Canon and Medical Teaching in Italian Universities after 1500*. Chicago: University of Chicago Press, 1987.

———. "In Search of the Origins of Medicine: Egyptian Wisdom and Some Renaissance Physicians." In *Generation and Degeneration: Tropes of Reproduction in Literature and History from Ancient through Early Modern Europe*, edited by Valeria Finucci and Kevin Brownlee. Durham, N.C.: Duke University Press, 2001.

———. *Medieval and Early Renaissance Medicine: An Introduction to Knowledge and Practice*. Chicago: University of Chicago Press, 1990.

Smith, Bruce. *The Acoustic World of Early Modern England: Attending to the O-Factor*. Chicago: University of Chicago Press, 1999.

———. *Homosexual Desire in Shakespeare's England*. Chicago: University of Chicago Press, 1991.

Solerti, Angelo. *Le origini del melodramma*. Turin: Bocca, 1903.

———. *Le rime di Torquato Tasso*. 3 vols. Bologna: Romagnoli-dall'Acqua, 1900.

Soranus. *Gynecology (Gynmaeciorum libri IV)*. Translated by Owsei Temkin. Baltimore: Johns Hopkins University Press, 1956.

Sorella, Antonio. *Magia, lingua e commedia nel Machiavelli*. Florence: Olschki, 1990.

Sorkow, Harvey. *In re Baby M*. 525 A.2d 1128, 1164. (N.J. Super. 1987) (opinion of J. Harvey Sorkow).

Spallanzani, Lazzaro. "Osservazioni e sperienze intorno ai vermicelli spermatici." In *Opuscoli di fisica animale e vegetabile*. Modena: Società Tipografica, 1776.

Sperling, Melitta. "Spider Phobias and Spider Fantasies. A Clinical Contribution to the Study of Symbol and Symptom Choice." *Journal of the American Psychoanalytic Association* 19.3 (1971): 472–98.

Speroni, Sperone. "Dialogo del tempo di partorire delle donne." In *Opere*, 2 vols. Rome: Vecchiarelli, 1989.

Stallybrass, Peter. "Fetishizing Gender: Constructing the Hermaphrodite in Renaissance

Europe." In *Body Guards: The Cultural Politics of Gender Ambiguity*, edited by Julia Epstein and Kristina Straub. New York: Routledge, 1991.

———. "Transvestism and the 'Body Beneath': Speculating on the Boy Actor." In *Erotic Politics: Desire on the Renaissance Stage*, edited by Susan Zimmerman. New York: Routledge, 1992.

Stannard, Katherine, and Richard Kay, eds. *Herbs and Herbalism in the Middle Ages and the Renaissance*. Aldershot: Ashgate, 1999.

Stella, Pietro. "Strategie familiari e celibato sacro in Italia tra '600 e '700." *Salesianum* 41 (1979): 73–109.

Stephens, Walter. "Tasso's Heliodorus and the World of Romance." In *The Search for the Ancient Novel*, edited by James Tatum. Baltimore: Johns Hopkins University Press, 1994.

———. "Witches Who Steal Penises: Impotence and Illusion." *Journal of Medieval and Early Modern Studies* 28 (1998): 495–529.

Sterba, Richard. "On Spiders, Hanging and Oral Sadism." *American Imago* 7 (1950): 21–28.

Stevenson, Walter. "The Rise of Eunuchs in Greco-Roman Antiquity." *Journal of the History of Sexuality* 5 (1995): 495–51.

Stewart, Pamela. *Retorica e Mimica nel Decameron e nella commedia del Cinquecento*. Florence: Olschki, 1986.

Stoller, Robert. *Presentations of Gender*. New Haven: Yale University Press, 1985.

Straparola, Giovan Francesco. *Piacevoli notti*. In *Novelle italiane: Il Cinquecento*, edited by Marcello Ciccuto. Milan: Garzanti, 1982.

Sumberg, Theodore. "La *Mandragola*: An Interpretation." *Journal of Politics* 23 (1961): 320–40.

Taruffi, Cesare. *Storia della teratologia*. Bologna: Regia Tipografia, 1881.

Tasso, Torquato. *The Creation of the World*. Translated by Joseph Tusiani. Binghamton: State University of New York, Medieval and Early Renaissance Texts and Studies, 1982.

———. *Dubbi e risposte intorno ad alcune cose e parole concernenti alla Gerusalemme liberata*. In *Appendice alle opere in prosa di Torquato Tasso*, edited by Angelo Solerti. Florence: Successori Le Monnier, 1892.

———. *Gerusalemme liberata*. Edited by Anna Maria Carini. Milan: Feltrinelli, 1961.

———. *Jerusalem Delivered*. Edited by Ralph Nash. Detroit: Wayne State University Press, 1987.

———. *Lettere*. 2 vols. Edited by Cesare Guasti. Florence: Le Monnier, 1901.

———. "Il messaggiero." In *Dialoghi*, edited by Bruno Basile. Milan: Mursia, 1991.

———. *Il mondo creato*. In *Le opere*, edited by Bruno Maier, vol. 4 of 5 vols. Milan: Rizzoli, 1964.

Taviani, Ferdinando. *La commedia dell'arte e la società barocca: La fascinazione del teatro*. Rome: Bulzoni, 1969.

———. *Il segreto della commedia dell'arte: La memoria delle compagnie italiane del XVI, XVII e XVIII secolo*. Florence: Usher, 1982.

Thomasset, Claude. "La Femme au moyen age: Les composantes fondamentales de sa ré-presentation: immunité-impunité." *Ornicar?* 22–23 (1981): 223–38.

Thompson, Charles. *The Mystic Mandrake*. New York: University Books, 1968.

Thorndike, Lynn. *A History of Magic and Experimental Science*. 8 vols. New York: Columbia University Press, 1941.

Todd, Dennis. *Imagining Monsters: Miscreations of the Self in Eighteenth-Century England*. Chicago: University of Chicago Press, 1995.

Tommasi, Francesco. *Reggimento del padre di famiglia*. Florence: Marescotti, 1580.

Tornielli, Agostino. *Annales sacri, et ex profanis praecipui, ad orbe condito ad eumdem Christi passione redemptum*. 2 vols. Antwerp: Moretum, 1620.

Traub, Valerie. *Desire and Anxiety: Circulations of Desire in Shakespearean Drama*. New York: Routledge, 1992.

———. "The Psychomorphology of the Clitoris; Or, the Reemergence of the *Tribade* on English Culture." In *Generation and Degeneration: Literature and Tropes of Reproduction in Literature and History from Antiquity to Early Modern Europe*, edited by Valeria Finucci and Kevin Brownlee. Durham, N.C.: Duke University Press, 2001.

Trotula of Salerno. *The Disease of Women (De mulierum passionibus)*. Translated by Elizabeth Mason-Hohl. Los Angeles: Ward Ritchie Press, 1940.

Trumbach, Randolph. "The Birth of the Queen: Sodomy and the Emergence of Gender Equality in Modern Culture, 1660–1750." In *Hidden from History: Reclaiming the Gay and Lesbian Past*, edited by Martin Dauml Duberman, Martha Vicinus, and George Chauncey Jr. New York: New American Library, 1989.

Tuana, Nancy. *The Less Noble Sex: Scientific, Religious, and Philosophical Conceptions of Woman's Nature*. Bloomington: Indiana University Press, 1993.

Uberti da Cesena, Grazioso. *Contrasto musico. Opera dilettevole*. Rome: Ludovico Grigniani, 1630.

Valenti, Cristina. *Comici artigiani: mestiere e forme dello spettacolo a Siena nella prima metà del Cinquecento*. Ferrara: Panini, 1990.

Vallisnieri, Antonio. "Riflessioni intorno la maniera sinora creduta del nascere degl'insetti." In *Opere fisico-mediche*. Venice: Sebastiano Coleti, 1733.

Valverde, Giovanni. *Anatomia del corpo humano*. Rome: Salamanca et Lafréri, 1560.

Varchi, Benedetto. *Lezzione . . . sopra la generazione de' mostri, e se sono intesi dalla natura, o no*. In *Lezioni di M. Benedetto Varchi*. Florence: Giunta, 1590.

Varolio, Constantino. *Anatomicae, sive de resolutione corporis humani libri IIII*. Frankfurt: Wechel and Rischer, 1591.

Vernant, Jean Pierre. *Myth and Society in Ancient Greece*. Translated by Janet Lloyd. Brighton: Harvester Press, 1980.

Vesalius, Andreas. *Observationum anatomicarum Gabrielis Fallopii examen*. Venice: Francesco de' Franceschini da Siena, 1564.

———. *On the Fabric of the Human Body*. Translated by William Richardson. San Francisco: Norman, 1998.

———. *Tabulae anatomicae*. In *The Illustrations from the Works of Andreas Vesalius of Brussels*, edited by J. B. de C. M. Saunders and Charles O'Malley. Cleveland: World Publishing, 1950.

Watts, Sheldon. *Epidemics and History: Disease, Power and Imperialism.* New Haven: Yale University Press, 1997.

Wittkower, Rudolph. "Marvels of the East: A Study in the History of Monsters." *Journal of the Warburg and Courtauld Institutes* 5 (1942): 159–97.

Zacchia, Paolo. *Quaestiones medico-legales.* Lyon: Huguetan and Ravaud, 1661.

Zambelli, Paola. "Le Problème de la magie naturelle à la Renaissance." In *Magia, astrologia e religione nel Rinascimento.* Warsaw: Accademia Polacca delle scienze, 1972.

———. "Topi o Topoi?" In *Cultura popolare e cultura dotta nel Seicento,* edited by Paolo Rossi et al. Milan: Franco Angeli, 1993.

Zatti, Sergio. *Il Furioso fra epos e romanzo.* Lucca: Pacini Fazzi, 1990.

———. *L'uniforme cristiano e il multiforme pagano: Saggio sulla Gerusalemme liberata.* Milan: Saggiatore, 1983.

Zayika Hanafi. *The Monster in the Machine: Magic, Medicine, and the Marvelous in the Time of the Scientific Revolution.* Durham, N.C.: Duke University Press, 2000.

Žižek, Slavoj. *Enjoy Your Symptom: Jacques Lacan in Hollywood and Out.* New York: Routledge, 1992.

———. *The Sublime Object of Ideology.* London: Verso, 1989.

Zorzi, Ludovico. *L'attore, la commedia, il drammaturgo.* Turin: Einaudi, 1990.

INDEX

Abortifacients, 45, 59

Abortion, 24

Abraham, Karl, 102

Achillini, Alessandro, 14n

Actors, 82n, 194–200, 203–6, 207n, 221, 228, 256n, 257–59

Actresses, 231–33

Adelman, Janet, 14n

Ademollo, Alessandro, 232–33n, 237n, 259n

Adriani, Marcello Virgilio, 93

Africanus, Leo, 219

Agrippa, Cornelius, 51

Alberti, Leon Battista, 106n

Alciati, Andrea, 136, 269

Alderotti, Taddeo, 13

Aldrovandi, Ulisse, 68–69, 134n, 136, 138, 146n

Alvarez, Francisco, 124n, 144n, 147n

Amenorrhea, 22. See also Menstruation

Andreini, Giovan Battista, 214n, 259

Andrews, Richard, 81n, 195n, 197n

Angelini, Massimo, 53n, 60n, 139n

Angelini Bontempi, Giovanni Andrea, 245

Anglicus, Bartholomaeus, 96

Apollonio, Mario, 231n

Aquilecchia, Giovanni, 92, 97–98

Aquinas, Thomas, 18n, 72, 255, 270

Arachnophobia. See Spiders

Arachnid fantasies. See Tarantism

Archenholtz, Johan, 242

Archilei, Vittoria, 229, 233

Aretaeus of Cappadocia, 168

Aretino, Pietro, 4, 164, 169n, 221n

Arias, Francisco, 231n

Ariosto, Ludovico, 30, 32, 55, 57, 67, 125, 160–88, 195, 200, 214, 237. See also Orlando furioso

Aristotle: and eunuchs, 28, 247; and generation, 7, 9–11, 15, 20, 23, 25, 42n, 50, 51n, 54, 60, 72, 107, 121, 128–30, 143, 146, 209, 215, 244, 266, 267; and pneuma, 25, 50

Arnaldus of Villanova, 207

Ascoli, Albert, 67n

Augustine, 18n, 72–73, 76, 133, 144, 219, 268, 271n

Averroes, 72

Avicenna, 7, 20, 72, 107

Baby M, 80–82, 92

Bairo, Piero, 19, 24

Balatri, Filippo, 226, 239n, 262n

Balzac, Honoré, 241n, 277

Bandello, Matteo, 30–31, 41, 58, 62, 89, 253, 256–57

Barbagli, Marzio, 29n, 120n, 230n

Barberi-Squarotti, Giorgio, 171n

Barbier, Patrick, 230n, 239n, 247n, 251, 273n

Barbirato, Giorgio, 161n, 164n

Barthes, Roland, 244, 277

Bartholin, Thomas, 53

Basile, Adriana, 233

Basile, Bruno, 49n, 144

Battaglia Terme, 48n, 217

Baudrillard, Jean, 77–78n

Beauty: in men, 155n, 162–63, 171–77; in women, 21, 82, 111, 125, 151, 172, 173

Beckett, Samuel, 95n

Beer, Marina, 161n

Behn, Aphra, 150

Bell, Rudolph, 10n, 57n

Bellamy, Elizabeth, 155n, 175n

Benedetti, Alessandro, 212

Berardi, Antonio Maria, 262

Berengario da Carpi, Jacopo, 14, 42, 60

Berriot-Salvadore, Evelyne, 212

Bianconi, Lorenzo, 228, 259

Bibbiena (Angelo Dovizi) 6, 30, 33, 169, 184, 190–223. See also *Calandria*

Biondo, Michelangelo, 97

Birth. *See* Generation

Blaze, Castil, 234

Blondel, James, 136

Blood, 14n, 15, 26, 47–50, 70, 102, 131

Blumenfeld-Kosinski, Renate, 132n

Boccaccio, Giovanni, 30, 62, 65–66, 84, 111n, 161n, 167n, 179, 194n, 207

Boiardo, Matteo, 138, 166n

Bolognetti, Giovanni, 267–68

Boose, Lynda, 151–52

Boswell, John, 254n

Botteri, Inge, 20n

Bracciolini, Poggio, 66

Bragaglia, Anton Giulio, 232n, 259n, 262n, 276n, 278n

Brockbank, William, 9n

Brower, Gary, 240n, 247n, 256n

Brownlee, Marina, 137n

Bruno, Giordano, 74–75, 222

Bullough, Vern, 10n; and Bonnie Bullough, 260n

Burney, Charles, 238n

Burshatin, Israel, 213n

Butler, Judith, 3n, 208, 220

Caccini, Francesca, 233

Caccini, Giulio, 235, 236n

Caccini, Margherita, 233

Cadden, Joan, 216n, 218n, 261n

Calandria (La), 6, 30, 190–223. *See also* Bibbiena

Camillo, Giulio, 70

Campanella, Tommaso, 55, 58, 76, 96–97, 101n, 129, 139, 143, 212, 249

Campeggi, Ridolfo, 71

Camporesi, Piero, 28n, 31, 40, 43n, 66, 77, 93, 95n, 249n, 251n

Canal, Pietro, 234n, 265n

Canale, Florian, 176

Canossa, Romano, 214n, 222n, 272n

Capra, Galeazzo Flavio, 53–54

Cardano, Gerolamo, 17, 59, 74

Carnival, 53, 200, 259, 276

Carter, Tim, 229n, 232n, 236n

Casanova, Giacomo, 210, 241, 275, 276

Casserio, Giulio, 244

Castiglione, Baldassarre, 11–12, 20, 101, 104n, 105, 172, 173n, 190n, 196

Castracani, Castruccio, 84, 117

Castrati, 5, 6, 34–36, 208, 210–11, 226–30, 233–47, 253–79

Castration: practice, 5, 6, 238–39, 245–57; psychoanalytical and metaphorical, 30, 33–34, 98–99, 102, 104, 108, 110–11, 115, 117, 125–26, 151, 174n, 179–81, 186, 200, 208, 211, 273–74, 277; real (bilateral

orchiectomy) 36, 227, 245–46, 249–
57, 260–77. *See also* Castrati; Eunuchs;
Testicles

Castro, Antonio Arjona, 237n

Catamenia. See Menstruation

Céard, Jean, 144

Cecchi, Domenico (Cecchino de Castris, Il
Cortona), 250, 262, 275

Celletti, Rodolfo, 235n

Celsus, Cornelius, 8n, 39n, 248

Cesalpino, Andrea, 74

Chojnacki, Stanley (1), 147

Chojnacki, Stanley (2), 29n, 120n, 207n

Cicero, 133

Cipolla, Bartolomeo, 269

Circumcision, 218n, 227, 243, 251n, 253;
female (clitoridectomy), 145–46, 219,
243, 251n

Clark, Elizabeth, 80n

Clement IX. *See* Rospigliosi, Giulio

Clementi, Filippo, 199n

Clitoridectomy. *See* Circumcision: female

Clitoris, 14n, 19n, 102–5n, 210, 219, 273–
74

Cocco, E., 197

Codronchi, Giovan Battista, 27n, 44n

Cohn, Samuel, 249n

Coke, Edward, 167n

Colombo, Realdo, 14n, 16n, 23n, 97, 105n,
132n, 218, 247n, 267n

Conception. *See* Pregnancy; Sexual intercourse; Womb

Corago (Il), 258

Corbiau, Gérard, 5n

Cornaro, Alvise, 169n

Corruption. *See* Putrefaction; Worms

Cortese, Isabella, 48n, 266n

Crawford, Patricia, 22n

Cremonini, Cesare, 13

Cressy, David, 59n

Croce, Giulio Cesare, 27n

Cross-dressing, 3–6, 33, 45, 191–92, 200–
209, 217, 221, 237

Cuckoldry, 29, 32, 166, 176

Daciano, Giuseppe, 33

Dame, Joke, 248n

D'Amico, Jack, 91n, 197

Da Molin, Giovanna, 230n

D'Anania, Lorenzo, 144n

D'Ancillon (C. D'Ollincan), 262, 278

D'Ancona, Alessandro, 61n, 197–98n

Dante, 11, 75, 229

Da Porto, Luigi, 30

Darmon, Pierre, 139n, 264–65

Daston, Lorraine, 216–17n

d'Auvermont, Magdeleine, 52

Davidson, Nicholas, 271n

da Vinci, Leonardo, 14–15n, 109n, 129

De Conches, Guglielmo, 22

Delaney, Carol, 80

Della Casa, Giovanni, 97, 106

Della Mirandola, Pico, 105

Della Porta, Giambattista, 17, 18–19n, 45n,
56, 68, 71–72, 87, 139

Della Terza, Dante, 148n

Del Panta, Lorenzo, 230n

De Martino, Ernesto, 100, 109n

Dentice, Luigi, 234n

De Sepulveda, Juan Ginés, 73

De Sommi, Leone, 198

De Villanova, Arnaldus, 176

Devils, 64–65, 146, 214, 272

De Zayas, Maria, 137n, 163

De Zerbis, Gabriele, 60

Di Conti, Nicolò, 244–45

Dionisotti, Carlo, 190n

Dioscorides, 93–94

Dissection, 9n, 13, 14n, 23n, 28n

Domenichi, Lodovico, 18, 52, 55n, 135

Donato, Luciano, 217n

Doni, Giovanni Battista, 239n

Doubling, 175, 182, 192. *See also* Twins

Duchartre, Louis, 198n

Durling, Robert, 8n

Empedocles, 209

Epstein, Julia, 217n

Erizzo, Sebastiano, 61–62

Ethiopia, 32, 57, 74, 121–22, 125n, 129, 136, 143–56

Ethiopians. *See* Ethiopia

Eunuchs, 28, 122, 149n, 153, 208, 234–35, 240, 244–47, 250–51, 254n, 255–57, 260–61, 263, 267, 269, 277–78; "natural" eunuchs (Reifenstein's syndrome), 242–43, 249. *See also* Castrati

Evirati. *See* Castrati

Falloppio, Gabriele, 14n, 17n, 19, 46, 97, 105n, 135n, 268

Family structures, 28–29, 120, 255, 263–64

Farinelli (Carlo Broschi), 5n, 239n, 254n

Fausto-Sterling, Anne, 242n

Favorinus, 243n, 261

Ferguson, Margaret, 153n

Fermentation, 36, 47, 69. *See also* Putrefaction

Ferroni, Giulio, 91n, 193n, 202n

Festa Campanile, Pasquale, 208

Ficino, Marsilio, 20, 47, 134

Filipczaz, Zirka, 10n

Filmer, Robert, 80

Finucci, Valeria, 7n, 14, 64n, 141–42n, 148n, 166n, 173n, 175n, 204n

Fioravanti, Leonardo, 24, 48n, 56, 210, 249, 251n

Firenzuola, Angelo, 40, 54n, 172

Flaumenhaft, Mera, 83n, 91n

Folengo, Teofilo, 40

Fontaguzzi, Giuliano, 261n

Fonte, Moderata, 64, 68n, 88n

Foucault, Michel, 35n, 120–21, 217n, 264, 265n, 277

Foundling, 84, 117, 156, 233

Fracastoro, Girolamo, 46, 250

Franceschetti, Antonio, 164, 184n

French, Roger, 9n

Freud, Sigmund: and castration, 34, 98, 102, 110–11, 176, 180, 211, 227, 244n, 272–74, 277; and family, 120, 151; and narcissism, 109, 175; and Oedipal logic, 108, 110, 154, 179, 186; sexuality, 15n, 181; and the uncanny, 202, 211

Galen, 8, 11, 13n, 16, 31, 50, 98–99, 128, 135, 168, 207, 209, 212, 216, 247, 267, 271

Galilei, Celeste, 43

Galli Stampino, Maria, 229n

Garber, Marjorie, 17n

Gareffi, Andrea, 184n

Garzoni, Tommaso, 42, 45n, 55, 64, 65, 70, 115n, 134n, 238–39

Gélis, Jacques, 134–35n

Gelli, Giovan Battista, 22

Generation, 2, 12; anal, 40, 57, 41; bestial, 56–65; from blood, 39; from ear, 41; from leg, 39; from *molae*, 53; from putrefaction, 56, 68–75; from snow, 40, 70n; from sperm donor and noncoital, 81–83, 117, 151; from spilled or discarded semen, 41–44, 66–67; from wind, 51, 52n; in dream, 52–53; influenced by maternal imagination, 123–24, 134–42, 151; panspermic, 44, 50–53; spontaneous generation, 25, 31, 49n, 68–69, 72–77; without women, 39, 66–67, 70–73

Genua, Marco Antonio, 132

Gerbino, Giuseppe, 235n

Germain, Marie (Germaine Garnier), 6, 243

Gerusalemme liberata, 30, 32, 121–28, 143,

147–57, 203, 240. *See also* Tasso, Torquato

Getto, Giovanni, 150

Gilino, Corradino, 101

Ginzburg, Carlo, 31, 44n, 70, 164n

Gioberti, Lorenzo (Laurant Joubert), 56–57, 98–99, 138n, 168

Girard, René, 152n, 170

Gl'ingannati, 3, 4, 195, 196n, 204, 222

Gl'Intronati. See *Gl'ingannati*

Gliozzi, Giuliano, 73–74n, 136n

Gloyne, Howard, 100

Goethe, Johan Wolfgang, 258

Goldstein, Robert, 36n

Gollaher, David, 251n

Gonorrhea. *See* Syphilis

Gonzaga, Guglielmo, 232, 234, 257, 265

Gonzaga, Vincenzo, 198n, 232, 233n

Gozzi, Carlo, 95

Grazzini, Anton Francesco (Il Lasca), 86n, 200, 252–53

Green, Monica, 8n

Greenblatt, Stephen, 10n, 201, 217n

Gregory XIV, 44

Gregory of Tours, 251n

Grendler, Paul, 44n, 61n

Grosrichard, Alain, 138n, 140n

Grubb, James, 217n

Guainerio, Antonio, 17–18, 20, 23, 87, 131

Guarini, Giambattista, 198

Gunsberg, Maggie, 206

Hammond, Frederick, 260–61n

Handsomeness. *See* Beauty

Hanson, Ann, 16n

Harpies, 56, 57

Heat. *See* Humors

Hegel, Friedrich, 137

Heliodorus, 30, 148

Herdt, Gilbert, 40n

Heriot, Angus, 234n

Hermaphrodites, 16n, 32, 34, 190, 215; and sex, 54–55, 102n, 105, 213–19, 223, 241n, 242, 245

Hermaphroditism. *See* Hermaphrodites

Herophilus, 267n

Hill, John, 51–52n, 70n

Hippocrates. *See* Hippocratics

Hippocratics, 7–8, 11, 24, 45n, 140, 146, 267n

Homer, 63

Homosexuality, 18, 108, 125n, 167, 170, 211, 221–22, 249–50, 260n, 264, 271n, 276

Homunculus, 69–70, 73, 95n

Horowitz, Maryanne, 10n

Huarte, Juan, 16n, 63, 136, 141n, 151, 207, 212, 240

Huet, Marie-Hélène, 121n, 142n

Humors, 6, 11, 13, 15n, 26, 47, 55, 96–97, 105, 135, 176, 212–13, 242–43, 247

Hypermasculinity, 165–70

Hysteria, 177–78, 182, 185

Imagination. *See* Generation: influenced by maternal imagination

Imperiali, Giovanni, 58

Impotence, 86, 267n; and the devil, 213–14, 278

Infertility. *See* Sterility

Infibulation: female, 219; male, 247–48

Inghirami, Tommaso, 197–98

Innocent III, 269

Innocent XI, 262

Intermedi, 228, 235, 258n

Irigaray, Luce, 170, 272

Isidore of Seville, 128, 133, 143

Ivanovich, Cristoforo, 228n

Jacquart, Danielle, 9n, 16n, 23n, 50n, 97, 101n, 104n, 168n

Javitch, Daniel, 161n, 165n
Jones, Ann Rosalind, 217
Jordan, Constance, 51n
Juvenal, 277

Keiser, Dorothy, 233
Kirkendale, Warren, 232n
Kirshner, Julius, 207n
Klapisch-Zuber, Christiane, 29n
Kristeva, Julia, 142n, 156, 177n, 240
Kuefler, Martin, 39n, 263n
Kuen, Thomas, 29n, 120n

Lacan, Jacques, 7, 34, 111, 155, 166n, 167,
    184–87, 272, 275
Lafitau, Joseph-François, 136
La Fontaine, Jean, 163
Landucci, Luca, 132n
Laplanche, Jean, 179
Laqueur, Thomas, 9n, 12n, 14n, 55n, 105n,
    106–7, 138n, 146n, 217n, 219n, 273
Larivaille, Paul, 127n
La Torre, Felice, 9n, 39n, 105n
Latour, Bruno, 2
Lavarda, Sergio, 29n
Law: and dowries, 29; and generation, 28,
    263–71; and inheritance, 29
Lazar, Lance, 41n
Le Cat, Nicholas, 137
Lemay, Helen, 10n, 17n, 86n
Leprosy, 101
Liceti, Giuseppe, 133n
Liceto, Fortunio, 134n, 143n
Little, Ralph, 99
Livy, 91, 111n
Loraux, Nicole, 66
Lucian, 39
Luther, Martin: and Philip Melanchton, 133

MacGrath, Aidan, 263n, 268n, 271n
Machiavelli, Niccolò, 18, 30, 32, 45, 80–

117, 169, 178, 195n, 198n, 200. See also
    Mandragola, La
Maclean, Ian, 9n, 13n, 135
Magnus, Albertus, 9, 51, 86, 89n, 98–99,
    130, 216
Maimonides, Moses, 218
Maiorano, Gaetano, 262n
Malespini, Celio, 56, 132n
Malizia, Enrico, 44n, 266n
Malleus Maleficarum, 64n, 213-14, 272–73n
Malpighi, Marcello, 15, 49n
Mandragola, La (The Mandrake), 32, 45,
    81–117. See also Machiavelli, Niccolò
Mandragora. See Mandrake
Mandrake, 83, 88–98, 92–96, 103–4, 108,
    176
Marchesi, Luigi, 262n
Marinella, Lucrezia, 206n
Marinello, Giovanni, 17, 20, 24, 42n, 140,
    151, 266–67
Marino, Giambattista, 5, 228
Martin, Dale, 26, 169n, 173n
Martin, Helen, 10n
Martin, Ruth, 44n
Martinelli, Caterina, 233
Martinez, Ronald, 88n, 91n
Martini, Gabriele, 4n, 222n
Masochism, 178, 276
Massa, Niccolò, 10, 18, 102, 107n
Matazone da Caligano, 40
Matrix. See Womb
Mattioli, Pietro, 94, 100
McClary, Susan, 237n
McLaren, Angus, 12n, 16n, 21n
Melancholia, 15n, 94, 154, 168, 176, 181–82,
    206–7, 220n, 226
Melicow, Meyes, 260
Menaechmi, 193, 197, 202
Menstruation, 10, 20, 22, 23n, 36, 76, 90,
    96, 98, 135n, 138n, 168; and conception,
    20–21, 56, 130–31; and phobias, 22, 27, 36

Mercuriale, Girolamo, 48, 100, 109n
Mercurio, Girolamo, 21, 45, 141, 213, 266
Midwives, 23, 45, 132. *See also* Menstruation; Pregnancy
Migiel, Marilyn, 149n
Milk, 14n, 26, 27, 46; animal milk, 153–54n
Miscegenation, 25, 32, 60
Mohlo, Anthony, 207n
Molae, 36, 53–54, 56, 138
Molza, Tarquinia, 232
Monsters, 25, 44, 62, 68, 98, 121–22, 129–38, 144–53, 211
Monstrosity. *See* Monsters
Monstrous femininity, 57, 124, 127, 134, 144, 150
Montaigne, Michel de, 279
Montesquieu, Charles, 241n, 276n
Monteverdi, Claudio, 229, 234n, 236
Moreschi, Alessandro, 227n, 247n
Morlini, Girolamo, 54
Mulvey, Laura, 174n, 274–75
Munro, Alexander, 13n
Mussato, Albertino, 62

Narcissism, 33, 105, 109, 114, 155n, 163, 169, 173–77, 183–86, 202, 220, 273
Newcomb, Anthony, 231n
Newman, Lawrence, 102n
Nicander of Colaphon, 93
Niccoli, Ottavia, 23n, 60n, 80n, 99n, 131–33n
Nicholson, Eric, 199n
Noonan, John, 49n, 270n

Olivo, Ippolito, 265
Orchiectomy. *See* Castration
Orgasm, 14–17, 25, 36, 47, 89
Orgel, Stephen, 198n
Orlando furioso, 30, 33, 57, 67, 160–88, 203. *See also* Ariosto, Ludovico
Ottonelli, Giovan Domenico, 199n, 231n
Ovid, 50, 62n, 67n, 160, 218

Padoan, Giorgio, 91n, 193–200n
Paleotti, Gabriele, 136
Pallavicino, Ferrante, 57
Papal Bulls, 35, 41n, 44, 231, 232, 235n
Parabosco, Girolamo, 195, 221n
Paracelsus, 8n, 18n, 44, 61, 69–73, 107, 134–35
Pardo, Mary, 164n, 173n
Paré, Ambroise, 6n, 56–59, 64, 131, 134–35, 140, 151, 209, 216, 219, 246, 251–52
Parini, Giuseppe, 278–79
Park, Katharine, 86n, 134n, 216–17n, 219
Parker, Geoffrey: and Lesley Smith, 230n
Parronchi, Antonio, 83n, 103n
Pasqualigo, Zaccaria, 243
Pasteur, Louis, 2, 36
Penis, 13, 17, 20, 35, 54–55, 89, 102, 106, 108, 113, 167, 204, 207, 211–19, 223, 242n, 244–52, 266n, 272–73; cures for penis-related problems, 248, 250–51; penectomy, 251–52; penis envy, 102n, 111, 112
Peri, Jacopo, 229–30, 232n
Perocco, Daria, 89–90
Persio, Antonio, 140–41, 151
Peschel, Enid, and Richard, 246n, 260n
Peter of Abano, 260–61n
Petronio, Alessandro, 48
Phallic mother, 108, 110
Phallus, 33, 54, 108, 110, 154, 169, 177, 207, 272, 275
Piccolomini, Alessandro, 195, 221n
Pico della Mirandola, Gianfrancesco, 42
Pinto-Correia, Clara, 49n
Pio, Emilia, 12
Pirrotta, Nino, 229n
Pisetzki, Rosita Levi, 4n
Pitkin, Hanna, 85, 91n
Platina (Bartolomeo Sacchi), 48
Plato, 168
Plautus, 193–94

Pliny, 39, 55n, 59, 138n, 173n

Pneuma, 25, 26, 50

Poliziano, Angelo, 39n, 228

Pollution, 26, 46, 57, 73, 77, 98–101. *See also*
    Fermentation; Putrefaction; Worms

Pomata, Gianna, 14n, 131n

Pomponazzi, Pietro, 64, 73, 133n

Pontano, Giovanni, 100

Povoledo, Elena, 229n

Pregnancy: aided by baths, 85; fanciful,
    39–42; male pregnancy, 38; panspermic,
    44, 50–53. *See also* Semen; Sexual inter-
    course; Urine; Uterus; Womb

Prierio, Sylvester, 64

Primal scene, 179

Prostate, 14n, 246, 260n

Prostheses, 6, 190, 205, 208–11, 214

Prostitutes, 4, 57, 106, 113, 170, 193, 199n,
    265n, 272n

Putrefaction, 6, 25–27, 31, 36–38, 47, 49, 58,
    68–77, 97

Quint, David, 115n, 124n, 144n, 147n

Quintilian, 260

Rabelais, François, 41

Ramponi, Virginia, 233n

Randolph, Charles, 93–94, 95n

Ranke-Heinemann, Uta, 45n, 51n, 132n,
    271n

Rapp, Richard, 230n

Rebhorn, Wayne, 88n

Redi, Francesco, 49

Reguardati, Benedetto, 168–69

Renzetti, Emanuela, 19n

Riddle, John, 59n

Ridolfi, Roberto, 81n

Ringrose, Kathy, 234n, 255n

Rivière, Joan, 33n, 166n

Rocke, Michael, 167n, 221, 222n, 249n,
    276n

Romano, Giulio, 164

Romei, Giovanni, 44n

Rosa, Salvatore, 226, 256

Rosand, Ellen, 236n

Rospigliosi, Giulio, 259

Rosselli, John, 231–37n, 253n

Rossello, Timoteo, 48, 248

Rousselle, Aline, 246n

Ruggiero, Guido, 167n, 222n, 249n, 265,
    276n

Ruscelli, Girolamo, 19, 248

Russo, Luigi, 91n

Ruzante (Angelo Beolco), 195, 253

Saccardino, Costantino, 71

Salernitano, Masuccio, 30

Saliceto (da), Guglielmo, 248–49

Sanchez, Tomas, 264

Sannazaro, Jacopo, 41

Sanudo, Marin, 199n

Sassonia, Ercole, 73, 145

Savonarola, Michele, 9, 16, 18–21, 87, 96,
    100, 266n

Scaglione, Aldo, 161n

Schiebinger, Londa, 9n, 12–13n, 40n, 266n

Schiesari, Juliana, 114, 153n

Schnapp, Jeffrey, 84

Schor, Naomi, 277

Scoglio, Egidio, 197n

Scott, Joan, 3n

Sedgwick, Eve, 170, 250n

Seed. *See* Semen

Segal, Eric, 202n

Semen: female, 14–16, 50, 52n, 63, 104, 107,
    128, 270–71; male, 10–16, 20, 26, 35–36,
    43, 47, 50, 57, 69–70, 73, 76, 83–85, 104,
    107, 128–29, 168, 216, 245, 263, 266–72;
    sperm donor, 81, 84; third seed, 209

Senesino (Francesco Bernardi), 278

Sercambi, Giovanni, 161n

Serpents. *See* Snakes

Serpetro, Niccolò, 38

Sexual intercourse: and abstinence, 20, 23, 168, 173n; anal sex, 18n, 66, 260–61n; and baby's sex, 16, 19, 21, 42n, 129–31; and conception, 15–23; and concoctions, 17–24; and dietary recommendations, 17–21, 266n; and disease, 46; and foreplay, 16–18; and herbals, 18–19, 24, 88; and the law, 28, 263–71; and menstruation, 22, 130–31; and orgasm, 19; and pollution, 26–27, 47; and positions, 15–19; and power of imagination, 25, 32–34, 135–42; resulting in man's "pregnancy," 39, 65–67; and timing, 15, 20, 88; violent or excessive, 20, 89, 130, 168; with animals, 59; with devils, 64–65, 213, 214, 272

Sforza, Caterina, 27n

Shakespeare, William, 38, 95, 125n, 168

Shemek, Deanna, 166n

Sherr, Richard, 234n, 238–39n, 265n

Siface (Giovanni Francesco Grossi), 261–62

Silverman, Kaja, 154n

Silvius, Jacobus, 26n, 267n

Sinatti D'Amico, Franca, 44n

Siraisi, Nancy, 8–9n, 13n, 39n

Sixtus V, 44–45, 231, 235, 263–64, 269, 271n, 272n

Smith, Bruce, 198n, 222n

Snakes, 56, 68–69, 75, 94; women fed on snakes, 98–99

Sodomy, 66. See also Homosexuality; Sexual intercourse

Solerti, Angelo, 126n, 226n, 229n

Soranus, 8, 16, 140

Sorella, Antonio, 92n, 103n

Sorkow, Harvey, 80–81, 116

Sorlisi, Domenico, 262

Soul, 45n, 74, 132

Spacciani, Cesare, 263

Spackman, Barbara, 114

Spadones. See Castrati

Spallanzani, Lazzaro, 49

Sperling, Melitta, 102n

Sperm. See Semen

Speroni, Sperone, 21n, 41–42

Spiders, 99–104, 108; spider woman, 32, 98, 103–4, 108

Stallybrass, Peter, 34, 205, 217n

Stella, Pietro, 255n

Stephens, Walter, 148n, 214n

Sterility, 22n, 35, 86, 178; female, 24, 85, 94–96, 244n

Stewart, Philip, 277n

Stoller, Robert, 102n, 274

Straparola, Giovan Francesco, 63–64

Sumberg, Theodore, 83n, 112

Sumptuary legislation, 5, 29, 44n, 106

Syphilis, 46, 89, 101, 145, 168n, 250, 255

Taiani, Rodolfo, 19n

Tarabotti, Arcangela, 4n

Tarantella dance, 32, 101

Tarantism, 99–104

Tasso, Torquato, 30, 32, 58, 68, 75, 76, 95, 114, 116, 121–57, 240. See also Gerusalemme liberata

Taviani, Ferdinando, 155n, 231n

Tenducci, Giusto, 241, 263n

Testes. See Testicles

Testicles, 14, 35, 85, 107, 211–13, 239, 241–43, 245–54, 256, 260, 263–69, 272–73; women's "testes," 13–14, 105, 107, 267n, 269, 271

Thomasset, Claude, 9n, 16n, 23n, 50n, 97, 101n, 104n, 168n

Thompson, Charles, 93

Thorndike, Lynn, 69n

Tommasi, Francesco, 268

Tornielli, Agostino, 136

Transvestism. See Cross-dressing

Traub, Valerie, 167n, 220n

Trotula, 8n

Tuana, Nancy, 9n, 12n

Turci, Mario, 43n

Twins, 23n, 33, 45n, 131–34, 184, 190–95,
201–2, 215

Uberti da Cesena, Grazioso, 254

Urethra, 27, 66, 86n, 245

Urine, 27, 48, 65–66, 86–87, 94, 96, 219,
252

Uroscopy. *See* Urine

Uterus, 10, 14, 16, 21–23, 89, 107; prolapsed,
23n, 55, 212n

Vagina dentata, 57, 114, 252. *See also* Uterus

Valenti, Cristina, 198n

Valerio, Gian Francesco, 162

Vallisnieri, Antonio, 49n

Valverde, Giovanni, 9n, 105

Varchi, Benedetto, 60, 134, 136

Varolio, Constantino, 219

Vasectomy, 245–46

Venereal diseases. *See* Syphilis

Venexiana (La), 200, 203, 205, 220–21

Vernant, Pierre, 28

Vesalius, Andreas, 9, 14n, 15, 97, 103–4, 219

Virgil, 51, 52n, 57, 68, 126n

Virginity tests, 86–87

Vittori, Loreto, 237, 258, 261

Vocal cords, 198

Voltaire, 59

Warburg, Aby, 205n

Weaver, Elissa, 4n

Wig, 4, 7

Williams, David, 63n

Witchcraft. *See* Witches

Witches, 43–44, 46n, 65, 213

Womb, 23–24, 83–84, 142–43, 153, 209,
212; cleansing of, 24, 89–90; containing
animals, 56–59; containing extraneous
bodies, 53–58; decomposing, 58; displaced, 23, 87; greedy, 102–4; poisonous,
83–84, 89, 96–101, 104, 111. *See also*
Uterus

Women: and birthmarks, 138; as contaminators, 90, 96–97, 101–2; as failed men,
15; as having a venomous body, 96–99

Worms, 27, 47, 56, 71, 75–77. *See also*
Putrefaction; Sexual intercourse: and
pollution

Zacchia, Paolo, 55, 60, 218, 246n, 269

Zambelli, Paola, 71, 74

Zatti, Sergio, 156, 184n

Zeuxis, 173

Žižek, Slavoj, 181n

Zorzi, Ludovico, 196n

Valeria Finucci is Associate Professor of Italian at Duke University.

Library of Congress Cataloging-in-Publication Data
Finucci, Valeria.
The manly masquerade : masculinity, paternity, and
castration in the Italian renaissance / Valeria Finucci.
p. cm.
Includes bibliographical references and index.
ISBN 0-8223-3054-7 (cloth : alk. paper)
ISBN 0-8223-3065-2 (pbk. : alk. paper)
1. Masculinity — Italy — History.   2. Paternity — Italy —
History.   3. Castration — Italy — History.   I. Title.
HQ1090.7.18 F56   2003
305.31'0945 — dc21   2002010947